STUDIES IN
SPEECH AND DRAMA

STUDIES IN
SPEECH AND DRAMA

IN HONOR OF
Alexander M. Drummond

NEW YORK / RUSSELL & RUSSELL

PREFACE

THE essays contained in this volume are offered to Professor Drummond by twenty-five of his pupils and colleagues, past and present, as a mark of their respect and admiration for a distinguished leader in the field of study to which they are devoted.

In the thirty-five years during which he has given to Cornell University an example of masterly teaching both of undergraduates and of graduate students, his influence has extended to many institutions throughout the nation, and in various councils his judgment has been of weight. On his sixtieth birthday he may well look back, if he is minded to do so, upon a noteworthy development of academic instruction and scholarship in Speech and Drama. He may reflect that he has had no small part in the movement by which college studies in these subjects have been broadened, teachers strengthened through a more vigorous discipline, and the best standards of humanistic research brought to the higher study of speech, public address, and the theatre.

To honor the significant part which Professor Drummond has played in this development by his teaching, his writings, and the influence of his example, is but one purpose of the contributors to this book. They hope, too, that the papers here included reflect in a measure the breadth of his interests and the range of his curiosity. And above all they wish to express their gratitude and warm affection.

July 15, 1944.

The committee in charge of the planning and editing of this volume was composed of Donald C. Bryant, Barnard Hewitt, Karl R., Wallace, and Herbert A. Wichelns, Chairman. The photograph was kindly supplied by Barrett Gallagher of New York. In correcting the proofs, Russell H. Wagner lent generous aid.

CONTENTS

ALEXANDER M. DRUMMOND

ALEXANDER M. DRUMMOND

By Hoyt H. Hudson

THERE must be thousands of us now, scattered across the continent, each of whom will say that he did his hardest (and probably his best) strokes of work at the instigation of Alexander M. Drummond. Most of us were his students, some were his colleagues, some his actors or sceneshifters, and some merely happened to serve on a committee with him. The word "instigation," used above, is of course too strong. We worked at Drummond's very deferential and cooperative suggestion. Perhaps we even thought it was our own idea, although later we recalled that the big fellow was in the vicinity when the idea arrived.

He likes ideas, even his own, but they always suggest to him things to do. One has a feeling that an idea unassociated with action or potential action somehow lacks reality for Drummond.

So . . . after first making him appear to be a slave-driver and then proving that he is a grubby pragmatist, one is obviously off on the wrong foot, and had better take a new start. Suppose we try quoting Drummond. He is talking about school dramatics—and he might be talking about college dramatics:

For every sincere and honest production is there one tawdry and artificial? For every fine play presented to the community is there one of third or fourth rate? For every pupil who is the better for participation in dramatics is there one spoiled? For every school play coached by a director of adequate training, is there one coached by a teacher confessing no training at all? For every administrator demanding trained directors and artistic productions, is there not one insistent only on having plays, and on "having plays that pay"? Is the public taste of the community being elevated or catered to? . . . Choose a good play and don't spoil it.[1]

That machine-gun fire of interrogation is part of the man. He always thinks up more questions than any other two people put

1. From "Dramatics and Speech Training," in *A Course of Study in Speech Training and Public Speaking for Secondary Schools,* edited by A. M. Drummond, New York, 1925, p. 230.

together. And those questions aren't rhetorical. He wants answers. By the time you have answered his questions you have worked your fool head off. And you find that he has a new set of questions.

Suppose we try the narrative approach. A veteran of the fall and winter campaign of 1920-21 may be pardoned if he falls into garrulous reminiscence. Drummond took over the chairmanship that fall, and, among other things, he wanted to build up the graduate work in rhetoric and public speaking. So he and Everett Hunt founded a seminar. They took a few of us through Aristotle's *Rhetoric* (it is quite possible that we were the only group in any American university then giving attention to what is now a perennial best-seller), Cicero's *De Oratore,* and Quintilian's *Institutiones.* The three works occupied most of the academic year, though somewhere early in it we also polished off Plato's *Phaedrus* and picked up something about Isocrates and the Sophists. Things began to happen. We found that there were articles we wanted to write. We saw chances to apply classical dogmata in our dealings with modern material. We suddenly discovered that swatting over old books or swinking over long papers was fun.

There was Drummond, you see, asking questions, never knowing anything but showing an almost pathetic willingness to learn. He wasn't exactly dull, but he was stubborn as all get out. Somehow we couldn't let him down; we had to educate him. It is true that he seemed to have read everything. Burke, American orators, English historians, Reynolds' *Discourses,* Demosthenes, the psychologists—all of them got into the pot somehow. When we had been especially adventurous and had marched out on a lone hunt, whether in our reading or our thinking, we were likely to meet Drummond there—coming back. And always there seemed to be two main defenses or arsenals of defense that we could never break through or exhaust. On the one side was a realistic common sense, a farm boy's tough-mindedness, whence he shot volleys that riddled anything fantastic or finespun, compelling us to keep our feet on the ground. On the other side was the solid framework of his own thinking on the subject of art, a subject on which he has always been willing to talk all night, sometimes after talking on it a good share of the day.

He has long since turned over the work in rhetoric to other members of his expanded department and has given himself to dramatics. The drama courses at Cornell have never been designed to train professionals, though they have produced a few, better grounded than most in the principles of their craft. Drummond, it would seem, has never been interested primarily in teaching his graduate students technique—how to do this or that. Rather, he has expected them to know a lot about the theatre and its ways. Most directors of work in dramatics are interested in performances. Drummond has been more interested in the aesthetic of the theatre, with performances taking their place as illustrative examples, as raw material, as exercises.[2]

His classroom method is aimed at bringing out a fair interpretation of the thought of others and a clear formulation of one's own. In his discussion of papers read before him, as in all of his associations with a student, this teacher contrives to make a person think and act for himself. His method might be described as controversial and critical. Perhaps Socrates has something to do with it. Students recall no instances of being told precisely what to accept or to believe, or what must be done. Something similar prevails in the rehearsal room. The Boss will rarely tell his actors how to do it. He tries to get them to discriminate the real from the phony, and lets the individual discover his own way of recreating thought, emotion, and movement with apparent (or real) spontaneity.

One of the most valuable lessons Drummond teaches, in connection with the exploration of aesthetic theory, is to avoid suppositions and to take an author on his own terms. Let Lee Simonson criticize Gordon Craig for sets too high to fit the proscenium of the contemporary theatre, and Drummond will remind you that Craig has consistently pleaded for a special

2. For most of the pages dealing with Professor Drummond's work as teacher and director I am indebted to an account written by Dr. Colby Lewis, who also collected the opinions and comments of former students.

theatre of his own. Let the critic whose mind is bounded by modern custom dismiss with haughty superiority some device of an older theatre as "unreal," and Drummond will show you the truth of that device to its own day and its possible advantage to ours. This tolerance, this fairness to the terms of others, naturally extends to Drummond's method of direction, which is notable for respecting the validity of the text, observing the stage directions, seeking carefully the author's meaning, and avoiding an "effect" which will distort the play's intention.

He makes one realize the connection between meaning and effective speech. And as the rhetorician is allied to the grammarian, actors at Cornell are reminded of the old and useful practice of parsing, nor do they escape without some knowledge of loose, compact, and periodic sentences, and cumulative thought structure. The papers they submit and the theses they write are carefully corrected for English style, so that one former student can say, "I learned more about clear, coherent writing from the Boss than I did from all the courses I took in the English department, and I was an English major." Another sums up Drummond's contribution thus:

I have learned to look closely and thoroughly into the meanings of words (long before Adler!) until the *habit* of exact understanding and critical evaluation now appears to be as well established as this body-and-mind permits. Professor Drummond's tendency to leave out linking steps during lecture, his close and trenchant questioning, his seeing six meanings in a line where I had seen one or two, his keen perception of nuances and implications—all help to mark the man and his reasonably perceptive student. I have rarely run up against a more penetrating mind, and I doubt whether we can find his superior, intellectually, in our field.

One more point about Drummond's teaching. For every statement or theory he gives you he will also give you immediately eight anti-statements and nine contrary theories. To some he appears always to be playing the part of devil's advocate. Whatever you think, it begins to seem, is wrong. As a result, a student of Drummond's is rarely in a hurry to make up his mind. Sometimes he may seem unable ever to come to a decision. This is the price of a tolerance such as led Leibniz to observe,

"It may sound strange, but I approve of everything I read, for I know well in how many ways things can be grasped." Yet Drummond does have his convictions and wants his students to have theirs. For his purpose is not to prove the student wrong but to force him to meet an attack with facts, with reasoning, and with active thought. One who responds fully and positively to this technique gains a kind of intellectual toughness, a thickness of skin which serves him well many times in later life.

Drummond sets a goal that is difficult, usually impossible, to reach. The student is hardly in danger of becoming self-satisfied. One observed that Drummond does not belong to the pat-'em-on-the-back school but rather to the throw-'em-in-the-water-and-let-'em-swim school. Yet such a generalization is obviously too strong when one considers the infinite pains he takes with the poor swimmer. Undemonstrative as he appears to be, his insight does not fail to see the latent spark, where there is one. More stimulation results from the Boss's "Pretty good" than from all the honeyed compliments of flatterers. As one student wrote: "He gets out of us what he does because we realize that if we do our best he will respect us."

Turning to Drummond's work as a producer of plays, it is almost enough to say that his knowledge of all departments of production distinguishes him as a true director in the Craigian sense. His lighting and scene design are grounded not only in a sense of theatrical effectiveness but also in an acquaintance with the compositions of good painters, sculptors, and architects. The newer among his friends are sometimes amazed at the way he can dissect and explain the construction of a painting, or, on another occasion, rearrange their furniture to a plan at once more pleasing and more practical.

Despite this talent, Drummond seems to regard design and decor as subsidiary to thought and action. Certainly he is not the primarily visual director that Alexander Dean is said to have been. He has sometimes at least hinted his agreement with Aristotle's dictum that spectacle is the least important of the elements of drama, and more than hinted his allegiance to those chapters in which Aristotle wrote: "The plot ought to be so constructed that, even without the aid of the eye, he who hears the tale told will thrill with horror and melt with pity at what takes place"; and "Tragedy, like epic poetry, produces its true effect without action; it reveals its power by mere reading." His approval of these passages shows the rhetorician in him. It underlies, one guesses, his fondness for Shaw and his success with Shavian productions. Conversational delivery, thoughtful speech, variety of utterance, resistant flexibility, relatively continuous flow of modulated sound—such considerations animate Drummond's concern with the voice as the actor's chief instrument. Speech is primary with him, because words carry the burden of the dramatist's meaning—and the translation of meaning is his foremost objective as a director.

How many times one can hear him ask the actor, "What do you mean?" Every question, indeed, is a variation on this theme: does this help elicit the idea? That is why an "effect," no matter how striking, is discarded. Drummond is not so pictorial as was Dean, nor so esoteric as Stark Young; and one correspondent doubts that he can get his actors to dance Shakespeare "as Shakespeare must be danced"—but he can get his actors and directors to find the meaning of whatever play he touches and, what is more, to deliver that meaning to an audience. One likes to think that he adheres more to Coquelin than to Stanislavski, but Drummond probably would object to putting it that way. He wants, and gets, meanings. In the words of a former student: "As a director of drama, Professor Drummond has remained a plain 'business man,' because he has never deviated from the simple rule that a production has business to do with an audience."

One who has worked under Drummond, and with him, and who has watched him at work with others finds difficulty in summing up the real power of the man, which is to a great degree an executive power. Yet the moment that is said there comes the realizaton that his artistic power is as great. The combination is almost unique in him. Nothing has been said as yet about his own plays—his original and striking expressionistic *Traffic Signals,* his fine regional plays, *The Cardiff Giant* and *The Lake*

Guns. Perhaps it is supposed to be a secret, but Drummond also likes to paint in oils, and would have covered more canvasses if he had not been pretty well occupied with other tasks. Among these other tasks there was, for some years, the New York State Country Theatre; the record of that would make, and will make when it is set down, a rather fine story. Nothing has been said about his consuming interest in upstate New York local history. Yet he has spent many hours in collecting lore, and he appreciates the character of his region as well as any man living.

Best of all is the fact that Drummond has always been willing to talk—to share talk, to listen to talk, to play at talk, to talk things out, to revel in talk. A masterly raconteur, in his storytelling he contrives to be artful while remaining homespun. He takes seriously and gratefully the friendships, the good hours of companionship, the give-and-take of academic life. Yet back of it all is his faith in honest work. He has maintained completely democratic and humane standards in all his professional relations as well as in his personal life, recognizing no distinctions of race, position, or wealth, but only distinctions of intellectual quality and performance. So we end about where we began. A former student contributes this:

You ask me what the greatest lessons were that I learned from him. Though this may seem hopelessly general, I say that I appreciate more than anything else the increase of knowledge of the interplay of cause and effect on human nature—the realization that unless I keep at it, make every gain count, quickly set about filling in blanks as I see them, nothing on earth can stop a decline—though that may happen anyway.

The writer of those words is not the only student Drummond has put the fear of God into. Yet there is more to his philosophy and personality than that, more than has been said here or can be said. Perhaps a close observer, remembering that our subject is one who has given a life to teaching the arts and crafts of speech, can find help here toward answering the old questions of the relation of thought to speech, of speech to action, of art to life. We are led to believe that action can be informed by thought and discussion, that words can grip things, that eloquence is more than sound, that art can mesh gears with reality. But let us not mar our portrait, and our tribute, by probing for a moral. The rest of this volume, designed as a tribute, is also essential to the portrait.

STUDIES IN
SPEECH AND DRAMA

Musical Drama as a Union of All the Arts

H. Darkes Albright

Such terms as *unity* and *synthesis* are commonplace in modern theories of dramatic production. In this country, as well as in England and on the continent, critics and aestheticians have come to insist on some sort of fusion of contributory arts as a basic concept in theatrical theory. The designer and director are described as blending on the stage varied colors, sounds, planes, and masses. The actor is represented as correlating the arts of time with the arts of space. All who work in the theatre are looked upon as borrowing from architecture and music, painting and sculpture, literature and the dance, and then organizing the contributions of these separate arts into a single dramatic design.

But the notion of fashioning a unified art of the theatre from the stuff of other arts is by no means a new one: musical drama, conceived as a synthesis of appeals to "the eye, the ear, and the understanding," dates back at least to the Renaissance. The difficulties underlying any combination of independent arts, inherent in all types of dramatic presentation, have of course been more complicated and at the same time more pronounced in the case of musical-dramatic forms. Operatic performances, with their complex blending of musical, scenic, and poetic appeals, have always presented problems of unification unparalleled in other fields of dramatic activity. As an ideal, however, if not an actuality, musical drama has consistently challenged the attention of theatrical theorists and innovators, from the sixteenth to the twentieth century.

The present study attempts to trace the varying poetic, musical, and scenic relationships in the evolution of musical drama, and to examine the aesthetic theory underlying these relationships at significant stages in their development. Particular emphasis is laid on Wagnerian and post-Wagnerian proposals, although sufficient earlier material has been introduced to insure the clarity and continuity of the whole.

§1

Three centuries and a half ago Beaujoyeulx formulated an ideal which has, broadly speaking, served as an objective for musical drama down to the present time. In October, 1581, in the preface to his glamorous and then quite original *Circe*,[1] he wrote:

I have breathed life into the ballet and made it speak; I have given to comedy voice and melody; and by adding to them several unusual and sumptuous displays and ornamentations, I can say that I have in one well-proportioned whole satisfied the eye, the ear, and the understanding.

Beaujoyeulx's *Circe* used the choreographic, musical, and scenic conventions of contemporary royal *mascarades,* and put them all to the service of the aesthetic principles expounded by the Academy of his day. From this Academy, organized by Antoine de Baïf, had come the earliest of what might be called musical-dramatic theory. De Baïf's *Académie de Poésie et de Musique,* founded in 1567, and composed of poets, musicians, and interested persons of culture, hoped to resuscitate the measured chant of Greek lyrical verse. Its plan was to give France a choric poetry and a theatre where poetry, music, and the dance could be fused into an ensemble basically similar to that of the Greeks.[2] Within a few years, however, the Academy's patronage was removed, and its activity ceased.

The researches and experiments of Count Giovanni Bardi and his Florentine "Chamber" of art-enthusiasts were to have more lasting and perhaps more tangible results.[3] Like de Baïf's French group, which had preceded it by several decades, the Florentine Academy was never completely to fulfill its neoclassic ambitions. But the first solo songs and the first dramatic recitative were developed at Florence, and from these evolved the musical principles of Italian opera.

The earliest extant example of a work in the new monodic style is Jacopo Peri's *Eurydice* (text by Ottavio Rinuccini), given in 1600 in honor of the marriage of Maria de' Medici to Henry IV of France. Generally accredited as the first real "opera,"

Eurydice was distinguished from its predecessors by a complete and relatively unified musical setting of its text, and by the use throughout of dramatic recitative.[4] The scenes were interspersed with simple choruses, and the final chorus included a dance. The music, according to Parry, was simple, and rarely expressive in itself; its limited duty was apparently to accompany and support the poetry. The ideal of the composer seems to have been satisfied "with setting the words to any succession of sounds which could conveniently be sung."[5] Giulio Caccini also set Rinuccini's entire libretto to music, publishing it in Florence in 1600 with a dedication to Count Bardi.

Both Caccini and Peri have left theoretical discussions justifying their aims and beliefs—the former in the preface to his *Nuove Musiche,* a collection of musical efforts in the new style, and the latter in his preface to *Eurydice.* Caccini begins his preface by objecting to the singer's use of trills and ornaments merely for display. He then confesses his debt to the Florentine Academy, and continues:

For these wise and noble personages have constantly . . . determined me to place no value upon that music which makes it impossible to understand the words . . . but to hold fast to that principle so greatly extolled by Plato and other philosophers: "Let music be first of all language and rhythm and secondly tone."[6]

He relates his early experiences in thus seeking a method of direct, eloquent, and dramatic solo expression, and concludes by reiterating his objection to the use of either vocal ornament or musical device for its own sake. Peri's discussion is in a similar vein. Like Caccini, he was guided by two quite definite aims: first, a revival of what he imagined to have been the Greek methods of declamation and delivery; and second, a rational adaptation of musical setting to poetical text.

In the earliest days of the opera, then, the position of music in the poetical-musical relationship was clearly defined. To the Parisian and Florentine academicians, music was meant to imitate the patterns of natural speech. Its function in a musical drama was simply to accompany and color the words, which in themselves carried the burden of dramatic significance. A poetical text was the basic substance of the art-work; any musical text was distinctly subsidiary.

But as, in the succeeding century, the art of music developed in resources and complexity, it began more and more to assume a leading place in the operatic scheme of things. By 1640, the focus of musical-dramatic activity had shifted to Venice, where the now familiar *aria* had begun to establish its popularity. By the time of Scarlatti (1658-1725) and his Neapolitan successors, an Italian tendency had become a tradition: to make the units of the musical-dramatic scheme musically complete and self-dependent, and to consider a musical drama as merely a kind of framework upon which to hang a number of independent musical movements. In Italy, as elsewhere on the continent, critics noted the "reign of the singer"; and the policies of operatic composition and production were often based on the relative popularity, financial value, and personal vanity of the leading *virtuosi*.

By 1767, Gluck felt called upon to write that he sought to restore music to "its true function, that of supporting the poetry."[7] At the most, he insisted somewhat later, operatic music and poetry must stand in a position of equality, and neither must appear to dominate the other. Theoretically, ". . . the voices, the instruments, the tones, even the pauses, should strive for one end—expression—and the agreement between the words and the song should be such that neither the poem should seem to be made for the music nor the music for the poem."[8] To what extent such a relationship is possible, and to what degree the arts are then to maintain their own identity, Gluck did not discuss; but he was in some measure resisting the trend of musical-dramatic evolution. In any case, most late eighteenth- and early nineteenth-century dramatic music was no longer a sort of auxiliary color in the poet's palette, a secondary and inferior contributing element in a musical-poetical combination. Matured and developed in its own right, music was gradually assuming a position as the basic substance of musical drama.

It was essentially on this point that Richard Wagner rebelled, and on this point that he based his theoretical objections to all operas before his time. "The error in the art-genre of the opera," he wrote, "consists herein: that a Means of Expression (Music) has been made the end, while the End of Expression (the Drama) has been made a means."[9] His own "ideal" and "universal" art was built, he contended, on a completely different formula, on a formula in which neither music (as in the opera) nor poetry (as in the spoken drama) was to take precedence, and in which the center of interest was to lie in what he chose to call "the true dramatic action." In Wagner's opinion, music had gradually been betrayed into an unnatural and impossible position in which it had lost sight of its own limitations; instead of being content to remain simply a "supremely mighty organ of expression," music had fallen into the "error of desiring to plainly outline the thing to be expressed." His new drama, the Art-work of the Future, was to be expressed "from within outward," and was to be conceived as a union of all the "humanistic" as well as "plastic" arts. A Wagnerian music-drama, so Wagner believed, was a combination of self-dependent arts, each at high intensity, the result being presumably greater and more effective than the individual arts in separation.

§2

Before examining in detail the Wagnerian conception of a union of all the arts, it will be necessary to pay some attention to the *mise en scène* as a contributory element in musical drama. It is to be noted that before Wagner the scene had received little consideration as a necessary and functional part of operatic theory; earlier writers in Italy, as in Germany and France and England, were concerned primarily with the musical-poetical relationship. From the time of the academies, authors as well as critics assumed the presence of scenes, machines, and divertisements, but they apparently did not consider that these factors posed a basic problem with regard to an organic fusion of contributory appeals. Dryden, for example, in his preface to *Albion and Albanius* (1685), took pains to explain at some length his theories of operatic composition, discussing plot, motivation, the necessary language for recitative and aria, and the like.[10] Of scenes and machines, however, and of their design or execution, he mentioned only that these he "had from Mr. Betterton." The settings presumably "enhanced" the whole, and served as "ornament" and "decoration," and there the matter ended.

But if in the seventeenth century scenic elements were not yet looked upon as forming one part of a synthetic whole, their presence was nonetheless regarded as indispensable. Opera was simply not opera without showy landscapes or palatial pseudo-architecture, without magical disappearances or celestial apparitions. The technical tricks of earlier *intermezzi, ballets de cour,* and masques were used not merely in occasional operatic productions, but were assumed to be requisite to all of them. Causal relationships in this matter are of course obscure, but it is possible that the mythological and quasi-historical libretti were chosen as much for the opportunities they afforded by way of scenic display as for their musical adaptability. The musical-dramatic form was novel, but so was the elaborate scenery; and the stage machinist was exalted as never before.

All of the earliest operas, in short, necessarily included a spectacular setting as fundamental to their appeal. In this, however, they were not unique; for, whatever the relationship from period to period between the setting and the action, the presence of the spectacular has always remained an important factor in operatic production. It is difficult to say specifically why this should have been the case. It may be that spectacular divertisements and technical wonders in the *mise en scène*—present in early productions as a sort of new toy—gradually became traditional, and have lasted for no other reason. Certainly this is true in regard to the ballets of the French opera. The importance of Wagner's *Tannhäuser* affair at the Paris *Opéra* has perhaps been exaggerated, and doubtless there were other comparatively irrelevant factors contributing to the difficulty; but the fact remains that Parisian audiences traditionally expected a *ballet-divertissement* at the end of the second act, and—motivation or no motivation—they tried to force Wagner to insert one in *Tannhäuser.*

It is possible, too, that the tradition of opera as a showpiece of showpieces is allied to the festival nature of the occasions for which, in its earlier years, it was usually prepared. On the other hand, the explanation may lie chiefly in the spectator-auditor's need for variety or for relief from tedium. Even in productions where musical values are paramount, it is possible that the average opera-goer has needed something to absorb his attention at moments of low musical intensity or at moments of transition from musical unit to musical unit. Again, perhaps music has usually needed a sort of "program," and possibly a visual program is more attractive to the average listener than a printed one.

However, even though a spectacular scene has always been associated with musical-dramatic production, the relationship existing between the scene and the action has not always been identical from period to period. The broader outlines of this changing relationship are of interest in the present discussion. In the seventeenth century, stage scenery—as exemplified by the work of Torelli on the continent and of Davenant and Webb in England—was stage decoration: the scene was an ornamental or pictorial background (possibly illustrating some phase of the action), before which the actor moved. The so-called "picture-architecture" of the eighteenth century,[11] on the other hand, was no longer merely decorative or ornamental; it was meant to deceive the eye, to give the illusion of a particular and real place. The typical eighteenth-century setting was still conceived fundamentally in two dimensions, although some of the units in the foreground may have been built-up. But it began the tendencies which culminated in the nineteenth-century illusionistic setting, with a multitude of practicables and a predominantly built-up foreground, and with the ideal of indicating, so far as contemporary means allowed, a real place in which the actor moved. In other words, compared with the decorative scene of the earliest operas, the setting for Rossini's *William Tell* was concerned with a certain archeological exactitude, a particularization of locale, a realism of a sort. Here was a *place in which,* rather than a *decoration before which* an actor moved. Consequently, the relationship of the actor and the action to the setting—

although in both cases the setting might have been "spectacular"—was in each case basically different.

Broadly speaking, the particularized, realistic operatic setting in which the nineteenth-century actor-singer performed bore a closer functional relationship to the actor and the action than any previous type of setting. Richard Wagner developed the logic of such a scene to what was from his point of view its ultimate conclusion. "The setting," said he, in effect, "must act." Word-speech is but conditioned and arbitrary; its only possible appeal is to the intellect. Tone-speech (that is to say, music) appeals directly to feeling, through the senses: it can express what to word-speech is "unutterable." Its rightful companion in appealing directly to feeling is the *mise en scène,* the movements and gestures of the actors, as the actors are related one to another and to the setting in which they move.

Shakespeare, in Wagner's view, appealed neither to the ear nor the eye, but primarily to the intellect; Mozart appealed only to the ear, since the actor-singer's pantomime and the setting before which he performed were simply understanding-appeals and were "unrelated to the music." In neither case, Wagner implied, was there complete synthesis of all possible sense-appeals to feeling. In neither case was there that union of all the arts toward which he believed musical drama had blindly been striving.

§3

Assuming that we take Wagner at all literally, what are the possibilities in his concept of a union of all the arts? And what implications has that concept for any theoretical combination of visual and auditory appeals in a dramatic work? It is perhaps unnecessary to point out at the start that critics of musical drama, from Addison to Tolstoi, have considered it extravagant and irrational entertainment at best, and have agreed to the extent of calling it impossible as a unified work of art. Sheldon Cheney was expressing a popular point of view when he wrote, in *The Theatre:*

We all of us go to hear and see [opera] . . . for various reasons, social and otherwise. It may be the music of Wagner, or Chaliapine, or Urban's new settings, or the new dresses and the debutantes in the boxes; but did any of us ever see a perfect opera production, or even one that held together, in that sort of unity that we experience at a symphony concert, or in reading or hearing . . . [a poem]? Opera is essentially a mixed, broken thing, with beautiful and compelling patches. . . . But . . .[the Florentines] founded a sort of music-drama that has been much with the world ever since; that has, indeed, pre-empted its biggest and showiest theatres for three hundred years. . . . The operatic stage holds its important place in all sophisticated communities, through criticism, calumny, and repeated proofs of its unimportance.[12]

But let us note some of the inherent conflicts and contradictions in musical drama, as they are manifested in production. How, for example, can music and poetry blend, in anything approaching Wagnerian synthesis, especially if each is still to maintain essentially its own nature and its own intensity? However often we may by analogy call poetry musical, our chief pleasure in true poetry does not spring from purely tonal qualities; it springs rather from a subtle blending of moods, ideas, and emotions as these are evoked by word-association. To appreciate poetry, in any commonly accepted sense of the term, we must give it all our attention, and we simply must understand the words. To ask that the average opera-goer—in the midst of the distracting ensemble of operatic production, and despite the accompanying orchestra—should first actually understand the words of the piece, and then appreciate them poetically, is probably to ask the impossible. Again, speech (whether in prose or in poetry) is developed by progression, by a more or less continuous forward movement. Music, by its very nature, needs for its development frequent repetitions and longer intervals of time. Such conflicts must remain so long as poetry is poetry and music is music. To speak of a mystical Wagnerian synthesis of the two, each at the maturity of its development—a synthesis in which each art would be stronger and more effective than in separation—is to speak in figures.

What of music and the *mise en scène?* As to the stage setting itself, the *mise en scène* is a passive, static thing; while music is by comparison an active, changing, moving element. It has always been possible, of course, to change in setting from day to night, from gaiety to depression, from a free and open space to an oppressive and enclosed one; but these broad distinctions only partially solve the problem. Wagner's moving panoramas (as in *Parsifal*) were an attempt at a solution. So, possibly, were the processions, motivated or otherwise, so frequently introduced by Wagner and the opera composers before him.

But it is obvious that the setting can only partially move in harmony with the music, and then only for comparatively short durations of time. The actor-singer, of course, can move; and at times, as in a ballet, a dance, or a march, he can move in rhythm with the music. But if his entire movement pattern is to become dance, as logically it must if it is to be completely synthesized with the music, he is in even worse difficulties than before. For if he dances, he tends to caricature, so to speak, that semblance of reality which a drama as opposed to a dance or a ballet must maintain. In practice, moreover, it is inconceivable that the actor-singer's movement and gesture should approach complete harmony with the music. So long as he sings, he must necessarily postpone most of the possible expressive movements and gestures, and any continuous or strenuous movement is a priori out of the question.[13]

It is clear that such practical difficulties with a musical-poetic-scenic synthesis must condition our acceptance of the Wagnerian concept. If it is remembered that Wagner practically denied the legitimate existence of any other art except this synthesis, his position bcomes even more indefensible. Sculpture, painting, poetry, and music, he argued, have matured to the limit of their possibilities; and consequently they can no longer hold any real significance for the art-observer when they are presented in separation. Actually, as several of Wagner's critics have indicated long since,[14] it is precisely because the various arts have matured and have developed in self-dependence that they now tend to obstruct or cancel one another when presented simultaneously. Once music, like the other arts, had developed toward specialization and independence and had matured and grown complex in resources, it was something entirely different from "music" in

the time of the Greeks or the Florentines—to whom Wagner insisted, in a sense, he was returning. It is obviously impossible to
disentangle the arts completely one from the other. But it is a
mistake to regard poetry, music, and painting as merely translations into different artistic language of the same fixed quantity
of imaginative thought; or to assume that one art or combination of arts can now satisfy for all people every diversity of
intellectual and emotional need.

§4

The difficulties in Wagner's position suggest a factor which
he himself nowhere discussed, but which helps considerably to
clarify the relationships between the arts: the factor of *conflicting intensities*. Putting aside for the moment the question
of the *mise en scène*, what is to be said in this connection of
poetry and music? Historically, as we have seen, there have
been three sharply defined conceptions as to the poetical-musical
relationship. First, to the Parisian and Florentine Academies,
music (or what was then called music) was meant to imitate the
patterns of natural speech, to accompany and to color the movement of the poetry. Second, to the pre-Wagnerians and probably
to most of the nineteenth century, music was definitely the
basic substance of the art-work—the poetic function being merely to furnish a background for the music, to suggest to the
mind a channel along which the comparatively vague and general emotions of the music might flow. Finally, Wagner's concept was a combination of self-dependent arts, each at high intensity, and each greater and more effective in combination than
alone.

It has already been suggested that time and musical evolution
have disposed of the first of these conceptions and have made
possible the second; and that Wagner's proposal, at least as he
expressed it in his prose works, seems difficult to accept. It is all
very well to assume in theory that we can assimilate as a unity
a synthetic work of art in which the scene, the poetry, and the
music are allied on practically equal terms and at equally high
intensity. It is all very well to assume further that each part of

such a combination can only serve to assist us in receiving and understanding the whole. But in practice one is likely to find that the contributory elements in such a combination merely obstruct or cancel one another, and that the ensemble effect merely distracts the senses and confuses the mind.

But there remains still a fourth possibility: to blend music and poetry at low pressure, so to speak, lest the relatively high intensity of each merely distract from the effect of the others. It is to some such scheme as this that Roger Fry subscribes when he finds in Congreve's and Handel's *Semele* the ideal poetic and musical relationship. Troubled for some years by the problem of opera as a "genuine" form of art, Mr. Fry confesses, he found it usually "only a jumbling together of different arts, leaving now one and now another sticking out in either pleasurable or painful prominence." Moreover, this was true particularly with Wagner; it was precisely at the moments of greatest dramatic intensity that the mixture became least manageable. But at a Cambridge production of *Semele,* his impressions were notably different.

I was told [he writes] by people of taste that Congreve's words were absurdly bad. I found them admirably suited to their purpose. Congreve . . . knew where to keep his emotional pitch. He knew that any intense poetical quality of words must either be lost in song or must intrude impertinently on the musical effect, so he gave to his words just as much generality and colourlessness as was consistent with clear sense and good writing. . . . The poetry, by no means despicably written, makes so little claim on the attention that music has it all its own way, and yet takes its clue from the words and derives from them a certain clearly-felt direction. . . . Then Handel came along and took all Congreve offered, and though he had been left free to fill the grand rôle, to be the essential esthetic creator, he did not presume. He kept his music well in hand, and though he had much the largest liberty of anyone, he knew he might not do quite what he would if he were alone. . . . Though we have far more attention free for music than for anything else, we have not quite our whole attention; sense and sight still occupy a corner of it. . . . And Handel, too, keeps, I think, the same humorous aloofness from dramatic intensity that Congreve did.[15]

Perfect cooperation between the arts, Mr. Fry concludes, becomes difficult "in proportion as they reach a high pitch of intensity or completeness of expression."

The problem of conflicting appeals is of course especially acute in the matter of the *mise en scène*. Despite Wagner's beliefs and pretensions, it is evident that he solved his own difficulty—when he solved it—through the overpowering intensity of his music. Adolphe Appia has called Wagnerian music "omnipotent," "of infinitely strong intensity," "developed according to its own bidding."[16] Romain Rolland has spoken of the demons of Wagner's orchestra as alone being capable of combating the tyranny of his *mise en scène*. "Let the Rhine," he has written, "overflow the stage; let the clouds beat against one another amidst the thunder-claps; let a rainbow-bridge be thrown across the atmosphere: his music will always be a thousand times more potent than his machines, and its dominating force can always mould the tremendous mass of competing elements into a single work of art."[17]

That is to say, the laws of unity in a synthetic art admit of only two possibilities: either there is mutual subordination of contributory appeals (as in *Semele*), or the imperious intensity of one of them must impose its own unification. This is essentially what Professor Prall—a writer on aesthetics of markedly different background and temperament from Appia's or Rolland's—suggests as the key to unification in any of the "mixed" arts of modern times. The character of the specific beauty in a theatrical production, he concludes, is determined through emphasis on one type of structure, one sort of aesthetic material, one particular art, over another; and on the "subordination of all subsidiary technique and all subsidiary materials."[18]

§5

Wagner himself believed both the opera and the symphonic poem unquestionably less perfect than his own art-form—in the case of the symphonic poem on the ground that the characters, events, and ideas in this form were left wholly to the imagination, while in his music-drama they were indicated or suggested visually on the stage. The results are sometimes the observer's loss. The emotional and poetic values in Wagner's scripts are too often disturbed by the grossly unideal presence of the average actor, by the reduction of one's imaginative conceptions to the tawdriness of wire and paint and canvas. The sheer practicality of trap doors and built-up levels, of property animals drawn jerkily on a wire, of robot-like actors marching to unearthly music, has destroyed more than one opera-goer's poetic vision. There is a point beyond which sound design, good taste, and expert technique in actual presentation cannot go; there is a point at which the visual, scenic contribution in such a union of all the arts becomes too difficult to assimilate.

Experiences of this sort in the operatic theatre have led several post-Wagnerian critics to set forth musical-dramatic theories of their own. Might not the ideal musical drama, they ask, be conceived as a form of program symphony? Ought not the scene (substituting, so to speak, for a "program" in the literal sense) merely to furnish for the observer a kind of orientation, a kind of rational basis for the whole? The situation suggests to Ernest Newman a simile from Browning's *The Ring and the Book*—that of the jeweler who finds it advantageous to mix a certain amount of alloy with the gold while he is working on a ring, but who afterwards burns it out with a spirit of acid, leaving simply the circlet of pure gold. Similarly, the composer of the symphonic program opera can use the scenic and poetic alloy "in the conceptual stages of his work to give coherence to the tissue of it," but leave only a minimum of the alloy "visible in the completed work itself." To vary the simile, he can use poetry and the scene as his scaffolding, but as his scaffolding only; the trouble with musical drama, ideally considered, is that it "too often shows the scaffolding projecting at a score of points through the finished building."[19]

Viewed in this light, the proper function of the scene is to frame or at most to decorate unobtrusively the appeal of the music. It is not the business of the scene to compete with the music, to insist on any sort of independent appeal on its own terms and in its own idiom, but merely to lend to the music and the drama a base, so to speak, a visible milieu for the changing events. And even this visible base must remain at an absolute minimum in production; the ideal musical-dramatic work will have fundamentally no scene at all, except (particularly in the conceptual stages of its development) by way of suggestion and orientation.

Adolphe Appia's criticism of the Wagnerian setting has taken a somewhat different direction. In the main, his reaction to such proposals as Mr. Newman's would have been that they include only part of the picture. They consider the scene primarily as a meaningful and rational (that is to say, what Appia himself called a "symbolizational") factor; the secret of the difficulty in synthesizing the scene with music and with poetry lies in failing to raise the intensity of the scene as *an expressional factor.*

Wagner himself had originally made a somewhat similar distinction, in that he looked upon his own scene as a "sense-appeal to feeling," but branded the typical operatic setting as merely an "understanding-appeal, unrelated to the music." But in Appia's opinion, Wagner never discovered how to make his presentational form—his scene—agree with his adopted dramatic form: he rode into battle "girded with a powerless realistic convention, a fossilized principle of production." Wagner's use of a representational scene rather than an expressional one led, according to Appia, to the necessity that the music and the poetry alone carry the burden of expressing "from within." Consequently the poem and particularly the music had to be developed in their own right at infinitely high intensity; in Wagnerian music-drama, the music was omnipotent, developed according to its own bidding. In any true synthesis of the arts Appia believed, the synthesis implies not merely combination, but mutual subordination. In Wagnerian works, however, the conflict between the high expressional intensity of the music and the naturalistic, non-expressional character of the scene denied the possibility of real synthesis. The cause of failure at Bayreuth, both before and after the Master's death, was simply that the Wagnerian scene was never brought up to the expressive level of the concepts underlying the Wagnerian dramas.[20]

To Appia, then, the question of relative intensities in visual appeal was not primarily one of rational or meaningful elements. That, to him, was simple; the less "symbolization" required, in theory and in practice, the better. A more fundamental question is this: how can the level of intensity be raised expressionally, spiritually, aesthetically?

Even here there is a possible difficulty, a difficulty which Appia apparently did not foresee, or at least did not discuss. If the scene is to be intensified expressionally, in its own right and on its own terms, how then can it guard against serving as an aesthetic end in itself? How can the observer fail to regard it, ultimately, as an independent artistic entity, not functionally subordinate to the action, the music, and the dramatic ensemble? A setting raised aesthetically to a high degree of intensity or completeness of expression may tend to be more potent (and hence in effect more distracting) than a simple and comparatively realistic one that is without definite expressional and artistic pretensions. In theoretically removing one contradiction from his union of the arts, it is possible that Appia merely substituted another, and perhaps a more difficult one.[21]

Appia's remarks on conflicting intensities and his insistence on a "mutual subordination of elements" imply, of course, that his system meant to take into account *any* distraction from what he termed the "musical-poetical idea"; and in the main an expressive but unobtrusive scene may be taken as his ideal. In any case, the assumption that the *mise en scène* ought in production to be held to some theoretical minimum—either rational or expressional—is not, in the final analysis, a solution to the basic problem. Clearly, if musical dramas are to be produced at all, there must be a musical-dramatic scene, as there always has been and evidently always will be; and the apparently immortal tradition that an opera is the showpiece of showpieces does not lighten the difficulty. So long as there is any scene, any visual orientation, any visual expressiveness, there will be the inevitable possibility of conflicts of attention and of visual distractions from the poetic or musical appeals. Musical drama remains what its critics have called it for centuries: a dream, a concept, an ideal, an art of contradictions. So complex, so varied, so numerous are its contributory appeals that to unify them all seems impossible of achievement.

But that very complexity serves to emphasize and to clarify the basic problems of synthesis which are present, in varying ways and to varying degrees, in all forms of modern dramatic production. It has become increasingly evident since Wagner's time that unification of the arts on his special terms is an unlikely achievement. No single work of art can be conceived as a mere sum of lesser ones; and cooperation between the several arts becomes difficult as each maintains its own fullness or completeness of expression. The constituent elements and the structural principles of the subsidiary arts are, obviously, transformed in the process of fusion. Various combinations are possible; and various centers of emphasis on one type of aesthetic material or structure or on one kind of art over another may make up the sequence of these combinations. But too great a variety or complexity of contributory appeals must necessarily exceed the assimilative grasp of the spectator.

NOTES

1. A copy of this work is preserved in the National Library at Paris, and it is reprinted in P. Lacroix, *Ballets et Mascarades de Cour de Henri III à Louis XIV* (Geneva, 1868), I. A significant portion of the preface is quoted in Enid Welsford's *The Court Masque* (Cambridge, 1927), pp. 248-249.

2. Mathieu Augé-Chiquet, *Jean-Antoine de Baïf* (Paris, 1909), pp. 431-456.

3. C. Hubert H. Parry, *Music of the XVIIth Century* (Oxford, 1902), chap. 2. See also W. J. Henderson, *Some Forerunners of Italian Opera* (New York, 1911), pp. 172 ff.

4. The so-called "new style" was known as *stile rappresentativo*, or on occasion as *stile parlante*. Peri and Rinuccini called their work *Tragedia per Musica;* but in time a commoner name for the form was *Dramma per Musica*. By 1650, the title *Opera in Musica* had come into use, and this was gradually reduced to the later "opera."

5. Parry, *op. cit.*, p. 35.

6. Quoted in Henderson, *op. cit.*, pp. 222 ff.

7. From the preface to *Alceste*, quoted by Ernest Newman in *Gluck and the Opera* (London, 1895), pp. 238-240.

8. From a letter to *Journal de Paris*, October, 1777; quoted by Newman, *op. cit.*, pp. 171-172.

9. "Opera and Drama," in *Prose Works*, tr. William Ashton Ellis, 8 vols. (London, 1893-1899), II, part i, 17. The present summary of Wagner's theory is drawn from his own statement of the case, chiefly in "Opera and Drama" and "The Art-work of the Future" and in his correspondence (e.g., with Roeckel and

Uhlig). Both here and elsewhere, however, I have been influenced by Ernest Newman's brilliant analyses: *A Study of Wagner* (London, 1899), *Wagner as Man and Artist* (London, 1914), and *Richard Wagner* (New York, 1933 ff.).

10. *The Works of John Dryden*, ed. W. Scott and G. Saintsbury, 18 vols. (Edinburgh, 1882-1893), VII, 228-241.

11. As exemplified by the work of the Bibbienas, who developed the false-perspective system suggested by Andrea Pozzo (1642-1709). In "picture-architecture," the scene was conceived as a series of two-dimensional cutouts, which, when placed at their proper position and viewed at the correct distance, gave an illusion of a whole.

12. (New York, 1935), pp. 484, 215.

13. Martin Shaw records, however, that in at least one instance Gordon Craig successfully trained his actors to combine singing with relatively violent expressive movement. Writing of *Dido and Aeneas*, produced by the Purcell Operatic Society during the season of 1898-1899, under Craig's direction, the English musician observes: "The production . . . was the beginning of a new era in theatrical art. . . . The most remarkable of the players themselves were the chorus. . . . They had to sing their choruses crawling, leaping, swaying, running—any way that Craig fancied. How they did it I do not know, but they did. Most of them had no stage experience at all. Perhaps that was as well, for I am sure a Covent Garden chorus would have struck at the first rehearsal." *Up to Now* (London, 1929), p. 26.

14. E.g., Walter Pater, *The Renaissance* (London, 1925), p. 130; John Palmer, *The Future of the Theatre* (London, 1913), pp. 46-49; Newman, *A Study of Wagner*, pp. 179, 201-202.

15. Roger Fry, *Transformations* (London, 1926), pp. 33-34.

16. *Die Musik und die Inscenierung* (Munich, 1899), p. 157.

17. *Les Origines du Théâtre Lyrique Moderne* (Paris, 1895), p. 137.

18. D. W. Prall, *Aesthetic Judgment* (New York, 1929), p. 274.

19. *Wagner as Man and Artist*, p. 339.

20. Appia's Wagnerian criticism is presented most fully in the latter portions of *Die Musik und die Inscenierung*. See also: *La Mise en Scène du Drame Wagnérien* (Paris, 1895) and *L'Oeuvre d'Art Vivant* (Geneva, 1921).

21. It is interesting to note that on the occasion of one of his few major appointments as a practical *metteur en scène* (at La Scala, in 1923, for Wagner's *Tristan*), Appia's settings were severely criticized. They were criticized, however, not for any theoretically over-intense expressional appeal, but for their utter simplicity of line, color, and general arrangement. The Italians, accustomed to vivid, colorful, and detailed representations, were unwilling or unable to see any virtue in Appia's style and method. Gordon Craig, on the other hand, defends Appia's work at Milan, contending that he was given neither the support nor the freedom necessary to realize his ideas. See Craig, *Fourteen Notes* (Seattle, 1931), pp. 10-11.

Stanislavski and the Idea

EDWIN DUERR

§1

For the rhapsode ought to interpret the mind of the poet to his hearers.—PLATO's *Ion*.

So THOROUGHLY has the Stanislavski[1] system of acting captivated the American theatre mind, especially in the schools and universities, that any faultfinding with its methods and aims is likely to be thought bumptious. The system is generally considered ineffably wise and holy and final. It is supposed to be beyond criticism. That sort of adulation ought to be smashed.

After all, the Stanislavski system is not the beginning and end for all actors, nor the only measuring stick for acting. There are other somewhat tenable theories of acting. There are other theatre men who have thought about acting. Lorenz Kjerbühl-Petersen published the results of his extensive examination into the psychology of acting at about the same time that *My Life in Art* appeared, and came, though academically and without the charming patness of a system, to conclusions almost diametrically opposed to those of Stanislavski.[2] Alexander Tairov (1885–) directed his Kamerny Theatre on principles constantly contradictory to and critical of those advocated by Stanislavski.[3] Vsevolod Meierhold (1863–), a member of the Moscow Art Theatre at its founding and an assistant to Stanislavski, broke decisively with the tenets of that theatre and, in his search for a style, continually and vigorously fought the Stanislavski methods; he worked, he said, toward finding the thought of the author and revealing it to an audience in a theatrical form. Eugene Vakhtangov (1883-1922), one of Stanislavski's most brilliant pupils, eventually adhered only to part of his master's teachings as he went on his own way to set up radically different theories of acting;[4] and Stanislavski admitted that Vakhtangov finally discovered what "he himself had sought for years, and could not find."[5] Stark Young (1881–), the perceptive American theatre critic, is "convinced that in many cases the Stanislavski system has done harm."[6] He has said that in *My Life in Art* "there is not one remark that gave me any sense of the creative surprise, the authentic right, the illumination, that comes from a man inside an art."[7]

Even if the Stanislavski system is the "only organic technique of acting in the modern theatre,"[8] it is not aesthetically final. It has its shortcomings.[9] It has its faults. Despite the juicy premiums it offers—a full-length mirror for the would-be actor fondly to look into, some thin psychology for the scientifically-minded student to dabble at, and definite lessons for the teacher to lean on—the Stanislavski system can, too frequently for comfort, be more harmful than helpful to apprentice actors. That danger derives from the fact that the Stanislavski system of acting ignores the playwright, and therefore demotes the director to a position where, instead of properly serving the author, he becomes an impotent coach of a kind of acting which is artistically beside the point. Any scheme of acting which almost completely disregards the initial and predominant creator in the theatre is not merely self-centered but inimical to the whole art of the theatre.

The fact that the Stanislavski system of acting neglects instead of emphasizing the playwright can be proved by an examination of the system.

That examination begins, as it must, with a salute to Stanislavski as a lovable and sincere person, as a warm and humble teacher, who devoted a long lifetime to the art of acting. Ambitious as no one before him had been to define its mysteries, a patient and tireless servant to the theatre he indubitably cherished, he was determined to pour out its truths for the benefit of all as simply as one pours water from a glass. But his findings cannot be accepted because of the virtues and the shine of the man. Formulated by Benedict Arnold or by Squire Cribbs, by René Descartes or by Elsie Dinsmore, they must stand on their own as a guide to actual theatre rehearsal and performance.

Any critical examination of the system also begins with

hesitating care and enormous difficulty, since in *An Actor Prepares,* and in *My Life in Art* which introduces it, there are many contradictions and confusions, much jumping and overlapping, and many slippery terms. "The vast creative experience of Stanislavski comprises such a variety of data, so many enunciations, that for any assertion about his art theories one can always find in his statements or his practice sufficient basis for a counter-statement."[10] Nevertheless, in all his teachings there is a basic line. Criticism must isolate this basic line (although it might also prove profitable to discover exactly how "every good director makes the system his own, thus transforming it somewhat,"[11] and to learn why such adaptations are necessary). Criticism, moreover, must follow the line where it goes and not stop where it starts.

Obviously, and with acumen, Stanislavski began his investigations by codifying, dilating, and explaining the age-old fundamentals of acting; and his general arrangement and treatment of those fundamentals, at the familiar point, is right. His findings there, rightly derivative, are highly personal and seminal and exciting; his teaching there is compulsory for all who would either know or practice acting.

Stanislavski uncovered a number of laws of stage art underlying the biologic nature of the actor's creative work. We are fully entitled to treat those laws as universally valid—possessing the same value for the proletarian actor as for the bourgeois, for the actors of Shakespeare's time as for those of the Italian comedy. We have the full right to maintain that it is necessary for any actor to be concentrated upon the stage; to distribute his muscular energy efficiently; to seek his attitude to the surrounding environment; to act without concerning himself with feelings; to motivate ("justify") his behaviour on the stage; to disclose the inner meaning of the author's text (the "subtext" under the words); to recreate the biography and life conditions of the character; to perform not for himself but for his partner; to struggle against stereotypes; and so forth.[12]

But these orthodox principles of acting do not constitute the basic line of the Stanislavski system; they are only its starting point. The basic line moves on from there. Stanislavski went from this codification and elaboration of the perennial essentials of acting to a new definition of acting.

The basic line in its entirety has been adequately summarized by many:

The cardinal principle of that system is that through conscious means we reach the subconscious. The preparation trains the pupil's "inner creative state," helps him to find his "super-objective"; and "through the line of action" it creates "a conscious psycho-technique," and in the end leads him to the "region of the subconscious."[13]

Stanislavski's system is built upon the slogan "The spectator is to forget that he is sitting in the theatre." For this reason the actor has to renounce his own ego; he has to live the life of the character and become one with the soul of the character he portrays. He has to hypnotize himself to such a degree that he can physically and spiritually give himself over to the re-living of another person.[14]

When the actor has found the nature and origin of his emotions, then he must say "I am this person." There can be no separation between the actor and his part. . . . Upon arrival at this stage one comes to grips with the spiritual values of the play. . . . And if the actor sees into the spirit, then the audience will. Finally, when he has grasped the image in its physical, mental or psychological, and spiritual aspects, there remains only to work with his own will power, to will himself to act as the image should. Then is his character complete.[15]

In Stanislavski's own words, "in our art you must live the part every moment that you are playing it, and every time."[16]

Our type of creativeness is the conception and birth of a new being—the person in the part. It is a natural act similar to the birth of a human being. . . . If you analyze this process you will be convinced that laws regulate organic nature, whether she is creating a new phenomenon biologically or imaginatively. . . . Nature's laws are binding on all, without exception, and woe to those who break them.[17]

In short, the basic line, the core, of the Stanislavski system is a definition of and a recipe for the art of acting which confuses art and nature without any perceptive acknowledgment of their differences. For Stanislavski the differences between art and nature are unimportant in the actual teaching of acting. Knowing that all artists are men who feel truly, he comes to the conclusion that all men who feel truly are artists, are actors. He is magnanimous. He is also illogical.

Never in his basic chapter of *An Actor Prepares,* "When Acting Is an Art," does Stanislavski mention or examine any of the other arts in order to determine their common distinguishing characteristics. Art to him is nature, and nature is art, and that is all you need to know. Acting is living.

But perhaps Stanislavski is only unintentionally unskillful in his definition. Perhaps he did not care to *prove* acting an art. Perhaps, without finding the correct terms to label his aims and methods, he intuitively knew that acting was an art and always hoped he was perfecting it as such. A man may wrongly or weakly define what he rightly knows and aims to teach.

Does Stanislavski, while bungling his definition or minimizing its abstract importance, indicate in *An Actor Prepares* that he is aware of the characteristics, the essentials, the principles of an art? He does. But in his system of acting he almost invariably disowns that knowledge.

§2

Perhaps it can be granted, without tangling too much with too many aesthetic theories, that "emotion towards life is the primary stuff of which art is made,"[18] that art's "business is to transmit emotion,"[19] and that "emotions are attached to events and objects in their movement. They are not, save in pathological instances, private."[20] Furthermore, it is generally held to be true that in our reaction to a work of art—whether we appreciate the emotion in and for itself,[21] or whether we evaluate the emotion for its reaction upon actual life[22]—there is always "the consciousness of purpose, the consciousness of a peculiar relation of sympathy with the man who made this thing in order to arouse precisely the sensations we experience. . . . We feel that he has expressed something which was latent in us all the time, but which we never realized, that he has revealed us to ourselves in revealing himself."[23] In other words, in an art object, although not in a natural object such as a rose, a sunset, or a woman loved, we are always aware of the artist, of his mind, of an attitude, *of an idea.*

The artist, so peculiarly and inexplicably gifted in his attitude toward life that he can see "things detached and therefore more vividly, more completely, and in a different light,"[24] is compelled in some way to reproduce or imitate or express the event or the object which is causing his own emotion in such a way that the emotion is communicated to others. But unless the emotion communicated is part of an inclusive and enduring idea it is merely an automatic reflex.[25] A thought or an idea (particularly in the language arts), an attitude or a perception, always arranges and controls the emotions and thereby comes into existence. What is fundamental to and characteristic of an art work, *what differentiates it from nature,* is an emotionalized and emotionalizing idea. In architecture, for instance, "A competent designer instinctively chooses a theme, a leit-motif, for a given structure, and allows it to influence all his choice of form and line within that structure."[26] In music, "given the quality of mind—to use a clumsy phrase for lack of a better—capable of significant ideas, the rest of the work of composition is largely a matter of mechanics. . . . Music consists of ideas and their treatment."[27] In the novel *War and Peace* Tolstoy is "in perfect and serene control of his idea."[28]

To bring the point to the theatre:

Poetry, or art, as Plato says, is a general name signifying that process by which something is where something was not before. We may say that the something that has arrived consists of a form and an idea; the idea was never born till it has the form to express it, the form never exists without the idea to determine it. An idea, whatever other form of existence it may have, does not exist in the theatre until it achieves a theatrical body. A play can exist only in theatre terms.[29]

In summary, the playwright as artist is an individual who can see in his material, in people and events and in his own experiences, "an essential characteristic"; he can find in it "something that is his idea, . . . that which will be for him permanent and ideal, and will remain for him when the material has faded"; and he will be driven to find that theatre form, or technique, inevitable to the expression or creation of his idea, by the desire either to communicate it to others, or "to free his idea from the confusions and accidents of the original material and to leave it essential."[30] Moreover, "the idea is translated into the terms of every part" of the play: into terms of this section and that section, this moment and that, this character and that, and the like; it is also translated into terms of acting, and directing, and decor, which are all additional parts of the play; for

in the theatre the creative process does not stop with the completion of the playwright's script. Every step in the production is creative, and every step affects the living quality of the play. A line drawn by the scenic artist, an actor's way of smiling, the color of a woman's dress, may mar the completeness of the whole design.[31]

The difference between an artist and a man who has intentions but cannot create them into art appears in the absence of the style that might accomplish this translation of idea into form. Minor artists and imitators, apart from the significance of such ideas as they possess, are what they are because they are able to put the essential characteristic not through all the parts of a work, but only in this part or that.[32]

The idea of the play can be, with many gradations, vitally and sensitively tragic or comic; it can be perceived and revealed in various moods, and under the trappings of any period. It can be expressed in a style which is naturalistic, realistic, romantic, fantastic, expressionistic. It can variously depend on plot, characterization, language, speech, movement, and decor in a combination which is unified and varied as it follows the principles of fitness and the laws of relationships in order to attract and hold the attention of the audience.

That acting, when there is any, is a part of the play will be admitted even by those who regularly swoon before Aristotle when he maintains, in general, that the idea of the play may be apparent in its structure and incidents upon a mere reading.[33] Certainly acting can and should serve the expression of the play's idea instead of changing or even nullifying the playwright's idea.

Actors can have faith and a sense of truth, a belief in their emotions and their actions, a sincere inner feeling—actors can be true to nature—and never once serve the idea of the play, never once express that idea except accidentally. A director can coach his actors to be true to nature without ever once being sure that they will be true to the idea of the play. Actors and their director, or their teacher, can best and most dependably express a play's idea only by continuing where the playwright left off. This means that they must find the idea, and perhaps believe in it, as an "essential characteristic" of life which is to be preserved or communicated by theatrical emotional expression as a part of the play. This means that actors and directors must always know, and therefore be taught to know, the crucial difference between art and nature.

It is, of course, highly probable and perhaps unavoidable that the actors in seeing the idea might thereby interpret the idea, and consequently seek a form for their own interpretation of the idea; they might even comment on the idea. That is an incidental matter. The main point is that actors, not as human beings, but as human beings who are artists, must never expunge all idea from a play, nor take it for granted, nor minimize it. The main point is that actors should be taught, not merely to live on stage, but to act on stage.

Now Stanislavski realizes the quality, if not the importance, of that distinction between nature and life. Throughout his system of acting he knows that acting must be true to nature, must be true psychologically to the actor, to his "inner feelings," so that each and every moment on stage will be "saturated with a belief in the truthfulness of the emotion felt, and in the action carried out."[34] But now and then Stanislavski also recognizes—and this is the significant but hidden and always forgotten point—that acting must be true to something else. He is sometimes certain that the actor's faith and sense of truth must be "transformed into a poetical equivalent by creative imagination."[35] He sometimes knows that acting is a process of "initiating, clarifying, transforming simple everyday realities into crystals of artistic truth."[36] He writes: "The greater part of life is devoted to unimportant activities. You get up, you go to bed, you follow a routine which is largely mechanical. That is not the stuff of the theatre. . . . We are challenged to fight . . . for an idea."[37] He is at times sure that the actor must seek for "one dominating idea that would absorb everything."[38] This idea or main theme "must be firmly fixed in an actor's mind throughout the performance. It gave birth to the writing of the play. It should also be the fountain-head of the actor's artistic creation."[39]

In other words, Stanislavski knows that the actor must be true, first, to nature, and true, second or concurrently, to an idea—which is largely the playwright's idea. He proceeds further to develop this point by saying that "in reality life builds the line but on the stage it is the artistic imagination of the author that creates it in the likeness of truth."[40] "The thoughts, feelings, conceptions, reasoning of the author are transformed"[41] into the actor's own. The "inner significance of the play" will not usually be discovered until the actor thoroughly studies the play "by following the steps the author took when he wrote it."[42] "The actor takes the thoughts in the lines of his part and arrives at a conception of their meaning. In turn, this conception will lead to an opinion about them, which will correspondingly affect his feeling and will. . . . The direct stimulus for the mind we can find in the thoughts taken from the text of the play."[43]

Stanislavski speaks more concretely of this point by referring to his own experience with the soliloquy in the final act of Gorki's *The Lower Depths* which demanded the impossible of him—

to give a universal significance to the scene, to say the soliloquy with such profound implications of deeper meaning that it became the central point, the denouement of the play. . . . I tried to get down to the roots of that soliloquy, to the fundamental idea of the play. I realized that my version had had no real kinship with what Gorki had written. My mistake had built up an impassable barrier between me and the main idea.[44]

Furthermore, Stanislavski's knowledge that the actor must be true to more than nature, that he must be simultaneously and finally true (1) to nature and (2) to the play, is granted and agreed to by Harold Clurman, one of the staunch American advocates of the system, when he announces his conviction that "the Stanislavski system is primarily concerned with the interpretation of plays in the most literal sense of the word . . . that the whole of the actor's technique to Stanislavski is mere virtuosity . . . unless it relates to giving a living body, a human breath to the *meaning* of the play."[45]

But knowing that foundation fact, the essential difference between nature and art, does Stanislavski teach his actors to be true to nature and to art? Although Stanislavski's definition is wrong and dangerously inconsistent with his knowledge of the art of acting, does he in his system as set down in *An Actor Prepares* teach the art of acting?

§3

The Stanislavski student actors are taught continually how to be true to nature, to life. That point is admitted by all, and gladly admitted, since life is the source of art and surely the very stuff of the theatre. But such teaching should be only preliminary to the main training; thus merely *An Actor "Prepares."* Acting as an art will not come into existence, life will not be translated into "the likeness of things absent," until the students are taught (1) how to find the idea and, almost simultaneously, (2) how to express that idea in terms of the theatre. The first is a prerequisite, obviously, to the second. Criticism, therefore, focusing its attention on this prerequisite fundamental, and overlooking Stanislavski's inept definition of his theory, can ask whether or not the Stanislavski system teaches the student actors the necessity of finding an idea to express.

The answer is an emphatic *no*. Nowhere in all his writings, despite the fact that he somewhat furtively agrees with Constant Coquelin's sound observation that "if I refuse to believe in art without nature I will not in the theatre have nature without art,"[46] does Stanislavski teach his students to be true to art, to find an idea to express. Most of his talk and his exercises in *An Actor Prepares* is devoted to training the students truly to live their parts and to rely *only* upon nature. In practice the system so consecutively emphasizes an inner feeling of truth to nature that the preliminary preparation for the art of acting becomes verily the perfection of the art, and is therefore defined loosely as being the art.

In his actual teaching Stanislavski forgets his own declarations to the effect that nature, life, experience, and a true inner feeling are the sources of art but never the substitutes for it. He forgets that the soil and the seed and the rain are necessary to the flower, but are not the flower. Talma's cry at the deathbed of his father might be the source of his cry of pain in a play, but it is a changed and a new cry when used on stage. The source of Dasha's deeply-stirred emotions in the scene from *Brand* may be the fact that not long ago she herself had lost a child;[47] the original grief is part of her real experience; but it is more than that, is something else, whenever it becomes part of the expression of a perceived idea. The weeping may have in it and behind it a personal verification; it may require some personal nourishment; but assuredly until it has in it Ibsen's idea it is merely mimetic or recalled weeping.

When Director Torstov (Stanislavski), for instance, in one of his exercises tells his students who are acting out the burning of the money that "if every little auxiliary is executed truthfully, then the whole action will unfold rightly"—when he tells them that he does not *believe* the counting of the non-existent banknotes, and then proceeds to deepen one student's "physical actions, movement after movement, second by second, until coherent sequence" is achieved and the class can see "to what an extent of realistic detail you must go in order to convince our physical natures of the truth of what you are doing on the stage"[48]—he is demonstrating not how to act, not how to express an idea, but only how to re-live sharply and fully and with belief the truth of experience. Loyal only to nature, he is merely teaching them verification and verisimilitude, and dangerously assuming that all men who feel deeply and honestly are artists, that Beethoven and Olin Downes and Jack Jones, when they sensitively and truthfully recall a pastoral experience, are each fully capable of composing symphonies.

Surely no one can prepare actors to express an idea so long as he blamefully omits to tell them that experiencing the validity of the playwright's material is not the same thing as perceiving the idea in that material which they as actors must actively and finally express. No one can soundly prepare actors unless he instructs them to proceed from the truth of emotions and actions to the truth of an idea. No one can correctly prepare actors until he warns his students that "there is no locale, character or action that would mean the same if isolated to itself."[49] Stanislavski does not teach acting when he forgets, or does not know how, to compel his charges to differentiate between life and art.

In all the exercises, as well as in all the warm explanations, of *An Actor Prepares* Stanislavski teaches only the truth of emotions and actions, the truth of nature, nothing more. He does not constantly and correctly fix attention on the idea to be expressed in the exercise of hunting for the brooch (pp. 35-37), of closing the door (pp. 40, 42-43, 154-158), of lighting the fire (pp. 40-41, 43); of communicating with the object of one's love (p. 218). These isolated and improvised scenes are never once acted, first, on a level of living and natural and honest truth, and then acted, second, on another level in accordance with the perception and expression of a dominant idea in a whole play. The Stanislavski students are taught thoroughly, but only that "feelings, drawn from our actual experience, and transferred to our part[s], are what give life to the play."[50] The students learn to appreciate nature and life, and to neglect acting and art.

Therefore these student actors following the Stanislavski system will henceforth tend to be totally unaware that banknotes would be counted one way in a scene from a Molière farce and another way in a Molière high comedy; and yet differently in a play by Bernard Shaw, and differently again in a play by Maxwell Anderson; and counted one way in a Shaw play written when he was thirty years old, and differently in another play written when he was sixty; and one way in an Anderson play as directed by Harold Clurman, and still differently in the same play as directed by Guthrie McClintic; and yet differently if the scene came near the beginning of the play and not near the end, and again differently if the playwright wished to emphasize the scene and not to subordinate it.

The playwright is emphatically ignored in *An Actor Prepares* even when Stanislavski as teacher leaves his own original improvisations and takes up the discussion or enactment of definite scenes from actual plays. Even then he continues to stress truth to nature at the expense of truth to an idea. He rarely, and never correctly, mentions the idea of a play and its scene; he never guides or drives the students to search for "an essential characteristic"; he is always almost completely oblivious of the playwright's mind. Thirteen different playwrights are discussed in the book.[51] But to his class these playwrights are as individual as so many quills, typewriters, or printing presses—and as unhuman; they are robots or voder-men minus perceptive minds and stylistic skills. They are men minus any ideas.

Of course, often aware of the inconsistency between his knowledge and his teaching, Stanislavski does tiptoe around the edges of his negligence and find it unfortunate that many actors frequently "are incapable of dissecting a play and analyzing it"; and then he can promptly kill his point with a subsequent but inept analysis of *The Inspector General*. Wise in saying that all actors "must subject the unit to a process of crystallization,"[52] he can then immediately proceed to neglect Ibsen entirely in his dissection of *Brand*,[53] and rather blur the theme of *Le Malade Imaginaire*.[54] Stanislavski does venture a consideration of idea in the chapter on "The Super-Objective" when he tells the class that "Dostoyevski was impelled to write *The Brothers Karamazov* by his lifelong *search for God*. Tolstoy spent all of his life struggling for *self-perfection*. Anton Chekhov wrestled with the *triviality* of bourgeois life and it became the leitmotiv of the majority of his literary productions."[55] He is sure that "the actor has to point up the super-objective [idea] himself, make it deeper and sharper,"[56] and that the super-objective must be "in harmony with the intentions of the playwright" while arousing "a response in the soul of the actors."[57] Then he can minimize, or rather kill, his whole point with the observation that this idea, this "intellectual main theme . . . will be right but it will lack some charm for the actor. It can serve as a guide but not as a creative force."[58] In other words, Stanislavski confusedly makes obeisance to his knowledge of the essentials of art, and to the principles advocated by Vakhtangov; but he continues to teach his students only to be true to their inner feelings as the best and sole preparation for the art of acting! He continues to search for the characters' psychological motivations and to disregard entirely the playwright's philosophical intent. He continues to teach true emotionalizing and to skip the emotionalized and emotionalizing idea.

The unfortunate and dangerous result of such skimpy and abortive teaching, or preliminary teaching which is but partly and wrongly preliminary, is that the students are left with the notion that whatever they have been doing or watching in the classroom exercises is acting. Surely as tomorrow comes they will tend always thereafter to depend only on life, on honest personal experience and belief; they will tend to maintain that that is acting. Rarely will they learn the value and potency of an idea; rarely will they know the necessity of finding an idea to express while acting in a play.

The disciples of Stanislavski's system will at once rush in to say that the playwright's idea is included in the "complete given circumstances" since "given circumstances" can always cover what you have forgotten to include. But certainly the playwright and his idea deserve a more important place than merely among the etcetera. Why should the relevancy of the idea be taken for granted? Why not award the playwright an emphasis at least equal to the emphasis given to nature? Actors must be emphatically taught that

the totality of the natural object which has been perceived empirically has been broken up. The artistic choice has already been made by the author. . . . It follows from this that there can be no question in dramatic art of a conventionalized imitation of a given aspect of nature. . . . The art of the actor means at least the art (of the author) seen through the temperament (of the actor).[59]

Actors must be taught constantly from beginning to end, whatever else they are taught, that "every dramatist has his own peculiar mental outlook, his works reveal it, and the actor must reflect it . . . ,"[60] that all parts are "characteristic of the brain that created them" and that since they have "the accent of the author, the actor must have it."[61]

Surely no competent teacher of acting can propose that this

essential "given circumstance," the prerequisite discovery of the idea, needs no emphasis and can be left merely to chance, to the kindness of time. Yet this is precisely what Stanislavski advocates throughout his system! He teaches his students that nature will become art, that the translation of the true inner feeling "will appear by itself after you have studied our whole system of acting."[62] "Time is a splendid filter for our remembered feelings—besides it is a great artist. It not only purifies, it also transmutes even painfully realistic memories into poetry."[63]

Graduates of the Stanislavski system are consequently supposed to wait for something to do in art without ever knowing what it is they will be called upon to do, and without being trained to do it. The system may therefore be said to lead the would-be actor from the conscious (re-living nature and believing in it) to the subconscious, or inspiration, or creation (waiting passively for an idea to come to all men who truly feel). Nature, without effort or vision, is transmuted by time into art!

I have seen this poor waiting in a production of Evreinov's *The Chief Thing* as acted by a serious, talented group of students who had arduously and faithfully practiced the Stanislavski system for two years on an average of five hours a day. Their acting was always inwardly true in every way to nature, believable as life itself to each of the actors and to most of the audience. Yet for all this achievement the result was pathetically murderous to the playwright's specific idea that theatricality is one of our happy and fruitful instincts. The lack of an idea to express was also in all probability behind Stanislavski's own failure to "incarnify" his role in Pushkin's *Mozart and Salieri*,[64] and behind Gordon Craig's refusal to accept Stanislavski's "humdrum naturalness and simplicity," which robbed his interpretation of all poetry in the Moscow Art Theatre production of *Hamlet*.[65]

Stark Young, in reviewing that theatre's production of Alexei Tolstoy's *Czar Fyodor* in New York, wished that the cast might have achieved "not the studied naturalness that we take daily as the ways of men, but the form, the magic of distance and scope, the conscious arrangement, the artifice and logic that would create in my mind the idea."[66] And those who argue that the same company notably discovered and luminously expressed the essential ideas in the four major Chekhov plays always forget that those plays were successfully produced before 1905, and that Stanislavski did not formulate his system of acting until 1907 nor start teaching it until 1911.[67]

The Stanislavski system of acting, as a deductive analysis of the Moscow Art Theatre company's acting, cannot teach anyone why or how that acting found the idea in *The Cherry Orchard* but failed to find it in *Czar Fyodor,* and *The Blue Bird,* and *The Life of Man,* and *Mistress of the Inn.* It leaves "seeing the idea" to the whims of time, to accident, or to rare racial inevitables.

Criticism therefore holds that the system can be more harmful than helpful, and that it can even be inimical to the whole art of the theatre because in its basic line it does not differentiate between nature and art; because the basic line of the system, bearing "the same relation to subconscious creative nature as grammar does to poetry,"[68] places such an emphasis upon the grammar that the student actor is misled into believing that this grammar is the desired poetry. Criticism maintains that the system cannot purposively prepare a favorable ground for inspiration; it is positive that the system cannot be used as a test for valid acting since it ignores the playwright and the idea.

If only Stanislavski had correctly defined an art and, then and therefrom, the art of acting; if only he had been intelligently articulate; if only he had thought consecutively with the zing of rightness, he might have found it necessary and relatively easy to teach his student actors to look for an idea to express in their acting. Possibly he might have taught more warmly and brilliantly what all alert American directors and teachers of acting must now teach and demand as they go beyond the basic line of the Stanislavski system toward the art of acting.

For instance, Stanislavski could have included in *An Actor*

Prepares an exercise for the class in which, under various definite circumstances, a girl must welcome home after long absence her brother, and set him immediately to avenging his father's murder. The students would then be drilled for pages, for days, until they individually found the true inner feelings, the honesty of the experience, a belief in the objectives, the actions, and the emotions. Next and most important the students would be taught to go from life to art; to find this "recognition scene" as part of a play, or many plays; to see an idea; to learn how the author's perception of life transforms the true-to-nature scene into something else; to discover that their acting must differ fundamentally with the expression of different ideas; and finally to distinguish between art and life. They could be taught by some such method that all true and well directed acting aims to express an idea, and that right and conscious aim is more dependable than a mere reliance upon the powers of time.

The aim of the acting in this same scene as placed in the plays of Aeschylus, Sophocles, and Euripides—although perhaps each experience might be identically "lived"—would differ in accordance with the idea to be expressed. In Aeschylus, as a whole, the tragic conflict is usually an abstract one between moral principles seen in the case of certain human beings; in Sophocles the conflict in moral principles is embodied in one man; in Euripides the conflict is related, almost psychologically, to society. The three *Electra's*, for example, are three different variations on the same theme—are what three different artists saw in the same incident—are three different visions or transformations of the same actual happening. If actors merely live truthfully the experience of the happening without the playwright's idea, they are giving an audience only the incident and not the individual transformation of the incident. If Stanislavski were fully teaching acting, he would teach his students to create differently, in terms of idea, the three "recognition scenes" in the three *Electra's*.

He would teach his students next that it is the individual playwright's original idea being expressed therein which so definitely changes this basically similar scene when it is used by Hugo von Hofmannsthal for his *Electra* in a way vastly different from the Greeks' use of it. The ancient "recognition scenes" begin:

[AESCHYLUS]

O thou that art unto our father's home
Love, grief and hope . . .
     the saviour that should be.

[SOPHOCLES]

Ah, dear, dear friends and fellow-citizens, behold Orestes here who has feigned dead, and now by that feigning hath come safely home!

[EURIPIDES]

O my brother, thou art come at last, and I embrace thee, little as ever I thought to.

The von Hofmannsthal scene begins:

O let my eyes look on you! Do not touch me.
Go on your way. I am ashamed before you.
I do not know how you can look at me. . . .
And yet I was the daughter of a King.
I think that I was beautiful: and when
At night before my mirror, I blew out
The lamp, I felt, and with a maiden thrill,
My naked body through the heavy night
Shine, as a godly thing immaculate.

Next he would teach his actors to aim differently in playing the same scene, with almost identical circumstances, but for another idea, as it is used by Robert Turney in his *Daughters of Atreus:*

I am myself again. This face. This face! These hands at last. The cruel vigil paid. The moment come! But have you come with arms on vengeance bent?

He would teach them a different style of acting a similar scene, with its new idea, in Eugene O'Neill's *Mourning Becomes Electra (The Hunted):*

ORIN (*with a boyish brotherly air* . . .) You certainly are a sight for sore eyes, Vinnie! How are you, anyway, you old bossy fuss-buzzer! Gosh, it seems natural to hear myself calling you that old nickname again. Aren't you glad to see me?
LAVINIA (*affectionately*) Of course I am!

In other words, if students are taught only to enact an actual incident, the audience will be left to find whatever ideas it can in the incident; and each member of the audience will find perhaps a different idea. If students, however, are trained to enact an actual incident as illustrating an idea which either Sophocles or O'Neill found in it, the audience might come nearer to comprehending or at least experiencing the specific idea intended to be communicated. In other words, there is a vast and fundamental difference between the actual case history of a modern New York matricide and the story of Orestes as set down by Aeschylus.[69] Put another way, knowledge of the psychology of the actual "living" of a character is not the same thing as knowledge of the psychology of attracting the attention of, and communicating an idea to, an audience in the theatre.

By the method of using similar scenes from *actual plays* for the purpose of translating life into art most teachers can truly prepare the ground for the coming of inspiration in the actor's expression of an idea. Actor students can be taught to find the different ideas, for instance, in the Amphitryon story in the different versions by Plautus, Molière, Dryden, Behrman-Giraudoux, and others. Actors can be taught to approach and to act differently the basically similar scenes between Lady Percy and Hotspur in 1 *Henry IV* (ii. 3) and between Portia and Brutus in *Julius Caesar* (ii. 1). Teachers can assign an exercise in which two students, a boy and a girl, enact a love scene on a park bench until they have perfected the playing for a true inner feeling. Then the scene can be translated into the expression of an idea, into art, as next they variously act the scene as it is designed in Chekhov's *Uncle Vanya* between Vanya and Helena (ii), in Molnar's *Liliom* between Liliom and Julie (i), in O'Neill's *All God's Chillun Got Wings* between Jim Harris and Ella Downey (i. 3), in O'Casey's *Within the Gates* between the Artist and the Young Whore (ii), in Odets' *Golden Boy* between Joe and Lorna (ii. 1), and even perhaps in the Quinteros' *A Sunny Morning* between Doña Laura and Don Gonzalo.

Not merely life itself as truly experienced, but the idea in it which is to be expressed, will lead student actors to playing such scenes correctly, just as only the *idea* will turn the characterization of Shylock comic or tragic, or what not, and design still another completely different Shylock for St. John Ervine's *The Lady of Belmont*. The *idea* that Yank delineates and expresses in O'Neill's *The Hairy Ape* is much more to the point than his individual psychology. The twinkling *idea* of Shaw and nothing else will lead the actors to playing rightly the final scene in *The Doctor's Dilemma* between Jennifer and Dr. Ridgeon. The comic *idea* and not the real experience of an eighteen-hour starvation will shape the hilarious acting of the "banquet" scene of the John Murray and Allen Boretz farce *Room Service* (ii) when Davis, Binion, and Miller "eat ravenously, wildly . . . guzzle, gorge and stuff themselves until every plate is clean, every cup dry."

A play is someone's idea about life. Therefore if actors are properly to serve a play, they must communicate to an audience the idea of the play, or an idea imposed upon the play. Furthermore, any valid system of acting must, above all else, teach apprentice actors eventually to express an idea.

When the Stanislavski system of acting is carefully examined, it can be proved faulty in theory and in practice. It is at best incomplete. It is far from being aesthetically final because it does not teach actors, emphatically and always, to hunt for an idea and then to express it in their acting.

NOTES

1. Throughout this article, including all quotations and titles, the transliteration used ends in *i* instead of *y*, since Constantin Alexeiev (1863-1939) adopted for a pseudonym the name of a Polish actor; and the final *i* is usually Polish, the final *y* Russian, as in Paderewski and in Stravinsky.

2. See Lorenz Kjerbühl-Petersen, *Die Schauspielkunst* (Berlin and Leipzig,

1925), trans. as *Psychology of Acting, a consideration of its principles as an art,* by Sarah T. Barrows (Boston, 1935).

3. See Alexander Tairoff, *Das Entfesselte Theater, aufzeichnungen eines regisseurs* (Potsdam, 1927).

4. For a popular summary of the work of Meierhold see Norris Houghton, *Moscow Rehearsals, an account of methods of production in the Soviet theatre* (New York, 1936), pp. 85-117; for the work of Vakhtangov see pp. 125-148.

5. R. Ben-Ari, "Four Directors and the Actor," *Theatre Workshop* I (January-March 1937), 67; trans. by Harry Elion from a chapter in the author's *The Habima* [in Yiddish] (Chicago, 1936). This article discusses many of the differences in the methods of Stanislavski, Meierhold, and Vakhtangov.

6. Stark Young, "His Art in Life," *New Republic* 94 (March 30, 1938), 222.

7. *Ibid.,* p. 223. For his comments on *An Actor Prepares* see "Preparing Actors," *ibid,* 89 (January 20, 1937), 359.

8. Harold Clurman, "Founders of the Modern Theatre," *Theatre Workshop* I (January-March, 1937), 75.

9. I sense in the pages of *An Actor Prepares* that the teacher himself knows that his lessons only partly solve some acting problems; and I have heard many times that Stanislavski had planned to write a sequel to that book dealing almost entirely with external form in acting.

10. V. Zakhava, "Can We Use Stanislavski's Method?" trans. Mark Schmidt and ed. Molly Day Thatcher, *New Theatre* XI (August, 1935), 16: originally appeared as B. [E?] Zakhava, "The Creative Method of the Vakhtangov Theatre," *Soviet Theatre,* XII (1931), 6-16.

11. Clurman, *op. cit.,* p. 79.

12. Zakhava, *op. cit.,* p. 18.

13. Young, "Preparing Actors," p. 359; taken from Constantin Stanislavski, *An Actor Prepares,* trans. Elizabeth Reynolds Hapgood (New York, 1936), p. 266.

14. Ben-Ari, *op. cit.,* p. 66.

15. Houghton, *op. cit.,* p. 75.

16. Stanislavski, *An Actor Prepares,* p. 18.

17. *Ibid.,* pp. 294-295.

18. Jane Ellen Harrison, *Ancient Art and Ritual* (New York, 1913), p. 223.

19. *Ibid.,* p. 248.

20. John Dewey, *Art as Experience* (New York, 1934), p. 42: "Emotion belongs of a certainty to the self. But it belongs to the self that is concerned in the movement of events toward an issue that is desired or disliked."

21. See Roger Fry, *Vision and Design* [1920] (Harmondsworth, Middlesex, England, 1937), pp. 32-33.

22. See [Leo] Tolstoy, *What is Art?* [1898] *and essays on art,* trans. Aylmer Maude (London, 1930).

23. Fry, *op. cit.,* pp. 33-34.

24. Harrison, *op. cit.,* p. 210.

25. See Dewey, *op. cit.,* p. 42; Harrison, *op. cit.,* p. 34.

26. Walter Dorwin Teague, *Design This Day, the technique of order in the machine age* (New York, 1940), pp. 177-178.

27. Christian Darnton, *You and Music* (Harmondsworth, Middlesex, England, 1940), p. 22.

28. Percy Lubbock, *The Craft of Fiction* [1921] (London, 1932), p. 28.

29. Stark Young, *The Theatre* (New York, 1927), p. 68; see also John Howard Lawson, *Theory and Technique of Playwriting* (New York, 1936), p. x. "The

52   STUDIES IN SPEECH AND DRAMA

form or essential structure is to a poem what the soul, or 'form' . . . of an animal is to its body. Doubtless this is a conception in which the philosophy of Socrates and Plato has a common ground with that of Aristotle; it seems to be a fundamental conception for all human thought." (Lane Cooper, *Aristotle on the Art of Poetry* [New York, 1913], p. xxiv).

30. See Stark Young, *Glamour* (New York, 1925), pp. 71-73.
31. Lawson, *op. cit.*, pp. x-xi.
32. Young, *Glamour*, p. 78.
33. See Aristotle, *Poetics*, VI, 19; XIV, 1; XXVI, 3.
34. Stanislavski, *An Actor Prepares*, p. 122.
35. *Ibid.*, p. 151.
36. *Ibid.* See also Bernard Bosanquet, *Three Lectures on Aesthetic* [1915] (London, 1931), pp. 7-8. "Say you are glad or sorry at something. In common life your sorrow is a more or less dull pain, and its object—what it is about—remains a thought associated with it. There is too apt to be no gain, no advance, no new depth of experience promoted by the connection. But if you have the power to draw out or give imaginative shape to the object and material of your sorrowful experience, then it *must* undergo a transformation."
37. *Ibid.*, p. 205.
38. *Ibid.*, p. 241.
39. *Ibid.*, p. 258.
40. *Ibid.*, pp. 241-242.
41. *Ibid.*, p. 233.
42. *Ibid.*, p. 238.
43. *Ibid.*, p. 234.
44. *Ibid.*, pp. 174-175.
45. Clurman, *op. cit.*, p. 80.
46. C. Coquelin, *The Art of the Actor* [1886], trans. Elsie Fogarty (London, 1932), p. 81.
47. Stanislavski, *An Actor Prepares*, p. 143.
48. *Ibid.*, p. 126.
49. Young, *The Theatre*, pp. 52-53.
50. Stanislavski, *An Actor Prepares*, p. 155.
51. Beaumarchais on pp. 194-195; Chekhov on pp. 160, 179; Gogol on pp. 105-106; Goldoni on p. 258; Gorki on pp. 173-174; Griboyedov on pp. 188-189, 257; Hauptmann on pp. 150-151; Ibsen on pp. 113-119, 142-147, 151-153, 263; Maeterlinck on pp. 150-151, 166, 192; Molière on p. 257; Ostrovski on p. 217; Shakespeare (*Hamlet* on pp. 165, 252-253, *Macbeth* on pp. 140-141, *Othello* on pp. 2-11, 16-17, 26-27, 103-104, 122-163, 165, 171, 200, 205, 235, 241, 252, 280-283); and Sophocles on p. 160.
52. *Ibid.*, p. 109, 115.
53. *Ibid.*; see also pp. 115-119, 263 ff.
54. *Ibid.*, pp. 257-258.
55. *Ibid.*, p. 256.
56. *Ibid.*, p. 257.
57. *Ibid.*, p. 284.
58. *Ibid.*
59. Kjerbühl-Petersen, *op. cit.*, pp. 142-143.
60. Coquelin, *The Art of the Actor*, p. 87.
61. *Ibid.*, pp. 88-89.
62. Stanislavski, *An Actor Prepares*, p. 151.
63. *Ibid.*, p. 163.

64. Constantin Stanislavski, *My Life in Art*, trans. J. J. Robbins (Boston, 1927), p. 549.

65. *Ibid.*, p. 523.

66. Young, *Glamour*, p. 52.

67. See Stanislavski, *My Life in Art*, pp. 458-467; and also p. 526.

68. Stanislavski, *An Actor Prepares*, p. 266.

69. See Frederic Wertham, *Dark Legend, a study in murder* (New York, 1941), for a picture of a contemporary matricide, and a study of the psychiatric process and the psychiatrist at work.

Expression in Stage Scenery

Barnard Hewitt

ALTHOUGH stage scenery today, like theatrical art in general, is predominantly realistic, and although most plays are produced today in forms of scenery which crystallized at the beginning of this century, there has been in recent years considerable experimentation. We have seen Shakespeare and some contemporary non-realistic plays set in abstract plastic settings. We have seen attempts to adapt painted perspective scenery to the needs of the modern theatre. More significant, perhaps, is the greater and greater simplification and abstraction which the realistic setting itself has undergone, until sometimes nothing has been left of the box set but the skeleton of a window or the texture of walls. Scenery has even been discarded almost altogether, not only in Shakespeare but also in a realistic play like *Our Town*.

Such experimentation, however unsystematic and varied in aim, is surely a sign of dissatisfaction with the established forms. Other signs are not wanting that stage scenery is inadequate to many of today's demands. Jo Mielziner says that he designs his settings for the two or three most important scenes of a play.[1] Although there may be some exaggeration in this statement, it serves to call attention to the large element of compromise at present inherent in scene design. Robert Edmond Jones apparently feels that the actor suffers under the necessary compromise and that the scenery actually gets in the way of the performance. "Would not a setting be more effective," he asks, "if it were merely an indication of the atmosphere of the play offered to the audience for a moment at the beginning of the performance and then taken away again?"[2] He goes further; he implies that scenery as we know it is a major obstacle to the growth and development of theatrical art: "The best thing that could happen to our theatre . . . would be for the playwrights and actors and directors to be handed a bare stage on which no scenery could be placed, and then told that they must write and act and direct for this stage."[3]

Why this dissatisfaction? Why is scenery inadequate to the demands of our theatre? We need not look far for an answer. Scenery today, both realistic and non-realistic, is predominantly three-dimensional. In spite of simplification, in spite of the development of revolving stages and wagon stages to-shift the plastic realistic setting, in spite of the ingenious use of light to alter the appearance of the plastic abstract setting, three-dimensional scenery remains relatively inflexible. This inflexibility might not be so apparent if we did not have at hand for comparison the theatre of the moving picture with its infinitely flexible scene. Not only can the moving picture make many more major changes in scene than are possible on the stage, but it can make minor changes from moment to moment, and is thus able to express scenically every slight development in the dramatic action. Even the realistic setting, so inflexible on the stage, can become highly expressive on the screen, as for example in the melodramas directed by Alfred Hitchcock. And when the screen abandons realism, as in the subjective film *The Eternal Mask* or in the animated cartoon, setting becomes a major means of dramatic expression. For a stage production of *The Doctor in Spite of Himself*, Sganarelle's hut can be built and painted to resemble a comic face, but for the screen Mr. Disney can animate that face so that it weeps, laughs, winks, squints, closes its eyes in mock horror, and, in short, becomes a major participant in the farcical action.

It is possible that the radio theatre also has contributed to the current dissatisfaction with stage scenery. The theatre of the air perforce does without all visual means of dramatic expression, but in losing stage scenery it has gained freedom of setting. By means of vocal descriptions, sound effects, and music, it can shift its setting almost at will.

In comparison with the moving picture and the radio, the stage appears extremely limited in its ability to express place. On the other hand, stage plays, influenced doubtless by the drama of screen and radio, are making greater and greater demands on the limited scenic expressiveness of the stage. Stage scenery in its present forms is increasingly inadequate to the requirements of the drama. The time is ripe for the molding of new theatrical forms, for the development of new means of expressing place. The theatre is ready for change.

What will be the nature of this change? In what direction is theatrical art likely to move? A glance at the history of the theatre should help us to answer that question, for it will serve to remind us of the different means of expressing place in the theatre of the past. It will remind us also that scenery has not always been a major means of expressing place, and that the scenic artist has always been limited and guided by technical conditions.

We have no direct knowledge of the beginning in Greece of theatrical art, but the assumption is that it began without scenery. The place of the dramatic action and the place of the performance were one and the same, a flat circular space around an altar. The first scenery doubtless appeared when the place of the dramatic action was no longer the place of the performance. The altar was then transformed by means of scenery into the rock to which Prometheus was bound or into some other object required by the action and suggestive of the place of the action. Because the audience nearly surrounded the playing space, this scenery was necessarily three-dimensional, and probably because machinery had not been developed for shifting it quickly, it remained permanent throughout the play. Though this first scenery suggested place and consequently to some extent mood, it was important less as a means of such direct expression than as a focus and physical support for the acting. When expression of place was of special importance to the action or the mood, the playwright depended largely on verbal description by the characters and choruses.

Scenery as background appeared with the scene house, a permanent building designed primarily as a dressing and storage house. Different kinds of temporary fronts could be attached to the scene house, and painted panels could be fastened between the pillars of its porch, providing greater scope for the expression of place. Because there were no machines for swiftly shifting this scenery, and because artificial light was not used, such expression remained limited to changes from play to play. In all probability this background scenery remained relatively general, allowing the playwright to describe in words, if he so desired, the exact location of different episodes in the same play. The background scenery, like the scenery built around the altar, was expressive mainly through its physical support of the acting, for which it provided a new focus and a variety of levels and entrances. Although Greek playwrights tended to keep their plays within the limitations of the generalized permanent setting, they felt its inflexibility, and often, in order to indicate changes of place within the play, resorted to such conventional devices as the *exostra, ekkyklema,* and *pariaktoi.*

No fundamental change occurred in the form and functions of scenery through the rest of the classical period. In the Roman theatre the area and variety of the acting space were reduced without increasing the expressiveness of the scenery.

When the theatre was reborn in the Middle Ages, it shared the sprawling character of all medieval art. The episodic mystery plays required that many different places be represented as specifically as possible. The medieval theatre developed a tremendous stage with a dozen or more specific playing spaces set around or at the rear of an unlocalized space, a dozen stages in one. Each of a dozen of the episodes of the mystery play was acted on a different stage in a setting as solid and detailed as ingenious artisans could make it. The episodes in which place was less important were played in the neutral area. Scenery did not have to be shifted. Even expense was no item, for performances were infrequent, and the Guilds bore the cost of production. Because the audience tended to surround the playing space, and performances took place under natural illumination, scenery remained three-dimensional. It retained its function of supporting the acting, a base capable of great variety from stage to stage, and it gained immeasurably as a means of direct expression through its greater freedom to indicate place. It is probable that sometimes—for example, in the scenes at Hell Mouth—scenery tended to overshadow the actor. The next great theatre, that of Elizabethan England, was professional and unsubsidized. It inherited from the medieval theatre a form of play characterized by many brief scenes and by the frequent shifting of the place of the action, but it could not afford the costly medieval method of staging. Moreover, artificial illumination had not yet been turned to theatrical use. Consequently the Elizabethan stage developed a largely permanent generalized setting, which in essentials was much like that of the Greek theatre, though in appearance of course very different. With its forestage projecting into the auditorium, its permanent architectural background, resembling almost any English city street, its two inner stages, permanent entrance doors, and permanent balcony windows, the Elizabethan stage was a marvelous machine for acting. It provided an acting base of great area and variety, and it permitted a conventional indication of change of place by the shifting of the action from one part of its permanent structure to another. Specific expression of place was, however, limited to such moveable scenery as could be used in the two inner stages (on which the sightlines were extremely bad) and to such properties as could be carried on and off the forestage by the actors. Scenery had lost the direct expressiveness it had gained in the medieval theatre.[4] When place was important to the action, the playwright resorted to verbal description.

As long as production took place out of doors under natural illumination and partly in the midst of the audience, scenery could be made directly expressive only at great cost. However, when the theatre moved indoors under artificial illumination and the stage was set behind the proscenium arch, it was discovered that two-dimensional scenery painted in the newly developed technique of linear perspective could be used effectively. At first two-dimensional painted scenery replaced three-dimensional scenery in the background only; the scenery in the acting area was still built in three dimensions. Under these conditions the plastic unity of actor and setting, which had characterized theatre art since its beginning, was lost, but a visual unity could still be maintained. A variety of background could be achieved cheaply and easily. As the technique of scene painting improved, the desire for still greater flexibility, and no doubt the desire also for still greater economy, led to the use of two-dimensional painted wing pieces in the acting area. Thus the stage could be set with a single great perspective painting by the simple expedient of cutting the painting up into backdrop, wings, and borders. Since all the scenery was then two-dimensional, it was cheap to make, and it was easy to shift by means of a fundamentally simple system of windlass, pulleys, and ropes. This type of scenery permitted great variety and tremendous elaboration; it was free to express place as specifically as one might wish and to express mood with no limitation but the imagination of the scenic artist.

Scenery, however, had lost its organic relation to the action of the play as expressed through the physical movement of the actor. Even the visual unity of actor and setting was gone. Scenery had become background merely, a tremendous illustration to the text of the actors' movement and speech. There can be little doubt that a good deal of scenery's gain was at the expense of the actor. He was deprived of the aid of a varied playing base, for the stage floor was denuded in order that the background might be more elaborate and varied. Moreover, the perspective painted scene was most effective under a flat, shadowless illumination, an illumination which made the three-dimensional actor less expressive.

In the latter half of the nineteenth century, scenery as illustration became unacceptable to a world which had absorbed the scientific concept of environment. Human action had come to be regarded as inseparable from its environment, of which it was considered to be the product. Unity of setting and actor could be restored only by making scenery once more three-dimensional. The painted perspective scene gave place in interiors to the box setting with three walls and a ceiling, and in exteriors to a setting with at least the foreground built up in three dimensions on the stage floor. Since the notion of environment is scientific rather than imaginative, setting had to be an exact reproduction of real place; so it became not only three-dimensional but also extremely specific. The more solidly realistic the setting, the more expensive to build and the more difficult to shift. The more specific the setting, the less is it capable of change in appearance under changing light. In its new forms scenery retained and developed the power to express place with exactitude, and it retained the power to express mood within the limits of realism, but it lost almost all flexibility. The actor, re-endowed with a setting which supported the action physically as well as emotionally, and once more plastically lighted, gained in comparative prominence, though this gain was somewhat reduced by the convention of realistic acting which demanded that he sink himself in the setting.

The restrictions of the realistic style quickly stirred up rebellion in a variety of experiments, all of them involving some modification in the notion of the function of stage scenery and of its form. Perhaps the first of these was the replacement of the idea of scenery as environment in the scientific sense by the idea of scenery as environment in the dramatic sense. A particular setting should grow not out of imitation of any real place but out of the physical demands of the action. In form it should express mood rather than place. This was the abstract architectural setting demanded by Gordon Craig. Adolphe Appia, rebelling against the disunity of the wing-backdrop type of production, had arrived at much the same conception of setting. Freed from the bonds of factual detail, scenery gained tremendously in its ability to express mood, and it gained also in potentiality for change under changing light. But it remained three-dimensional, and consequently retained much of the inflexibility of realistic scenery. It was much less capable of change from scene to scene than was the painted setting against which Appia rebelled.

Bakst for the Ballet Russe and a number of painter-decorators for the plays of Maeterlinck and other symbolists revived the painted setting, using it without realism for the expression of mood rather than of specific place. Thus liberated, scenery tended once more to overshadow the actor.

Other experiments have had for their aim the greater subordination of setting to actor. Such was Copeau's purpose when he developed a permanent setting a good deal like that of the Elizabethan theatre. The ultimate in subordination of setting to actor appeared in constructivism which purged the setting of all direct expression in order to make it a stimulator of physical action.

Production today, though predominantly realistic because most plays are written in the realistic convention, reflects to some degree most of the counter-realistic experiments. Constructivism did not develop into a popular style, but its influence is still felt in the use of action-promoting elements in other styles of setting. The desire to concentrate attention on the actor has undoubtedly been a factor in some of the scenery-less productions of the past few years. Though the revival of painted scenery led to no large-scale movement, it is still used occasionally, as in Chaney's setting for *Twelfth Night*. The strongest non-realistic scenic current is that which Craig and Appia set in motion. Most non-realistic plays are set today in a relatively abstract architectural setting, and this type of setting has been carried to a high point of perfection, for example, in Norman Bel Geddes' production of *Hamlet* and in Max Reinhardt's production of *The Eternal Road*. In both, light was used to transform from scene to scene the appearance of a large permanent structure composed of many levels and various forms.

In the main current of realistic production the skill of the engineer has been utilized to make flexible the factual three-dimensional scenery required for most plays. Revolving and wagon stages have been used with ingenuity to move quickly and easily the settings for the play requiring several changes of place. But the realistic play has grown more and more episodic, until it has quite overtaxed the machinery. Designers have been forced to greater and still greater simplification until the realistic setting has come very close to abstraction, for instance, in the skeletal forms of Mielziner's settings for *Two on an Island* and in the omnipresent brick walls of Morcom's settings for *Native Son*.

With the simplification of scenery, both realistic and non-realistic, there has been a growing tendency to rely more and more upon light to express place and mood. This was perhaps best illustrated by Orson Welles' production of *Julius Caesar* on low platforms set against the bare back wall of the stage. He used a changing pattern of light in place of moveable scenery. This is well along the road toward the disuse of scenery.

Should scenery be discarded and replaced by other means of expression? Or can it be made more flexible? Realistic three-dimensional scenery can expect no more help from the machines, and is in danger of losing its character through extreme simplification. Abstract three-dimensional scenery has probably achieved the greatest flexibility possible through the manipulation of light, but it is possible to imagine abstract three-dimensional scenery which could be made to change its form actually as well as apparently. In fact, an attempt to construct such scenery was made some years ago.

The fervencies and paradoxes of Gordon Craig's writings have tended to obscure his genuine contributions to theatre theory, among others his analysis of scenery as a means of dramatic expression. He saw that scenery can be indirectly expressive, as it was in the Greek and Elizabethan theatres, by supporting and stimulating the physical movements of the actors.[5] He saw also that the abstract plastic setting can be made to change in appearance by changing the light thrown upon it, and can thus be made directly expressive of the developing dramatic action.[6] But he was not satisfied with the scenic expressiveness obtainable by those means, and he realized that if the setting was to become fully expressive, it must achieve motion. It must become capable of changing its shape, not in the intermissions behind the curtain, not *apparently* by means of the shifting play of light, but *actually* before the eyes of the audience.[7]

The desire to make the setting change by degrees instead of sharply between scenes seems to be comparatively new in the theatre. Hubert von Herkomer was moving in that direction when he modelled his realistic exteriors in order to be able to imitate the changes which occur in real landscape under the changing light of day.[8] And Appia's conscious use of light to unite actor and abstract setting led him to utilize it also as a means of altering the appearance of the setting in accord with the development of the dramatic action.[9] The notion of actual fluidity of setting seems to have been original with Craig, however.

Craig apparently did not succeed in his one attempt to make the setting thus mobile,[10] but his failure does not mean that it cannot be done. In fact it is surprising that Craig's failure has not already inspired someone with engineering training to develop a type of screen and the necessary machinery to permit the composition in space and time of a background expressive of the developing dramatic action. Although apparently it did not occur to Craig, it is not impossible to imagine the development of machinery for varying the stage floor in response to the changing demands of the physical action. Such inventions should not be beyond the ingenuity of this age of machinery, and they would increase tremendously the expressive possibilities of the abstract plastic setting. It is doubtful, however, if such development can ever be a major solution to the problem of scenic expression. The necessary machinery will almost surely be expensive, and great though its contribution might be to the flexibility of the abstract setting, it would still carry the limitations of all such machinery. Moreover, it would solve the problem for only a small proportion of the plays being written today.

Another possible direction of change lies along the way suggested by such productions as Orson Welles' *Julius Caesar* and Jed Harris' *Our Town*. Scenery can be discarded and other means of expressing place and mood can be developed in its place. The potentialities of light, on which Welles largely depended in his *Julius Caesar,* have probably already been fully exploited, for as Appia long ago pointed out, the expressive power of light depends almost wholly on what it illuminates. If we liberate light from the fixed forms of scenery, we necessarily deprive it of a large part of its expressiveness.

Although, as seems likely, the expressive possibilities of light have already been mapped, the expressive possibilities of sound are only beginning to be guessed at. Harold Burris-Meyer pointed out in 1935 that sound is as controllable and therefore as dramatically useful as light.[11] Since then he has been experimenting with the dramatic uses of the control of intensity, pitch, quality, direction, apparent distance, and form (reverberant or non-reverberant) of vocal and non-vocal sound. By controlling reverberation he has found it possible to give to dialogue the peculiar character it has in a huge cathedral, in the cramped quarters of a dungeon, and in other physical surroundings of real life.[12] The possibilities of this means of expression have caught the imagination of Robert Edmond Jones: "A magical new medium of scenic evocation is waiting to be pressed into service. Imagine a Voice pervading a theatre from all directions at once, enveloping us, enfolding us, whispering to us of scenes 'beautiful as pictures no man drew.' "[13]

All this suggests a theatre in which auditory expression will to a great extent supplant visual expression. Before accepting this as the only possible direction in which our theatre can move, we should ask why visual expression has proved inadequate to the demands made upon it. It must be obvious that in our time the greatest obstacle to expressiveness in stage scenery is the notion, which came into the theatre with realism and was strengthened by the Craig-Appian scheme for non-realistic production, that a plastic unity must exist between actor and setting. We have seen in the past that the period of greatest scenic expressiveness was the period of painted perspective scenery, a period in which the setting was almost wholly independent of the actor. As sporadic attempts have shown, it is not enough merely to revive the painted setting. A new visual technique is needed. And there are indications that scenery may actually throw off the yoke of plastic unity, not by a return to the painted technique of the past, but by the development of a new technique of projection. Jo Mielziner combined projected scenery with realistic three-dimensional pieces in *Two on an Island,* and with abstract three-dimensional pieces in *Journey to Jerusalem.* This may be a tentative first step along a road of infinite possibilities. Robert Edmond Jones, sensitive to all the currents of theatrical change, clearly points the way when he says: "In the simultaneous use of the living actor and the talking picture there lies a wholly new theatrical art."[14]

Some attempts have already been made to combine the moving picture and the living actor, the best known perhaps those of Piscator some years ago in Germany, but little has yet been done in this country, nor anywhere in a systematic fashion. And systematic experiment, of the kind which Burris-Meyer is carrying on in the dramatic use of sound, will be needed to solve the problems which will inevitably present themselves. Ordinary projected scenery is static and permits of a visual unity with the actor, but, once the projection moves, even this visual unity is lost, and we are faced with a problem in the focus of attention.

On the stage as we know it, actor and setting are presented simultaneously. The moving picture does not have to present actor and setting at the same time; the camera eye can shift from actor to setting and back again with the greatest of ease. If moving pictures are used as scenery in the theatre, almost surely a technique must be developed for shifting attention from the actor to the screen and back again. This may mean that the theatre will have to assume a good deal of the episodic form of the moving picture, alternating episodes of expression by the actor with episodes of projected scenic expression.

If the theatre adopts the moving picture, both plastic and visual unity between actor and setting will be lost. The actor may find his playing space restricted in extent and variety, but the gain in scenic expressiveness will be tremendous. Scenic expression on the stage has always been restricted by the single viewpoint of its audience; whereas the screen, whose audience sees through the moveable eye of the camera, enjoys complete freedom of scenic expression. If the stage is able to adapt the camera eye to its own needs, it will enjoy much of the same freedom.

Thus the way seems open for the theatre to move in two quite different directions. The stage may become once more a platform, backed by infinite space or perhaps by drapes or flats neutral in color and in form. On this platform actors may present plays without the aid of scenery, the necessary expression of place being supplied by light, by vocal descriptions (those of the visible actors or those of an unseen narrator), by descriptive sound effects, and finally by the intensity, pitch, quality, direction, apparent distance, and degree of reverberation of their own voices, mechanically controlled and distributed. The substitution of light, voice, and sound effects for scenery holds possibilities for the development of a strongly auditory theatre art, in the tradition of the Greek and Elizabethan theatres. On the other hand, the moving picture screen may become an integral part of the stage. We can imagine a number of small, bare acting platforms and lighting arrangements which will permit instantaneous shift of attention from one acting platform to the screen, to another acting platform, back to the screen, and so on. In the combination of the living actor with the moving picture lies the possibility of a strongly visual theatre art, in the tradition of the theatre of painted perspective.

NOTES

1. Quoted by Norris Houghton, "The Designer Sets the Stage, VI," *Theatre Arts Monthly* XXII (February, 1937), 116.

2. *The Dramatic Imagination* (New York, 1941), p. 146.

3. *Ibid.*, p. 135.

4. George Fullmer Reynolds' recent study, *The Staging of Elizabethan Plays at the Red Bull Theatre 1605-1625* (New York, 1940), casts doubt on the long-accepted reconstruction of the Elizabethan stage. If Dr. Reynolds is right, scenery in the Elizabethan theatre was like scenery in the medieval theatre, although probably not so extensive, elaborate, and costly.

5. *Towards a New Theatre* (London, 1913), p. 41.

6. *Scene* (Oxford, 1923), pp. 19-26.

7. *Ibid.*, p. 20.

8. "Scenic Art I," *Magazine of Art* XV (1892), p. 259.

9. Adolphe Appia, *Die Musik und die Inscenierung* (Munich, 1899), p. 78.

10. The famous production of *Hamlet* at the Moscow Art Theatre, described by Stanislavski, *My Life in Art*, tr. J. J. Robbins (Boston, 1924), pp. 519-522.

11. The Dramatic Use of Controlled Sound, a paper delivered before the Acoustical Society of America (April, 1935).

12. Harold Burris-Meyer, "Theatrical Uses of the Remade Voice, Subsonics and Reverberation Control," *Journal of the Acoustical Society of America* XIII, 1 (July, 1941), 16-19.

13. Jones, *op. cit.*, p. 140.

14. *Ibid.*, p. 17.

Color Music

WALTER H. STAINTON

MOBILE color as an independent art form has interested in the course of the centuries a strange company of philosophers, scientists, and musicians. Many of these, fascinated by the possibilities of an art combined of sound and sight, have based their work on the false premise that there is a simple relationship between colors and the notes of the musical scale. In considering the relationship between the senses, Aristotle proposed the theory that "if either contrary or diverse qualities are to be simultaneously perceived there must be an absolutely individual psychical unity which can yet be viewed in two different ways at the same time."[1] Newton was intrigued more by the prospect of a mathematical relationship between music and the colors of the rainbow than by a psychical unity of sight and sound. He attempted to divide the colors of the prismatic spectrum into seven intervals proportional to the intervals of the musical scale. Later he realized that the intervals were dependent upon the nature of the refracting material.[2] The false notion of a simple parallelism between the spectrum and the octave has interested others, but cannot be said to have influenced the course of practical experimentation with the art of mobile color.

The first to envisage such an art and to create a device for realizing it appears to have been Louis Bertrand Castel, a Jesuit priest.[3] His *Esprits, Sallies et Singularities du Père Castel,* published (posthumously) in 1763, contained a chapter entitled "Clavessin pour les yeux." It described an instrument in which, when the player depressed a key, a string was plucked, and simultaneously a lighted area of translucent colored cloth was exposed.

Other experimenters during the next century and a quarter described and built crude instruments. Bainbridge Bishop, of Essex County, New York, constructed a projection instrument attached to a parlor organ. At first he used daylight as his source of illumination, but later he turned to the then new electric arc.

The rapid progress of science at the end of the nineteenth century made an auspicious time for the development of a color organ. The greatest of American physicists recognized this, and his imagination was caught by the possibilities. Said Michelson, lecturing in 1899:

> If a poet could at the same time be a physicist, he might convey to others the pleasure, the satisfaction, almost the reverence, which the subject [light waves] inspires. The aesthetic side of the subject is, I confess, by no means the least attractive to me. . . . Indeed, so strongly do these color phenomena appeal to me that I venture to predict that in the not very distant future there may be a color art analogous to the art of sound—a *color music*, in which the performer, seated before a literally chromatic scale, can play the colors of the spectrum in any succession or combination, flashing on a screen all possible gradations of color, simultaneously or in any desired succession, producing at will the most delicate and subtile modulations of light and color, or the most gorgeous and startling contrasts and color chords! It seems to me that we have here at least as great a possibility of rendering all the fancies, moods, and emotions of the human mind as in the older art.[4]

But the poet-physicist did not appear. Had Michelson himself chosen to answer his own challenge, the progress of color music would, undoubtedly, have been hastened.

It may well be that Michelson's vision was inspired not only by his study of light waves but by knowledge of the experiments of A. Wallace Rimington, from whose invention, made about 1893, all modern color music dates. Rimington was a painter and a teacher who constructed, and later patented, an intricate color organ. This first instrument, or a similar portable model, was demonstrated in London, at St. James Hall, on June 6, 1895. Rimington's organ consisted principally of fourteen optical projection systems using electric arcs as light sources, each system equipped with a number of delicately balanced shutters for controlling the hue and brightness of the projected light. Apparently both carbon bisulphide prisms and selectively absorbing filters were used to produce color. A keyboard of several octaves enabled the operator to play the light on a textured white fabric screen placed opposite the instrument at the end of a large room. By suitable controls, the visible spectrum might be spread over the entire keyboard, or over a single octave with tones of "paler and deeper intensity" over the higher and lower octaves.

Though he believed that the art would have its chief development in connection with music, Rimington did not fall into the error of attempting to relate sight and sound in any simple manner. He did, to be sure, use a musical keyboard, and he did divide the spectrum-band in accordance with the octave. But this was for convenience only. And it should be said, with emphasis, that he did not assign various colors to specific notes of the musical scale. Rimington himself states his position clearly:

In the earlier days of my experimental work I was perhaps inclined to think of it [the analogy between light and sound] as of more value as a working hypothesis in the construction of some of my instruments than I do at present, and there is, no doubt, a certain fascination about its mysterious possibilities; but I cannot too clearly guard myself from being understood to lay any great stress upon the probability of its existence.[5]

An observer, viewing a composition played upon Rimington's instrument, saw a uniformly lighted area (broken only by the texture of the screen) which changed in hue, saturation, and brightness, slowly or rapidly according to the will of the operator. Apparently one or more areas of a second color might be projected upon the colored background. Rimington held, however, that form, if used at all, should be indefinite or merely decorative and not in any sense realistic, that a cloud form might add interest to slow compositions, but that, in rapid compositions of color, form would be an unnecessary complication.[6] While Rimington himself, as well as other and less interested observers, appears to have preferred slow color changes, he thought that some compositions in rapid tempo might be acceptable after the spectator had had a certain amount of training.[7]

Opinions regarding the success of Rimington's color music as an art form differ widely. Rimington was, however, able to arrange an extended series of concerts, and for more than two years he toured England with his bulky equipment.

One of a number of experimenters of the twentieth century was Mary Hallock Greenewalt, an American musician. She devised a keyboard instrument for playing lights on a fulled silver-fabric curtain. Her principal use of mobile color appears to have been as an accompaniment to piano music. While the Greenewalt instrument seems not to have advanced the art of color music, the inventor recognized an important limitation of all color instruments, namely, the limited lighted area or field of projection:

It may be that while color play on such a curtain, or on other objects or surfaces on a stage in front of an audience, will constitute an important feature of this new art, yet, after all, this is but a part of the main object. To produce its maximum effect, or, conversely, to express most fully the emotions of the performer, the illumination *of the whole interior* must be played upon. This is because of the very wide seeing angle of the eye—both horizontally and vertically —and because illumination, like the atmosphere, is all pervading, and surrounds the whole person, and the whole assemblage of persons. A play on that enveloping illumination must be had if the highest expression of this new art is to be conveyed.[8]

G. A. Shook, a physicist, describes his mobile color apparatus in considerable detail. All instruments constructed by him have had four essential parts:

1. A stationary light source—generally and preferably a standard projection lamp.
2. A movable optical device for distorting the light source into effective shapes to be imaged on a screen [a black-bordered, matte-white surface] as mobile color motifs.
3. A lens for projecting these shapes on a distant screen.
4. A rotating color disk to cause a continuous flow of colors through the motifs.[9]

The distorting devices used to produce the motifs are short-focus lenses, cylinders, prisms, and diffusing glasses. The color disk is made of segments of colored glass or gelatine between two glass plates. With some choice of direction and speeds, a motor-driven gear train rotates the distortion and color disks.

An apparatus of this kind, though it may produce the most remarkable colored patterns, is hardly more than an elaborate effect machine such as is known to the theatre, and would be an effect machine no less if the disks were turned by hand at the will of an operator. Shook has experimented with the combination of music and color, but with no thought of trying to establish a fixed relationship between sound and light.

Thomas Wilfred, a Danish-born American citizen, has done more than anyone else to advance mobile color as an art. His instrument (or more exactly, series of instruments) called the Clavilux has been in process of development over a period of many years—before he came to America in 1916 and after his first recital in 1922. Wilfred's own description of his instrument lacks details:

Clavilux, a keyed projection instrument which makes possible the use of light as a medium for aesthetic expression. . . . The instrument consists of a number of projectors grouped before a large white screen and controlled from a keyboard that is either attached to the projectors or placed at a distance. The keys slide in grooves grouped in tiers, each comparable to a pipe-organ manual. A tier contains three sets of keys connected with the form, colour and motion-producing devices in the corresponding projector in which a strong beam of white light from an incandescent lamp, after passing through the three devices, is projected on the screen as one or more mobile images depending in form, colour and motion upon the positions and movements of the various keys. A skilled player may select to play a silent visual composition previously written by another artist and recorded by means of a special notation system.[10]

The reluctance of the inventor to disclose in detail the mechanism of his instrument has been due to the fact that he has utilized well-known optical principles in ways which, while highly ingenious, have not, perhaps, been patentable. To any technically-minded observer, Wilfred's use of variously shaped incandescent lamp filaments is clearly evident. Indeed, once noted, these projected filaments become a source of distraction in almost every composition played. At least one observer has noted also "the silhouettes that serve as static participants in a composition."[11]

Wilfred has always insisted that color music is an independent art. Though music is sometimes used as a prelude, his compositions are performed in silence. His few attempts to combine the mobile color of the Clavilux with music have, like earlier attempts of other experimenters, been marked by indifferent success. On one occasion, performing with the Philadelphia orchestra, Wilfred interpreted with his colored lights the music of Rimsky-Korsakoff's symphonic suite "Scheherazade." Some in the audience reported that the play of colors intensified the music, but most found that the two sensations were incompatible and that Wilfred's usual avoidance of a union of the arts was the right course.[12]

Because Wilfred's compositions are all relatively complex, no description can be altogether satisfactory. Stark Young has most nearly succeeded:

When you sit at the keyboard you first select your form that is to open the composition, your solo figure; then you select your color and the way it is to be introduced into the form and into space. It may be introduced as a plain rising or falling mass of color; or it may come in fibres, interlacing, juxtaposing or superimposing. Then your form may move independent of your color, the two may move together, or either one move while the other remains stationary. Or several forms may be introduced, moving in different rhythms, thus creating a visual counterpoint.[13]

A more recent review makes still other suggestions concerning the nature of Wilfred's compositions, at the same time implying clearly the limited range of the Clavilux:

He [Wilfred] is at present concentrating on two objectives: increased depth and heightened contrast between sharply defined and amorphous shapes within a single composition. New "stops" have been added to the instrument on which he plays. These enable him to introduce subtle blendings of color and a more complex rhythm of movement.[14]

All mobile color instruments thus far considered have had one characteristic in common: the color music is produced at the time of projection either by a human player or by a mechanism which permits some variation by the operator. There is another device now in use for producing color music. Potentially at least, the motion picture film with its associated mechanism is capable of projecting images far beyond the range even of the Clavilux. Potentially also, color music through the motion picture film might reach far larger audiences than Wilfred could ever hope to reach with his unique instrument.

The borderline between the "avant garde" and the "abstract" film, and the film of color music cannot be clearly defined, but many non-realistic films from the earliest days of the cinema to the present may be considered the "primitives" of the color music film. Among those who have experimented with the medium are Viking Eggeling, Fernand Leger, Man Ray, Len Lye, and Oskar Fischinger. Fischinger's films, for example, show "abstract motion including pure line, line and plane mass, plane mass in color, solid in color, and a combination plane mass and solid in color."[15]

Far from the primitives are the films of Disney. These are not in general considered color music, yet they have shown their creator's increasing interest in color, and his increasing command of its possibilities, until in "Fantasia" we have a demonstration of the potentialities of the motion picture film for producing color music. At least one observer, as early as 1936, foresaw the turn Disney's imagination would take, and in effect predicted "Fantasia."[16] In this work, the Bach "Toccata and Fugue" is accompanied on the screen with brilliant colors flowing and merging as a background for lacy figures in constant change. One critic, who started to write that the fluid patterns on the screen were intended to create the mood of detached reverie suitable for the enjoyment of the music, found himself writing instead that they created the mood for the enjoyment of the entire program.[17] Color had triumphed over sound. Of course, the music of "Fantasia" came first, and we are told that the patterns in light are those which might pass through the mind while one is listening to the music. Regardless of original intent, however, the visual accompaniment of the "Toccata and Fugue" (and indeed of all other parts of the film as well) is to most observers the significant aspect of "Fantasia." As one reviewer put it: "The effects achieved are nevertheless Walt Disney plus Bach or Beethoven. And the audience applauded exactly where it would have applauded had the score been composed by a Hollywood musician."[18] An earlier experimenter offered mobile color as an accompaniment to music; Disney may have intended his work to be a mere accompaniment; but the prime response of the audience has been to the screen, not to the musical score.

To predict a future for color music would be idle speculation. Color music engages the attention of few persons who call themselves artists, largely, perhaps, because of the complex mechanisms involved in experimentation. If there is a future for the art, its considerable cost of development will, presumably, be borne by a large corporation. The color musician can make no significant progress without the assistance of engineers and craftsmen—and a great deal of money.

To indicate some of the possibilities of development is not difficult. Color music, while utilizing to the fullest extent the advances of science and technology, must deal with ideas rather than with things. In its highest forms, paralleling the highest forms of music, it must be rigidly conventionalized. It must provide pure visual experience without the trappings of the realistic motion picture.

Color music will develop, if not independently of music, at least without theories of a simple relationship between sound and sight. That ghost has been laid to rest permanently by the facts of science. "If the name colour music can be applied with justice to a sequence of coloured lights, the justification must be based solely on the mental states produced by the arrange- ment and not on any dualogy, real or fancied, between the spectrum and the octave."[19] Sound, if used at all, will be the accompaniment and will be specially composed.

Color music appears infrequently to have been considered as painting in movement. In many respects, however, it is closer to painting than to music. For this reason it seems improbable that there will ever be a standardized color organ, correspond- ing, for example, to the pianoforte in sound music. Yet it would be possible to fix by convention the range of effects which a given instrument might be built to produce. Indeed, a symphonic group of instruments, each with its individual range of effects, immediately suggests itself as being capable of the grandest conceivable mobile color.

The simplest instrument, not unlike that of Rimington, would be capable of projecting uniformly on an extended white surface, in any time sequence desired, all the visible hues in a wide range of saturation and intensity. Screen brightnesses approaching daylight levels would be desirable. Both instantaneous and dissolving changes would be possible with this simple instrument. The compass of such an instrument might well be sufficient to serve as accompaniment for music, though too limited to hold interest long if played independently.

Successively more complicated instruments, placing fewer limitations upon the demands of the player, might be devised, and with each instrument an art of color music, conventionalized upon the limitations of the particular instrument, might be developed. One instrument might permit simple division of the screen color, another might introduce certain non-geometric shapes. The possibilities for varieties of color instruments appear greater, if that be possible, than the varieties of musical instruments.

Wilfred's Clavilux is well up the scale toward complete flexibility, but neither the Clavilux nor any other instrument of its type can approach the range of the motion picture film. One minor use of the motion picture film might be to reproduce at will the entire repertoire of a color organ such as the Clavilux.

Color motion picture photography of moving patterns in light or of moving objects in space offers the most obvious method of making reproducible color music. There are, however, other methods of using the color film. Klein[20] discusses a number of these. The cartoon technique of Disney and others permits a free play of the imagination of the artist. Colored papers and solid models may be used in modifications of the cartoon technique but are limited in range. Methods of coloring film directly have been tried with some success, notably by Len Lye in "The Rainbow Dance" and other abstract films.

In summing up the advantages of the motion picture film Klein says:

The composer is offered limitless scope as to the class of composition he desires to create. No instrument and no collection of instruments and performers could compete with the reproductive powers of the film. This applies to every expressive factor, colour, shape, form, movement, synchronization, rapidity of change, subtlety of gradation, etc. There is probably nothing that the human visual imagination can conceive which the colour film could not be caused to record.[21]

A considerable advance in the art of color music will have been made when the restricted area of a relatively small screen ceases to limit the artist and the response of the observer. Looking at a screen in a dark room, as has been well said, is "analogous to observing the outer world through the mouth of a cave." As already noted, Greenewalt realized the limitations of a small screen as early as 1926. To replace the small, plane screen, Klein's proposed hall of color music is modest in its requirements. Three-dimensional color music encompassing the entire visual field of every one of a group of observers seated near the center of a section of a spherical shell is practicable. The technical problems of three-dimensional projection, the synchronization of many projector mechanisms, and the exact registration of projected patterns have, very largely, been solved.[22]

If a great artist and a wealthy patron can some day be brought together, a color music to meet the most extravagant demands of the human imagination will be evolved.

NOTES

1. *De Sensu and De Memoria,* trans. G. R. T. Ross (Cambridge, 1906), p. 32.

2. *Opticks: or, a Treatise of the Reflections, Refractions, Inflections and Colours of Light* (London, 1721), pp. 110, 111. Newton's method of division is described in R. A. Houstoun's *Light and Colour* (London, 1923), pp. 12-14.

3. Adrian Bernard Klein, *Coloured Light* (London, 1937), p. 2. A history of color music is given in Chapter I. This book is the third edition of the author's *Colour-Music the Art of Light* (London, 1926).

4. A. A. Michelson, *Light Waves and their Uses* (Chicago, 1903), pp. 1-2; quoted by permission of the University of Chicago Press.

5. *Colour-Music* (New York, 1911), p. 32.

6. *Ibid.,* pp. 71, 72.

7. John W. N. Sullivan, "An Organ on which Color Compositions are Played," *Scientific American* CX (February 21, 1914), 163, 170.

8. "The Light-Color Player," *Transactions of the Illuminating Engineering Society* XXI (April, 1926), 414.

9. "Design of Mobile Color Apparatus," *ibid.*, XXIV (June, 1934), 428.

10. "Clavilux," *Encyclopædia Britannica* (14th ed., 1932), V, 784.

11. Edward Alden Jewell, "Development of the Color-Organ," *New York Times* (June 16, 1935), Sec. X, p. 8.

12. "Clavilux," *Outlook* CXLII (January 27, 1926), 130; George Vail, "Visible Music," *The Nation* CXV (August 2, 1922), 120.

13. "The Color Organ," *Theatre Arts Monthly* VI (January, 1922), 29.

14. Edward Alden Jewell, "Clavilux Recital Given by Wilfred," *New York Times*, November 2, 1940, p. 18.

15. Hubert C. McKay, "The Ciné Amateur," *American Photography* XXXII (November, 1938), 820.

16. Adrian Bernard Klein, *Colour Cinematography* (London, 1936), p. vii.

17. Bosley Crowther, "Walt Disney's 'Fantasia' . . . ," *New York Times*, November 14, 1940, p. 28.

18. Franz Hollering, "Films," *The Nation* CLI (November 23, 1940), 513.

19. R. A. Houstoun, *Light and Colour* (London, 1923), p. 172.

20. Klein, *Coloured Light*, p. xxvii *et seq.*

21. *Ibid.*, p. xxix.

22. The Eastman Kodak "Hall of Color" of the 1939-1940 New York World's Fair used eleven synchronized projectors (they were not, however, conventional motion picture projectors) on a semi-cylindrical screen twenty-two feet high by one hundred eighty-seven feet in circumference.

Senecan Influence in *Gorboduc*

MARVIN T. HERRICK

§1

GORBODUC, or Ferrex and Porrex, by Sackville and Norton, has long occupied the position of a minor Elizabethan classic. Students of the drama know that *Gorboduc,* first presented at the Inner Temple in 1561-62,[1] is the first blank-verse tragedy in English; few take the trouble to read it. Historians of the sixteenth century mention *Gorboduc* as an important milestone in the development of Elizabethan tragedy; few take the trouble to examine it carefully. Those historians and critics who have studied the play have found it either a political admonition to Queen Elizabeth or a capital example of Senecan tragedy.

It is the Senecan influence that I propose to examine now. The political message in the play seems fairly clear. The authors were much exercised about the Tudor succession and evidently hoped, by dramatizing the perils of disunity, to strengthen Elizabeth's sovereignty. The Senecan influences, however, are not so clearly or easily defined. In 1887, H. Schmidt[2] published a study of *Gorboduc* in which he asserted that the "classical influence is due only to Seneca." In 1893, John W. Cunliffe[3] attributed the external form of the English play to Seneca and decided that Seneca was also responsible for the long speeches, the sententious precepts, and some of the thought. In 1908, Felix Schelling[4] said that *"Gorboduc* is pure Seneca." In 1910, Homer Andrew Watt,[5] in the most detailed examination yet made, demonstrated that *Gorboduc* is, in part, a native outgrowth from the medieval morality play. Watt agreed with Cunliffe that the external form is Senecan, and he concluded his examination of Senecan parallels with this modification of Schmidt's statement: "All the classical traces in *Gorboduc* may be due to the influence of the Senecan tragedies." In 1939, Howard Baker[6] declared that the emphasis upon Senecan influence in *Gorboduc,* and in other Elizabethan tragedies as well, is a "blighting critical fiction."

Baker, in his attack on Schmidt, Cunliffe, and Watt, presents
several good arguments. He argues that the five-act structure of
Elizabethan tragedy comes primarily from classical comedy, that
the Chorus is descended from medieval expositors and from
commentators in the metrical tragedies (e.g., *The Mirror for
Magistrates*, 1559-1610), that the Messenger is common enough
in medieval mysteries and moralities, that the Ghost—which
does not appear in *Gorboduc*, to be sure—is an "essential convention" in the metrical tragedies (e.g., *The Mirror for Magistrates*). Bloody horror, melodramatic rant, and sententious precepts are, says Baker, no special gift of Seneca to the Elizabethans, who found Thyestean banquets in Ovid, melodramatic
rant in Herod of the mysteries, and sententious precepts in the
speech of their own forefathers. Far from agreeing with Schmidt
and Watt, that the classical influence in *Gorboduc* is due to
Seneca, Baker finds *Gorboduc* merely classical in general, by no
means Senecan in particular.

I believe we may grant Baker every one of his arguments and
at the same time contend that he has not yet discredited the
importance of Senecan influence in *Gorboduc*. Sackville and
Norton surely owe much to the native English mysteries and
moralities. They are also heavily indebted to the English metrical tragedies, to the *Mirror for Magistrates* and to that poem's
model, *The Fall of Princes* by John Lydgate. Nevertheless,
when we say with Baker that the native traditions in English
drama are important, we need not say, as does Baker, that
Seneca is unimportant. Both influences are important. Though
the five-act structure probably starts from the plays of Terence,
Seneca's tragedies, by the time they were well known in England,
were divided into five acts. The authors of *Gorboduc* could
have found Renaissance authority[7] for ending each act with a
sententious choral passage, but they probably borrowed the device from the Tudor translations of Seneca's tragedies.[8] Seneca
does use Messenger and Ghost. Seneca does pile bloody horror
upon bloody horror. Seneca's rant is often very good rant, and
was much relished by the Elizabethans. The *sententiae* in
Seneca's tragedies were extremely popular in the sixteenth cen-

tury, sharing a place in the poetic anthologies,[9] such as Mirandula's *Illustrium Poetarum Flores* and the *Polyanthea,* with extracts from Virgil, Ovid, Horace, Plautus, and Terence. On the other hand, Baker has successfully challenged the easy assumptions of critics who dismiss *Gorboduc* as merely Senecan. His arguments, in my judgment, have reopened the case. He has suggested that the classical background of the English play may be complex and not "pure Seneca." Therefore I propose to re-examine *Gorboduc,* testing the Senecan parallels adduced by Schmidt, Cunliffe, and Watt, searching for Senecan parallels that may have been overlooked by these critics, and trying to identify other influences, classical, medieval, and contemporary, which have helped to shape the play.

§2

As every one familiar with *Gorboduc* knows, each of the five acts is preceded by a dumb show which summarizes the action to follow. This dumb show is Italian in origin, not classical. The dumb show before the first act exhibits the old story of the bundle of sticks, which are easily broken one by one but unbreakable when bound together.

Hereby was signified that a state knit in vnitie doth continue strong against all force, but being diuided is easely destroyed; as befell vpon Duke Gorboduc diuiding his land to his two sonnes, which he before held in monarchie, and vpon the discention of the brethren to whom it was diuided.

The ultimate source of this pantomime is doubtless the well-known fable of Aesop. The tragic interpretation, however, may go back to Lydgate's conclusion to the story of Thebes in his *Fall of Princes:*

As this tragedie doth to you discure,
Kyngdamys deuyded may no while endure. (1. 3842-43.)

If the authors of *Gorboduc* did consult Lydgate's story—Sackville, for one, knew Lydgate well, as did all the contributors to the *Mirror for Magistrates*[10]—they would have been referred to Seneca's tragedies.[11] The *Thebais* of Seneca, even in its fragmentary form, would have offered the most convenient dramatic source for the tragedy of a divided kingdom. Another play of Seneca, *Thyestes,* to which Lydgate also refers,[12] would have offered sensational material for the horrors of strife between brothers. Thyestes, when invited by his brother Atreus to return and share his rule, says: "The throne holds not two."[13] Aegisthus, in Seneca's *Agamemnon,* says that "neither throne nor bed can bear a partnership."[14] Eubulus, the wise secretary of King Gorboduc, expresses the same opinion: "Within one land one single rule is best."[15] The Chorus of Act 1, which moralizes upon the preceding action, enlarges upon the danger of a divided reign and predicts the coming fall of Gorboduc, who

> A myrrour shall become to princes all
> To learne to shunne the cause of suche a fall.

It should be pointed out that both Statius and Lucan also speak of the dangers of divided rule.[16]

Videna, Gorboduc's queen, opens the first act with a complaint:

> The silent night, that bringes the quiet pawse
> From painefull trauailes of the wearie day,
> Prolonges my carefull thoughtes, and makes me blame
> The slowe Aurore, that so for loue or shame
> Doth long delay to shewe her blushing face;
> And now the day renewes my griefull plaint.

Schmidt and Watt have compared this speech with the opening lines of Seneca's[17] *Octavia:*

> Iam vaga caelo sidera fulgens
> Aurora fugat, . . .
> age, tot tantis onerata malis,
> repete assuetos iam tibi questus.

(Now shining Aurora drives the wandering stars from heaven. . . . Lead on, weighed down with all thy woes, renew thy now accustomed plaints.)

In part, the parallel is fairly close. But there is no mention in Octavia's speech of Aurora's delay because of love or shame. Ovid, in a celebrated passage that both Marlowe and Shake-

speare have imitated, presents a nocturnal lament and describes
Aurora, who deserts her aged husband's bed, as "more shameful
than any woman in heaven."[18] The notion of shame may also
owe something to Lydgate, who thus describes the goddess in
his *Troy Book:*

> Abasched rody, as I can diffyne,
> Only of fer that is femynyne,
> For a-schamyd durst[e] not be seyn
> Because sche had so longe a-bedde leyn
> With fresche Febus, hir owne chose knyght.[19]

Another famous nocturnal lament, which has doubtless influenced the authors of *Gorboduc* here, is that of Dido in the
fourth book of the *Aeneid.* The phrase "silent night," for example, was commonly recognized in the sixteenth century as
Virgilian.[20] Thomas Cooper, whose *Thesaurus* (first published
in London in 1565) was standard authority for Elizabethans,
attributes the phrase to Virgil. So does Textor in his *Epitheta*
(Basle, 1549). It looks as if Videna's speech was based upon
Virgil, Ovid, Seneca, and possibly Lydgate.

There is further evidence that Seneca's *Octavia* has come to
mind during the writing of this scene. Videna's tirade against
the injustice of Gorboduc, who is planning to deprive her
favorite son, Ferrex, of half the kingdom, is reminiscent of
Octavia's bitter complaints about the injustice of her husband
Nero. Octavia implores Jove to destroy this "tyrant of the
world."[21] Videna prays that Jove will punish Gorboduc and his
counselors.[22] One of the themes in *Gorboduc* is a protest against
tyranny. From Chaucer and Lydgate to Sackville's *Complaint,*
Nero has been a favorite example of the tyrant, and the best
dramatic treatment of Nero is in Seneca's *Octavia.*

In the second scene of Act 1, Gorboduc announces his plan of
dividing the realm between Ferrex and Porrex. His counselors
debate the merits and demerits of the plan. Eubulus, the secretary, who strongly objects to dividing the kingdom, presents the
best arguments. Eubulus recognizes two grave dangers: (1) the
overwhelming greed for power that exists in men, (2) the suscep-
tibility of youth to fraud and flattery. Both of these objections

are good Senecan doctrine and appear time and again in the
tragedies as well as in Seneca's philosophical writings. Eubulus
says:

> Suche is in man the gredy minde to reigne,
> So great is his desire to climbe alofte,
> In wordly stage the stateliest partes to beare,
> That faith and iustice and all kindly loue
> Do yelde vnto desire for soueraignitie. (262-66.)

The Chorus of Act 3 presents a more elaborate statement of the
same argument. Oedipus, in the *Thebais,* speaks of his two
sons, who are quarreling over the kingdom, as abandoning all
right, all filial love in their greed for sovereignty. "Their hearts,"
says Oedipus, "are crazed with lust for rule."[23] Eteocles, the
younger son, admits that "empire is pleasing at any price."[24]
Seneca's Hippolytus, in a celebrated speech on the superiority
of the country over the city, attributes the ills of mankind to
greed and "cruel thirst for power."[25] The Nurse in *Octavia*
names as chief among the long series of crimes that have afflicted
Rome "lust for sovereignty."[26] An often quoted chorus in *Hercules Oetaeus* teaches the same lesson of the evils of greed and
desire for power.[27]

Eubulus, in Act 1, Scene 2, warns the King against trusting
power to youth:

> Arme not vnskilfulnesse with princely power. (325.)

Eubulus fears lest the "fraude"

> Of flatteringe tongues corrupt their tender youth
> And wrythe them to the wayes of youthfull lust,
> To climyng pride, or to reuenging hate. (352-54.)[28]

Seneca (the character), in trying to restrain Nero, says: "It is
more necessary that fiery youth be ruled."[29] Agamemnon, in
trying to restrain young Pyrrhus at Troy, says: "Ungoverned
violence is a fault of youth."[30] And Agamemnon adds: "No one
holds violent rule long."[31] Atreus, who distrusts everybody, is
especially distrustful of youth: "Youths readily listen to the
worse precepts."[32] Atreus sees that his own sons have small
chance of escaping evil: "Though none should teach them the

ways of fraud and crime, the throne will teach them."[33] The Chorus in *Hippolytus* says: "Cruel lust conquers pure men; fraud reigns high in the palace."[34]

Eubulus (330-31) and the Chorus (Act 1) point to Phaethon as the example of rash youth who brings ruin to the world. In the next act (2. 1. 203-08) Dordan, counselor to Ferrex, also refers to Phaethon:

> Lo, such are they now in the royall throne
> As was rashe Phaeton in Phoebus carre;
> Ne then the fiery stedes did draw the flame
> With wilder randon through the kindled skies
> Than traitrous counsell now will whirle about
> The youthfull heades of these vnskilfull kinges!

Watt has called attention to two parallels in Seneca,[35] and Baker[36] has reminded us that the famous story of Phaethon is in Ovid's *Metamorphoses*. Nevertheless, the moralizing upon Phaethon is more Senecan than Ovidian. Beyond the statement that the "middle course is safest,"[37] Ovid does not emphasize any lesson in the story; but the two choruses in Seneca, as usual, moralize. Sackville and Norton, however, could have found Phaethon as the example of rash, ungoverned youth in Chaucer and Lydgate, both of whom moralize on the story.[38] Evidently Phaethon had long been a conventional symbol of rash behavior.

In the dumb show before Act 2, a king refuses a glass of wine but accepts a gold cup of poison, drinks it and dies—signifying that a clear glass (i.e. the wholesome counsel of a faithful friend) holds no poison, but that the "delightfull golde filled with poyson betokeneth flattery." The Chorus (Act 2) summarizes the lesson:

> Loe, thus it is, poyson in golde to take,
> And holsome drinke in homely cuppe forsake.

Watt has called attention to a familiar phrase in Seneca: "Poison is drunk from gold cups."[39] Hippolytus expresses a similar idea: "The proud drink from anxious cups of gold; how delightful to lap from the spring with bare hand."[40] Thomas Cooper's *Thesaurus* says: "*Bibunt auro sollicito superbi*. Seneca. Drinke in golde, but with feare of poysonyng." The Chorus of *Hercules*

Oetaeus, probably with Atreus and Thyestes in mind, says: "In golden cups the wine is mixed with blood."[41]

I have no doubt that this emphasis, in *Gorboduc,* upon the evils of pride, fraud, and flattery owes much to Seneca. I think it is likely that Sackville and Norton drew also upon Erasmus and possibly upon Erasmus' chief authority, Plutarch. Chapter 2 of Erasmus' *Education of a Christian Prince* is entitled "The Prince Must Avoid Flatterers." Early in the chapter we read: "This pest [the flatterer] has a pleasing sort of poison."[42] Plutarch discusses flatterers and parasites in his essay *How to Tell a Flatterer from a Friend* and in his even more famous essay on the *Education of Children.*[43]

Ferrex protests that he has no evil designs; he hopes that the prince of Hell may torture him with Tantalus' thirst or Ixion's wheel or Tityus' vulture if he ever wished harm to his father.[44] Sackville and Norton did not have to go to Seneca for Tantalus, Ixion, and Tityus; they could have found them in many places, notably in Ovid and even in Lydgate.[45] Nevertheless, Ferrex is not merely mentioning these famous sufferers; he is calling down their particular punishments upon himself. Likewise, Seneca's Deianira, the wife of Hercules, asks Pluto for the same punishments, adding the stone of Sisyphus to the other three tortures.[46] Likewise, Theseus, when he realizes that he has driven his son to death, asks for the same punishments.[47]

There is a phrase in Dordan's reply to Ferrex which also may be Senecan. Dordan, in speaking of the father Gorboduc, says: "While yet the Fates do lende him life to rule" (25). This conception of man's life and all his possessions as a loan from Fate or Fortune is prominent in the Stoical philosophy of Seneca.[48] The same idea appears in the old morality play of *Everyman,*[49] however, and we cannot be sure that the authors of *Gorboduc* were directly indebted to Seneca.

Hermon, a parasite, undoes by his flattery the good counsel of Dordan. Hermon urges Ferrex to violence:

> But, if the feare of goddes and secrete grudge
> Of Natures law, repining at the fact,
> Withholde your courage from so great attempt,

> Know ye that lust of kingdomes hath no law:
> The goddes do beare and well allow in kinges
> The thinges [that] they abhorre in rascall routes. . . .
> Thinke you such princes do suppose them-selues
> Subject to lawes of Kinde and feare of gods? (140-51.)

Schmidt and Watt have found parallels in the *Agamemnon*. Clytemnestra says, "There is a law for the throne, another for the private bed,"[50] and Aegisthus, "This they think is the greatest pledge of kingship, if whatever is unlawful to others is lawful to them alone."[51] I find another parallel in a speech of Atreus which is perhaps even more apt. Jasper Heywood, in 1560, translated it as follows: "Such holines, such piety and fayth, Are private goods: let kings runne one in that that likes their will."[52]

Watt suggests that we have here, in Seneca and in Sackville and Norton, an expression of the divine right of kings. What we have, however, is quite the contrary. All of the speakers, Clytemnestra, Aegisthus, Atreus, and Hermon are wicked people with wicked designs. The good characters in Seneca's tragedies and the good characters in *Gorboduc* respect the laws of Nature and the laws of man. Seneca, the good counselor of Nero, for example, tries to dissuade the tyrant from his ruthless course. Seneca tells Nero that an emperor should put off his wrath, refrain from bloodshed, cherish the fatherland, give peace to the world, and so, like Augustus, win heaven and deification.[53] It is the Senecan villain who defies Nature's law and man's law. The Chorus in *Medea* speaks of the "sacred covenants of the universe."[54] Polynices is overwhelmed by his brother's disregard for Nature's laws.[55] The wicked Lycus, in *Hercules Furens,* admits that he rules "without fear of laws."[56] Octavia says that her wicked mother (Messalina) was "unmindful of the laws."[57] Octavia's Nurse says that Messalina, in her greed for empire, broke Nature's laws and every right.[58] The Nurse in *Hippolytus* solemnly warns Phaedra that her unlawful passion will overturn Nature.[59] Theseus, believing that his son is guilty of incest, reviles him for disobeying Nature's laws.[60] Likewise, the good characters in *Gorboduc,* Eubulus, Philander, the Chorus, Gorboduc himself, reverence Nature and the law. Philander, for example, says:

> Nature hath her ordre and her course,
> Which being broken doth corrupt the state
> Of myndes and thinges, euen in the best of all.[61]

Hermon's advice is bad advice; his flattery is turning Ferrex to unnatural, evil ways. Dordan, the good counselor of Ferrex, expresses the proper judgment of such sentiments:

> O Heauen! was there euer heard or knowen
> So wicked counsell to a noble prince? (2. 1. 162-63.)

Hermon is descended from the medieval and classical parasite, but Sackville and Norton have transformed him into a Senecan villain whose wicked counsel, which awakens pride and lust for empire, turns Ferrex into a villain.

Porrex, the younger son, needs little prompting from his parasite (Tyndar). He determines to attack his brother before Ferrex attacks him:

> Shall I geue leasure, by my fonde delayes,
> To Ferrex to oppresse me all vnware?
> I will not. But I will inuade his realme,
> And seeke the traitoir prince within his court!
> Mischiefe for mischiefe is a due reward. (2. 2. 52-56.)

Watt refers to a fairly close parallel in *Thyestes*. Atreus, plotting vengeance, on his brother, says:

> For which ere he prepare himselfe, or force to fight entend,
> Set fyrst on him, least while I rest he should on me aryse.
> He wil destroy or be destroyd in midst the mischiefe lyes,
> Prepard to him that takes it first.[62]

I suspect that "mischiefe for mischiefe is a due reward" may also owe something to a line from *Agamemnon*, translated by Studley as "The safest path to mischiefe is by mischiefe open still."[63] According to Senecan ethics, mischief is punished by mischief, for crime always recoils upon its author.[64] Philander, the good counselor of Porrex, sees that the young prince is about to bring ruin to all:

> Lo, here the end of these two youthful kings,
> The fathers death, the ruine of their realmes! (67-68.)

Therefore Philander determines to make a final, desperate appeal to the King to avert this calamity. Likewise, Antigone, in the *Thebais,* makes an appeal to Oedipus to restrain his sons, whose madness is bringing civil war to the realm.[65]

The Chorus of Act 2 moralizes on the dangers of pride in ungoverned youth.

> When growing pride doth fill the swelling brest,
> And gredy lust doth rayse the climbing minde,
> Oh hardlie maye the perill be represt.

No tragic poet, I believe, has more consistently emphasized the peril of "swelling pride" than has Seneca.[66] *Tumidus* in the tragedies usually means "swollen with pride"; Cooper says that *spiritus tumidi* is Senecan.

Gorboduc, who has now learned of Ferrex's intentions, opens the third act with a speech that has long been labeled Senecan. The early lines of this speech are:

> O cruel Fates! O mindful wrath of goddes!
> Whose vengeance neither Simois stayned streames
> Flowing with bloud of Troian princes slaine,
> Nor Phrygian fieldes made ranck with corpses dead
> Of Asian kynges and lordes, can yet appease! (1-5.)

The phrase "O cruel Fates," according to Baker, is merely conventional. So it is; it is conventionally Senecan in the sixteenth century. According to Cooper's *Thesaurus,* both *dira fata* and *dura fata* (commonly translated by Elizabethans as "cruel fates") are taken from Seneca. Certainly Seneca repeatedly uses both phrases.[67] "Simois stayned streames," as Watt and others have pointed out, looks like an echo of a line in *Agamemnon.*[68] Gorboduc's speech as a whole is, I believe, reminiscent of Seneca's *Troades.* Gorboduc obviously thinks of himself as a descendant, by way of Brutus, of the Trojans, and he thinks of ruined Britain as further evidence of the "mindful wrath of goddes," whose "still-continued rage pursues our lyues."[69] Seneca's Hecuba, when she sees the ruins of Troy about her, cries: "The gods are not yet satisfied."[70] Gorboduc's phrase (14-15), "Hecuba, the wofullest wretch that euer lyued to make a myrrour of," may owe something to Chaucer's "the wofulleste wyght that evere was."[71] It may also be inspired by a complaint of Seneca's Hecuba.[72] It is surely a verbal echo of a chorus added by Heywood to his translation of the *Troades:*

And Hecuba that wayleth now in care,
That was so late of high estate a Queene,
A mirrour is to teach you what you are
Your wavering wealth, O Princes here is seene.[73]

Gorboduc's "happie Pryam" (16) may be an echo of Seneca's *felix Priamus.*[74]

Philander brings the King more bad news, that Porrex is invading his brother's realm. Gorboduc feels that nothing can stop his sons now:

In vaine we trauaile to asswage their mindes,
As if their hartes, whome neither brothers loue,
Nor fathers awe, nor kingdomes cares, can moue,
Our counsels could withdraw from raging heat. (3. 1. 92-95.)

Likewise, Oedipus, in the *Thebais*, when he hears that his sons are preparing civil war, feels that nothing can stop them now: "No respect for their wretched father, nor for their fatherland, moves them; their frantic hearts rage with lust for empire."[75]

Philander begs Gorboduc not to despair:

Yelde not, O king, so much to weake dispeire! (104.)

Eubulus says:

But now, O noble prince, now is no time
To waile and plaine, and wast your wofull life.
Now is the time for present good aduise.
Sorrow doth darke the iudgement of the wytte. (135-38.)

Likewise, Antigone urges her despairing father to stand firm and unyielding against calamities.[76] The thought in Eubulus' phrase, "Sorrow doth darke the iudgement of the wytte," is Senecan, and occurs more than once in the tragedies. The best parallels are in the *Troades*. Helen says that great grief lacks reason, or, as Jasper Heywood translates, "care do cause the want of wit, and reasons rule denye."[77] Ulysses says: "Sorrow is an unreasonable judge."[78]

When a Messenger brings news that Porrex has already invaded his brother's kingdom and slain Ferrex, Gorboduc calls upon Heaven to punish both his son and himself.

O Heauens, send down the flames of your reuenge!

> Destroy, I say, with flash of wrekefull fier
> The traitour sonne, and then the wretched sire! (163-65.)[79]

Though exhortations to Heaven for fiery vengeance are commonplace and conventional, the pattern of thought in this
speech is distinctly Senecan. Thyestes, for example, asks Jove
to blast with flames both Atreus and himself.[80] Likewise, Medea
calls upon Jove to prepare his "avenging flames" (*vindices
flammas*) and strike either Jason or herself, since both are
guilty.[81]

The dumb show before Act 4 presents three Furies:

Alecto, Megera, and Ctesiphone, clad in black garmentes sprinkled
with bloud and flames, their bodies girt with snakes, their heds
spred with serpentes in stead of heare; the one bearing in her hand
a snake, the other a whip, and the third a burning firebrand; ech
driuing before them a king and a queene, which, moued by furies,
vnnaturally had slaine their owne children: the names of the kings
and queenes were these: Tantalus, Medea, Athamas, Ino, Cambises,
Althea.

The Chorus of Act 4 says of these Furies:

> The dreadfull Furies, daughters of the night,
> With serpentes girt, carying the whip of ire,
> With heare of stinging snakes, and shining bright
> With flames and bloud, and with a brand of fire.

Schmidt calls these Furies Senecan. Baker suspects that their
origin is more complex. Baker is right, for the Furies here represent a very complex outgrowth from classical and medieval
sources. The phrase, "daughters of the night," is not Senecan.
Ultimately it is Aeschylean, but Sackville and Norton could
have found it in Virgil, Ovid, Chaucer, and Lydgate.[82] Seneca,
in his tragedies, speaks of Tisiphone and Megaera, but not of
Allecto. Statius, in the *Thebaid*, uses Tisiphone and Megaera.
Ovid names Tisiphone and Alecto, but never Megaera. Virgil
names all three, as do Dante, Chaucer, and Lydgate.[83] The snaky
locks and torches are conventional, and invariably accompany
the Furies. The black garments may be Senecan,[84] but the garments sprinkled with blood probably come from Ovid or
Virgil.[85] Seneca does not gird his Furies with snakes; Ovid and

Dante do.[86] The whip may come from Virgil, or Seneca, or Statius.[87] The names of the Furies' victims also come from various sources. Tantalus and Medea, to be sure, are from Seneca's *Thyestes* and *Medea*. Athamas, Ino, and Althaea are from Ovid's *Metamorphoses*. Cambyses, who was notorious for his madness, drunkenness, and murders, may go back to Herodotus, though suggestions may have come from Seneca's prose works and from Lydgate.[88]

Videna's long speech, which comprises the whole first scene of Act 4, has been called Senecan. Schmidt and Watt compare lines 1-8 with *Medea* 1-55. There does seem to be some parallel between Videna and Medea, that is, between mothers who prepare to kill their sons for vengeance. But there is also a parallel between Videna and Ovid's Althaea,[89] who appears in the dumb show with Medea. Another parallel in both situation and thought is offered by Alcmena's lament in *Hercules Oetaeus*. Videna mourns the loss of Ferrex, Alcmena the loss of her son Hercules. Videna says:

> Why should I lyue, and linger forth my time
> In longer life to double my distresse?

Alcmena says: "Why do I waste the day complaining, Why, O wretched life, dost thou endure?"[90] Even closer in phrasing is a complaint of Oedipus in the *Thebais*: "Why do I, lingering, drag on this life?"[91]

After her lament over the dead Ferrex, Videna curses Porrex in a tirade that may owe something to Agrippina's tirade against her son Nero.[92] Videna, who calls Porrex a monster and a tyrant, says:

> Moughtest thou not haue reached a mortal wound,
> And with thy sword haue pearsed this cursed wombe
> That the accursed Porrex brought to light,
> And geuen me a iust reward therefore? (54-57.)

Watt has found a Senecan parallel in the *Thebais*. Jocasta tells her sons to attack her, to strike the womb that bore the brothers.[93] Closer, in my judgment, is the cry of Agrippina when her son's murderer attacks her. The Chorus in *Octavia* recounts how Agrippina begged the murderer to sheathe his sword in her womb: "It is this must be torn by the sword, this which bore such a monster."[94]

Videna asks why Porrex, in his greed for blood and death, could not have chosen some other victim than his own brother. Jocasta, in the *Thebais*, uses a similar argument to halt the battle.[95]

Finally, Videna renounces Ferrex as a changeling:

> Rutheless, vnkinde, monster of natures worke,
> Thou neuer suckt the milke of womans brest,
> But from thy birth the cruell tigers teates
> Haue nursed thee! Nor yet of fleshe and bloud
> Formde is thy hart, but of hard iron wrought;
> And wilde and desert woods bredde thee to life! (71-76.)

Schmidt and Watt have found parallels in Virgil and Seneca.[96] The details in the Senecan parallel are much closer to the English speech.

In Act 4, Scene 2, King Gorboduc summons Porrex and tells him that his monstrous crime deserves death:

> Euen natures force doth moue vs to revenge
> By bloud againe, and iustice forceth vs
> To measure death for death, thy due desert. (25-27.)

The Chorus (Act 4) says:

> Blood asketh blood, and death must death requite.

The thought here is obviously Biblical; it is an expression of the Mosaic law.[97] But the thought is also classical, appearing in both Aeschylus and Euripides, and in Ovid as well.[98] The phrasing here, however, is much closer to Lydgate, to the 1559 edition of the *Mirror for Magistrates,* and to Sackville's *Complaint.*[99] I do not find either thought or phrasing specially Senecan. Apparently "blood for blood and death for death" was a more or less proverbial expression in the sixteenth century.

A sentence from Porrex's reply to his father is obviously taken from Chaucer. Porrex says:

> Then saw I how he smiled with slaying knife
> Wrapped vnder cloke! (122-23.)

The well-known line in the *Knight's Tale* reads:

> Ther saugh I . . .
> The smylere with the knyf under the cloke. (1999.)

The editor of *Ancient British Drama* (London, 1810) and Hazlitt[100] caught this borrowing, but modern commentators have neglected it.

After Porrex is banished, Arostus says to the King:

> How full of chaunge, how brittle our estate,
> Of nothing sure saue onely of the death. (152-53.)

Complaints about the fickleness of Fortune are, to be sure, commonplace in classical, medieval, and Renaissance literature, and they abound in English poetry from Chaucer on. Nevertheless, the peculiar pattern of thought here is certainly Senecan. There are numerous parallels in the tragedies, but the closest parallel is in one of the *Moral Epistles:*

> Nihil non lubricum et fallax et omni tempestate mobilius. . . .
> nihil cuiquam nisi mors certum est.
> (Everything is slippery, deceitful, and more changeable than any
> weather. Nothing is sure for anyone but death.)[101]

That Englishmen of the sixteenth century thought of complaints about Fortune as specially Senecan is evident from a passage in the 1559 *Mirror for Magistrates:*

> O morall Senec true find I thy saying,
> That neyther kinsfolke, ryches, strength, or fauour
> Are free from Fortune, but are ay decaying.[102]

Arostus goes on to say that the King should not let "Nature's power" overcome his just vengeance. But Gorboduc cannot bring himself to kill his son Porrex:

> Many can yelde right sage and graue aduise
> Of pacient sprite to others wrapped in woe,
> And can in speche both rule and conquere kinde,
> Who, if by proofe they might feele natures force,
> Would shew them-selues men, as they are in-dede. (159-63.)

Theseus expresses the same sentiment when he hears that his

son Hippolytus has been killed. Studley's translation (*c.* 1567) reads:

O Nature that prevaylste too much, (alas) how dost thou binde
Whyth bonds of bloud the Parents breast? how love we thee by
    kinde?
Maugre our Teeth whom guilty eeke we would have reft of breath?
And yet lamenting with my teares I doe bewayle thy death.[103]

Marcella, a waiting woman, enters to announce that Videna has murdered Porrex. She cries:

Is all the world
Drowned in bloud and soncke in crueltie? (169-70.)

Schmidt and Watt have pointed to *Hippolytus* 551-52:

Hinc terras cruor
infecit omnes fusus et rubuit mare.
(Hence streams of blood stained all the land and the sea grew red.)

The Senecan passage was well known in the sixteenth century; Mirandula quotes it and Cooper says: *"fusus cruor inficit terram* Sene."[104]

Gorboduc, when he hears of this latest crime, cries:

O hatefull light!
O lothsome life! O sweete and welcome death! (192-93.)[105]

This speech is probably Senecan; there are several fairly close parallels in the tragedies. Alcmena, after she has lost her son, cries:

quid misera duras vita? quid lucem tenes?
(Why endure, O wretched life? Why cling to the light?)[106]

Hyllus, in the same play, cries:

Pro lux acerba, pro capax scelerum dies!
(O grievous light, O day filled with crimes!)[107]

Octavia cries:

o lux semper funesta mihi, . . .
lux es tenebris invisa magis!
(O light, ever dismal to me! O light more hateful than the dark!)[108]

Jocasta, in *Oedipus,* says: "Death is welcome."[109] Theseus in

Hippolytus, Hecuba in *Troades,* Cassandra in *Agamemnon,* and Deianira in *Hercules Oetaeus* express the same idea.[110]

Another phrase of Marcella—"pale death pressing within his face" (225)—may owe something to Seneca, although the most celebrated *pallida mors* is Horatian.[111]

The concluding stanza of the Chorus (Act 4) is similar in sentiment to the moralizing of Theseus in *Hercules Furens:*

> O happy wight that suffres not the snare
> Of murderous minde to tangle him in blood!
> And happy he that can in time beware
> By others harmes, and turne it to his good!
> But wo to him that, fearing not to offend,
> Doth serue his lust, and will not see the end.

Theseus says that he who rules mildly, without bloodshed, he who holds his own spirit in check, shall live happily, and he concludes:

> sanguine humano abstine
> quicumque regnas; scelera taxantur modo
> maiore vestra.

(All ye who rule, abstain from human blood; your sins are more severely punished.)[112]

The last act witnesses the collapse of Britain in civil war and rebellion. The wranglings of the courtiers over the proper treatment of the mob, which has risen and killed both Gorboduc and Videna, are similar to debates in Seneca's *Octavia.* The British nobles advocate ruthless suppression of all the people. So does Nero in *Octavia.* Eubulus, while he condemns the people for their violence, expresses a more moderate policy. Eubulus fears the power of the mob:

Ye see, my lordes, what strength these rebelles haue. (5. 1. 74.)

The Nurse in *Octavia,* who, together with Seneca and the Prefect, represents moderation, says that the strength of the people is great.[113] Seneca warns Nero that the people will crush the man they hate.[114] The Prefect tells Nero that no one can check the madness of the mob,[115] and advises him to punish only the ringleaders. Likewise, Eubulus advises pardon for the people upon

condition that they give up their ringleaders for punishment.[116]
Eubulus argues that the people are naturally fickle and will soon
desert their leaders.

> So giddy are the common peoples mindes,
> So glad of chaunge, more wauering than the sea. (72-73.)

Schmidt and Watt have found a close parallel in *Hercules
Furens* 170, where the Chorus speaks of the mob as "more wavering than the sea" (*fluctuque magis mobile vulgus*). Since the
phrase occurs in a passage that was well known—it is quoted
in both Mirandula and the *Novissima Polyanthea*—it doubtless
has come to mind here. But, except for this one phrase, the
thought of Eubulus seems much closer to a chorus in *Octavia*.

> O funestus multis populi
> dirusque favor, qui cum flatu
> vela secundo ratis implevit
> vexitque procul, languidus idem
> deserit alto saevoque mari.

(O deadly and fearful to many is the people's favor, which has
filled their ships' sails with a fair breeze and borne them far, then,
languishing, has failed them on the deep and raging sea.)[117]

While the idea of a fickle, faithless mob is very common in
classical, medieval, and modern literature, there is evidence
that Sackville was familiar with this chorus in *Octavia*. There is
a note at the end of the author's manuscript of the *Complaint*
which, according to Miss Hearsey's transcription, reads as follows: "remember Magister Burdeus [?] promise for the showing
of Senecas chore [?] touching the captation of auram popu-
larem."[118] The only chorus in Seneca which treats specifically
of the popular favor is the one in *Octavia*. The chorus of
Hercules Furens remarks only incidentally on the "mob more
wavering than the sea." We find still further evidence in the
Complaint that it was probably Sackville who was responsible
for the last act of *Gorboduc*.

> Oo let no prince put trust in comontie
> nor hope in faith of giddie peples mind
> but let all noble men take hede by me
> that by the profe to well the pain do find

lo wher is truth or trust or what doth bind
the vain peple but they will swarve and swaie
as chaunce bringes chaunge to drive and draw that waie.[119]

Fergus, Duke of Albany, plans to seize the throne during the popular uprising. He believes that his chances for success are good:

And though they should match me with power of men,
Yet doubtfull is the chaunce of battailles ioyned. (158-59.)

Schmidt and Watt refer here to a speech of Jocasta in the *Thebais*.[120] Thomas Newton's translation (1581) is fairly literal:

Of warre, the doubtful hazardes all set downe before thy syght,
And throughly weigh thuncertayne chaunce that longes to martial
    fight.
Though al the power of Grece thou bring thy quarrel to mayntayne,
And though great armed multitudes of Souldiours thou retayne:
Yet chaunce of warre stil doubtful hanges.[121]

Although comments on the doubtful chance of war abound in classical writers, the authors of *Gorboduc* may have had Seneca in mind here; the passage is quoted in Mirandula under *de Bello*.

Arostus, taking the place of the Chorus, brings the play to a close with a long speech predicting ruinous times for Britain but prophesying that right will finally triumph:

For right will alwayes liue and rise at length,
But wrong can neuer take depe roote, to last. (5. 2. 278-79.)

"A noble conclusion," says Courthope, "and quite unlike the moral of Seneca's plays."[122] Watt agrees with Courthope. Baker says, "Certainly the real morality of *Gorboduc* is the reverse of Senecan morality."[123] But I do not believe that the morality of *Gorbuduc* is the reverse of Senecan morality. The morality of Seneca's tragedies is naturally complex, for various dramatic characters express various sentiments. There are many complaints in the tragedies about the injustice of Fortune, as there are in *Gorboduc*. No character in Seneca's tragedies, so far as I know, says specifically that right will always win and wrong perish. But Seneca certainly tells Nero that Augustus, though

tossed to and fro by Fortune, finally won long life and deification by following justice and virtue.[124] Certainly Theseus in
Hercules Furens says that the just and mild ruler is the one
who lives long and wins heaven.[125] Furthermore, I think we
should take some account of Seneca's philosophical writings,
for the Elizabethans associated the tragedies with the prose
works. Seneca's moral position in his philosophical writings is
clear enough. He maintains that man's natural instinct is good
and that this instinct strives against wrong.[126] "Virtue," says
Seneca, "is never lost to view."[127] Again he says that the true
good—i.e. wisdom and virtue—never perishes.[128] We must remember that for three hundred years in England Seneca had
been a leading arbiter of morals; he was pre-eminently the
"moral Senec." We must remember Sir Philip Sidney's famous
remark on *Gorboduc:* "It is full of stately speeches and well-
sounding phrases, climbing to the height of Seneca's style, and
as full of notable morality."[129] Another Elizabethan essayist,
William Cornwallis, published some *Discourses upon Seneca
the Tragedian* in 1601. These discourses are moral comments
on celebrated passages from the tragedies. Most of Cornwallis'
arguments are directed towards good government. In commenting on the beginning of the first chorus of *Agamemnon,*[130]
which speaks of the uncertain tenure of kings, Cornwallis says
that there would be no complaining about Fortune if sovereignty were justly administered; for, says he, "nothing can
perish that hath truth and justice for the foundation."[131] I
suspect that Seneca stimulated Sackville and Norton in much
the same way.

§3

To recapitulate, I believe that the predominant classical
influence in *Gorboduc* is Senecan. But the literary background
of the English tragedy, as any careful student of Elizabethan
drama might suspect, is complex; it is classical, medieval, and
contemporary. I believe that Sackville and Norton thought of
Gorboduc as a continuation of the Trojan tragedy, and therefore
allied not only to Virgil's *Aeneid* and Seneca's *Troades* and

Agamemnon but to Lydate's *Troy Book* and *Fall of Princes,*
to Chaucer's *Troilus,* to the English chronicles, to the *Mirror
for Magistrates.* It is quite clear, in fact, that the authors
thought of *Gorboduc* as the final chapter in the Trojan tragedy.
Dordan, Philander, Gorboduc, and the Chorus speak of the
royal family as the last seeds of Brutus, the last remnants of
the Trojan line.[132]

Undoubtedly the strife between brothers owes much to Seneca's *Thebais* and *Thyestes,* and probably something to Statius
and Lydgate as well. The important political issues in *Gorboduc*
are complex, but they evidently owe something to *Octavia* and
to passages from other Senecan tragedies. In the sixteenth century Seneca was an arbiter of both moral and political education. In the early part of the century Erasmus gives the following advice to princes:

After Plutarch, I would readily assign the next place to Seneca,
whose writings are wonderfully stimulating and excite one to enthusiasm for [a life of] moral integrity, raise the mind of the reader
from sordid cares, and especially decry tyranny everywhere.[133]

Erasmus, to be sure, is thinking of Seneca's epistles and essays.
At the beginning of the next century, 1601, William Cornwallis
says of the *Moral Epistles,* "Seneca of morality is the best."[134]
Then, in the same essay, he says: "Among Poets Seneca's Tragedies fit well the hands of a Statesman." I have already referred
to Cornwallis' *Discourses upon Seneca the Tragedian.* Elizabethans, when writing about kings, about good rule and about
tyranny, would naturally turn to Seneca, to his philosophical
writings and to his tragedies.

So far as I can make out, then, the literary sources of *Gorboduc* fall into a pattern that is fairly typical in the sixteenth century. Among native English sources, which are unquestionably
important, there are the morality plays, the chronicles, Lydgate,
Chaucer, and the *Mirror for Magistrates.* Among the classical
sources, there are Seneca, Virgil, Ovid, probably Statius, possibly Plutarch and Lucan. An examination of many another
Elizabethan tragedy would point to similar sources. Partly
morality play, partly chronicle play, *Gorboduc* is also a tragedy

in the classical manner, that is, in the Senecan manner. As such, it is a true prototype, I believe, of the greater historical tragedies of Marlowe and Shakespeare.

NOTES

1. First published, with a corrupt text, in 1565. The first authorized edition was in 1570, and it is this text, as printed in Adams's *Chief Pre-Shakespearean Dramas*, that I now follow.
2. "Seneca's Influence upon Gorboduc," in *Modern Language Notes* II (1887), 56-70.
3. *The Influence of Seneca on Elizabethan Tragedy.*
4. *Elizabethan Drama* (Boston, 1908), II, 401.
5. *Gorboduc; or, Ferrex and Porrex*, in Bulletin of the University of Wisconsin, No. 351.
6. *Induction to Tragedy: A Study of a Development of Form in Gorboduc, The Spanish Tragedy, and Titus Andronicus.*
7. See Minturno, *De Poeta* (Venice, 1559), p. 255.
8. See *Seneca His Tenne Tragedies Translated into English, Edited by Thomas Newton.* Tudor Translations (London and New York, 1927).
9. There are many extracts from Seneca's plays in the *Illustrium Poetarum Flores* by Octavianus Mirandula and in the *Polyanthea* by Nanus Mirabellus, Domenicus. Mirandula's *Flores* appeared in over a dozen editions between 1539 and 1630; there were two London editions, in 1598 and 1611. The *Polyanthea* was first published at Venice in 1507. I have used this first edition and the revised, enlarged *Novissima Polyanthea* (Venice, 1616).
10. See Marguerite Hearsey's edition of Sackville's contribution to the *Mirror for Magistrates—The Complaint of Henry Duke of Buckingham* (New Haven, 1936).
11. See *FP* 1. 3580. Sackville probably also knew Lydgate's more extended version of the story, *The Siege of Thebes*.
12. *FP* 1. 4203.
13. non capit regnum duos. *Thy.* 444.
14. nec regna socium ferre nec taedae sciunt. *A* 259. (This quotation is in Mirandula.)
15. *Gorboduc* 1. 2. 259.
16. *Thebaid* 1. 130; *Pharsalia* 1. 92-93. (Both passages are in Mirandula.)
17. According to modern classicists, *Octavia* is not by Seneca; but it passed with Elizabethans as Senecan.
18. femina non caelo turpior ulla foret. *Amores*, 1. 13. 36. For other references to Aurora's aged husband Tithonus, see Virgil, *Aeneid* 4. 585; Seneca, *Agamemnon* 822-4; Statius, *Thebaid.* 2. 134-37.
19. *TB* 3. 5-9. Aulus Gellius, whose *Noctes Atticae* was well known in the Middle Ages and Renaissance, says that the old Roman poet Laevius called the blushing Aurora "shame-colored": [*Laevius*] *rubentem Auroram pudoricolorem appellavit.* Gellius, 19. 7. 6.
20. sub nocte silenti. *Aeneid* 4. 527.
21. *orbis tyrannus. Oc.* 250.
22. *Gorboduc* 1. 1. 57-67.
23. regno pectus attonitum furit. *Theb.* 302.
24. Imperia pretio quolibet constant bene. *Theb.* 664.
25. imperii sitis cruenta. *Hip.* 542-43. (A large part of the long speech is quoted in Mirandula.)

26. regni cupido. *Oc.* 144. Cf. 157-59.

27. *HO* 604-39. (Mirandula quotes most of this chorus.)

28. Gorboduc is actually speaking here, but he is answering Eubulus. Cf. Arostus in 1. 2. 122-29.

29. Regenda magis est fervida adolescentia. *Oc.* 446. This line is quoted in both Mirandula and the *Novissima Polyanthea.* Thomas Cooper assigns *fervida adolescentia* to Seneca.

30. Iuvenile vitium est regere non posse impetum. *Troades* 250.

31. violenta nemo imperia continuit diu. *Ibid.,* 258. (Both of these quotations are in Mirandula.)

32. Peiora iuvenes facile praecepta audiunt. *Thy.* 309. (In Mirandula.)

33. Vt nemo doceat fraudis et sceleris vias, regnum docebit. *Thy.* 312-13. (In Mirandula.)

34. vincit sancto dira libido, fraus sublimi regnat in aula. *Hip.* 981-82. Cf. *HO* 611-12. (Both passages are in Mirandula.)

35. *Medea* 599-606; *HO* 675-82.

36. *Induction to Tragedy,* p. 210.

37. medio tutissimus ibis. *Met.* 2. 137.

38. See Chaucer, *Hous of Fame* 940-59; Lydgate, *Reson and Sensuallyte* 4200-26.

39. venenum in auro bibitur. *Thy.* 453. (In Mirandula.)

40. sollicito bibunt
auro superbi; quam juvat nuda manu
captasse fontem!
  —*Hip.* 518-20. (In Mirandula.)

41. aurea miscet pocula sanguis. *HO* 657. (In Mirandula.) Cf. Juvenal, 10. 25-27; Ovid, *Amores* 1. 8. 103-04.

42. *Education of a Christian Prince,* trans. Lester K. Born (New York, 1936), p. 193.

43. Judging by the extracts in the *Novissima Polyanthea* under *adulatio,* Plutarch and Seneca were the leading authorities on flattery. See Seneca, *On Benefits,* 6. 33; *De Ira* 3. 8. 5; *De Tranquillitate* 1. 16; *Natural Questions,* Preface to Bk. 4; *Moral Epistles* 45. 7; 59. 11; 116. 5; 123. 9.

44. *Gorboduc* 2. 1. 16-21.

45. See *Met.* 4. 457-61, 10. 41-44. Lydgate, in the *Troy Book* (3. 5461-64), omits Tityus but adds Sisyphus.

46. *HO* 938-47.

47. *Hip.* 1221-31.

48. See *De Tranquillitate* 11. 1; *Ad Polybium de Consolatione* 10. 4; *Moral Epistles* 120. 18.

49. See *Everyman* 161-65. Probably the thought was proverbial in the sixteenth century. Prince Hal (1 *Henry IV* 5. 1. 127) says to Falstaff: "Why, thou owest God a death."

50. lex alia solio est, alia privato in toro. *A* 264.

51. id esse regni maximum pignus putant,
si quidquid aliis non licet solis licet. *A* 271-72.

52. Sanctitas pietas fides privata bona sunt; qua iuvat reges eant. (*Thy.* 217-18; *Seneca his Tenne Tragedies,* I, 62.)

53. See *Oc.* 472-78. The same idea is expressed in his philosophical treatise *Ad Polybium de Consolatione* 7. 1-2.

54. sancta foedera mundi. *M* 605-06.

55. See *Theb.* 478.

56. sine legum metu. *HF* 400.

57. legum immemor. *Oc.* 261.

58. See *Oc.* 155-64.

59. *Hip.* 173-77.

60. *Hip.* 914.

61. *Gorboduc* 1. 2. 220-22. Cf. Chorus (Act 2), 7-12; 4. 2. 16-27; Chorus (Act 3).

62. *Th.* 201-04. I quote Jasper Heywood's translation (1560), in *Tenne Trage-dies*, I. 62.

63. per scelera semper sceleribus tutum est iter. (*A* 115.) See *Tenne Tragedies*, II. 106.

64. The following quotations from *HF* and *A* are in Mirandula:
auctorem scelus
repetit suoque premitur exemplo nocens. *HF* 735-36.
Quod metuit auget qui scelus scelere obruit. *A* 151.
Quas non arces scelus alternum
dedit in praeceps? *A* 77-78.
sceleris pretium maius accepi scelus. *Theb.* 269.

65. See *Theb.* 288-94.

66. See *Thy.* 607-22; *HF* 384-85; *A* 248; *Tr.* 253; *Tr.* 1-6; *A* 81-86; *Oc.* 624-31.

67. *Tr.* 1056; *M* 431; *Hip.* 1271. Cf. *Ad Polybium de Consolatione* 3. 3. Cf. Sackville, *Complaint*, st. 45. Cf. Lydgate, *Troy Book* 3. 1975.

68. fluctusque Simois caede purpureos agens. *A* 214. Cf. Virgil, *Aeneid* 6. 87-88; *Culex* 306-07.

69. *Gorboduc*, 3. 1. 8-9. Cf. Philander's words in 2. 2. 75-77.

70. non tamen superis sat est. *Tr.* 56.

71. *Troilus and Criseyde* 4. 516-17.

72. *Tr.* 1061-62. Heywood's translation in 1559 (*Tenne Tragedies*, II, 49):
I beare the smart of al their woes, each other feeles but his
Who ever he, I am the wretch all happes to me at last.

73. *Tenne Tragedies*, II, 15. Hecuba, to be sure, was virtually a symbol of tragic despair in the sixteenth century. See *Hamlet* 2. 2. 584-86.

74. *Tr.* 157, 162.

75. non patris illos tangit afflicti pudor,
non patria; regno pectus attonitum furit. *Theb.* 301-02.

76. *Theb.* 182-99. Cf. Jocasta's speech to Oedipus in *Oe.* 81-86. (Both passages are in Mirandula.)

77. *Tr.* 902-03. *Tenne Tragedies*, II, 43.

78. est quidem iniustus dolor rerum aestimator. *Tr.* 545-46. Cf. *HO* 1402-03; *Oc.* 52-54.

79. Gorboduc expresses a similar wish earlier in the act (22-26).

80. See *Thy.* 1085-88.

81. *M* 531-37.

82. [Allecto] virgo sata Nocte (Virgil, *Aeneid* 7. 331; cf. 12. 847); sorores Nocte genitas (Ovid, *Met.* 4. 451-52); O ye Herynes, Nyghtes doughtren thre (Chaucer, *Troilus* 4. 22); nyghtes doghter (Lydgate, *TB* 3. 547; cf. *Siege of Thebes* 858-61).

83. See Dante, *Inferno* 9. 38-48; Chaucer, *Troilus* 4. 24; Lydgate, *Siege of Thebes* 858-61; *TB* 3. 5446-47.

84. See *A* 763.

85. See *Met.* 4. 482-83; *Aeneid* 6. 555.

86. See *Met.* 4. 483; *Inferno* 9. 40. Cf. Virgil, *Aeneid* 6. 570.

87. *Aeneid* 6. 570-71; *Culex* 219; Seneca, *HF* 88, 982; *M* 961-62; *HO* 1002; Statius, *Thebaid* 1. 112; 9. 153.

88. See Herodotus, 3. 30-38; Seneca, *De Ira* 3. 14; *Moral Epistles* 86. 1; Lydgate, *FP* 3. 1681-87.

89. See *Met.* 8. 478 ff. The words of Eubulus, in 5. 2. 240-41, offer further evidence that the authors of *Gorboduc* may have had Medea or Althaea, or both, in mind. Eubulus, commenting on Videna's murder of Porrex and her own punishment, says:

Thus wreke the gods when that the mothers wrath
Nought but the bloud of her owne childe may swage.

90. quid diem questu tero? quid misera duras vita? *HO* 1774-75.

91. quid segnis traho quod vivo? *Theb.* 47-48.

92. See *Oc.* 593 ff.

93. *Theb.* 447. Cf. *HO* 992-93; Deianira begs her son Hyllus to strike her womb.

94. utero dirum condat ut ensem: "hic est, hic est fodiendus" ait "ferro, monstrum qui tale tulit." *Oc.* 369-72.

95. See *Theb.* 559 ff. Cf. Statius, *Thebaid* 11. 329-53.

96. *Aeneid* 4. 365-67; *HO* 143-54.

97. See *Genesis* 9. 6; *Exodus* 21. 12; *Leviticus* 24. 17.

98. See Aeschylus, *Agamemnon* 1338-42; Euripides, *Electra* 1093-95. In Ovid's *Metamorphoses* (8. 483) Althaea, when she decides to destroy her son Meleager, cries "Death must be atoned by death" (*mors morte pianda est*).

99. Blood shad for blood is fynal recompence (*FP* 1. 7049; cf. 2, 3899; 3. 886); Deth quit for deth; loo, heer his fynal meede! (*FP* 2. 3913); Moordre quit for moordre (*FP* 8. 3372); For blood axeth blood as guerdon dewe (*Mirror for Magistrates*, ed. Campbell [Cambridge, 1938], p. 99); And see yf blood aye aske not blood agayne (*Complaint*, st. 12); that deathe for deathe coulde be but iust rewarde (*ibid.*, st. 24).

100. *Lectures on the Dramatic Literature of the Age of Elizabeth* (1820).

101. *Moral Epistles* 99. 9. Cf. *HF* 190, 870-74; *Tr.* 1-7, 259-64; *Hip.* 978-80, 1123-48; *Oe.* 52; *A* 52-107; *Thy.* 391-92, 596-622; *HO* 640-42, 1099; *Oc.* 377-79, 452. Cf. *On Benefits*, 6. 33.

102. *Mirror*, ed. Campbell, p. 132.

103. *Tenne Tragedies*, I, 177. *Hip.* 1114-17. (The Latin passage is in Mirandula.)

104. Cf. effusas omnes irriget terras cruor. *Thy.* 44.

105. Cf. *Gorboduc* 5. 2. 106-08.

106. *HO* 1775.

107. *HO* 1419. Cooper says that *lux acerba* is Senecan.

108. *Oc.* 18, 20.

109. mors placet. *Oe.* 1031.

110. *Hip.* 1201-02; *Tr.* 1170; *A* 750-51; *HO* 1021. Cf. Polyxena's "O deth, welcome!" in Lydgate's *Troy Book* 4. 6821.

111. Horace, *Odes*, 1. 4. 13. Cf. mors avidis pallida dentibus, *HF* 555. Cf. Sackville's *Complaint*, st. 53.

112. *HF* 745-47. Cf. *Oc.* 471-78. (Mirandula quotes both passages.)

113. Vis magna populi est. *Oc.* 185.

114. *Oc.* 455.

115. *Oc.* 866-67.

116. *Gorboduc* 5. 1. 85-92.

117. *Oc.* 877-81. (These lines are in Mirandula and the *N. Polyanthea.*)

118. *Complaint*, ed. Hearsey, p. 92. Cf. p. 27.

119. *Complaint*, st. 61. Miss Hearsey refers to Valerius Maximus (Bk. V, ch. 3), to his illustrations of Roman ingratitude. The idea is widespread in classical and medieval literature. Lydgate repeatedly speaks of the fickleness of the "commons." See *FP* 3. 2162-70, 2198, 2921-26. Virgil's *incertum volgus* (*Aeneid* 2. 39)

was well known. For that matter, there are two other phrases in Seneca's tragedies that were well known: non aura populi et vulgus infidum bonis (*Hip.* 488); et
numquam stabilis favor vulgi praecipitis movet (*Thy.* 351-52).

120. *Theb.* 625-29.

121. *Tenne Tragedies,* I, 133.

122. *History of English Poetry,* II, 371.

123. *Induction to Tragedy,* p. 34.

124. See *Oc.* 471-91.

125. See *HF* 739-47.

126. *Moral Epistles* 94. 31.

127. Nulla virtus latet. *Ibid.,* 79. 17.

128. Nam illud verum bonum non moritur . . . sapienta et virtus. *Ibid.,* 98. 9.

129. *Defense of Poesy,* ed. Cook, p. 47.

130. *A* 57-59.

131. I have used the London edition of 1632. There are no page numbers.

132. See *Gorboduc* 1. 2. 160-65; 2. 1. 194-96; 2. 2. 75-77; 3. 1. 6-10; Chorus
(Act 3), 12-13.

133. *Education of a Christian Prince,* trans. Born, p. 200.

134. *Of Essayes and Bookes,* in *Essayes,* first published in 1601. I quote from
the 1632 edition.

Some Plays in the Repertories of the Patent Houses

Arthur L. Woehl

A SOUND understanding of the Restoration theatre demands recognition, not always given, of the continuity of tradition connecting the theatre of Elizabeth with that of Charles II. From the vantage point of history, differences between the two theatres have more often been given prominence. We therefore read of the Restoration as the age in which audiences were small and select, the age of scenic innovation, or the age of heroic tragedy and artificial comedy.

Audiences of the Restoration were, however, like others in their demands for variety. Scores of heroic tragedies turned out for critical playgoers were more satisfying to their authors or to a few connoisseurs than to the public generally, which quickly detected the superiority of Elizabethan models. A few early examples of the artificial comedy of manners were perennially favored by reason of their novelty and topical humor, but, for the best of these, audiences had to wait until 1675 for *The Country Wife* and until 1700 for *The Way of the World*. Lacking a large popular repertory from other sources, it would have been impossible to attract audiences, which, though small, did not remain select. The managers, therefore, turned to the treasury inherited from the Elizabethans for plays which many had seen and remembered, and whose freshness and vigor attracted others.

For over a quarter of a century from 1660, these plays were the core of the repertories of both patent houses. Our discussion is concerned with the manner in which the managers divided and used the older plays while they added to the repertories the works of contemporary authors.

It is important to remember, first of all, that the years 1642 and 1660 are convenient dates of reference rather than absolute limits. The playhouses did not all close in 1642 to remain idle until 1660. Puritan fury against theatrical entertainment, although strong enough to bring about the passing of Parliamentary edicts against theatres from 1642 on, was by no means so unified as is sometimes implied. If the nobility were not unanimous in support of King Charles and the Restoration, the common people were likewise not fused into a solid bloc of opposition to places of public amusement. There were many who saw no reason to include in their religious dogma a ban on theatregoing. The edict of Parliament passed in 1642 has a tone of mild admonition:

Fasting and Prayer having bin often tryed to be very effectuall . . . are still enjoyned; and whereas publike Sports doe not well agree with publike Calamities, nor publike Stage-playes with the Seasons of Humiliation, this being an Exercise of sad and pious solemnity, and the other being Spectacles of pleasure, too commonly expressing Iaciuious Mirth and Levitie: It is therefore thought fit, and Ordeined by the Lords and Commons in this Parliament Assembled, that while these sad Causes and set times of Humiliation doe continue, publike Stage-playes shall cease, and bee forborne.[1]

The edict was not taken too seriously. For this we have abundant proof in subsequent public clamor and in printed diatribes against the theatre, more Parliamentary prohibitions, and frequent arrests of actors by the soldiery. The players steadfastly continued performances throughout the period of civil war, and even had the temerity, at times, to appeal to Parliament for the relief of their economic condition.[2] Open defiance of the edicts of Parliament was, nevertheless, dangerous, and the risk of discovery could not be faced daily. Hence the plays which were given were necessarily those for which casts could be hastily recruited. New productions involving preparation and scenery were not likely to be undertaken. Therefore the old and familiar plays were kept alive, and a bridge connecting the pre-Commonwealth and Restoration theatres was built.

Another important bond connecting the two theatres was the talent of two men—Thomas Killigrew and William Davenant. They were alike in many respects: both were loyal servants of the King; both shared his exile; both were playwrights; and both had wide acquaintance in Court circles, an important factor in the re-establishment of the theatre after the Restoration. During the exile, Killigrew was Charles's representative at Venice, where he continued to write plays. Davenant had been appointed leader of an expedition to introduce French artisans into Virginia, but Commonwealth agents, informed of the date of departure, intercepted the ship on which he sailed. He was taken to England, tried, and sentenced to be hanged. After a term spent in prison, he was pardoned.[3] With his release, the re-establishment of the theatre in England got under way. He made no secret of his plans, publishing a printed text of *The Siege of Rhodes,* and announcing the intended performance to his friend Bulstrode Whitelock, Lord Commissioner of the Treasury, on the date of publication.[4]

There has been much emphasis on the importance of *The Siege of Rhodes* as a milestone in the history of the Restoration theatre. Dryden[5] has called it the first example of heroic rhymed tragedy. As dialogue accompanied by music and embellished with scenery in the manner of the Italian operas, it escaped classification as a prohibited play. When it was first presented as a private performance at Rutland House, much of the dancing characteristic of the Italian opera had to be omitted because of limited stage space. As a safeguard against criticism, Davenant employed former court musicians (never suppressed by law) as actors. These innovations entitle *The Siege of Rhodes* to consideration as the first important production of the Restoration. He had presented previously, on May 23, 1656, another dialogue with music, *The First Day's Entertainment at Rutland House,* as a private performance. And there is reason to believe that he was operating companies in several theatres prior to April 1, 1656.[6] Now, by heralding *The Siege of Rhodes* with a printed text, and averting criticism with the presentation of an opera instead of a play, he was attempting the transition to outright public performances. He accomplished this in 1658, when he presented a second part of *The Siege of Rhodes* and gave daily performances of *The Cruelty of the Spaniards in Peru* and *The History of Sr Francis Drake* at the Cockpit in Drury

Lane. Within a year and a half, three companies were regularly presenting plays in London: one, composed of young actors, opened at the Cockpit in Drury Lane, another company of veterans occupied the Red Bull, and a third company under William Beeston played for a time during the summer of 1660.

With the return of Charles II from France, Davenant and Killigrew joined forces to obtain a monopoly on theatrical performances in London. Davenant had been granted a patent by Charles I in 1639, and although it had been revoked the same year as a result of strong opposition, Davenant now argued for a new patent on the evidence of this old grant.[7] There was new opposition this time: from Attorney-General Palmer, and also from the old Master of the Revels, Sir Henry Herbert, who was eager to regain his rights and perquisites for the licensing and censoring of plays. Davenant and Killigrew, however, used their influence at Court to overcome their opponents, and the patents were granted on August 21, 1660. Davenant's patent authorized the establishment of a company and playhouse under the patronage of His Royal Highness, the Duke of York. The company was recruited from the group of younger actors who had been playing at the Cockpit. Killigrew's theatre had the patronage of His Majesty the King. Killigrew took over the veteran actors from the Red Bull. Having recruited their companies, the managers next sought plays for them to act. Colley Cibber tells us[8] that the older plays were divided as follows:

All the capital plays . . . of Shakespear, Fletcher, and Ben. Johnson, were divided between them, by the approbation of the Court and their own alternate choice. So that when Hart was famous for Othello, Betterton had no less a reputation for Hamlet.

Genest[9] denies the existence of such an agreement because all the best of Jonson's plays were acted at the King's theatre, while none appears to have been acted by the other house. He adds that Cibber is not to be depended upon as to events which happened before his time.[10] It is true that, for many years, Jonson's plays were presented solely by Killigrew's players, but Cibber is supported in his statement about a division of plays by the following record printed by Nicoll[11] from the Lord Chamberlain's documents. The date is December 12, 1660.

Whereas Sr William Davenant, Knight has humbly p^rsented to us a proposition of reformeinge some of the most ancient Playes that were playd at Blackfriers and of makeinge them, fitt, for the Company of Actors appointed under his direction and Comand, Viz: the playes called the Tempest, Measures, for Measures, Much adoe about nothinge, Rome and Juliet, Twelfe night, the Life of Kinge Henry the Eyght, the Sophy, Kinge Lear, the Tragedy of Mackbeth, the Tragedy of Hamlet prince of Denmarke, and the Dutchesse of Malfy, Therefore wee haue granted vnto the sayd Sr William Dauenant, liberty to represent the playes aboue named by the Actors vnder his comand, notwithstandinge any Warrant to the contrary, formerly granted.

The document further states that the actors of Davenant's company have the sole right to present these plays. In addition, Davenant was given the right to his own works, and two months' right to "The Mad Lover, The Mayd in ye Mill, the Spanish Curate the Loyall Subject Rule a Wife and Haue a Wife and Persiles prince of Tyre." The Duke's theatre, therefore, had exclusive acting rights to nine plays of Shakespeare, one of Denham (*The Sophy*), and one of Webster (*The Duchess of Malfi*); and the rights for two months to another play of Shakespeare (*Pericles*), four of Fletcher, one of Fletcher and Rowley (*The Maid in the Mill*).[12] There is no mention of plays to be assigned to Killigrew, which may indicate a supplementary private agreement between the managers concerning other plays. The performance records show a remarkable exclusiveness in the repertories of the two theatres.

Pepys's *Diary* is our most important contemporary record. He writes of seeing Heywood's *Love's Mistress, or The Queen's Mask* at the Duke's house on March 2, 1660/1, and again at the King's house on March 11. The respective entries are as follows:

After dinner I went to the theatre, where I found so few people (which is strange, and the reason I do not know) that I went out again, and so to Salsbury Court, where the house as full as could be; and it seems it was a new play, "The Queen's Maske," wherein there are some good humours: among others, a good jeer to the old story of the Siege of Troy, making it to be a common country tale. But above all it was strange to see so little a boy as that was to act Cupid, which is one of the greatest parts in it.

After dinner I went to the theatre, and there saw "Love's Mistress" done by them, which I do not like in some things as well as their acting in Salsbury Court.

This is the only instance I have found of the same play presented by both companies. Pepys records a performance by the King's company of *Rule a Wife and Have a Wife* on February 5, 1661/2. This play was free for Killigrew's players, since Davenant's two months' right to it had long ago expired.

Davenant's managerial shrewdness, in all probability, accounts for the choice of most of the plays assigned to him on December 12, 1660. He chose plays which he thought his company could do well, or plays for which he had special plans. Killigrew's company, it should be borne in mind, was made up of the older and more experienced actors.[13] Some of them were famous in the roles of Othello, Iago, Cassio, and Falstaff. These are characters in three of the four plays of Shakespeare most used by the King's company, as we shall see later. But Davenant had Betterton in his company, and Betterton's Hamlet was supreme from the very beginning of the Restoration period. In 1661 Pepys says that Betterton did the part "beyond imagination." On May 28, 1663, having seen the play again, he has "fresh reason never to think enough to Betterton." And the entry of August 31, 1668, suggests that the diarist has seen the play repeatedly, and leaves no doubt that his judgment is unaltered.

To the Duke of York's playhouse, and saw "Hamlet," which we have not seen this year before, or more; and mightily pleased with it, but above all with Betterton, the best part, I believe that ever man acted.

Colley Cibber prefaces his analysis of Betterton's Hamlet with the following statement:

Betterton was an actor, as Shakespear was an author, both without competitors! form'd for the mutual assistance and illustration of each other's genius! How Shakespear wrote, all men who have a taste for nature may read, and know—but with what higher rapture would he still be *read,* could they conceive how Betterton *play'd* him. Then might they know, the one was born alone to speak what the other only knew to write![14]

Davenant's exclusive right to the presentation of his own plays was an advantage he would not overlook, and may well have offset the other company's use of Jonson's plays. This, of course, is not a judgment of the relative literary merits of the two authors, but a recognition of the contemporary popularity of some of Davenant's works. It is presumed that Killigrew had the right to his own plays also; but of his plays only *Claricilla* and *The Parson's Wedding* were used repeatedly after the Restoration. They did not compete in popularity with Davenant's *The Wits, Man is the Master, Unfortunate Lovers, The Playhouse to be Lett,* two parts of *The Siege of Rhodes,* and some highly successful adaptations which Davenant had ready or planned to make.

It must have been these adaptations which he had in mind when he presented a proposition for "reformeinge some of the most ancient Playes . . . and makeinge them fitt." He had very early sensed the growing demand for spectacle, had, in fact, been the one to stimulate it. His experience with the scenic mounting of plays was long, dating from the pre-Commonwealth masques. Although Inigo Jones had died (1652), John Webb remained to continue collaboration with Davenant on new scenic miracles. From *The First Day's Entertainment at Rutland House* in 1656, to the legal opening of the theatres four years later, Davenant's productions show a growing reliance upon scenery as a means of attracting audiences. The stage at Rutland House was too small for the spectacles he aimed eventually to produce, but he planned steadily for the day when he would have a theatre and stage large enough for the elaborate machinery he needed.[15] The stage at Salisbury Court, where his company played during the first year after the opening of the theatres, was more adequate. The new theatre at Lincoln's Inn Fields opened[16] with the first and second parts of *The Siege of Rhodes* and *The Wits,* staged more magnificently than had been possible up to that time. Music, dancing, and scenic transformations were henceforth so characteristic of all his productions that the theatre came to be known as "the Opera." On February 18, 1661/2, Pepys wrote:

Having agreed with Sir Wm. Pen to meet him at the Opera . . . I went thither and saw "The Law Against Lovers," a good play and well performed, especially the little girl's dancing and singing.

The Law Against Lovers was Davenant's version of Shakespeare's *Measure for Measure* and *Much Ado About Nothing*, reworked into one play and dressed up with singing and dancing. Two weeks later, on March 1, 1661/2, Pepys writes:

To the Opera, and there saw "Romeo and Juliet," the first time it was ever acted. I am resolved to go no more to see the first time of acting, for they were all of them out more or less.

The actors may have been less to blame than the author, for this was James Howard's version of Shakespeare's play, provided with happy and tragic endings for alternate performances.

Late in 1663 Davenant was preparing another of the Shakespeare plays assigned to him. Pepys hears from his shoemaker "of a rare play to be acted this week of Sir William Davenant's. The story of Henry the Eighth with all his wives."[17] When he saw the performance, on January 1, 1663/4, it did not much impress him.

Went to the Duke's house, the first play I have been at these six months, according to my last vowe,[18] the so-much cried-up play of "Henry the Eighth"; which, though I went with resolution to like it, is so simple a thing made up of a great many patches, that, besides the shows and processions in it, there is nothing in the world good or well done.

Davenant next used *Henry V*, not mentioned in the grant of December, 1660. This play was given in an adaptation by the Earl of Orrery. Pepys records his impressions of the play on August 13, 1664:

To the new play, at the Duke's house, of "Henry the Fifth": a most noble play, writ by my Lord Orrery; wherein Betterton, Harris and Ianthe's[19] parts most incomparably wrote and done, and the whole play the most full of height and raptures of wit and sense, that ever I heard; having but one incongruity, that King Harry promises to plead for Tudor to their Mistress, Princesse Katherine of France, more than when it comes to it he seems to do; and Tudor refused by her with some kind of indignity, not with a difficulty and honour that it ought to have been done in to him.

The plays just mentioned had all been furbished with an elaborate scenic display unknown in Shakespeare's time. But *Macbeth* and *The Tempest* were reserved for special treatment which clearly entitled them to be called opera. *Macbeth* emerged especially successful, with the double advantage of operatic treatment and the excellence of Betterton in the title role. Pepys admired the production more each time he saw it:

To the Duke's house, and saw "Macbeth," which though I saw it lately, yet appears a most excellent play in all respects, but especially in divertisement, though it be a deep tragedy; which is a strange perfection in a tragedy, it being most proper here, and suitable.[20]

The "divertisement" consisted of the singing and dancing which were liberally added, and the effects produced by machines which enabled the witches to fly. There were other alterations and additions in this production after the Duke's company moved from the theatre in Lincoln's Inn Fields to the new house in Dorset Garden (1671). Meanwhile, Davenant and Dryden had altered *The Tempest*. Pepys writes, November 7, 1667:

At noon resolved with Sir W. Pen to go to see "The Tempest," an old play of Shakespeare's, acted, I hear, the first day. And so my wife and girl, and W. Hewer by themselves, and Sir W. Pen and I afterwards by ourselves: and forced to sit in the side balcony over against the musique-room at the Duke's House, close by my Lady Dorset and a great many great ones. The house mighty full; the King and Court there; and the most innocent play that ever I saw; and a curious piece of musique in an echo of half sentences, the echo repeating the former half, while the man goes on to the latter; which is mighty pretty. The play has no great wit, but yet good above ordinary plays.

These adaptations of Shakespeare were popular enough to be given repeatedly at the Duke's house. *Twelfth Night* was not so popular, and Pepys does not mention *Pericles*. Up to spring, 1669, when his *Diary* ends, Pepys had also seen at the Duke's house the following plays: Massinger, *The Bondman;* Heywood, *The Queen's Mask;* Davenant, *The Siege of Rhodes, The Wits, Man Is the Master, The Unfortunate Lovers;* Cowley, *Cutter of Coleman Street;* Porter, *The Villain, A Witty Combat;* Samuel Tuke, *The Adventures of Five Hours;* Stapylton, *The Slighted Maid;* Orrery, *Mustapha, Tryphon;* Etherege, *Love in a Tub, She Would if She Could;* Carlell, *Heraclius;* Caryl, *English Princess;* Carey, *Wedding Night;* Shirley, *School of Compliments;* Dryden, *Sir Martin Mar-All;* Tomkins, *Albumazar;* Shadwell, *The Sullen Lovers, Royal Shepherdess;* Habington, *Queen of Arragon;* Ford, *The Ladies' Trial.*

Turning now to the plays used by Killigrew, we find that up to 1665 only four of Shakespeare's plays were performed.[21] *Othello,* which had the benefit of Burt, Clun, and Hart in the chief roles, seems to have been given more often than the others. Pepys thought ill of *A Midsummer Night's Dream,* ". . . which I never had seen before, nor shall ever again, for it is the most insipid ridiculous play that ever I saw in my life." And although Lacy was famous in the part of Falstaff, Pepys has no praise for either *The Merry Wives of Windsor* or *Henry IV.* As the acting at the King's house declined, even *Othello* was disappointing, as Pepys indicates on February 6, 1668/9:

To the King's playhouse, and there in an upper box . . . did see "The Moor of Venice": but ill acted in most parts, Moone (which did a little surprize me) not acting Iago's part by much so well as Clun used to do: nor another Hart's, which was Cassio's; nor indeed Burt doing the Moor's so well as I once thought he did.

There were frequent performances of Jonson's plays at the King's house, with *The Silent Woman, Bartholomew Fair,* and *Cataline's Conspiracy* especially favored. Pepys also saw *The Alchemist,* and thought *Volpone* "a most excellent play: the best I think I ever saw, and well acted."[22] Downes also records performances of *The Devil's an Ass, Every Man in His Humour, Every Man Out of His Humour,* and *Sejanus.* Lowe[23] observes that Downes (prompter at the Duke's house) had most of his information from Charles Booth (prompter at the rival theatre), and that he could not have known at first hand of the plays at the King's house. He concludes, therefore, that we have few particulars of the plays at the King's house, even if we combine the list given by Downes with that of Pepys. Nevertheless, the *Diary* yields a long list of plays given by Killigrew's company.

Beaumont and Fletcher share first place with Jonson in performances of the older plays. Pepys mentions: *The Beggar's Bush, The Scornful Lady, The Knight of the Burning Pestle, The Maid's Tragedy, The Humorous Lieutenant, The Wildgoose Chase, The Sea Voyage, Philaster, The Island Princess, Rule a Wife and Have a Wife, The Tamer Tamed, The Faithful Shepheardesse* (Fletcher), and *The Custome of the Country* (Fletcher and Massinger).

Other plays of the older playwrights include: *Argalus and Parthenia,* Glapthorne; *Love's Mistress, Queen Elizabeth's Troubles,* Heywood; *Claricilla, The Parson's Wedding,* Killigrew; *Jovial Crew, Northern Lass,* Brome; *The Goblins, Discontented Colonel,* Suckling; *The Cardinal, Changes, Hyde Park,* Shirley; *The City Match,* Mayne; *Flora's Vagaries,* Rhodes; *Chances,* Duke of Buckingham (an adaptation from Fletcher); *The Virgin Martyr,* Massinger and Dekker.

The plays of the newer playwrights are more prominent at the King's house than at the Duke's house during the first eight years of the Restoration. Dryden's early plays,[24] *The Wild Gallant, The Rival Ladies, The Indian Emperour, The Maiden Queen,* and *An Evening's Love* were presented by the King's company. His brothers-in-law, the Howards, were authors of other popular plays, as follows: Sir Robert Howard, *The Committee, The Surprizall, The Duke of Lerma;* the Hon. Edward Howard, *The Change of Crowns, The Usurper;* the Hon. James Howard, *The English Monsieur, The Mad Couple.* Sir Robert also collaborated with Dryden on *The Indian Queen.* The Earl of Orrery, whose plays were usually given at the Duke's theatre, gave *The Black Prince* to the other house. The Duchess of Newcastle supplied *The Humorous Lovers* in 1667, and the Duke of Newcastle's *The Heiress* was produced in 1668/9. Lacy, King Charles's favorite actor, wrote *Monsieur Raggou* and *The Tam-*

ing of a Shrew, or Sauny the Scot. The latter play appears to
have been introduced into the repertory along with infrequent
performances of Shakespeare's original. Pepys writes on April
9, 1667:

To the King's house, and there saw "The Tameing of a Shrew,"
which hath some very good pieces in it, but generally is but a mean
play; and the best part "Sawny," done by Lacy; and hath not half
its life, by reason of the words, I suppose, not being understood, at
least by me.

At the same playhouse, on November 1, 1667, he saw the
Shakespearean play again, this time describing it as "a silly play
and an old one."

Beginning in 1665, performances at both theatres were continued under difficulties. The great plague and the fire in 1665
and 1666 closed the playhouses for about a year and a half. On
February 12, 1666/7, Pepys was told by Killigrew that his audiences were only half as large as before the fire. Plays and performers at both theatres so offended the King on several occasions that actors were forbidden to play, or playhouses were
closed altogether. Killigrew's actors grew restive under his management. Davenant was more successful in dealing with his
company, but his management came to an end on April 7,
1668. Pepys writes on that date:

To the King's playhouse, and there saw "The English Monsieur,"
(sitting for privacy sake in an upper box): the play hath much mirth
in it as to that particular humour. After the play done I down to
Knipp, and did stay her undressing herself: and there saw the several
players, men and women, go by; and pretty to see how strange they
are all, one to another, after the play is done. Here I hear Sir W.
Davenant is just now dead; and so who will succeed him in the
mastership of the House is not yet known.

Two days later he records:

I up and down to the Duke of York's playhouse, there to see, which
I did, Sir W. Davenant's corpse, carried out towards Westminster,
there to be buried. Here were many coaches and six horses, and many
hacknies, that made it look, methought, as if it were the buriall of
a poor poet. He seemed to have many children, by five or six in the
first mourning-coach, all boys.

The settlement of Davenant's affairs was complicated by a reassignment of shares in the theatre and company, plans for the new theatre to be built in Dorset Garden, and the financial depression which affected both houses at this time. Davenant's son Charles, and two principal actors of the company, Betterton and Harris, were appointed managers. One of the first readjustments to be made was a new division of plays between the companies. From the warrant volumes of the Lord Chamberlain, Nicoll[25] prints two lists. The first, dated August 20, 1668, is an enumeration of the plays to be allotted the Duke's theatre; the second, dated January 12, 1668/9, contains those assigned to the King's house. The first is short, listing only twenty-three plays; the second contains 108 titles. A summary of these plays by authors will serve in lieu of a complete catalogue of the plays named.

The plays which are henceforth to be the property of the Duke's men, "and none other," are: three each by Fletcher, Chapman, and Shakespeare; two by Ford; one each by Jonson, Fletcher and Rowley, Beaumont, Shirley, Shirley and Chapman, Markham and Sampson, Day, Mason, Habington. The company at the King's house is to have "part of His Ma^tes Servants Playes as they were formerly acted at the Blackfryers & now allowed of to his Ma^tes Servants at ye New Theatre": twenty-eight by Fletcher, twenty-one by Shakespeare, fourteen by Jonson; and others by Beaumont and Fletcher, Fletcher and Massinger, Massinger, Fletcher and Rowley, Cartwright, Shirley, Greene, Suckling, Carlell, Chapman, Field and Massinger, Barclay, Middleton, Brome, and the Duke of Newcastle.

It is at once apparent that the authors mentioned are nearly all pre-Restoration dramatists, indicating that these lists must be considered supplementary to the grant of older plays given to Davenant on December 12, 1660. His death may have made necessary an explicit listing of plays formerly divided between him and Killigrew by private agreement. The assignment of so many plays of Shakespeare to the King's company is noteworthy. Although they had used only *Othello, A Midsummer Night's Dream, The Merry Wives of Windsor,* and *Henry IV* up to 1665, they are now given virtually all the plays not previously used by the Duke's company. The exceptions are: *"The Three Parts of Henry ye 6, Timon of Athens, Troyolus and Crisseida."* These are given to the Duke's company, as is *The Poetaster,* a play of Jonson's which seems to have been neglected by both houses up to this time.

Pepys's accounts of the plays given at the patent houses frequently mention the presence of King Charles II, the first English monarch to attend the public theatre. Although we do not have a record of the King's comments on the plays he saw, his attendance at the theatres is recorded in the Lord Chamberlain's books of Royal Warrants for payment on performances seen by the King. Nicoll gives a list of these performances from 1666 to 1693.[26] These were not paid promptly, and sometimes the players had to appeal for the money.[27] When they were paid, £10 was the sum for a performance at either of the theatres, £20 for a special performance at the theatre or at Court. The lists are of interest for the preferences among plays and authors which they indicate. The King's company presented plays by the following authors: Dryden, the Howards, Lee, Wycherley, Orrery, Crowne, Dekker, Massinger, Duffet, D'Urfey, Fane, Flecknoe, Heywood, Lacy, Mayne, Mrs. Philips, Ravenscroft, Rhodes, Rowley, Sedley, Shirley, and the Duke of Buckingham. The popular authors were Dryden, the Howards, Shirley, Lee, and Wycherley; and there were more performances of Dryden's *The Indian Emperour* and *The Maiden Queen* than of any other plays.

The Duke's company presented for the Court plays by Shakespeare, Dryden, Davenant, Mrs. Behn, Betterton, Orrery, Caryl, the Duke of Newcastle, Cooke, Cowley, Crowne, Charles Davenant, D'Urfey, Etherege, Leanerd, Otway, Payne, Mrs. Philips, Pordage, Porter, Settle, Shadwell, Sedley, Shirley, St. Serfe, Tomkins, Ravenscroft, Tuke, and Marlowe. The Marlowe play was *Dr. Faustus,* not before mentioned in the repertory of either house. *Macbeth, Henry VIII, Hamlet,* and *The Tempest* were the Shakespeare plays given by the Duke's company for the King. Nine performances of *The Tempest* are recorded.

The first five (1667, 1668) were undoubtedly the Davenant-Dryden opera, and the last four (1674, 1677) the new opera by Shadwell. There is mention of "Anthony & Cleopatra," on February 12, 1676/7, but this is Sir Charles Sedley's play. The most favored plays given by the Duke's company were: Tuke, *The Adventures of Five Hours;* Etherege, *Love in a Tub* and *She Would if She Could;* Shadwell, *The Sullen Lovers* and *Epsom Wells;* Dryden, *Sir Martin Mar-all;* Ravenscroft, *The Citizen Turned Gentleman.*

It will be noticed that the Court saw a large number of contemporary plays, indicating its search for novelty and the King's patronage to new authors.

The Union of the companies in 1682 abrogated previous grants and provided for the acting of all plays by the Duke's company. Both companies had been working under difficulties for nearly a decade. The Duke's, under Betterton's leadership, had managed to carry through Davenant's plans for a new theatre in Dorset Garden, but they opened there in 1671 under an oppressive burden of debt. Less than a year later the Theatre Royal was destroyed by fire, necessitating the building of a new house for the King's company. Killigrew's problems were complicated by trouble with the actors, whom he had brought to a state of revolt by poor management. He was forced by his son Charles to turn over to him the managership of the company and theatre. Charles Killigrew's leadership worked no improvement, however, and within a few months (July 30, 1677) the King granted a petition of the actors for self-government. The next three years brought complete disorganization, so that when the Union was effected on May 14, 1682, it actually dissolved the company at the Theatre Royal. The actors of the Duke's company were so favored by the articles of Union that some of the younger members of the King's theatre went off to Scotland, while a veteran like Mohun had to petition the King for a continuation of the right to share in the profits he had received formerly.[28]

The Duke's company had begun the Restoration period under the handicap of inexperience, a disadvantage which Davenant overcame by introducing his spectacular operas. It had by 1682 been built up into a seasoned company which could compete equally with the veterans of the other house. The King's company had, on the contrary, deteriorated under bad management and the ravages of time. As early as January 11, 1668/9, Pepys had noted the decline at the King's theatre, reporting *The Jovial Crew* as "ill acted to what it was heretofore in Clun's time, and when Lacy could dance." There was, at the same time, a dearth of new plays of sufficient merit to attract diminishing audiences. Dryden records in his *Essay of Dramatic Poesy* (1668) that the plays of Beaumont and Fletcher "are now the most pleasant and frequent entertainments of the stage; two of theirs being acted through the year for one of Shakespeare's or Johnson's."[29] Nothing could better prove the influence of these Elizabethan writers during the Restoration, for new plays were being written at a rate which would have done credit to the Elizabethans themselves. Playwriting was the sole occupation of many of the nobility and gentlemen of the time. Doran lists sixty authors up to the Union in 1682, over one hundred for the whole period to 1700, and says that the number of authors exceeded the number of actors.[30] Many of the authors were "of the party who talked of the unpopularity of Shakespeare, and who for the poet's gold offered poor tinsel of their own."[31] Even in writing their own plays, they were unable to ignore the plots and situations in Shakespeare, Beaumont, Fletcher, Webster, Jonson, and other earlier playwrights. Some of their adaptations have already been mentioned. Just prior to the Union the chief poets turned to a fresh mining of Shakespeare. The King's house had *All For Love* (1677) from Dryden; *The History of King Richard the Second* (1680) and *The Ingratitude of a Commonwealth: Or the Fall of Caius Martius Coriolanus* (1681) from Tate. Dryden gave the Duke's company *Troilus and Cressida* (1679); Shadwell, *The History of Timon of Athens* (1677/8); Tate, *The History of King Lear* (1681); Crowne, *Henry the Sixth* (The Second Part 1679/80, The First Part 1681).

The Union, which might have thrown the older plays into

the discard, when the need for variety in the repertories of two theatres was reduced, actually seems to have given them new life. From George Powell's preface to *The Treacherous Brothers,* Genest[32] quotes the following statement:

Upon the uniting of the two theatres, the revival of old plays so engrossed the study of the house, that the Poets lay dormant, and a new play could hardly get admittance.

Through two decades the Restoration theatre found its main strength in plays written for another age. While it was developing the types of drama for which we now remember it, the Elizabethans provided current entertainment for its audiences and an inexhaustible supply of plots and ideas for its playwrights.

NOTES

1. Leslie Hotson, *The Commonwealth and Restoration Stage* (Cambridge, 1928), pp. 5-6.

2. *Ibid.,* Chapter I.

3. Karl Mantzius, *A History of Theatrical Art in Ancient and Modern Times, Authorized Translation by Louise von Cossel,* 6 vols. (London, 1909), V, 320-21. See also Hotson, *op. cit.,* pp. 138-39.

4. See Hotson, *op. cit.,* pp. 151-52.

5. In *An Essay of Heroic Plays.*

6. See Hotson, *op. cit.,* pp. 137-49.

7. Cf. J. Q. Adams, *Shakespearean Playhouses* (New York, 1917), pp. 424-31, and Hotson, *op. cit.,* pp. 199-200.

8. Colley Cibber, *An Apology for His Life,* Chapter IV.

9. John Genest, *Some Account of the English Stage, From the Restoration in 1660 to 1830,* 10 vols. (Bath, 1832), I, 404.

10. Cibber joined the Theatre Royal company in 1690. His *Apology* was first published in 1740.

11. Allardyce Nicoll, *Restoration Drama 1660-1700* (Cambridge, 1923), pp. 314-15.

12. In crediting authorship of Elizabethan plays, I have used as authorities *The Cambridge History of English Literature;* F. G. Fleay, *A Chronicle History of the London Stage* (London, 1890); and Felix E. Schelling, *Elizabethan Drama 1558-1642,* 2 vols. (New York, 1910).

13. Kynaston, who had gone over to the company shortly after the theatres opened, was a notable exception.

14. *Apology,* Chapter IV.

15. Cf. Lily B. Campbell, *Scenes and Machines on the English Stage during the Renaissance* (Cambridge University Press, 1923), Chapter XIV.

16. The date given by Downes in *Roscius Anglicanus* as "Spring 1662" is at variance with Pepys's account of a visit to the *opera* on July 2, 1661, "the fourth day that it hath begun, and the first that I have seen it."

17. Entry of December 10, 1663.

18. A vow against wine and plays made some time before October 31, 1662, and kept when convenient.

19. Pepys habitually uses this name for Mrs. Betterton, whom he greatly admired. She was famous for her interpretation of the part of Ianthe in *The Siege of Rhodes.*

20. January 7, 1666/7. See also entries for November 5, 1664; December 28, 1666; October 16, 1667.

21. Nicoll, *op. cit.,* p. 82 n., adds two more not mentioned by Pepys: *Julius Caesar* and *Titus Andronicus.*

22. January 14, 1664/5.

23. Robert W. Lowe, "Thomas Betterton," in *Eminent Actors,* ed. William Archer (London, 1890), pp. 98, 103.

24. Except for *Sir Martin Mar-All,* and *The Tempest* (collaboration with Davenant), which were both produced in 1667 at the Duke's house.

25. *Op. cit.,* pp. 315-16.

26. *Op. cit.,* pp. 305-314. For the summary I have used only performances given up to 1682, when the companies united. The performances listed after 1685 were, of course, for succeeding monarchs.

27. See Hotson, *op. cit.,* p. 254.

28. See Cibber's *Apology,* Chapter IV, and Nicoll, *op. cit.,* pp. 297, 327-28.

29. W. P. Ker, *Essays of John Dryden,* 2 vols. (Oxford, 1900), I, 81.

30. John Doran, *Annals of the Stage From Thomas Betterton to Edmund Kean,* 2 vols. (Philadelphia, 1890), I, 127.

31. *Ibid.,* I, 132 ff.

32. *Op. cit.,* I, 404.

Actors and Audiences in Eighteenth-Century London

WILLIAM ANGUS

THE common generalization is that in the eighteenth-century English theatre, as in the continental theatres of the period, the actor was dominant. Allardyce Nicoll, referring to the last half of the century, says:

All who have written on this period . . . have emphasized the fact that the actor and not the dramatist ruled the theatre. While this general dependence of the playwright upon the performer is to a certain extent true of all eras, the Quins and the Barrys, the Garricks and the Kembles seem to have exercised more influence upon the audiences than even a Betterton and a Cibber had done.[1]

It would be true also to say that the theatre manager ruled, and that the audience exercised a very considerable influence upon him and his players.

The importance of the actor who reached the first rank cannot be gainsaid. A leader in the profession had power, authority, influence, good social status, vanity, and a handsome salary. He was jealous of his prerogatives and none too modest in his attitude. But with all this he might be a thoroughly sincere artist according to his lights. His contact with the public, the audience, was intimate. He could take his discontent and his troubles directly to them and appeal for reward or redress. And they, in their turn, were equally direct in making known from the auditorium their approval or censure.

When the actor was manager too, he ruled indeed. After Garrick bought a part-ownership of Drury Lane Theatre (1747), he was not only the premier star but also manager and monarch. At the other theatre-royal, Covent Garden, John Rich managed, especially financially, but James Quin, his leading actor, enjoyed the privilege of arrogant deputy. Garrick and Quin—the one with some duplicity, the other with gruff bluntness—contended with the whims of their associates and the wills of their public, and saw to it that their own interests were re-spected and satisfied.

There were considered to be—then as now—three main classes of actors. A treatise on the art of acting written in 1750, Sir John Hill's *The Actor*, classifies the possible roles as "capi-tal parts," "subordinate characters," and "subaltern" parts. The smallest and least important parts were assigned to the most inferior of the three classes of actors, and the rank of the actors corresponded "with the length of their speeches, or the im-portance of the share they chance to bear in the action."[2] Any of the extant playbills of this period would provide a specimen of the way in which the superior and inferior performers were indicated. The "capital parts" were those which were printed in large, bold capital letters; and the actors' names appeared also in heavy capital type, sometimes even larger than that used for the name of the character. Chetwood, the prompter, printer, and bookseller, wrote in 1749 :

Formerly characters were printed in the playbills according to their rank in the Drama, as for example in Macbeth Duncan stood first in the bill, though acted by an inferior person; but latterly I have found it a difficult task to content ladies as well as gentlemen, because I could not procure letters large enough to please them; nay some were so fond of elbow room, that they would have shoved every one out but themselves, as if one person were to do all.[3]

The stars had precedence in all privileges and prerogatives; and perhaps the quality of their acting justified this discrimina-tion. At any rate, the "under players" usually deserved no more than they got. Some, *The Actor* tells us, "perform the parts of kings and princes, who would appear to much more advantage in the characters of footmen and bailiff's followers." And audi-ences "are patient under a sort of mediocrity in the performers of the lower characters." The subordinate parts were "usually carelessly play'd."[4] But this situation could not be remedied, it seems, because generally only inferior players would accept subordinate assignments.

Usually parts were assigned by the manager, but often the actors complicated matters by insisting upon choosing their own roles for either a premiere or a revival. When a part was once

assigned, especially for a premiere performance, the player regarded it as his personal property. It was his role upon every
revival of the play so long as he remained a member of that
particular company. The part was frequently given to him even
when he transferred to another theatre, unless a member of the
other house, by reason of seniority, retained priority of claim
upon the cherished role, even though advancing years rendered him unable to give a convincing performance of the
character.[5] Such a claim was occasionally relinquished, however,
perhaps for the sake of novelty and showmanship, but more
often through the courtesy of one actor toward another who
wished to attempt a new character for a benefit performance.
This property right was retained by the players until the turn
of the century (1799).[6] It was a pernicious privilege, a frequent
cause of dispute and discontent among the actors, of trouble for
the managers, and of censure from the critics.

The discontent was felt mainly among the under players,
while the disputes occurred mostly among the principals. Records seem to indicate that more or less serious squabbles were
frequent. Quin in his earlier days killed two of his fellow-
actors—each time, however, in self-defense. He once challenged
Charles Macklin to a duel (which the manager prevented) after
an entr'acte fist fight in the greenroom. Macklin had "pum-
melled his face damnably" so that he could hardly speak and the
audience hissed him. The quick-tempered Macklin's most famous greenroom quarrel, however, related to a particular wig
which he refused to allow anyone to wear but himself. He
attacked a would-be wearer with a cane, poked it through the
man's eye into the brain, and killed him.[7] The women, too, had
their greenroom tussles, some of which attained notoriety in the
public press from contemporary columnists and in the gossip
of the nearby taverns and coffee-houses where "were found the
wits in the afternoon, and the rakes at night."[8] In 1736 at Drury
Lane, for example, "Mrs. Cibber and Mrs. Clive waged a terrific
paper-war for the part of Polly in *The Beggar's Opera.*" This
controversy "amused the town, advertised the production, and
did no one any harm," as it "was more or less amicably settled
before it had gone too far."[9] Even an author might occasion dis-

putes, especially if he had written with some player or players in mind and exercised his acknowledged prerogative of casting the play himself. Dr. Young, for example, "created an uproar behind the scenes at Drury Lane in 1753 by assigning the chief role in *The Brothers* to Mrs. Bellamy when Garrick wanted it for Mrs. Pritchard."[10]

Those of the audience who could witness these feuds only from the auditorium probably learned of the scenes backstage from those who had access to the wings and the greenroom and from the other channels of publicity. It was usual to make public everything about the actors' professional and private lives. Exhibition was the watchword on either side of the footlights. For the most part, the theatre seems to have been regarded primarily as a grand social diversion for both the town and the actors, although for some of the latter it was also very lucrative. "The theatre was a meeting-place, a fashionable amusement rather than a place of art."[11] Art and serious professional work were apparently unknown except to a few earnest technicians like Macklin and Garrick. In general the conditions backstage did not promote such a professional attitude and regimen as prevails today. The fault was partly the actors', partly the spectators'; and both were to be found backstage. Visitors, especially if they were distinguished, were welcome.

The actresses and the actors vied with one another in enlarging the list of fashionables and noble personages whom they considered their "followers." To Bellamy, John Hill, who "swam into the green room" to congratulate her during *Romeo and Juliet,* was hardly worth her notice; she gloried in her counts and dukes, countesses and duchesses, lords and ladies. Macklin is reported as saying that when he pummeled Quin "there were many noblemen in the green-room . . . for the green-room was a sort of state-room then." Noblemen, beaux, and men-about-town were there at any and all times—before, during, and after the performances. They came and went, lounged and loitered, going out into the house to see a bit of the performance and returning again to chat among themselves or with the players. The performance mattered little. If a beau wished to detain an actress in the wings or even abduct her (at least with her tacit consent) he did so. The incident of one Metham running off with Lady Fanciful (Bellamy) between the fourth and fifth acts is often cited. But there seems to have been no fuming nor tearing of hair backstage. The audience grew impatient with the prolonged music between acts, but Quin made a pretty speech of apology and explanation and the audience was satisfied.[12]

Even the dressing-rooms of the actresses were far from being private sanctuaries. Doran writes that

the "tiring rooms" of the actresses were then open to the fine gentlemen who frequented the house. They stood by at the mysteries of dressing, and commented on what they beheld and did not behold. . . . The dressing over, the amateurs lounged into the house . . . and at the termination of the piece crowded again into the "tiring room" of the most favorite and least scrupulous of the actresses.[13]

John Jackson, who assumed the management of the Theatre Royal in Edinburgh as late as 1781, tells us:

It had been a custom, before the Theatre came into my hands, for gentlemen to procure admittance at the stage door, who most generally sought it under the impulse of inebriety. The green-room was consequently open to a variety of visitors; and the ladies' dressing-rooms liable to the obtrusions of effrontery or design.[14]

It may not always have been "the impulse of inebriety," however, that brought visitors into the ladies' dressing-rooms. Apparently, the only scruple that the higher type of actress had in this matter was a discriminating choice in the class of visitor admitted.

The wings and the regions backstage, however, held but a small portion of the audience. There were also the pit, the boxes, the first gallery, the upper gallery, and the stage; and each of these had, generally, its particular class of spectator. Several authorities have presented the distinctions, and John Hill indicates a difference when he tells us that a certain "Cephisa spoke her fears, her tenderness, in accents that affected even the galleries."[15]

The pit seems to have been occupied only by "men of letters or wit, by students of the Inns of Court, barristers, or young merchants of rising eminence,"[16] professional and coffee-house critics, who regarded themselves as competent arbiters of taste. Churchill, author of *The Rosciad,* was daily in the pit, down against the footlights, studying the performers. Samuel Johnson's place was in the pit. This section of the house was highly regarded by manager and actors and its good opinion was courted in preference to that of any other part of the auditorium.

The boxes were supposedly reserved for persons of rank, quality, or fortune, and they were the resort of the beaux, the fashionable, and the would-be fashionable customers. They were used by the socially prominent as places for display and ostentation. There, virtue and decorum were assumed to prevail; no disreputable or drunken persons were supposed to be admitted, and it was considered ill-mannered for a man to keep on his hat during a performance or to sit in a front seat if there were ladies in the same box. The ladies arrived (perhaps masked) just before curtain time (6 P.M.), their places having been kept, sometimes from three o'clock, by servants.

Little has been written of the first gallery; but the gods above, in the "footmen's gallery," could not be ignored. They were loud and rowdy. Doran says, "The most exacting portion of the audience . . . was to be found in the footmen."[17] The upper gallery had been opened to them gratis in 1697 by Christopher Rich—for applause and for word-of-mouth publicity—and they continued to abuse their privilege till 1780. In the upper gallery with them there were tradesmen, apprentices, and those members of the lower middle class who attended a play. Their reactions were lusty and uninhibited. When enraged, they expressed their wrath by hurling down half-sucked oranges and half-eaten apples, terrifying those below in pit and boxes. If the character underwent the hunger of Jane Shore or played some similar role, they obliged her with chunks of bread. So, if *Cephisa* "affected even the galleries," her achievement was worthy of note.

There were spectators also on the stage itself, who were, however, more poseurs than spectators. For many years ineffectual objection to this practice was expressed by critics, managers, and even by the actors themselves, boisterously seconded by the gallery gods. John Hill wrote in 1750:

Above all things it is absurd and monstrous to admit a part of the audience upon the stage and behind the scenes. . . . The indignation of the generality of the audience has never fail'd to express itself too severely against the people who place themselves there, to encourage them to make a practice of doing so.[18]

Dandies on the stage bowed to acquaintances out front and, in consequence, had to dodge missiles thrown at them from the gallery.

The custom was of long standing. The king decreed in 1664 that there should be no visitors behind the scenes and again in 1674, warning them that their being on the stage was hazardous for them and interfered with the operation of the machinery. From the beginning of the eighteenth century the managers repeatedly requested in the newspapers and at the bottom of playbills that gentlemen would "not take it ill" that they could not be admitted behind the scenes and on the stage. By the end of the fourth decade of the century they were being asked to keep out of the orchestra pit also. The following is typical of these playbill notes:

N.B. The audience having lately been much disgusted at the performance being interrupted by persons crowding on the stage, it is humbly hoped, none will take it ill that they cannot be admitted behind the scenes in future.[19]

Notices like that appeared, at times, continuously for a month.

It is evident that the actors "endured this custom," as Odell says, ironically.[20] Distinguished playgoers, who could pay for the privilege (and John Rich charged them 10s. 6d. apiece at the opening of Covent Garden in 1732), were continually admitted behind the scenes. They stood and crowded in upon the stage—except for important benefit performances, when they sat. For "in the particular instance of the benefit nights of favorite players, paying them the compliment of sacrificing to their interest the appearance of reality,"[21] as Hill says, there was built on the stage an amphitheatre supplemented by side boxes, so that the playing space was reduced to a kind of alcove.

Wilkinson, too, ridiculed this custom of stage seats. In his opinion "what was termed *building* on the stage, certainly was the greatest nuisance that ever prevailed over an entertainment." He adds that "custom reconciles many things"; and though it was "next to impossible for those ladies in the stage boxes to see at all, still it was the fashion." The following passage has been popular with latter-day scholars:

The stage spectators were not content with piling on raised seats, till their heads reached the theatrical cloudings. . . . But when that amphitheatre was filled, there would be a group of ill-dressed lads and persons sitting on the stage in front, three or four rows deep. . . . Mr. Quin as Falstaff . . . was several minutes before he could pass through the numbers that wedged and hemmed him in, he was so cruelly encompassed around.[22]

Or perhaps for the ghost of Hamlet's father, as for the shade of Ninus in Voltaire's *Semiramis,* waggish spectators had the opportunity to shout lustily, "Make way for the ghost! Room for the shade!" Opposition grew through the century until in 1762 the spectators really were excluded from the stage.

The admission charged tended to make the higher-class theatres not the resort of the mass of the people but, rather, the rendezvous of a comparatively small number of London's population. For the most part, the fashionable class was the support of these theatres. These people knew each other as well as the actors. They attended the programs night after night mainly to amuse themselves. Davies makes this clear by comparing the audiences of Paris and London in the eighteenth century. Discussing Aaron Hill, he writes:

Mr. Hill in adapting French plays to the English stage, forgot the distinguishing character of the two nations. The Frenchman, when he goes to a play, seems to make his entertainment a matter of importance. The long speeches in [French] plays . . . which would disgust an English ear, are extremely pleasing to our light neighbors: they sit in silence, and enjoy the beauty of sentiment, and energy of language; and are taught habitually to cry at scenes of distress. The Englishman looks upon the theatre as a place of amusement; he does not expect to be alarmed with terror or wrought upon by scenes of commiseration; but he is surprised into feelings of these passions, and sheds tears because he cannot avoid it. The theatre, to most Englishmen, becomes a place of instruction by chance, not by choice.[23]

Such a playgoer as the Englishman had to be catered to, and he was hard to please.

The benefit performance, which was the occasion of the "building on the stage," described by Wilkinson, necessitated considerable advertising and solicitation. An actor sought to attract as large an attendance as possible, and by varied means. He used the public press, inserting attractive notices or direct and familiar appeals. Sometimes he announced his coming benefit from the stage. He wooed his author-friends to write him prologues, epilogues, and even plays—perhaps a comic after-piece or a full-length main feature of the bill. He might have the services of an artist like Hogarth, who would design special tickets for the occasion. He might promise the audience some sort of novelty. He might also secure the services of some popular favorite, such as Peg Woffington, who was very obliging, or even Garrick, or another fellow-player to appear wth him. And—perhaps the worst practice of all, though, as Wilkinson says, use had rendered it familiar—he canvassed and solicited his friends directly and personally; that is, he "waited upon" his friends.

To Wilkinson this was a "degrading and painful custom"; it was "truly dreadful, the draggle-tailed Andromache in frost, rain, hail and snow, delivering her benefit play-bills from door to door." Even when recollected in the remote tranquillity of 1790, this practice called forth the following ejaculation:

Good God! what a sight! to actually behold Mr. Frodsham, bred as a gentleman, with fine natural talents, and esteemed in York as a Garrick, the Hamlet of the age, running after, or stopping a gentleman on horseback to deliver his benefit bill, and beg half a crown (then the price of the boxes).[24]

The popular favorites, however, could secure their audiences more genteelly. Like Bellamy, they could seek favors of duchesses in the latters' drawing-rooms and be rewarded bountifully. We have this actress' word for it that her benefit was, "as usual, very brilliant, and lucrative to an excess." At one of her annual benefits she "cleared upwards of eleven hundred pounds." "This," she writes,

was owing to several causes. I had for some time been allowed to be sole dictatress among the polite ranks in the article of dress. My judgment in this point was held in so much estimation, that the ladies would have been wretched who did not consult me relative to their birth-day or fancy cloaths.[25]

All this, of course, indicates the actor-audience relationship, which prevailed throughout the century and which the players utilized profitably. As Thaler says, "Relations between the players and their audiences—nobility and commoners alike—were, as a rule, much more intimate, direct, and personal than they are at present. . . . Distinguished performers *belonged* to the public."[26] So also, it seems, did all performers, as is clear from the accounts of the behavior of both players and spectators. Or, perhaps, it would be better to say that the theatre belonged to the public—both fashionable and otherwise—that regularly frequented its performances. The audience had been encouraged to consider themselves the ultimate judges in any and all theatrical matters, and eventually they bettered the instruction. They judged literary merit; they were the final court of appeal in all disputes—between players, between players and managers, and between managers and public; they expressed themselves—often in riotous protest—in matters of managerial policy.

True to Davies' description of them, they were especially intolerant of dullness. Genest, indebted to *The Gentleman's Magazine* of February, 1735, in his account of the first performance of Fielding's *The Universal Gallants,* tells us that

the audience sat quiet till the 3d act was almost over, in hopes the play would mend, but finding it grew worse and worse, they lost all patience, and not an expression or a sentence afterwards passed without its deserved censure.[27]

And that demonstration of disapproval—probably by hisses, catcalls, and groans—was relatively mild. In that case it was only a lack of literary merit that displeased them. When managerial policy or partisanship caused indignation or merely pique, their protests at times resulted in mob violence and wanton destruction of property that only stopped short at setting fire to the building. A footnote on a playbill of 1744 announced that "the great damages occasioned by the disturbances last night makes it impossible to perform on this day." And the next day's bill informed the public that the company could not play till the following evening, as the damages had not then been repaired.[28]

Audiences would brook no breaking of contracts or promises. We learn from Knight that

On the 23rd January, 1748, a disturbance happened at Drury Lane playhouse, occasioned by two of the principal dancers not being there to dance at the end of the entertainment, whereupon several gentlemen in the boxes and pit pulled up the seats and flooring of the same, tore down the hangings, broke partitions, and all the glasses and sconces.[29]

The same source tells us of an uproar on the night of January 25, 1763. Rioters, who were "gentlemen" disgruntled at being deprived of places on the stage, rebelled, ostensibly over being refused admission at half-price at the end of the third act. The leader of the mob

came to the front of the boxes, harangued the audience on the imposition of the manager, and pleaded vehemently *the right of the public to fix the prices of admission.* . . . Acts of outrageous violence were committed.[30]

"In a measure," says Thaler, "the players and managers themselves were to blame for such excesses. It is true, at least, that they invited interference by carrying to the public each and every little dispute of their own."[31] The audience reciprocated, being ready at any and all times to express their own views—if not always with violence, at least with frankness and emphasis. Manifestations of this, according to the occasion, took the form of heckling or of expressions of approbation and tolerance.

Even the premier star of a theatre-royal was not immune from ungentle treatment. Quin once made so long a pause before giving the expected answer, "I'll meet you there," that one of the pit shouted, "Why don't you tell the gentleman that you'll meet him?"[32]

Miss Bellamy gives us numerous examples of the direct exchange of incidental remarks between audience and performers. One typical instance of hissing and heckling was that of a Mrs.

Hamilton, who tried to stop the tumult by explaining that she had refused to play at Bellamy's benefit because the latter had said Hamilton's public were all tripe people. "With one voice they encored her, crying out . . . 'Well said, Tripe!' A title she retained till she quitted the theatre."[33]

Today encores are not called for at a play. But two hundred years ago approval was sometimes so expressed. For example, Quin, playing Cato, "received a whirlwind of applause and shouts of *'Booth outdone!'* . . . The well-known soliloquy, 'It must be so,' was encored! Mr. Quin readily complied."[34] In the records of the period other examples are to be found not only of speeches encored, but also of prologues and epilogues. A good deal of this behavior seems to have been merely "good, clean fun" and part of the night's entertainment. The English play-goer was in the theatre for a recreation to which he contributed himself—when he was in good humor. He usually took his theatre seriously only when it displeased him; otherwise he could be very tolerant and indulgent. Anecdotes illustrative of this are so numerous that it is difficult to select. One or two must suffice.

Miss Bellamy experienced grievous difficulty with her debut at Covent Garden, especially with recalcitrant colleagues at rehearsals. At the actual performance she had so bad a case of stage-fright that nothing could rouse her from her stupidity till the fourth act, as she herself relates. But of her very first entrance she writes:

I stood like a statue. Till compassion for my youth, and probably some prepossession for my figure, and *dress,* which was *simply elegant* . . . induced a gentleman, who was dictator to the pit, and therefore ludicrously denominated Mr. Town, to call out, and order the curtain to be dropped, till I could recover my confusion.[35]

Interruptions in the performance—like these and others—were not uncommon, but more often they were due less to stage-fright than to indignation that could not be suppressed. Especially if the audience were antagonistic, the actor was quick to express himself in his own defense with a vindication of some sort—reason, excuse, apology—or with a demand for an explanation from the hostile spectators. At one time, a Mrs. Horton, playing Phyllis in Steele's *The Conscious Lovers,* was hissed by an audience who wished rather to be charmed by a rival player who had been lured to another house:

> At last, she advanced to the front of the stage, and boldly addressed the pit: "Gentlemen, what do you mean? What displeases you, my acting or my person?" This shew of spirit recovered the spectators into good humor, and they cried out, as with one voice, "No, no, Mrs. Horton, we are not displeased: go on, go on."[36]

Performances were sometimes interrupted also by ludicrous mishaps, the like of which would not occur today even on the amateur stage or, if they did, would not now be countenanced, as they seem to have been by their audiences then. Furthermore, it would seem that many of the performers themselves were less concerned about their art than they should have been, certainly as professionals. Miss Bellamy, for example, tells us several times that she could not suppress laughter that did not belong in the play, the audience laughing with her. On the occasion of *The Prophetess, or the Fall of Dioclesian,* she was not above playing a practical joke that made a travesty of the play and brought about the fall of that Dioclesian. For the costume of a Roman emperor she advised the hero of the play to wear a full-bottomed wig as large as he could get and, to render himself more conspicuous, a hoop under his "lamberkins." Her serious air deceived the actor. To quote:

> Thus bedizened when he came on . . . there never surely appeared on any stage so grotesque a figure. The house was in a roar. But no one was more diverted with the humorous scene than myself. By this joke . . . was every person present, except the poor Emperor himself, indebted to me for a laugh which I thought would never have an end.[37]

She gives us no reason to believe that she perpetrated this trick because she had any grudge against the man. She made the drama of Antony and Cleopatra a merry play one night because of a mishap that occurred to evoke her laughter.

> Mrs. Kennedy happening unfortunately to have a ragged tail to her dress, pulled upon the stage after her the half of a kettle drum. . . . I could not refrain from bursting into a loud fit of laughter, in which the audience joined me. Nor could I compose my countenance till the asp had finished my night's duty.[38]

Her biography is enlivened with other examples of the free and easy, direct relationship between actor and audience—a relationship in which little thought was given to illusion. Her friend, Mrs. Kennedy, was indisposed one night when she was to play Zara in *The Mourning Bride*. But her sister, Mrs. Farrel,

who was about twenty years older than that lady . . . undertook to play the part. The audience expressed marks of disapprobation throughout the whole of her playing, but particularly so when she died. Upon which she rose from between the mutes, and . . . told the audience, that she was concerned she could not . . . give satisfaction; but, as good nature had induced her to undertake the part . . . she hoped they would excuse it. Having finished her speech, she . . . threw herself down again between the mutes, who covered her face with a veil.[39]

The audience and Bellamy herself laughed and "it was impossible to compose them for the rest of the evening." And that reminded her "of a similar laughable adventure that once befell Mrs. Hamilton," who

being very lusty, the scene-men found great difficulty to lift the chair into which she had thrown herself, upon her supposed death. Which she observing, she ordered them to set it down, and making her courtesy to the audience, walked off as coolly as if she was not to be supposed dead.[40]

Occurrences like those must have enlivened the evening's entertainment and have added relished bits of variety to programs that had a rather monotonous similarity night after night.[41] And from season to season no great amount of variety entered into the Londoner's theatrical fare. He saw the old plays (or new ones patterned on them) with little variety in staging, costuming, and acting.

Macklin and Garrick, both in 1741, broke with tradition, deviated from established custom in acting, and proceeded to fix their own stereotypes upon the various individual roles in their repertoire. There was a traditional manner of playing a certain part, with traditional business, and particular readings of the speeches. The omission of a word or the change of an inflection did not go unnoticed, especially by the frequenters of the pit. They were curious to know whether an actor would deliver such and such a speech better one night than the time before. They would compare the Romeo of Garrick and of Barry—perhaps running back and forth from one theatre to the other to do so. The actor's pronunciation had to satisfy the audience or else he was hissed; and a slip of the memory could be prompted by the audience as quickly and as accurately as by the prompter.

The playgoer of eighteenth-century London went regularly to his entertainment in the theatre in order to enjoy the intimate relationship that existed between him and his fellows, and between them and the performers. He knew the players too well, in their private lives, to regard the action presented to him on the stage as occurring in a world of its own, detached and distinct from his world in the auditorium. From these social contacts, and from his presence even at rehearsals, he had some acquaintance with the technical secrets of the profession. In the auditorium he was one of a large group or family, like the modern subscribers at the opera. The behavior of the audience was, however, more like that of spectators at a baseball game today; their cheers, loud remarks, and showers of missiles were part of the show. Quite often they functioned as referee in disputes, and always they enjoyed the prerogative of judge and jury of merit and reward. Those were palmy days indeed in the

"houses twain
Of Covent Garden and Drury Lane."

NOTES

1. *A History of Late Eighteenth Century Drama, 1750-1800* (Cambridge, 1927), p. 39.
2. *The Actor: A Treatise on the Art of Playing* (London, 1750), p. 141.
3. *A General History of the Stage* (London, 1749), p. 109.
4. *The Actor*, 2d ed. (London, 1755), pp. 155-156.
5. Hill in *The Actor* criticizes the conduct of the managers who cannot or who will not see the absurdity of giving such parts to such persons. In 1755 (2d ed.) he wrote: "It is no crime to be past five and twenty; but when she, who has twice that age, from her authority on the stage, takes from an actress of youth and figure such a character, she deserves to be exposed and laughed at."
6. Alwin Thaler, *Shakespeare to Sheridan* (Cambridge, U.S.A., 1922), p. 95.
7. J. T. Kirkman, *Memoirs of the Life of Charles Macklin, Esq.* (London, 1799), I, 140, 193.
8. Sir Walter Besant, *London in the Eighteenth Century* (London, 1902), p. 343.
9. Thaler, *op. cit.*, p. 118.
10. *Ibid.*, p. 38. See also George Anne Bellamy's *Apology*, II, 131-136.

11. A. Nicoll, *A History of Early Eighteenth Century Drama, 1700-1750* (Cambridge, 1925), p. 9.

12. Bellamy, *op. cit.*, II, 58-59.

13. Dr. John Doran, *"Their Majesties Servants"—Annals of the English Stage, from Thomas Betterton to Edmund Kean* (New York, 1865), I, 179.

14. *The History of the Scottish Stage* (Edinburgh, 1793), pp. 379-380.

15. *The Actor* (1st ed.), p. 76.

16. J. Fitzgerald Molloy, *Beaux and Belles of England* (New York, n.d.), I, 24-25.

17. *Op. cit.*, I, 388.

18. *The Actor* (1st ed.), p. 222.

19. John Genest, *Some Account of the English Stage . . . 1660-1830* (Bath, 1832), III, 533.

20. See G. C. D. Odell's *Shakespeare from Betterton to Irving* (New York, 1920), I, 284.

21. *The Actor* (1st ed.), p. 223.

22. Tate Wilkinson, *Memoirs of his Own Life* (York, 1790), IV, 109-115.

23. Thomas Davies, *Memoirs of the Life of David Garrick, Esq.* (London, 1780), I, 142-143.

24. *Op. cit.*, IV, 65, 67.

25. *Apology*, III, 51 (and cf. p. 1).

26. *Op. cit.*, pp. 88-89.

27. *Op. cit.*, III, 448.

28. *Ibid.*, IV, 139.

29. *David Garrick* (London, 1894), p. 111.

30. *Ibid.*, p. 187. (The italics are not in the original.)

31. *Op. cit.*, p. 146.

32. Sir Walter Besant, *op. cit.*, p. 428.

33. *Op. cit.*, III, 85.

34. J. Fitzgerald Molloy, *op. cit.*, II, 119.

35. *Op cit.*, I, 54.

36. Thomas Davies, *Dramatic Miscellanies* (Dublin, 1784), I, 103-104. He tells us of a somewhat similar experience of Peg Woffington's (pp. 31-32). And Bellamy relates several instances of the same sort.

37. *Op. cit.*, III, 50-51.

38. *Ibid.*, pp. 180-181.

39. *Ibid.*, IV, 50-51.

40. *Ibid.*

41. The nightly program of entertainment—humorous prologue, full-length play, humorous epilogue, an interlude of dancing and music, and a short farcical after-piece or a burlesque or pantomime—was the pattern familiar to the regular patrons.

The Stage Yankee

Jonathan W. Curvin

Exult each patriot heart!—this night is shewn
A piece, which we may fairly call our own.

THUS begins the stirring prologue which, one April night in 1787, introduced to the audience gathered at the John Street Theatre in New York a new comedy, "by an American citizen," Mr. Royall Tyler. Perhaps as the early scenes were played, skeptical theatregoers were tempted to question just how completely "our own" the play actually was. True, the characters made pointed reference to "the Mall" and "the Battery," and George Washington's name was introduced by the moralistic hero, Colonel Manly. But did these obvious devices make for a truly native drama? Was not *The Contrast* simply a transplanted English sentimental comedy, whose noble hero and heroine, in the face of ridicule by their gay and thoughtless acquaintances, "pursued unperturbed the path of solemn rectitude which leadeth to matrimony"?[1] Had not Tyler borrowed extravagantly from Sheridan? *The Contrast,* with its malicious gossip types, Letitia and Charlotte, and the affected dandy, Dimple, certainly echoed *The School for Scandal,* which Royall Tyler had seen performed only three weeks before.

Not until Act II, Scene 2, when Thomas Wignell, who had delivered the prologue, reappeared as Colonel Manly's Yankee "waiter," Jonathan, was the audience privileged to measure the originality of the New England playwright. In creating this one character, Tyler vindicated his claims; Jonathan was most assuredly "our own." There is a mild irony in the fact that the progenitor of a long line of stage Yankees should have been first interpreted by a British player, whose father had graced the London company of David Garrick.

In Tyler's Jonathan may be found the pattern from which were cut nearly all subsequent Yankees of the stage. In the structure of *The Contrast* he occupies a minor place; he figures in only three scenes, each of which might easily be omitted without damaging the main plot. Jonathan's station is humble; he serves Colonel Manly, late of Washington's army; and his associates, Jenny and Jessemy, are menials. Yet Jonathan himself is anything but humble. He prefers to be called "waiter" rather than "servant." He democratically insists, "I am a true-blue son of Liberty. No man shall master me: my father has as good a farm as the Colonel."

Jonathan has other sturdy virtues. He loathes affectation. The absurd posturings of the Anglomaniac Jessemy fill him with contempt. Unbroken, something of a child of nature, he scoffs at formalities. As the circumstances of his betrothal illustrate, a shrewd practicality governs most of his actions; he has pledged his word to Tabitha Wymen, whose father, the deacon, he has adjudged to be "pretty dumb rich."

The post-Revolution American, conscious of his own developing character, found embodied in Jonathan the very traits he fancied he himself possessed.[2] Yankee common sense, Yankee sincerity, and Yankee independence were all appealingly mirrored in this somewhat grotesque stage figure. When theatre audiences in New York, Philadelphia, and Baltimore applauded Jonathan, they indulged a pleasant self-approbation.

Tyler not only set the model of the stage Yankee as a representative national figure; he also established him in a role tailored for the comedian. Wignell was in his mind when he fashioned this near-caricature of a bumpkin among sophisticates. Jonathan is incredibly naive, and from his naivete derives much of his comicality. He mistakes a brothel for a meeting-house, and a theatre for an abode of Satan. Jessemy tricks him into courting the serving maid, Jenny, so that Jessemy shall appear more desirable by contrast. The gullible Jonathan falls easily into the trap. His speech, flavored with "gor," "buss," and "dang it," and pungent phrases like "by the living jingo," "thick as mustard," and "maple-log seize it!" further distinguishes him from the refinement of the other characters. He dominates every scene in which he appears. Wignell, astute enough to realize the comic potentialities of the character, heads the impressive list of actors who were to find in the Yankee a rich fund of material upon which to exercise their talents.

For some decades after *The Contrast* the Yankee character appeared only sporadically in native plays. This neglect is not surprising when we consider the almost total dependence of the American drama and theatre upon foreign importations. For years before the Revolution the struggling professional theatre had subsisted on standard British drama interpreted by English actors. When the native playwright first appeared, he either eschewed American subject matter altogether, as did Thomas Godfrey in *The Prince of Parthia,* or else, like Robert Rogers in *Ponteach,* he approached native material with a borrowed technique. The polemical satires during the Revolution, when most of the colonial theatres were closed on the recommendation of the Continental Congress, were for the most part "closet" dramas, written with no thought of production. After the Revolution the American playwright continued to make use of foreign sources, even extending his indebtedness, under the leadership of William Dunlap, to include France and Germany.

Plays with native values, furthermore, confronted a widespread public prejudice; audiences refused to acknowledge the worth of the local product. James Nelson Barker angrily scored the "hypercritics" who condemned the American while they exalted the English drama. "They can accompany the fop of an English play in his lounge through Bond-street, while an American personage, of the same cast, would most probably be knocked down, if he attempted a promenade in High-street," Barker asserted.[3] A few years later this playwright was to practice a convenient deception. He managed to present his play, *Marmion,* in Philadelphia with not even the cast aware that an American had written it.[4]

Lack of copyright laws threatened to rob the aspiring dramatist of his just financial reward. After writing his play, he could not prevent the performance of stolen and often mutilated versions of his original manuscript. Publication was even less desirable, for, once printed, a play passed out of the author's control entirely. None of these obstacles, however, could dissuade the playwright from tentative efforts to establish an American drama, and to incorporate with fair regularity his versions of the Yankee prototype.

In the same year that *The Contrast* was acclaimed, William Dunlap composed *The Modest Soldier,* which has not survived, but which from Dunlap's description[5] of the characters (a Yankee servant, a travelled American, an officer in the Revolutionary army, an old gentleman and his two daughters, one lively and the other serious), would seem to have closely resembled Tyler's comedy. In 1788 Samuel Low presented the managers of the John Street Theatre with his comedy of manners, *The Politician Out-Witted,* a piece which featured the garrulous Humphrey Cubb, a shrewd Yankee given to expressions like "worser," "sartin," and "I never larnt to cypher." A Yankee servant, Obadiah, has most of the liveliest speeches in *The Traveller's Return,* Judith S. Murray's domestic play, produced in 1796. Obadiah converses with the housemaid in this fashion:

OBADIAH. Oh! tarnation, tarnation, tarnation!
BRIDGET. Are you mad? (Shaking him violently.)
OBADIAH. Oh! I have broke—I have broke—I can't speak it—.
BRIDGET. Broke what?
OBADIAH. I have broke—I have broke th--the--the--what d'ye call it— . . .
BRIDGET. The--the--the--what d'ye call it! Now what the plague do you mean, Obadiah?
OBADIAH. Why that there glass thing, Bridget, by which folks find out when we should be cold and when we should be warm.
BRIDGET. I'll be hang'd, Obadiah, if you don't mean the thermometer.[6]

After the turn of the century, in *Jonathan Postfree,* by L. Beach, a Yankee drover has the title role. Much of the play's humor comes from the difficulties this rustic has in adapting himself to an urban environment. A. B. Lindsley created a similar comic situation in his *Love and Friendship, or Yankee Notions,* which the Park Theatre Company produced during the season of 1807-08. Captain Horner and his serving man, Jonathan, are engaged in peddling notions in Charleston, South

Carolina. Jonathan in particular finds the South hostile and confusing:

JONATHAN. Here I am, slick 'nough, and where to go next, be cust if I know. This must be Broad-street, and broad 'nough 'tis tewe, by gum! I've been walken' up it this good fifteen minutes, and darn'd 'f I've got acrost it yit. I must keep tewe eyes 'bout me, or I shall be intewe King-street, and the black-barded Jew'll shave the hair off my teeth. . . . This here Charleston's such a rotten hot place, there's no liven' in 't; then there's sich a tarnation sight 'f negurs black as the old feller 'imself, a body dan't stir but they has 'um at their nose or their heels. It beats all nater! Never fetch me, 'f I don't wish I was t'hum agin, with all my heart.[7]

The War of 1812 brought in its wake an era of confidence and prosperity, during which the people of the United States came to an even more fully developed consciousness of nationality.[8] Native critics appraised the deficiencies of American literature; at the same time they entertained hope for originality in creative writing. William Cullen Bryant contended in his essay, "American Society as a Field for Fiction," that the diverse aspects of the American social scene provided the best source of material for native writers. James Kirke Paulding urged his younger contemporaries to "give us something new—something characteristic of your native feelings."[9] And Emerson provided our intellectual Declaration of Independence in his Phi Beta Kappa address in 1837; here was a rousing plea for America to establish an original relation to philosophy and the arts, and to be no longer "fed on the sere remains of foreign harvests."[10]

Among the native dramatists were some intrepid and inventive enough to look about them for native themes to justify a truly national drama. James Nelson Barker has been mentioned as one who deplored the lack of encouragement granted the American playwright. Barker attributed this lack to "a superciliousness that freezes, a neglect that destroys."[11] Barker's own plays admirably illustrate his determination to use American materials. His early sentimental comedy of manners, *Tears and Smiles* (1806), had for its scene the playwright's native city, Philadelphia, and made use of Philadelphia customs for its subject matter; the story of Pocahontas as related by Captain John

Smith was the germ of *The Indian Princess, or La Belle Sauvage* (1808); and *Superstition* (1824) dealt with the Puritan persecution of witches and of non-conforming or opposing sects.

Mordecai M. Noah also exploited native material and drew upon recent realities of national life for his occasional dramatic contributions. Noah argued in his preface to *She Would Be a Soldier:*

National plays should be encouraged. They have done every thing for the British nation, and can do much for us; they keep alive the recollection of important events, by representing them in a manner at once natural and alluring. We have a fine scope, and abundant materials to work with, and a noble country to justify the attempt.[12]

The keenness of James Kirke Paulding's satirical thrusts against foreign cultures made his play, *The Bucktails; or Americans in England,* a powerful statement of the rising nationalism. *Fashion,* by Anna Cora Mowatt, first produced in 1845, promotes the same notion of America's cultural independence that had been so clearly implied in drama before it. Mrs. Mowatt denounced with an authority born of experience New York society's besetting sin, the habit of bending an obsequious knee to pretentious alien manners.

This struggle for a national drama became basically a struggle for the recognition of native and contemporary subject matter. Patriotic motives impelled the dramatist to mirror in his plays the scenes and the characters of his native land. He could scarcely do this and ignore the Yankee, the very epitome of the national spirit.

The stage Yankee became a symbol of national exuberance; he reflected the cockiness of a youthful nation which had twice been victorious over an older and favored opponent. He held sway in dozens of popular dramas, and up to the Civil War was more frequently acted in American theatres than any character. Playwrights gave him outlandish names: Welcome Sobersides, Jonathan Doolittle, Horsebean Hemlock, Obadiah Whitcher, Calvin Cartwheel, Deuteronomy Dutiful, Hiram Hireout, Truman Smelts. He might be a sailor, a peddler, a soldier, a teamster, an innkeeper, a wool-dealer, a policeman, or a farmer. His peculiar traits were often exaggerated, and he threatened at times to serve only as a clown; but nearly always there remained traces of the "real article." It may be said that the recurring presence of this vital figure chiefly distinguishes American comedy during the early nineteenth century. Between *The Contrast* of 1787 and *Fashion* of 1845, Yankee plays kept alive a maturing tradition. Their titles are all but forgotten, and their texts have been scattered or lost: *The Deed of Gift* and *The Forest Rose,* by Samuel Woodworth, in 1822 and 1825 respectively; *The Saw Mill,* by Micah Hawkins, in 1824; *Montgomery,* by Henry James Finn, in 1825; *Jonathan in England,* altered from George Colman's *Who Wants a Guinea?* in 1828; Stephen Glover's *The Cradle of Liberty,* 1832; George Stevens' *The Patriot,* 1834; Joseph Jones' *The People's Lawyer,* 1839, and his *Captain Kyd,* in the same year; R. C. McLellan's *The Foundling,* 1939; *The Yankee Peddler,* 1841, by Morris Barnett; and *The Brazen Drum,* 1842, by Silas S. Steele.[13]

The People's Lawyer, by Joseph S. Jones, bears examination as a play fairly representative of the Yankee genre. By modern realistic standards it seems an ingenuous piece; the hero is white, the villain black, and virtue enjoys an unequivocal triumph. John Ellsby, a scapegrace merchant's clerk, tricks his moralistic fellow employee, Charles Otis, into a compromising position. Falsely accused of having stolen his employer's watch, Charles is imprisoned. Then to his defense comes an honest young lawyer, Robert Howard, who befriends Otis and in the climactic courtroom scene wrings from the cowering Ellsby a confession of guilt.[14]

Such is the plot skeleton of *The People's Lawyer.* We look in vain for originality in its development, or for credible speeches and characters. The contrast, therefore, when the only character of real dimension happens upon the scene, is all the more striking. His presence, obviously, for he takes no active part in the resolution of the plot, is solely to amuse an audience in a theatre. Solon Shingle is a country teamster, who perpetually complains about such mundane hardships as driving cattle through the Boston streets, and losing a barrel of "apple sarse." He professes to have "fit in the Revolution." To nearly all his speeches he appends the tag phrase, "Jest so." The evil characters of the play consider him a garrulous old bore; the good folk credit him with genuine worth. Puzzled by city ways, he is ready at the close of the play to return to rural security:

SOLON. These city folks will skin me out of my old plaid cloak that I bought ten years ago; hat, boots and trousers, tu, far as I know. I've been here long enough. I'll follow arter the 'squire, find my Nabby, buy a load of groceries, and get home as quick as my team will go it. When I'm in this 'ere Boston I get so bewildered I don't know a string of sausages from a cord of wood. Jest so.[15]

Solon does not figure as a *deus ex machina* in the courtroom scene. Instead, he clowns merrily before the judge, goes to sleep and snores audibly, while the innocent Charles Otis is saved without him. It will be noted, on the other hand, that the playwright has favored Shingle with all manner of delights for the actor: choice exit lines; scope for elaborate incidental pantomime; and long soliloquies while no other characters are on the stage. No actor could fail to recognize that in *The People's Lawyer* it is not the lawyer, the hero, or the villain who is in primary focus and to an audience memorable; on the contrary, it is the appendage, the eminently actable Yankee. That the play should have had for its alternate title, *Solon Shingle,* was almost inevitable.

The printed evidence of the plays, however, tells but half the story of the Yankee's reign in the American theatre. To the actors themselves must go a large share of credit for his astonishing popularity. When James Nelson Barker in 1807 outlined the plot of his new play, *Tears and Smiles,* to Manager Warren of the Philadelphia Chestnut Street Theatre, the elder Joseph Jefferson "put in for a Yankee character."[16] Barker complied with the request, even though, as he admitted, he had never seen a Yankee at the time. *Tears and Smiles* apparently survived chiefly because of Jefferson's comic acting as the servant, Nathan Yank. He alone, according to Barker, kept the audience awake.[17] Samuel Woodworth was inspired to write *The Forest Rose* by his confidence in the ability of Henry Placide to do justice to the role of Jonathan Ploughboy, acquisitive farmer and shop-keeper. Ploughboy was a great favorite with the comedians. Alexander Simpson played it after Placide; J. S. Silsbee was Ploughboy for one hundred consecutive nights in London; Louis J. Mestayer appeared in the role for a long run in California. Chiefly because of the character and the actors who interpreted him, *The Forest Rose* held the American stage for over forty years. With this play the Yankee actor as a specialist came forward to exert his influence on the American theatre.

As the Yankee became in native playwriting a stock figure, there developed a group of American players so proficient in delineating the character on the stage that audiences identified the various Yankee roles with the particular mannerisms of these actors. Although now the plays often seem mere shells of trite situations and the Yankee a grotesque image of rustic credulity, nineteenth-century audiences evidently found in them a reality we have no adequate way of experiencing or testing. How could intelligent audiences reconcile so patent a stereotype with authentic characterization? The answer is to be found in the actors' consciously realistic style of playing.

James Henry Hackett early took advantage of the popularity of his Yankee monologues to incorporate them in his adaptation of George Colman's play, *Who Wants a Guinea?* in 1805. Hackett transformed the French Cockney, Solomon Gundy, into the Yankee, Solomon Swop, renamed the play *Jonathan in England,* and established himself as one of the foremost interpreters of the authentic Yankee.[18]

Perhaps the most successful of all impersonators of "Down East" characters was George H. Hill, whose career began in 1831 with his appearance as Jonathan Ploughboy. In this and similar roles[19] he shortly became famous throughout the United States and England as "Yankee" Hill. While the playwrights were making use of the Yankee character as a stage type, conventionalized, moving further and further away from the actual, and degenerating into a caricature, Hill drew upon his own observations to lend genuineness to the dramatists' feeble conceptions. His rich and truthful acting brought the characters to life; his generic portrayals maintained a nationalistic outline.

Repeated journeys to his native New England for affectionate study of its folk resulted in characterizations marked by truth, restraint, and simplicity.[20] Contemporary reports abound with references to these qualities in Hill's acting.

> We but echo public opinion, when we affirm, that in the exhibition of the quiet, dry humor, peculiar to *the* Yankee, par excellence, he stands unrivalled.[21]

> Mr. Hill's Yankee was the real critter. It was not, as are almost all the representations of other actors I have seen, a mixture of Western, Southern and Eastern peculiarities of manner and dialect, but the unalloyed, unadulterated down-easter. Mr. Hill did not merely imitate their tone, dialect, and manner, but felt and thought like them. It was this faculty, to use a hackneyed phrase, of throwing himself, body and spirit, into a part, which gave to his Yankee a richness and truthfulness not approached by any actor before or since his time. He did not merely put on a flaxen wig, a long-tailed coat, a short vest, a bell-crowned hat, and straps to his pantaloons long enough for suspenders, nor thus attired did he content himself by imitating the peculiar drawl and queer expressions of the Yankee, for the veriest bungler on earth can do all this, but the spirit of Yankeedom pervaded every action of his body, peeped from his expressive eyes with such sly meaning, that it was difficult for the time being not to believe it was a mistake in the bills, when they announced Mr. Hill as Major Wheeler, instead of announcing the veritable Major Wheeler himself.[22]

Other interpreters followed Hill and Hackett in the catalogue of plays built around the Yankee character. Danforth Marble and Joshua Silsbee had wide reputations. Marble's repertoire included *The Vermont Wool-Dealer; Sam Patch; Yankee in Time; Yankee Land; Down Easter;* and *Liberty Tree.* As Hackett had done in 1833 and Hill in 1836, Marble played in London, and met with enthusiastic reception from English audiences. *The London Court Journal* reported:

> His delineation of the Yankee character, the mixture of cunning, conceit, selfishness, fun and bombast, coupled with the habitual lazy drawl both of speech and action, is given with a truth that must be apparent to all. His stories are new, full of drollery, and capitally told. He must prove a good card to the management, and we congratulate both actor and lessee on this popular little theatre having

been the medium of introducing such a clever debutant to such a liberal lessee.[23]

Both Marble and Silsbee, Yankee born, sought in the villages and water fronts of New England for mannerisms of speech and authentic situations adaptable to performance on the stage. Silsbee was credited with perfecting an individual technique both new and original:

Faithfully as he performs the Yankee character, his performances are permeated with the natural humor of the man. His looks, gestures, and actions, even the arch twinkle of his eye, impress the spectator with ludicrous emotions, and his inflexible countenance, rigidly innocent of fun while his audience are in roars of laughter, gives an additional zest to the humor of the language and the absurdity of the situation.[24]

In the hands of John Edmond Owens the character of Solon Shingle became "a simple-minded, phenomenally shrewd old man from New England with a soul which soared no higher than the financial value of a bar'l of apple sass."[25] Owens was already a successful actor before essaying this role, but after his appearance in *The People's Lawyer,* the play became virtually his. Evidently Owens took the most careful pains to create a true portrait of the bemused rustic. L. Clarke Davis reported that Owens had made a personal study of his farm overseer, and had used the man as a model for his characterization:

Solon Shingle was not an inspiration of art, but rather a faithful copy from a peculiarly marked original. . . . Owens had the man he impersonated to sit to him for his picture, and the popularity and the merits of the performance rested upon the sure foundation of its wonderful fidelity to nature. As a copy, it was exact as a photograph, or as a landscape thrown upon a blank wall by the camera obscura, and almost as cold. There was perfection alike in the dress, the uncouth action, the awkward, rolling gait, suggestive of following the plow and straddling furrows, the shrewd, inquisitive habit, and the quaint patois, as true to the original in the pronunciation of each syllable as in the whole.[26]

William Winter tempered his praise of Owens' acting of the role with a critical rebuke for his excessive realism. The characterization, Winter believed, "would have been just as funny, and more endearing, if it had not been quite so literal."[27]

The procedure followed by Owens in basing his characterization on a known original was duplicated in 1876 by Denman Thompson with a somewhat similar conception, that of Joshua Whitcomb in the play of that name by George W. Ryer. This play served as a highly popular vehicle for Thompson until 1886, after which date, as *The Old Homestead*, it continued with Thompson in the leading role to win the approval of the American public for many years.[28] "Uncle Josh," a simple, lovable old farmer, dominates a negligible play. He is the logical successor of Solon Shingle and the earlier Yankee types. As Thompson acted the role, naturally, without exaggeration, he became for the thousands who saw the play, "the salt of the American race."[29] When Thompson took his play to Keene, New Hampshire, which was near the locale of the drama, the audience wanted their money back, on the ground that they got nothing for it but what they saw, free of charge, all about them every day. " 'It warn' no actin'; it was jest a lot of fellers goin' around and doin' things.' "[30]

The stage Yankee attained his centennial in *The Old Homestead*. From an inauspicious beginning in *The Contrast* as a comic servant, rural, uncouth, witty, and sympathetic, he had matured as a treasured symbol of Americanism. He found a secure place in dramas by our first nationalistic playwrights, and audiences in America and England persisted for decades in associating basic American traits with Jonathan's numerous theatre progeny. This was possible, even when the plays were often inconsequential fables and the Yankee a clown evolved from a ready-made formula, because of the dramatists' expert collaborators, the native actors. To the long line of ingenious players, from James Henry Hackett to Denman Thompson, must go major credit for preserving on the stage the unmistakable outline of the real Yankee.

NOTES

1. Oral Sumner Coad, *William Dunlap: A Study of his Life and Works and his Place in Contemporary Culture* (New York, 1917), p. 136.

2. Sidney George Fisher, *The Struggle for American Independence* (Philadelphia, 1908), I, 22-24.

3. See Barker's Preface to *Tears and Smiles*, reprinted in Paul H. Musser, *James Nelson Barker* (University of Pennsylvania, 1929), p. 141.

4. W. B. Wood, *Personal Recollections of the Stage* (Philadelphia, 1855), p. 188.

5. William Dunlap, *A History of the American Theatre* (New York, 1832), p. 77.

6. Perley Isaac Reed, *The Realistic Presentation of American Characters in Native American Plays Prior to Eighteen Seventy* (Columbus, Ohio, 1918), p. 61.

7. *Ibid.*, p. 73.

8. Albert Bushnell Hart, *The American Nation* (New York, 1905-07), XIII, 193.

9. From a letter to T. W. White in *The Southern Literary Messenger*, August, 1834, quoted in Amos L. Herold, *James Kirke Paulding, Versatile American* (New York, 1926), p. 87.

10. Ralph Waldo Emerson, *Complete Works*, ed. E. W. Emerson (Centenary ed., Boston and New York, 1903-1904), I, 82.

11. Musser, *op. cit.*, p. 56.

12. M. M. Noah, *She Would Be a Soldier, or The Plains of Chippewa* (New York, 1819), pp. 4-5.

13. These titles comprise only a part of the much longer list supplied by Reed, *op. cit.*, pp. 152-59.

14. See Alfred Bates, ed., *The Drama: Its History, Literature, and Influence on Civilization* (Philadelphia, 1904), XX, for the complete text of *The People's Lawyer*.

15. *Ibid.*, p. 230.

16. Dunlap, *op. cit.*, p. 377.

17. *Ibid.*, p. 378.

18. "I consider his Solomon Swop the most natural and unexaggerated Yankee I ever saw upon the stage." George Vandenhoff, *Leaves from an Actor's Notebook; or Anecdotes of the Green-Room and Stage* (London, 1860), p. 196.

19. Sy Saco in J. A. Stone's *The Knight of the Golden Fleece* and Solon Shingle in J. S. Jones' *The People's Lawyer* were among Hill's more successful interpretations.

20. See G. H. Hill, *Scenes from the Life of an Actor* (New York, 1853).

21. Quoted from *The Knickerbocker Magazine*, May, 1838, in George C. D. Odell, *Annals of the New York Stage* (New York, 1927-1941), IV, 206.

22. Dr. W. K. Northall, *Life and Recollections of Yankee Hill* (New York, 1850), p. 19.

23. Quoted in Falconbridge, *Dan Marble: A Biographical Sketch* (New York, 1851), p. 152.

24. Quoted in Oral Sumner Coad and Edwin Mims, Jr., *The American Stage* (New Haven, 1929), p. 174, from *Tallis's Magazine*.

25. Laurence Hutton, *Curiosities of the American Stage* (New York, 1891), p. 40.

26. L. Clarke Davis, "Among the Comedians," *Atlantic Monthly*, XIX (June, 1867), 757.

27. William Winter, *The Wallet of Time* (New York, 1913), I, 219. See also Mrs. John E. Owens, *Memories of the Professional and Social Life of John E. Owens* (Baltimore, 1892), p. 134, for a London review of *The People's Lawyer*: "The man who found a diamond amongst a heap of rubbish is not reported to have talked much about the rubbish. The play-goers will find Owens' *Solon Shingle* the diamond in the dust-heap; the piece is not worthy a second thought. The diamond has a bad setting; but anything more brilliant than the gem itself we have not seen."

28. See "The Old Homestead—The Greatest Popular Success of the American Stage," *Current Literature* (December, 1908).

29. F. E. McKay and Charles L. Wingate, *Famous American Actors of Today* (New York, 1896), p. 392.

30. Hutton, *op. cit.*, p. 44.

The Realism in Romanticism: Hugo and Wordsworth

LELAND SCHUBERT

§1

VICTOR HUGO's preface to *Cromwell* is the clearly expressed creed of the romantic theatre. It has been suggested that this famous pronouncement served romantic drama as Wordsworth's preface to *Lyrical Ballads* served romantic poetry. The parallel is not exact, of course, because Wordsworth spoke for only one aspect of romantic poetry. Romanticism is Wordsworth, but it is also Coleridge, Scott, and Byron. In the theatre, however, romanticism is Hugo, and Hugo is romanticism. De Vigny, Dumas *père*, Musset, and the others were merely followers and disciples of Hugo. The preface to *Cromwell* lays down in black on white the ideas and ideals of the romantic dramatists.

For the most part, of course, romanticism and realism are opposed—in theory and in practice. Mario Praz suggests that realism "loves to go out into the world, and live confidently and busily in the stirring multitude of external things." Romanticism, on the other hand, tends to turn inward and is "at least a withdrawal from these outer things into inner experience."[1] Realism is interested in what is outside of man rather than what is within him. L. A. Reid believes that realism is clearly opposed to romanticism; it is "a protest, explicit or implicit, against romanticism, a reaction to hard fact."[2] The truth of this theory is reinforced and more or less verified by nineteenth-century literary history. Champfleury, Flaubert, Zola—all were reacting against Hugo, Lamartine, and de Vigny: they were expressing a changed point of view. John Mason Brown describes it as the difference between nature that "borrows the enchantment of distance" and simple nature "observed through the myopic eyes of men and women avid for detail close at hand." He believes that realism is the commonplace, the factual, the scientific spirit, the slums—as opposed to the grotesque, the picturesque, the Gothic revival, and the cloak and sword of the romantic.[3] However brief these explanations are, they do suggest the generally accepted differences between realism and romanticism.

Yet the generally accepted distinction underemphasizes one facet of romanticism, as the discussion of the relative positions of Wordsworth and Coleridge shows. One the one hand, Wordsworth represents the romantic interest in truth-to-nature; and on the other, Coleridge represents the romantic interest in "far-away time, far-away clime." Both aspects belong to the idea expressed in the term *romanticism*. Some critics, unduly impressed by the popular distinction, or over-inclined to simplify and pigeonhole, have denied to the romanticist any impulse to truth-to-nature. Mr. Lescelles Abercrombie, for example, refuses to admit Wordsworth into his consideration of romanticism because Wordsworth does not fit into his picture of the romantic. "The mere fact," he writes, "that Wordsworth is the great figure of the romantic movement does not compel us to make *him* a romantic."[4] Mr. Abercrombie's arguments are neat and well organized. We may ask, however: If romanticism is not the product of a romantic age, what is? If Wordsworth is "the great figure in the romantic movement," is he not therefore a romantic? The difficulty lies in the critic's attempt to set up categories of strict mutual exclusiveness. Fortunately, the majority of critics have been less concerned for rigorous black-and-white definition, and have been quite willing to use *romanticism* as a term broad enough to include both contributors to *Lyrical Ballads*. In the theatre, Victor Hugo, by his own admission as well as by general critical consent, is a romantic. Corot and Géricault, in painting, as well as Delacroix and Gros, are romantics. Hawthorne, no less than Poe, is a romantic writer. In time, these men belong to the nineteenth-century romantic movement; and, in spirit, they subscribe to one or another of the several planks of the romantic platform. In their artistic work and in their occasional critical writings, Hugo, Wordsworth, Hawthorne, Corot, and Géricault exhibit and testify to qualities which place them at once in the romantic movement and in the movement which leads to realism.

It is not held here that these romanticists are realists. It is admitted that realism, as we now know it, did not appear until nearly a half-century after most of the great romantic artists had laid up their pens and their brushes. However, in some of its aspects, nineteenth-century romanticism seems to include elements which later developed into realism and naturalism. Romanticism seems to be, in part, one step in the tendency towards realism. The following pages will present evidence to support the belief that in romanticism—particularly in the theory of Hugo and Wordsworth—there is considerable realism.

§2

In the preface to *Cromwell* Hugo described the tremendous changes which had shaken the world from the time of Homer to the nineteenth century. With the coming of Christianity, he contended, two interesting literary phenomena appeared: the grotesque and the spirit of curiosity and examination. It was then that literature began, as nature had always done, to mix "but without confusing them, the dark with the light, the grotesque with the sublime, in other words, the body with the soul, the heart with the spirit." It is this change, Hugo adds, that marks

the fundamental difference which separates, in my mind, modern art from ancient art, the actual form from the dead form, or, to employ more vague but more approved terms, the *romantic* literature from the classic literature.[5]

Up to the point where Hugo says *romantic* he might well be talking about what we have come to think of as realistic; but in 1827, of course, there was no word in aesthetic philosophy for the realistic—except *romantic*.

During the primitive period, according to Hugo, literature was lyric; in the ancient period it was epic; in modern times it is dramatic. He then adds, "The ode sings of eternity; the epic solemnizes history; the drama paints life." The characteristic of the modern period, Hugo believes, is *la verité;* and drama, which is the representative literature of the modern period, lives "upon the real." Hugo believes that modern drama is *truth* because it does combine the grotesque with the sublime. This reminds us of the naturalists' insistence on the *whole* truth: the bad with the good, the ugly with the beautiful, the despair with the hope. Drama, says Hugo—and he is talking about modern *romantic* drama—is "the combination of two types, the sublime and the grotesque, which meet in drama as they meet in life and in creation." Clearly, Hugo sees the drama of his age as a true-to-life form of art. If he had known the word he might have described contemporary drama as *realistic*.

He becomes more specific. He describes the pseudo-classic stage setting to which he objects violently. The formal, un-localized setting of Molière and Racine, necessitated by observation of the absurd unities, distorts the action and characterization of the drama presented. "Where," he asks, "did anyone ever see a porch or a peristyle of that sort?" And he goes on to inquire:

What is more contrary—we will not say to verity; the scholastic considers it very cheap—but to verisimilitude? It results in everything being too characteristic, too intimate, too local to happen in the antechamber or on the street corner; that is to say, the whole drama takes place in the wings. On the stage, we see only what amounts to the elbow of the action; its hands are somewhere else. In the place of scenes we have recitations; in the place of pictures, descriptions. Solemn-faced personages—placed as in the ancient chorus, between the drama and ourselves—come to tell us about what is going on in the temple, in the palace, in the public square. Often we want to cry out, "True enough. But take us back there. It must be very amusing; it must be beautiful to see!"

The setting of a play, Hugo tells us, is a witness, "terrible and inseparable," a mute character, and it must be accurate and appropriate.

Turning for a moment to another of Hugo's works, the comments on Sir Walter Scott in *The Philosophy,* we find that Hugo greatly admires Scott, whom he compares to a magician "who does not deny his pen any truth." He is a writer who "wants his portraits to be pictures, and his pictures to be portraits." A few pages later, Hugo inquires into the proper intentions of the story-teller, and answers his own question:

It is to express a useful truth in an interesting story. And once this fundamental idea is chosen and the explanatory action is invented, should not the author, in order to develop it, seek a method of execution which gives to his novel a semblance of real life and to the imitation the likeness of the model?

Hugo believes that this "semblance of real life" and the "likeness of the model" are unquestionably to be desired. The novelist (or the dramatist) can approach closer to reality than the historian: his medium allows him to fill in the gaps with characteristic detail and to saturate the whole with imaginative, though accurate, local color.

Characteristic detail and local color are also revealed in the theatre. Under the control of art, Hugo tells us in the preface to *Cromwell,* the stage should reproduce the facts in reference to manners, customs, and peculiarities. The dramatist should fill in the details omitted by the historian, and he should harmonize the data which the historian gathers. The theatre should recreate the local color of the times which it presents: and local color, Hugo notes, is valuable only when it is "in the heart of the work," and not added on later. In this connection he points out that the poet must choose not the *beautiful,* but rather the *characteristic.* The dialogue of drama must be sincere and outspoken, easy and unaffected; it must avoid long, unnatural speeches; and, above all, it must be characteristic, i.e., faithful to the character who speaks it. Hugo cannot go so far as to rule verse out of drama, but he does circumscribe it:

Let us repeat, verse in the theatre should strip itself of all self-love, all undue claim, all coquetry. Here it is only a form, and a form which should admit everything, which asks nothing of the play, and, on the contrary, which should receive everything from it.

He is undoubtedly thinking of the elaborate, self-conscious, self-justified verse of the eighteenth-century drama. Hugo feels free to shock his hearers with unacademic run-on lines and out-of-place caesuras, because he seeks more realistic dialogue. He takes the hammer to theories and poetic systems (to use his own figure) and he chips off "the old plaster which masks the facade of art" when he states that because the only rules in art are "the general laws of nature which rise above all art," the poet "should therefore take counsel only from nature and truth."

In all fairness, however, it must be admitted that Victor Hugo was by no means a realist in the sense which that term has acquired. What his attitude would have been toward a Zola or even a Dumas *fils*, we can only guess. Though he might have found *Camille* palatable, he probably would have felt that *Thérèse Raquin* exceeded "the impassable limit which . . . separates reality according to art from reality according to nature." Hugo was neither a realist nor a scientist; he was a romanticist and an artist. He felt that "the truth of art should not be, as many have said, *absolute* reality. Art is not able to present the thing itself." This attitude he sums up concretely in a well-known passage:

Someone has already told us that the drama is a mirror which reflects nature. But if this mirror is an ordinary one with a plain and polished surface, it will reflect only a dull image of objects, without relief, faithful but faded: we know how color and luminosity are lost in a simple reflection. It is therefore necessary that the drama be a concentrating mirror which, far from weakening, concentrates and condenses the colored rays. It reflects a light from a mere glow; and a flame from a light. Only in this way is drama acknowledged by art.

Except for this insistence on the concentrating and condensing mirror, there is nothing of importance in the preface to *Cromwell* which applies exclusively to romanticism. Hugo might well be talking about realism. When he begs for scenes instead of recitations, pictures instead of descriptions; when he decries the old academic rules and demands that the poet "take counsel only from nature and truth"; when he argues for dramatic dialogue that is characterizing and that serves the play, rather than poetic dialogue that exists for its own sake; when he begs for a mixture of the grotesque with the sublime: when Hugo pleads for these changes, he sounds like Zola. Zola wrote:

"Thus, no more abstract characters in books, no more lying inventions, no more of the absolute; but real characters, the true history of each one, the story of daily life."[6] This is not to say that Hugo and Zola were cut from the same cloth. Hugo was not a naturalist interested in what Leon Deffoux calls the "literature of medical tendencies,"[7] as Zola was. He was not even particularly interested in daily life. But Hugo and Zola were both motivated by a desire to make their art more life-like. Both sought greater verisimilitude. Just as Zola was convinced that his art came closer to life than that of Hugo, so Hugo was convinced that he had pictured life more accurately than had Racine. Looking back on the work of the classicists, the romanticists, and the realists, we, in the light of our accurate photographic-techniques, can see that both Hugo and Zola were right in their claims. We can see this without passing judgment on the aesthetic value of these different periods and their styles. We can see, too, considerable realism in the romanticism of Victor Hugo.

§3

Whereas Hugo's concern with lifelike diction was only one among many of his revolutionary departures from neo-classic patterns, Wordsworth's concern with such diction was of primary importance. His contributions to *Lyrical Ballads* were written in what he thought to be "the real language of men." Throughout the preface to the 1800 edition of the poems, Wordsworth constantly stresses this point. He defends his use of the "language of prose" by quoting a passage from Milton and then by contending that:

a large portion of the language of every good poem can in no respect differ from that of good Prose. We will go further. It may be safely affirmed, that there neither is, nor can be, any *essential* difference between the language of Prose and metrical composition.[8]

We cannot deny that prose, by its very nature, is more realistic than verse. Wordsworth describes the delight found in "an indistinct perception renewed of language closely resembling that of real life." He says that he employs very little poetic diction because he aims to bring his language "near to the language of men." "The language of such poetry as is here recommended," he writes, "is, as far as is possible, a selection of the language really spoken by men." There are a dozen statements repeating this idea. Realistic romanticist that he is, Wordsworth wants his poetry to sound lifelife.

"I have wished to keep the Reader in the company of flesh and blood," he tells us, "persuaded that by so doing I shall interest him." Here, indeed, is a matter-of-fact attitude towards the craft of writing. Perhaps such self-conscious realism is not strictly legitimate; but it is none the less realistic. One could doubtless find numerous writers who have developed a realistic style in order to interest their readers: Sinclair Lewis certainly, and possibly John Erskine—to take a long leap. Wordsworth's "language really spoken by men," however, was no technical trick or device of salesmanship. It was an intrinsic part of his aesthetic philosophy. Like Hugo, and like the later avowed realists, Wordsworth was striving for what, within the limits of his medium, he considered to be truth-to-nature.

Truth-to-nature was his goal, even though the finished product was to be overcast with "a certain colouring of the imagination, whereby ordinary things should be presented to the mind in an unusual aspect." We are here reminded of Hugo's concentrating and condensing mirror. With Aristotle, Wordsworth agrees that "poetry is the most philosophic of all writing"; and he continues:

... it is so: its object is truth, not individual and local, but general, and operative; not standing upon external testimony, but carried alive into the heart by passion; truth which is its own testimony, which gives competence and confidence to the tribunal to which it appeals, and receives them from the same tribunal. Poetry is the image of man and nature.

Mr. Arthur Symons writes of Wordsworth's "sincerity" and of the "unapproachable fidelity to nature," which is its outcome.[9] It may be argued that Wordsworth's desire for "general and operative" truth rather than "individual and local" is no different from that of any great poet, that all universally significant art, however *unrealistic*, proceeds from such desires, and that the mere presence of such a statement in Wordsworth's preface does not necessarily imply a tendency towards realism, but the contrary. This might be true if it were not for the fact that throughout the preface he constantly supports the opposite theory. He says in one place, for example, that the present need for delicately sensitive men is the result of (among other things) theatrical exhibitionism, "frantic novels," and "idle and extravagant stories in verse"—all strictly imaginative and unrealistic types of literature.

The poet, Wordsworth says, is able to conjure up in himself feelings which "resemble passions produced by real events"; and, also, the poet "considers man and the objects which surround him as acting and re-acting upon each other, so as to produce an infinite complexity of pain and pleasure"—an almost Zolaesque conception. Wordsworth, like the true realists who came later, was consciously and actively seeking greater fidelity to nature. It is this *consciousness of effort* which distinguishes the realist's search for truth from the more general and somewhat unconscious search for truth apparent in all good art.

There is another point at which Wordworth resembles the later realists or, more specifically, Zola. He is willing to let science and art join forces for greater effect. He writes:

If the labours of the Men of Science should ever create any material revolution, direct or indirect, in our conditions, and in the impressions which we habitually receive, the Poet will sleep no more then than at present; he will be ready to follow the steps of the Man of Science, not only in those general indirect effects, but he will be at his side, carrying sensation into the midst of the objects of the science itself. The remotest discoveries of the Chemist, the Botanist, or the Mineralogist, will be as proper objects of the Poet's art as any upon which it can be employed, if the time should ever come when these things shall be familiar to us.

Uncertainty as to whether "the time should ever come" did not prevent Wordsworth's sensing the possible benefits from a union of science and art, nor did it inhibit the spontaneous expression of his joy at the thought of such an occurrence. Wordsworth anticipated Zola without knowing the extent to which Zola would force this union. Had he known, he probably would not have approved it, because Zola took the next step, and made, in his own mind at least, *science* synonymous with *art*.

Writing of the poems in *Lyrical Ballads,* Wordsworth states:

The principal object, then, proposed in these Poems was to choose incidents and situations from common life, and to relate or describe them, throughout, as far as possible in a selection of language really used by men, and, at the same time, to throw over them a certain colouring of imagination, whereby ordinary things should be presented to the mind in an unusual aspect; and further, and above all, to make these incidents and situations interesting by tracing in them, truly though not ostentatiously, the primary laws of our nature.

To this statement we can add a comment by Coleridge in which he discusses the philosophical basis for the poems.

For the second class, subjects were to be chosen from ordinary life; the characters and incidents were to be such as will be found in every village and its vicinity, where there is a meditative and feeling mind to seek after them, or to notice them, when they present themselves. . . . Mr. Wordsworth . . . was to propose to himself as his object, to give the charm of novelty to things of everyday.[10]

A more accurate definition of realism could scarcely be found than that suggested by Wordsworth and Coleridge. Let us look at Bliss Perry's definition of realism. Mr. Perry is discussing the novel, but the definition is valid for any type of literature.

Realistic fiction is that which does not shrink from the common-place (although art dreads the commonplace) *or from the unpleasant* (although the aim of art is to give pleasure) *in its effort to depict things as they are, life as it is.*[11]

Mr. Perry repeats this when he says that "there have been developed in the public mind three distinct conceptions of what constitutes realism in fiction." They are the "copying of actual facts," the "deliberate choice of the commonplace," and the "unpleasant." With the exception of the unpleasant, Mr. Perry's description applies to Wordsworth—to his theory as well as his practice. It was for the realists proper, who came after

Wordsworth, to add the unpleasant. Neither Wordsworth nor the world of art was ready for full-blown realism in 1800.

§4

It may be profitable to conclude this discussion of Hugo and Wordsworth as realistic romanticists by looking briefly at the development of the other arts, particularly in nineteenth-century France where romantic art attained its fullest expression. Such a glance will convince us that the appearance of realism in romanticism is neither accidental nor limited to the theory of Wordsworth and Hugo.

The French romantic painters were seriously concerned with truth to nature. We see, even in the work of a dreamy romanticist such as Corot, a tendency towards realism. John La Farge says of Corot:

The wet morning and the dewy eve, thus, were what he painted most—and on that side of representing moments in Nature, he was closely affiliated to those of his day who were moving more and more towards realism. . . . In such landscapes he placed figures . . . as if they had been really seen; they have the look of realism very often, and they are so seen in that they are intimately associated with the space that holds them, with an accuracy far beyond that of the majority of the most accurate representations.[12]

That the Barbizon painters were more than casually interested in nature is seen not only in their opposition to the preceding neo-classicists, who were involved in scholarly research and concerned with academic form, but also in their direct observation and close study of nature and natural phenomena. The light, airy quality of many of Corot's canvases appears to be his attempt to portray the effects of light on natural objects. It was the impressionists, more than half a century later, who advanced this idea and developed a successful technique. Impressionism, indeed, may with justice be considered the ultimate in realistic painting. But Corot was no less a realist at heart because he failed to carry the thing to its logical conclusion.

Eugène Delacroix, one of the least realistic among French romantic painters, was vitally interested in the faithful repre-

sentation of nature. In his *Journal* we find frequent references
to this. On October 5, 1822, he reminds himself: "Go see the
stage off, to make some studies of horses." Later he writes: "I
see some progress in my study of horses." On April 15, 1823, he
adds: "I must absolutely begin to draw horses. I must go to the
stables every morning." Though not a realist, Delacroix was
even less a classicist: he wrote on January 26, 1824, ". . . in
music, form predominates over substance, in painting, quite the
contrary is the case."[13]

Delacroix, like Corot, was moving in the direction of realism.
It was he who worked out and practiced the law of complemen-
tary color[14] which enabled the later realists to paint nature in
terms of the light rays reflected from objects in nature. Seldom
as realistic as Géricault, Delacroix was nevertheless a painter-
journalist. His trip to Algeria resulted in well painted repor-
torial studies such as the famous "Algerian Woman." "The
Massacre at Scio," likewise journalistic, is realistic in its technique and, what is more important to the present consideration,
this picture is contemporary in its subject matter. It is as modern (1824) as Hugo's dialogue and setting. Delacroix's *Journal*
is packed with detailed word-pictures of native life and background. Among his French subjects, "Liberty on the Barricade,"
though semi-classic in style, is as accurate in detail and local
color as it is up-to-date in its subject.

When we look at the work of Géricault, who has been called
by Réau a "scrupulous realist,"[15] we turn naturally to the well-
known picture, "The Raft of the Medusa." On July 2, 1816,
the frigate *Medusa*, with four hundred French soldiers and
sailors en route to Senegal, was wrecked on reefs near the Arguin
Islands. One hundred and fifty-two persons were put on a raft
where, for several days, they suffered from heat and rough water.
When the survivors were picked up by the *Argus*, only twelve
were alive. This incident was naturally one of the big news-
stories of the early nineteenth century. Géricault reported it
accurately. He was an ardent student of anatomy and natural
forms, and the human figures on the raft are distinguished for
their anatomical accuracy. The raft itself was carefully painted

from a miniature model which had been built at the painter's request by the carpenter who built the original raft for the *Medusa*. The painter spared no pains to make his picture as close to life as possible within the limits set by art—and even here he took some liberties. Like much romantic painting in France and elsewhere, "The Raft of the Medusa" is, as Mather describes it, "a bit of inspired journalism."[16] To quote Réau again: "Géricault, frank realist that he is, can only paint what he has seen or what he is able to reconstruct from visual memory."[17] There can be little doubt that Géricault, a thorough romanticist, indulged in considerable realism.

It was he who freed the painting of horses from the bonds of the earlier equestrian-sculpture techniques and from formal rigidity. When he went to England and attended the races at Epsom, he painted a series of pictures which are astonishingly realistic. Louis Horticq writes:

Until then horses ran in pictures by prancing like stone figures on a pedestal. Since then painters have caught from instantaneous photography more than one aspect among the innumerable positions of a horse who gathers and flings himself in galloping, which the eye has not been able to catch, and they have given up the flying gallop of Géricault. Still, that is the real position of horses who gallop *ventre-à-terre* over the turf of a race-course.[18]

(It is interesting to note that realistic painting is indebted to the observations of Géricault just as the moving pictures, the ultimate in realistic art, are indebted to the photographic experiments relative to running horses which Edward Muybridge made for Leland Stanford.)

One could go on at some length to list paintings by Géricault and Delacroix, Meissonier, Courbet, and Theodore Rousseau, and to cite comments by notable critics who point out and commend the realism in the works of these romanticists. Goya, with his interest in the affairs of his suffering and underprivileged contemporaries, could be mentioned. Innes and Leutze, the Corot and Géricault of America, could be offered as evidence, as could the sentimental Landseer and the nature-loving Constable in England. Among the actors, Frederick Lemaitre, for all his exaggeration, apparently carried on Talma's reforms in the direction of realism and made possible the more realistic acting of Got. Among the writers, Schiller and the Schlegels, Scott, Hawthorne, and even Poe could be listed. It seems clear, however, with no need for further examples, that Hugo and Wordsworth were not the only romanticists who sought verisimilitude, a reasonable fidelity to nature.

It seems equally clear that the realistic tendency is a part of what we generally call romanticism. We can account for this realistic strain in the romantic artists by admitting that they were seeking to represent nature as accurately as they knew how. They found the subjects and forms of their predecessors unfaithful to nature and inadequate for the representation of life as it appeared to be. If romantic art seems to be formless, it is because the romanticists found life relatively formless. If the subject matter of romanticism sometimes appears to be crude, it is because they found life relatively crude. They, like artists from the archaic Greeks to the Graeco-Romans, from early Christians to late medieval artists, sought to *represent* life by means of lifelike symbols. It is possible that all representative artists are realists: it is *our* fault, not theirs, that we label them classicists, romanticists, impressionists, or realists. Criticism sets up definitions and pigeonholes both artists and works of art. But, for the most part, art itself flows along in its own course and follows its own tendency—toward realism. From classicism to romanticism to realism, one impulse obtains: the artist's desire to represent life as he sees it.

NOTES

1. Mario Praz, *The Romantic Agony*, trans. Angus Davidson (London, 1933), p. 18.

2. L. A. Reid, *A Study in Aesthetics* (London, 1931), p. 371.

3. John Mason Brown, *The Modern Theatre in Revolt* (New York, 1929), p. 5.

4. Lascelles Abercrombie, *Romanticism* (New York, 1927), p. 16.

5. This and following translations from Hugo were made by the present author from *Oeuvres Complètes de Victor Hugo* (Paris, 1880).

6. Émile Zola, *The Experimental Novel*, trans. Belle M. Sherman, New York, 1895), p. 114.

7. Leon Deffoux, *La naturalisme* (Paris, 1929), p. 69.

8. This and other references to the Preface are from the 1800 edition of

Lyrical Ballads, printed in *Complete Poetical Works of William Wordsworth* (Boston 1911).

9. Arthur Symons, *The Romantic Movement in English Poetry* (London, 1909), p. 78.

10. Samuel Taylor Coleridge, *Biographia Literaria* (London, 1906), pp. 160-161.

11. Bliss Perry, *A Study of Prose Fiction* (Boston, 1902), p. 229.

12. John La Farge, *The Higher Life in Art* (New York, 1908), pp. 160-161.

13. *The Journal of Eugène Delacroix,* trans. Walter Pach (New York, 1927).

14. Cf. Louis Réau, in André Michel, *Histoire de l'art, depuis les premiers temps jusqu'à nos jours* (Paris, 1905), VIII, 135.

15. *Ibid.,* p. 120.

16. Frank Jewett Mather, *Modern Painting* (New York, 1927), p. 49.

17. Réau, *op. cit.,* p. 118.

18. Louis Horticq, *Art in France* (New York, 1911), p. 329.

Henry Irving, 1870-1890[1]

Edward J. West

IN THE years between 1870 and 1890, the London stage witnessed
the successful establishment, by T. W. Robertson and the Bancrofts, of a new realistic school of acting and production, in
opposition to the old training school of repertory and tradition.
The player of this school, though he had gained social and
artistic refinement, had lost stature by giving up the training
which should make him a skilled solo performer for that which
made him only an efficient team-worker.

The essential conflict in technique between the methods of
the old school and the new was related closely to the dramatic
conditions of the seventies and eighties. That period witnessed
a gradual change from a theatre in which the actor was dominant, to one in which the playwright was the figure of first importance. In other words, the actors who supported T. W.
Robertson and adopted his methods dwarfed themselves as
actors by so doing. For by developing the new technique based
on the reproduction of contemporary life, they came to believe
that the old careful training in elocution and deportment, in
fencing and the wearing of costumes, in the knowledge and
maintenance of tradition, was unnecessary. They thereby dis-
qualified themselves as interpreters of the traditional repertory
of Elizabethan tragedy and comedy, eighteenth-century comedy,
and nineteenth-century romance and melodrama. What they
could do, they did excellently, but increasingly they showed that
they could do only one thing. And after Robertson's death,
when no native dramatist arose to take his place, the frequent
revival of his few plays revealed their essential weakness. The
Bancrofts' attempt to produce Shakespeare and Sheridan by
Robertsonian methods proved that plays designed for the old
school actor were unsuccessful when acted with the new school
technique. In despair at the continued absence of a native playwright to provide them plays which they could act, the Ban-

crofts and their fellows turned to polite adaptations from the French.

Meanwhile, throughout the seventies, the old actors, aged or wearied survivors of the traditional school, attempted to win back their audiences by concessions to realism in the form of spectacular settings. But with the death of Samuel Phelps, the retirement of Buckstone, and the failure of Charles Dillon at Drury Lane, toward the end of the seventies the greater personalities of the older school disappeared from the London stage. The actor still remained dominant, however, in the persons of the new realists, the Bancrofts, the Kendals, Hare, Clayton and Cecil, Wyndham, who brought to the playing of modern French farce an old school gusto, and Irving and Terry, who effected by sheer genius a compromise between the old repertory and the new histrionic method.

But Irving and Terry were almost alone in the eighties in their attempt to cling to the older methods even in part, and certainly alone in their success in so doing. In the main, the actors whose technique shaped the tailor-made plays written to order by Pinero, Jones, and Grundy, were members of the new school of acting. And their technique was the new realistic method of the drawing-room comedy and the social problem play. The heritage of Garrick, the Kembles, Mrs. Siddons, Edmund Kean, and Macready had been, by 1890, wilfully sold for the Robertsonian roly-poly pudding, and the actor had himself prepared the way for a stage on which the play should supplant him as the center of interest. For the majestic dignity of the old school actor, he had substituted decorum; for the former's voice of thunder, he had substituted the ripple or chatter or mumble of colloquial conversation; for the knowledge of technique and tradition, he had substituted observation and imitation of contemporary manners; for training and experience he had substituted good looks and fine fashions; for the imaginative breadth of the tragedian he had substituted the mimetic detail of the character actor. Not how an actress was to treat the tradition of playing Juliet or Lady Macbeth, but how Paula Tanqueray or Lady Windermere was to solve her problem, not how the actor would handle the "points" in Hamlet or Lear, but how Michael was to react to "his lost angel," now interested audience and critics.

The members of the new school had steadily substituted small things for great things, a petty style for the grand style. In the power of Madge Kendal, the power of the small things, of the petty style, advanced as far as it could go; through the alchemy of Ellen Terry's charm, the smallness and the pettiness acquired a quality which was not their own. Through the sheer pertinacity and doggedness of Henry Irving, the authority of tradition and the power of the classical repertory were blended with the psychological interpretation and the character details of the new school to produce a completely personal and individualized style of acting. Somehow Irving succeeded overwhelmingly in playing the pieces and parts of the old school to an audience normally accustomed to the products of the new school and apparently satisfied with them.

Probably no actor has ever been so discussed and argued over as Irving, no actor so held up as the complete genius and the complete representative of what to avoid, no actor so analytically and so systematically praised and condemned. The trouble is that Irving stood for something more than a stage figure; as practically all critics admitted, he exercised upon all who came into contact with him the spell of a great personality. But the personality was in itself a histrionic creation. His disciple Martin-Harvey, denying Irving's success as due to the exploitation of personality alone, noted that Irving listed in *Who's Who* even his relaxation as acting, and argued that in any case an actor's personality grows in power as its possessor builds up his technical knowledge and equipment.[2] Irving himself frequently insisted: "The success I have made, such as it is, has been made by acting—by acting alone, whether good or bad."[3] And he believed that "the best school is practice, and there is no school so good as a well-conducted playhouse."[4]

This theory was supported by his own experience. In the course of his first two and a half years of provincial work, he played 428 parts, and before he settled in London, he played

160 more, while in London itself he added 83 others.[5] The truth obviously is that Irving, through the assumption of a possibly unparalleled range of characters, and through complete concentration upon his work, made himself, despite many physical handicaps, into an actor first, and then into a personality. To Ellen Terry, who certainly knew him as well as anyone, Irving was a man who substituted for genius a "faculty for taking infinite pains," his only real genius to her being "the genius of will."[6] When she acted with Irving at the Queen's in 1867 in *The Taming of the Shrew,* she found him lacking in technique ("he could express so little"), with "everything against him as an actor. He could not speak, he could not walk, he could not *look.* He wanted to do things in a part, and he could not do them. His amazing power was imprisoned, and only after long and weary years did he succeed in setting it free."[7]

This man who was to become the most prominent Shakespearean and traditional-part actor of his time first registered strongly in London as a modern character actor,[8] in the role of Digby Grant in James Albery's *Two Roses.* And luckily for him, who could never appear really natural on the stage, the character was that of an inveterate poseur. He was praised for the usual points in the new character acting: skillful make-up,[9] an infinitude of natural touches,[10] a capacity to produce on the stage actually observed details of individual human behavior.[11] But not content as practitioner of new school methods in new school plays,[12] Irving audaciously moved from the modern Digby Grant through the melodramatic Mathias to the classic and traditional Hamlet.

Since he intentionally deserted the field of modern comedy, it is worth while pausing to consider his own expressed opinions on the questions of the old and the new techniques. Recalling in the eighties that everybody had felt originally that he should identify himself with character parts, he stated his belief "that every part should be a character."[13] Nevertheless, his most successful parts in the classic repertory were those to which he could most efficiently apply the methods of modern character acting. His sound theatrical understanding made him realize that mod-

ern methods must be applied in a broad way, not in the quiet
and naturalistic fashion of most of the newer school. In a lecture
on acting, he said: "To appear to be natural, you must in reality
be broader than nature. To act on the stage as one really would
in a room, would be ineffective and colourless."[14] He believed
that the elevation of tragedy and the heroic should be merely
this enlargement of nature, not what he called "false inflation"
or "artificial declamation."[15]

Aware of the conflict between the schools, but with a prejudice in favor of the new, he thought "an actor who lapses from
a natural into a false tone is sure to find that his hold upon his
audience is proportionately weakened."[16] He thought that in
traditional parts an actor should make much but unobtrusive
use of the new naturalistic by-play, "the very essence of true
art," and of a capacity for listening, "one of the greatest tests
of an actor."[17] He developed the new principle of ensemble
playing into a fine art of handling huge crowds. Despite his own
practice of stealing the scene, he recommended sharing it: "All
the members of the company should work towards a common
end, with the nicest subordination of their individuality to the
general purpose."[18]

Accepting many principles of the new school, he naturally
had much criticism to make of the old or traditional methods.
Warily he admitted: "There can be no objection to the kind of
training that imparts a knowledge of manners and customs, and
the teaching which pertains to simple deportment on stage is
necessary and most useful, but you cannot possibly be taught
any tradition of character, for that has no permanence. Nothing
is more fleeting than any traditional method of impersonation."
He insisted that the attempt to play traditional parts with traditional interpretations resulted in formal and bodiless imita-
tions.[19] He explained and defended his own practice of seeking
new interpretations by claiming that the "natural dramatic
fertility" of a real actor, "with all the practical and critical skill
of his profession up to the date at which he appears, whether
he adopts or rejects tradition," gave "the personage being played
an individuality partly independent of, and yet consistent with,

and rendering more powerfully visible, the dramatist's conception."[20] In other words, there actually was no tradition "in Shakespearean acting; nor is there anything written down as to the proper way of acting Shakespeare."[21] Therefore the real actor is necessarily highly individual in his method: "The root of the matter is that the actor must before all things form a definite conception of what he wishes to convey. It is better to be wrong and consistent, than to be right, yet hesitating and uncertain."[22]

In his insistence on personal interpretation, Irving magnified the value of personality. Temperamental by birth, even a many-sided actor, he declared, would be impelled by "his natural idiosyncrasy . . . more strongly in one direction than in another."[23] Again he said: "There are only two ways of portraying a character on the stage. Either you can try to turn yourself into that person—which is impossible—or, and this is the way to act, you can take that person and turn him into yourself. That is how I do it."[24] This glorification of individual interpretation and natural idiosyncrasy could, of course, be extended to a defense of his mannerisms: "Have we not all mannerisms? I never yet saw a human being worth considering without them."[25] It could even be made to cover his much-debated peculiar pronunciations: "If a feeling is more accurately expressed, as in nature, by a variation of sound not provided for by the laws of pronunciation, then such imperfect laws must be disregarded and nature vindicated. The word should be the echo to the sense."[26]

But although he defied and denied tradition, and defended the new school methods of personal interpretation, he never made the new school mistake of confusing acting with representationalism. In his latter days, he objected to certain young players imported to support him from those strongholds of the new school, the Haymarket and the St. James's: "A lot of damned impostors. Get some *actors*."[27]

Having summarized his views on acting, let us see what his contemporaries felt about his allegiances in acting. Clement Scott, Bernard Shaw, and Irving's business manager, Bram

Stoker, all claimed to have recognized in him, in his earlier London parts, an outstanding representative of the new methods. In the seventies Hall Caine and Henry Barton Baker were notable as among the first to salute Irving as a new *mental* type of actor, as opposed to the older and more physical traditional type. This attitude was summed up by L. J. Claris when he referred to Irving in 1882 as "the Balzac of the stage."[28] His American tour in the early eighties brought much fresh, keen, and intelligent criticism. Ranken Towse immediately perceived Irving's work to be a strange confusion of the old and the new styles, in "conjunction with innumerable mannerisms of his own."[29] Another discerning critic, Henry Austin Clapp, maintained that Irving was lacking in the finest virtues of the old school: elocutionary variety, real power, the ability to sustain. Moreover, he noted the presence of a typical new school characteristic: "a series of light, disconnected touches or dabs," and labelled even the actor's Shylock and Hamlet as character parts.[30]

Two great acting contemporaries, Coquelin and Salvini, denied that Irving was a traditional actor at all,[31] and numerous critics agreed with them, linking Irving with the new school in such vague terms as "originality of conception" or "impersonation" or "psychological interpretation." On the other hand, Gordon Craig found him essentially a traditionalist, claiming: "He gathered to him all the old English traditions, he cut away from these traditions all that was useless to him, and then proceeded to display what was left, to exploit it further than it had ever gone before."[32] Certainly the accounts of eye-witnesses inform us that Irving retained carefully some of the older traditions: point-making,[33] "the traditional strut and stride of the Kemble and Siddons school,"[34] "an odd habit of stamping at times and walking towards the corner of the stage whenever he made some big point in a scene."[35] Frequently it was claimed that he was definitely indebted, even to the point of imitation, to former players. H. J. Byron, in 1880, traced much of Irving's success to his derivation from, and imitation of, Macready and Charles Kean.[36] Squire Bancroft and Gordon Craig also noted the influence of Charles Kean.[37] Irving admitted modelling himself originally, not only on Samuel Phelps, but on Charles Mathews as well.[38] Craig and others thought him indebted to Charles Fechter.[39]

We may conclude that he was a product of the older training who cannily made use of the methods of the newer, but his very successful blending of the two styles was the mark of an *actor*. Even when he played such an alleged new comedy role as Digby Grant, keen critics recognized that what aroused the audience was not the appeal simply of novelty in acting, but rather that of acting itself, of a bracing as opposed to "a weak and flabby performance."[40] This is the important point: despite the theorists who tried so desperately to align Irving accurately with the forces of one or other of the conflicting schools, the burden of the best criticism is that he had primarily to be considered as a man who understood that he was practicing an art deliberately, a man whose acting could be *analyzed* by critics and appreciated as to accepted technical details by his fellow-craftsmen. Such acting can only be accomplished by sure technique and calculated art. Bernard Shaw pointed out correctly that Irving "was stagestruck, and cared for nothing but acting."[41] This of course explains his lack of interest in the modern drama of his period, which called for mere representationalism, and his preference for what Ellen Terry called "fustian," the melodramas which formed so large a part of his repertory.

In relying for his strongest effects upon melodrama and melodramatic technique, Irving was again but following in the footsteps of Charles Kean and Samuel Phelps. Intelligent audiences, as well as professional critics, recognized that his greatest moments and his most successful parts were essentially melodramatic.[42] Melodramas gave him adequate opportunity, lacking in the modern realistic plays, for the display of his pantomimic power of pure acting, that is, of doing as opposed to mere looking and talking. They enabled Irving to *present theatre* to his audiences at a time when more and more actors were becoming content to serve merely as mouthpieces for playwrights, as puppets and pawns to theses.

Irving's first and greatest melodramatic success was with *The Bells* of Erckmann-Chatrian, in the Leopold Lewis version, first produced in 1871. The critics almost unanimously noted, in contrast to the Meissonier-like meticulousness in detail of the current realists, Irving's vigor, boldness, and power of playing, largely achieved through his skilled and trained "facial and hand play."[43] All audiences responded immediately to Irving's powerful interpretation, beginning with the finely pantomimic first entrance, many detailed records of which exist.[44] The role of Mathias brought Irving's strictly theatrical interpretation into comparison with the realistic one of his great French rival, Coquelin. Henry Arthur Jones, acknowledging Irving's melo-dramatic greatness as Mathias, contrasted the perfect training and technique of Coquelin with the imperfect vocal and physical control of Irving, but emphasized equally the imaginative and suggestive powers of the Englishman which the Frenchman lacked, and which enabled Irving to move his audiences emotionally as Coquelin could not.[45]

After *The Bells*, Irving's next strictly melodramatic venture was in Wills's version of *Eugene Aram*, a tailor-made vehicle designed simply to cast the limelight on the star, and adding nothing to his stature as an actor. But as Richelieu in 1873 he challenged comparison deliberately with Macready, and attempted a part which called for declamatory powers of the old school elocutionary sort. If critical reactions varied, audience reception was wildly enthusiastic. John Oxenford of the *Times* declared of the climactic fourth act curtain scene: "Here is tragic acting in the grandest style," and recorded with full approval the old-fashioned rising of the house, scarcely known in England since the electric days of Edmund Kean.[46] In contrast, the *Temple Bar* critic found Irving's playing not up to the Richelieu of tradition, but definitely better than could be offered by any contemporary actor.[47] Here certainly is the explanation of the rising of the pit at Irving: if he was not quite up to the vocal demands of Lytton's Cardinal, at least he was offering an audience, already unconsciously surfeited with the tea-and-cakes of Robertsonianism, the strong meat of melodrama and the wine of theatre; and the change of diet exhilarated them to a point where they did not question overmuch the quality of the meat or the vintage of the wine. These were good in *kind*, and the kind was of theatre, not of commonplace reproduction of the surface of life. If the acting was crude, it *was* acting, and its very vehemence over-excited an audience accustomed to the tameness of the miniaturists of the modern comedy stage.

Having in *Richelieu* challenged comparison with Macready in one of the latter's great roles, Irving proceeded, after an easy victory in Hamilton Aide's *Philip* in 1874, to attempt one of the younger Kean's greatest successes—the dual roles of hero and villain in *The Lyons Mail* of 1877. Most critical as well as audience approval went to the interpretation of the villain Dubosc, especially in the final scene of the play, when Irving put on one of those exhibitions of pure acting, independent of lines, which almost always aroused his audience to enthusiasm.[48] Ellen Terry, preferring the quieter interpretation of Lesurques the hero, may have been right in saying that Dubosc was an easy part for a real actor,[49] but the point seems to have been that Irving was an actor, and that in *The Lyons Mail* he was able to give his audiences the same sort of mysterious, supernatural, or at least completely uncommonplace thrill he gave them in *The Bells*.

The next year he attempted another of Charles Kean's favorite parts, the King in Boucicault's *Louis XI*, and found a third great melodramatic role, universally acclaimed.[50] Actors appreciated the finely detailed execution of the part, but some of the better critics doubted that it called for any true histrionic imagination. The final death-struggle gave Irving another chance for one of those detailed pantomimic solo-pieces with which he delighted more and more to stud his productions. A great American producer complained of "farceur's tricks," and of Irving's growing passion for a central limelight on himself and the rest of the stage in darkness,[51] but in the main his interpretation was compared very favorably with that of Charles Kean, not only in facial and vocal variety, but in power and magnetism,[52] and was even admitted to be superior to that of Ligier, the original French exponent.[53]

Still another Charles Kean success, the dual roles of the twins in Boucicault's version of Dumas's *The Corsican Brothers*, in 1880, exhibited Irving rather as manager than as actor, for the parts gave him little more scope for real acting than lately they afforded the younger Fairbanks in the movie version. In Charles Selby's farcical *Robert Macaire*, in 1883, Irving inserted another great melodramatic death-scene, contemporaneously declared "never surpassed in these times as an example of what a great actor can make out of the alliance of pantomime and intonation."[54] *Faust*, produced in 1885, was attacked as no better than a pantomime,[55] but amid all the scenery and music and trick-lighting, and despite the baldness and badness of Wills's lines, or in between them, Irving was actually doing some splendid acting, particularly in facial expression and in use of the eye,[56] in "the terrible eloquence" of his ever-moving fingers,[57] and in real emotional power, projected mainly through pure pantomime.[58] It took discerning critics to find the acting in *Faust* underneath the trappings; already in that play was obvious the danger which beset Irving the actor during the last half of the Lyceum period of glory. He worked for Irving the manager, one of the canniest readers of public taste of the day, and one of the finest stage-managers. Increasingly the taste was for spectacularly realistic melodramatic production, as the audience, surfeited with the tameness of modern comedy, demanded stronger and stronger sensationalism. Toward the close of our period, Irving followed up the financial success of *Faust* by producing *The Dead Heart* of Watts Phillips in 1889, and the *Ravenswood* of Herman Merivale in 1890, these spectacular melodramas anticipating the *Robespierre, Peter the Great, Madame Sans-Gêne,* and *Medicine Man* of the nineties. George Moore proposed a critical ban on such "pantomimic license" as Irving used in *The Dead Heart* in the scene where Landry, released from the Bastille, lay on the stage for several minutes, holding the audience's attention only by moans and facial expression. That Irving the actor was seizing one of the few chances to act offered to him by Irving the manager did not seem defensible to Moore. Moore also attacked the heavy realistic settings, objecting that formerly audiences had not demanded realism, being "gifted with a sense that is wanting in us."[59] He did not strictly identify this sense, but implied it was a taste for literature; I wonder if it may not have been a sense of what constituted legitimate acting, a sense to which Irving could offer satisfaction as actor, but a sense which Irving as manager preferred to ignore in large part.

In almost every one of the melodramatic parts we have briefly considered in Irving's repertory, the actor was praised for his finely picturesque quality, and as the melodramas he produced became more and more spectacular in nature, the actor was forced more and more, in such productions as *Faust* and *The Dead Heart*, to substitute the pictorial and the picturesque for the dramatic and the melodramatic. There is ample critical evidence that in sheer pantomime, in making the body and face of the actor constitute *theatre*, Irving had no equal in his time. Oscar Wilde told William Rothenstein that Irving showed his sense of the true value of the actor by choosing bad plays: "Remember, my dear Will, that good plays can be read; only the actor's genius makes a bad play bearable."[60] And he was right. The Lyceum manager could afford to present pictorial productions of bad scripts because the company was at least headed by two real players in Irving and Terry, or, as Thomas Wood Stevens phrased it:

The Lyceum stage was splendidly pictorial and utterly romantic; the cold light of Ibsen glimmered in the north, but never penetrated the rich chiaroscuro where Irving moved. A new historical poem by Lord Tennyson, or a new echo-play in which some lordly figure—Charles I, or Louis XI, or Dante, or King Arthur—strode and commanded and died, these were all the Lyceum needed, for the Lyceum had, by the grace of God, an actor.[61]

Examples of almost purely picturesque successes achieved by Irving the manager would include the productions of the undramatic scripts of Wills's *Charles I*, Tennyson's *Queen Mary* and *The Cup*, Fitzgerald and Wills's *Vanderdecken, The Lady of Lyons*, and the Lyceum revival of *Olivia*. Irving's interpretation of Dr. Primrose in the latter production invited comparison with Hermann Vezin's performance in the first production. Vezin was one of the finest products of the old school, but Irving was himself a product of that school, and was, "by the grace of God, an actor," and in whatever branch of his acting they considered him, even such captious critics as Shaw eventually admitted the presence of a dominating personality, greater in its total effects than any of its bad parts.

"An intractable face, a voice without charm, movements without grace, a faulty method of elocution," H. D. Traill summarized the bad parts in 1884, but the "mysterious quality" of the total effects, he decided, originated "no doubt in some hidden magnetism operating between the sensibilities of the actor and those of the spectator."[62] This magnetism obviously enough worked fairly surely and consistently, regardless of how bad a play he might choose as manager to exhibit his own melodramatic qualities or the picturesque qualities of himself and his leading lady. But how did this magnetism work for him in the Shakespearean repertory where he met his hardest tests and his strongest criticism, if not always his greatest successes?

Irving consistently attempted to substitute new interpretations of Shakespeare for the traditional ones, from which he was barred by deficiencies of voice and of emotional power. The new school intellectuality appealed to his age, which, in the voice of Edward Dowden, approved: "After all an actor's commentary is his acting!"[63] But the more sensitive critics of the time were dissatisfied with the new interpretations, and of the various reasons brought forward to account for Irving's failure to do justice to Shakespeare, all came to the same final point, that in his traditional parts Irving remained rigidly personal, and highly manneristic, whether the personal quality was condemned or admired. From the very beginning of his London career, there was awareness of the mannerisms. With pardonable irony, Irving remarked at the height of his career to Ellen Terry: "I was thinking how strange it is that I should have made the reputation I have as an actor, with nothing to help me— with no equipment. My legs, my voice—everything has been against me. For an actor who can't walk, can't talk, and has no face to speak of, I've done pretty well."[64]

In 1877 appeared the most famous attack on the mannerisms, *The Fashionable Tragedian,* in which William Archer and Robert W. Lowe asserted that, a good and potentially fine actor in his Digby Grant and Mathias days, Irving had been spoiled by success, and had come to concentrate on the less essential histrionic qualities, such as intellect and picturesqueness,[65] being content to walk "like an automaton whose wheels need oiling," and to speak "alternately from the pit of his stomach and the top of his head."[66] In colorful phrase they analyzed the limping, dragging walk, the spasmodic shoulder-movements, the head-noddings, the alternations in voice from *basso profundo* to *falsetto,* and the actual physical defects: "a weak, loosely-built figure," and a face limited to the expression of "abject terror, sarcasm, and frenzy."[67] The famous legs came in for special criticism, being accused of "stealing away from him," especially in *Macbeth* and *Richard III.*[68] Irving's famed originality was declared merely the result of "eccentric members,"[69] and for the authors the equally famed psychological subtlety made "of Hamlet a weak-minded puppy, of Macbeth a Uriah Heep in chain armour, of Othello an 'infuriated Sepoy,' and of Richard III, a cheap Mephistopheles."[70] In concluding, they admitted that Irving still possessed "the makings of an excellent actor," admirable in melodrama and comedy, but incapable of the highest tragedy, a man whose lack of really sound training in stage deportment and elocution and restraint had made him easy prey to the two dangers of a long-run system, "unexampled pecuniary success and indiscriminate adulation."[71]

Many explanations of the physical and vocal eccentricities of Irving were offered: deliberate development to meet the peculiar tastes of the age,[72] lack of control in moments of strong emotion,[73] "unconscious habit,"[74] a hangover from his provincial days in sensational melodrama and exaggerated comedy and farce,[75] an inability to portray real passion,[76] and a desire to become "an allegorical embodiment" of the intensity beloved of his aesthetic contemporaries.[77] A clear analysis of the actual defects was made by Clapp: "an alternate swallowing and double-edging of consonants, a frequent lapse into an impure

nasal quality, an exclusion of nearly all chest tones, the mis-
delivery of the vowels by improper prolongation or equally
improper abbreviation, an astonishing habit of confounding and
confusing vowel sounds," "very little resonance, and almost no
richness of tone," a high pitch and a narrow range, no sustained
power or variety in speech.[78] Clapp roundly declared that he
spoke "an Irving *patois*."[79] Shaw felt that the ridiculous "hys-
terical whinnying," resulting from his nasality in "rapid, violent,
energetic passages," forced him to abandon robust acting and
adopt the much-criticized slowness of playing, which made his
own acting more effective, but ruined that of the company,
particularly of Ellen Terry.[80] Gordon Craig alone has completely
defended the mannerisms: "He danced, he did not merely walk
—he sang, he by no means merely spoke."[81]

What was the effect of all these vocal defects and peculiarities
upon Irving's impersonations of traditional Shakespearean personages? Leaving aside for the moment the significance of a
great personality which may have been able to ride roughshod
even over Shakespeare and to assert triumphantly the power of
the actor, we must accept the almost unanimous verdict that
Irving never read Shakespearean verse to the satisfaction or
pleasure of good critics. Yet for all his inability to read verse as
verse, to make a real reading of a purple passage, Irving was
sensationally successful in certain Shakespearean parts, and
the reason certainly must be found in his meeting the tastes of
the age by giving his strong personality the real meat of great
parts to work upon, by applying the new intellectualized character methods to traditional roles, and by filling in, between the
lines he could not read properly, with naturalistic by-play. At
least, by re-establishing Shakespeare upon an English stage
dominated by Sardou and Sims, Irving, in the opinion of many
contemporaries, restored dignity and greatness to that stage.

Irving's Hamlet, in 1874, was epoch-making; it moved and
thrilled all London, but we of today have difficulty in deciding
exactly what made it so remarkable. Most critics emphasized
the intellectual or "thinking aloud" conception; many the absence of the "old extravagance," and of traditional point-

making;[82] and Edward R. Russell definitely noted the introduction into traditional tragedy of modern character acting.[83] This, surely, is the point. If Irving became the "only tragedian" of the seventies, it was because he alone had the cleverness—and the power—to play traditional roles by the new character methods. Joseph Knight was seriously worried at the revolutionary conception of Irving, at "the final abandonment of old traditions of acting and of conventions of declamation!"[84] but another veteran, Dutton Cook, found Irving's very much the accepted Hamlet, changed only necessarily by the Irving mannerisms, and to him the vocal deficiencies explained the much noted new method of reading the soliloquies.[85] It may be somewhat disconcerting to find it suggested that the revolutionary Hamlet of Irving was the necessary result of physical peculiarities and mannerisms, but it seems to me there is definitely something to the argument. Even the ecstatic Russell was struck by "a walk somewhat resembling that of a fretful man trying to get very quickly over a ploughed field," and by "a querulous piping impatience" of voice.[86] I am inclined to think that the audience which had already idolized Irving as Mathias, Charles I, Eugene Aram, and Richelieu, was predisposed in his favor, and inclined to argue that if the traditional Hamlet had not been like Henry Irving, then so much the worse for the tradition.

Certainly there does not seem to have been anything very wildly revolutionary in the business, and the main novelty in the reading seems to have been Irving's elocutionary weakness. A carefully built-up processional entrance for Irving's first appearance,[87] some new by-play and facial expression in the scene wherein Hamlet receives the news of his father's ghostly visitations,[88] a rather exaggerated bit of business in which, after dismissing the players, he put his tablets against a pillar and was seen writing "The Mousetrap" busily as the curtain fell,[89] the management of the play-scene, with the sinuous crawling toward the throne as the play proceeded, the wildness of the departure of the King, and the collapse into the throne-chair at the end,[90] the "daring and originality" in dispensing with the miniatures in the closet-scene,[91] a really interesting and well-executed duel in the concluding scene[92]—these were the most discussed of the first production's novelties, and they hardly seem, with the exception of the treatment of the closet and the play scenes, to be very startling. The main novelty of the 1879 revival was the emphasis of the scene with Ophelia,[93] a necessary compliment to the presence of Ellen Terry. In general, Irving's conception of Hamlet was almost universally praised, the execution almost universally condemned, so far as elocution was concerned. One surmises that it was the inexplicable spell of Irving's personality, the spell that apparently allowed him to break all the rules and come out successfully, that moved those of the audience who were moved.

At least, there was definitely something in Irving's Hamlet that evaded critical analysis; the critics might praise and the critics might damn, the cockney comedian might deride him: "Look at 'Enery Hirving! Look at 'is 'Amlet! Asthmatic, I grant you, but werry wulgar. Give 'im a song and dance and where is 'e?"[94] The point is that he gave himself the handicap of the song which Gordon Craig declared his vocal mannerisms to be, and of the dance—may we say the *danse macabre?*—of his physical mannerisms, and he seems to be among the immortals of the stage. It may not be a thought which will appeal to all critics, but an Irving seems to be greater than any of his parts or than the sum of his parts, even when these include Hamlet.

Irving imperilled his position as *the* Shakespearean interpreter of his day by following up the Hamlet with a production of *Macbeth* in the latter part of 1875. Odell has recorded the critical summary, that it is "easier to find excuses for Irving's Macbeth than to like it."[95] John Coleman's explanation of the failure was that Irving simply lacked "the requisite *guts*" to play the character.[96] At any rate, his Macbeth distressed all critics, who found only "the waspish petulance of an angry sick woman,"[97] or "spasmodic hysteria."[98] The spell may have held for a histrionically imperfect Hamlet, but for a completely misconceived and unpardonably badly executed Macbeth, no.

Irving's Othello of 1876 was not so successful as his Hamlet

nor so much a failure as his Macbeth. Dutton Cook wrote probably the most understanding review, based on his belief that the
actor should now be studied as an actor, not as a player of individual roles. That is, he emphasized that the physical mannerisms and limitations of Irving were directly opposed to the
traditional presentation of Othello, and therefore, he tried to
consider the performance on its merits as one *by* Irving, not as
one *of* Othello.[99] But Irving *was* temperamentally and physically
unsuited to play the Moor, and he removed, when he donned
the Oriental costume, all trace of Oriental calm—that calm
which is so necessary as contrast for the passion at the close—and
substituted feverishness, melodramatic starts, vehemence, and
extravagance.[100] Distress at the actor's lack of control and the
absence of a firm grasp of conventions and assured technique
was the common criticism.

In the 1881 revival, with Edwin Booth as co-star, the critics
almost to a man were forced to admit that Booth's sound and
conscientious old school and traditional performance was vastly
preferable to the attempted but not fully executed novelties of
Irving.[101] On the whole, I think we may count the revival of
Othello, so far as Irving in the title role was concerned, as a
success for Irving the manager, but a stalemate for Irving the
actor. But the revival as a whole gave him the chance to attempt
a new role. If Othello showed Irving's weakness, Iago gave him
an opportunity to display his dramatic strength, for Iago he
could conceive and execute by his already perfected means of a
combination of melodramatic and character acting, with its
proven strong appeal to contemporary tastes. Irving's main
points were his underlining of the humor of Iago, his handling
of the soliloquies in the untraditional, "thinking aloud" manner of his Hamlet; and his introduction of the famous business
of eating grapes and casting away the pits during the Cyprus
scene, a bit of business which might seem to the reader of today
a particularly obnoxious bit of "stealing." Many good critics
objected to the feverish and extravagant amount of business
and by-play; Cook made his objection specific:

Mr. Irving sat or lolled upon a variety of chairs and tables, toyed with a pen, with his swordbelt and trappings, used a poniard as a toothpick, rumpled his hair incessantly, waved a red cloak about him bull-fighter fashion, and otherwise occupied himself, naturally enough, no doubt, yet often superfluously, the necessary questions of the play being duly regarded.[102]

Of the reality of Irving's success in Iago there can be no doubt; of the histrionic impropriety of the means he adopted to win that success there can be no question. Too many of them were cheap, easy, obvious. A possible natural exuberance at finding a part so congenial, a very understandable desire to steal the stage from the American co-star, made him forget the important artistic necessity of order and proportion. To ride roughshod over the flimsy carcasses of his beloved melodramas was to prove the dominance of the actor upon the stage; but to distort Shakespearean tragedy for an actor's holiday was to suggest to many that there was a flaw in his artistic integrity. I fear I agree with them.

In *Richard III*, Irving probably scored his most universally conceded Shakespearean success. The performance did not create the sensation of his Hamlet, nor the amount of debate and dispute of his Macbeth or his Othello, but it satisfied everyone more completely. In *Richard III* he found the most thoroughly melodramatic of the Shakespeare plays which he played in London; in the leading character he found the most thoroughgoing character part in the Shakespeare plays he attempted, the one which most permitted of "the minute and special rendering of personal and physical traits and peculiarities."[103]

So far Irving had succeeded most surely in those Shakespearean parts which enabled him to use his melodramatic character acting methods; he had managed by intellect and personality to achieve a sensational Hamlet; he had failed conspicuously in the heroic parts of Macbeth and Othello. In Shylock he found another part to which he could with fair success adapt his character acting methods.

The break with tradition in the playing of the Jew was probably due as much to physical limitations as to real novelty of interpretation. Irving naturally always insisted that his acting of Shylock was the result of his deliberate conception,[104] but J. H. Barnes thought the real reason was Irving's discovery during rehearsals that he could not manage the traditional violent and vehement Shylock, and the resultant development of a Shylock whom he could portray.[105] Whatever the reason, and I am inclined to think that frequently his greatest successes were obtained rather by a compromise with his limitations than by deliberate choice, the Shylock he could portray was widely applauded. His attempt at passionate outburst in the Tubal scene was generally voted a failure, but the trial scene was almost universally praised as a masterpiece of the new naturalistic character acting, sacrificing all the traditional points of the great Shylocks of the past for a quiet dignity and a restrained intensity, and aiming at an effect of pathos and near-tragedy instead of the traditional melodramatic effect.[106] W. Graham Robertson objected, however, that, while "magnificent and unforgettable," this conception still "upset the balance of the play" and "ruined Portia's Trial Scene."[107]

Much as Irving's general triumph over Shakespeare's lines and his constant by-play were applauded, the greatest acclaim was given to his Shylock for two bits of pure pantomime. The first was the exit from the trial scene, described by George Pierce Baker thus: "Slowly, wearily, as if crushed, only rousing himself to look scornfully at Gratiano in answer to his taunts, he passed out and as he reached the door stumbled, with a sigh that expressed his hopelessness better than words."[108] The second was even more daring. If Irving stole the trial scene from Ellen Terry, at least he performed the untraditional and gracious act of allowing her the Belmont scene at the end, but he made up for it by resetting the scene of Shylock's house for a curtain call, and when the curtain rose to the always certain ovation at the end of the play, the audience saw Shylock enter the empty stage before his empty house, knock twice at the door, and look up patiently toward Jessica's window. Then the curtain fell. The effect was tremendous in its simple suggestiveness, and Irving had triumphantly taken back the play after generously giving it to Miss Terry in the last act.

The *Romeo and Juliet* of 1882 Irving succeeded in making splendidly pictorial, and in it he showed much of the mastery of crowds he had learned from the visit of the Saxe-Meiningers,[109] but unfortunately, as he himself later put it: "The most elaborate scenery I ever had was for *Romeo and Juliet,* but as I was not the man to play *Romeo* the scenery could not make it a success. It never does—it only helps the actor."[110] And before production, after reading the play to a group of friends, the actor remarked: "There, that is what I *want* to make of Romeo. Unluckily I know that on the stage I cannot come anywhere near it."[111] It would almost seem that Irving's Romeo was an unqualified failure. Yet Henry Arthur Jones, admitting that Irving's interpretation was "not the best all-around Romeo of his generation," declared it "the most impressive, the most imaginative, the most finely touched in its highest notes."[112]

Most critics colored Irving's Benedick in 1882 with the pleasure afforded them by Terry's Beatrice, and failed to see with her "Henry's rather finicking, deliberate method," and his complete failure to understand comic pace.[113] As Malvolio, his last Shakespearean role before 1890, Irving pleased few critics, and almost no audiences. The trouble, never diagnosed so far as I have found, was that Irving's pride would not allow him to play Malvolio as truly ridiculous, that his inadequate acting equipment prevented him from perceiving that it was not necessary always to "impersonate," that comic roles like the steward are best done when the actor remains outside the part, and offers a comment upon it, and that he could not bring himself to share honors with the players of Sir Toby, Sir Andrew, and Feste, while, without really good comedians in these roles, Malvolio himself can scarcely score.[114] At any rate, Irving conceived Malvolio as a pathetic, near-tragic figure, building up to a final exit much like that of his Shylock, designed to draw the sympathy of the audience. Possibly there were near-Irvingesque moments in the Malvolio, but on the contemporary evidence, I think we may safely judge the interpretation in Ellen Terry's words, "fine and dignified, but not good for the play."[115]

Irving's later Shakespearean roles, assumed for the first time after 1890, added nothing to change our judgment of him as a Shakespearean actor. He succeeded in those parts to which he could apply most surely and safely his well-founded melodramatic and character acting technique: Richard, Iago, Shylock; he failed most conspicuously in those where sound elocution and an heroic bearing were indispensable: Macbeth, Othello, Romeo; he wrested a success out of Hamlet by forcing his technique upon the character; he scored an easy victory with Benedick where his technique fitted well enough; he failed when he misapplied the technique to Malvolio. In other words, his Shakespearean successes were not accomplished by what one might justifiably regard as essential Shakespearean qualities: a fine voice, a trained delivery, a noble presence, a fine physique. Moments he could achieve in almost every part, by means of that gift for acting which was his as Brodribb and which he refused to develop fully by training and technique as Irving. He had the acumen to perceive that playing in Shakespeare would ensure and solidify his claim to greatness in acting, but I think he honestly preferred the fustian which distressed Ellen Terry so much, where his technique could perform more absolutely and more inevitably as purely histrionic power, unimpeded and unembarrassed by the presence upon the stage with him of great drama and a great dramatist. In other words, I question whether his playing in Shakespeare proved his versatility; rather do I think that he simply performed Shakespeare with his established technique.

Was Irving truly versatile? One difficulty in answering this question is the confusion which arises when it is assumed that different kinds of technique, of power, of means, are required necessarily to play in different kinds of drama. The critics who pointed out that he played in farce and high comedy, in sensational and romantic melodrama, in Shakespeare and contemporary poetic drama, merely achieved a Polonius-like cataloguing of types of drama. Those who picked out in different plays quietly intense and picturesque moments such as Irving could achieve by mere facial expression, commented rather upon his personality than his versatility. But by contrasting defi-

nite scenes in his varied repertoire with each other, certain
critics did suggest within Irving some real power of producing
effects different in kind by means different in kind, or effects
very like in kind by means subtly differentiated to give the
effect of individuality to each part. His versatility was not complete, as J. H. Barnes, who acted with all the great actors of his
time, pointed out; Irving lacked the comic vigor of Phelps and
the heroic and tragic power even of Charles Dillon, but "in all
his original creations, in all his character parts, in picturesque
melodrama and most of his comedy, he was preeminent."[116]

It is not fair to deny him versatility, as some have done, on
the ground that his characters were always recognizably Irving,
that he possessed mannerisms; every great actor has been,
after all, recognizably himself in each of his roles, being necessarily limited to acting in his own body and with his own voice.
But surely no actor of the late nineteenth century, after the
death of Samuel Phelps, at least none who possessed enough
power to reach the first rank, attempted so many and such
varied roles, and by some means or other, managed to bring so
many off with a measure of success. Irving's personality was
so strong that it impressed many observers to the point where
they denied the versatility, but I believe that his personality was
in itself a histrionic creation. There is abundant evidence that
Irving remade himself, or, as Gordon Craig would put it simply, that Brodribb made Irving.[117] In so doing, Bernard Shaw
might say, Irving proved himself again the age's "ablest exponent of acting as a fine art and serious profession."[118] Henry
Labouchere never tired of trying to explain to the age the spell
of its greatest actor, "a strange weird charm about his acting,"
"a peculiar individuality," which, although in many parts he
might be surpassed by several living actors, would make an
audience always vote for Irving's performance, right or wrong.[119]
Sixty years later, James Agate echoed: "He had that something
about him which made you rather watch Irving wrong than any
other actor right."[120] It matters relatively little what we call this
"something about him"—genius, magnetism, personality; the
essential point is that by virtue of his development of the qual-

ity within himself Irving grew from an undistinguished provincial player to become the leader of the stage in his time; regardless of his faults, as a critic in *The Edinburgh* noted in 1909, "an atmosphere emanated from him that conquered his audience, heart and head; and they worshipped him for it."[121]

He "conquered his audience," that is indeed the point; he won their interest and their plaudits not by obvious technique, as did Madge Kendal, cheap as some of his tricks may have been; not by instant charm, as did Marie Bancroft or Ellen Terry, or by warmly human qualities, as did his own leading man, William Terriss, or by mere and sheer eccentricity, as did Beerbohm Tree; he compelled them and forced them, wrestled with them and wrested them, first into accepting him and then into idolizing him as a creature aloof and remote, a truly unique and individual phenomenon. "It was natural to most people to dislike his acting," Ellen Terry finally decided, "they found it queer, as some find the painting of Whistler—but he forced them, almost against their will and nature, out of dislike into admiration. They had to come up to him, for never would he go down to them."[122]

Of course, Irving, as the dominant actor-personality of a period which saw the end of the actor's and the beginning of the playwright's theatre, was violently attacked for his devotion to Shakespeare and fustian and his neglect of Pinero and Jones. But critical sanity and good temper have come to recognize that his very insistence upon being greater than any part he played or any play he produced helped to create his eminence in an age which was deserting acting as *the* art of the theatre. Combining the traditional repertory and the old school flamboyancy with the new school psychology and realism, and projecting the blended techniques through the medium of his created personality, he held back for a short time the inevitable surrender of the stage to the dramatist. But unhappily, the strength of his personal quality made imitation of him, except for that of superficial eccentricities, impossible. He demonstrated the sovereignty of the actor over the playwright, but he showed no method that others could adopt or adapt. So the new school realists went on concealing acting as acting, went on substituting the representation of the surfaces of real life for the presentation of the depths of dramatic character. They covered their histrionic nakedness with the borrowed raiment of novelty of plot, power of thesis, or brilliance of dialogue. And when Irving died, histrionic greatness and robust glamor deserted the theatre. The last of the giants of tradition was gone; only pygmies, puppets in the hands of playwrights, remained.

NOTES

1. The material of this paper, in a much expanded form, originally formed a chapter in the author's Yale dissertation, Histrionic Methods and Acting Traditions on the London Stage from 1870 to 1890: Studies in the Conflict of the Old and the New Schools of Acting. Hence the dates. As it happens, Irving's London career began around 1870 and was firmly established by 1890, so that the period between these two dates includes all his important work.

2. Sir John Martin-Harvey, *Autobiography* (London, n.d.), pp. 330-331.

3. Joseph Hatton, *Henry Irving's Impressions of America* (Boston, 1884), p. 69.

4. Henry Irving, *The Drama: Addresses,* 2d ed. (London, 1893), p. 13.

5. Austin Brereton, *Henry Irving* (London, 1905), p. 68.

6. Ellen Terry, *The Story of My Life* (London, 1908), p. 97.

7. Ellen Terry, *Memoirs* (New York, 1932), p. 61.

8. The phrase is indefinite at best, although the thing was clear enough. William Archer ("The Drama," in T. H. Ward, *Reign of Queen Victoria,* 2 vols. [London, 1887], II, 590) defined character acting as "mimetic realism, the minute and unconventional reproduction of observed idiosyncrasies." It was designed to express the efforts of men like Tree, of no specific ability in any one special field of histrionic endeavor, no specific ability to create memorable interpretations of single parts, but rather an ability, especially through the use of make-up and external details, and through a multiplicity of bits of business and by-play, to give the impression externally of some credible human being, usually, as Tree himself once wrote, one "afflicted with either mental or physical eccentricity." See his "Some Aspects of the Drama of To-day," *North American Review* CLXIV (January, 1897), 71.

9. Shaw (*Bernard Shaw and Ellen Terry. A Correspondence* [New York, 1931], p. xx) noted the disguise as perfect.

10. See "The Theatres," *Saturday Review* LIII (January 7, 1882), 19; Clement Scott, "Our Play-Box," *Theatre* (March 1882), p. 166.

11. Bram Stoker, *Personal Reminiscences of Henry Irving,* 2 vols. (London, 1906), I, 9-10.

12. He told Squire Bancroft: "No actor can be remembered long who does not appear in the classical drama." Marie and Squire Bancroft, *The Bancrofts: Recollections of Sixty Years* (London, 1909), pp. 333-334.

13. Hatton, *op. cit.,* p. 72.

14. Irving, *op. cit.,* p. 57.

15. *Ibid.,* p. 51.

16. *Ibid.,* p. 52.

17. *Ibid.,* pp. 61-62.

18. *Ibid.,* pp. 63-64.

19. *Ibid.*, pp. 49-51.

20. *Ibid.*, pp. 3-4.

21. Hatton, *op. cit.*, p. 74; and cf. p. 113: "My principle has been to go straight to the author. I have not taken up the methods of other actors, nor modelled my work on this or that tradition."

22. Irving, *op. cit.*, p. 64; cf. Austin Brereton, *The Life of Henry Irving*, 2 vols. (London, 1908), I, 342, from a speech made in 1881: "About tradition I venture to say this—that it was all very well for those who invented it, but is simply injurious to those who merely imitate it."

23. Henry Irving, preface to *Diderot's Paradox of Acting*, trans. W. H. Pollock (London, 1883), p. xiii; cf. Irving, *Drama*, pp. 45-46, 56, 152-153, 160.

24. James Agate, *Ego 2* (London, 1936), p. 143.

25. Hatton, *op. cit.*, p. 75.

26. Irving, *Drama*, pp. 59-60.

27. Vincent Sternroyd, "Irving as Benedick," in H. A. Saintsbury and Cecil Palmer, *We Saw Him Act. A Symposium on the Art of Sir Henry Irving* (London, 1939), p. 233.

28. L. J. Claris, "Henry Irving, Actor and Artist," *Theatre* (March, 1882), pp. 157-158.

29. J. Ranken Towse, "Henry Irving," *Century* XXVII (March, 1884), 660-661.

30. H. A. Clapp, *Reminiscences of a Dramatic Critic with an essay on the art of Henry Irving* (Boston, 1902), pp. 220-227.

31. See Constant Coquelin, *The Art of Acting* (New York, 1936), pp. 68, 73; Salvini's remarks at Irving's death, *Athenaeum* (November 11, 1905), p. 656.

32. Gordon Craig, *Henry Irving* (New York, 1930), p. 17; and cf. p. 69.

33. H. M. Walbrook, "Henry Irving," *Fortnightly* CXLIX (February, 1938), 208.

34. "Henry Irving in 'The Bells,'" *Nation* XXXVII (November 1, 1883), 370.

35. Seymour Hicks, *Between Ourselves* (London, 1930), p. 122.

36. Quoted in Clement Scott, *The Drama of Yesterday and To-day*, 2 vols. (London, 1899), II, 85.

37. See Bancroft, *op. cit.*, pp. 327-328; Craig, *op. cit.*, p. 121.

38. H. Chance Newton, *Cues and Curtain Calls* (London, 1927), p. 25; Seymour Hicks, *Me and My Missus* (London, 1939), pp. 90-91.

39. Craig, *op. cit.*, p. 121; Newton, *op. cit.*, p. 25; E. B. Watson, *Sheridan to Robertson. A Study of the Nineteenth Century London Stage* (Cambridge, Mass., 1926), pp. 377-378.

40. Clement Scott, "Our Play-Box," *Theatre* (January, 1880), p. 36.

41. Shaw, preface to *Correspondence*, p. xxv.

42. See, e.g., Maud Howe Elliott, *Three Generations* (Boston, 1923), p. 151; James Agate, *Playgoing* (New York, 1927), p. 7; Maurice Baring, *The Puppet Show of Memory* (Boston, 1922), p. 52; B. Brooksbank, "Mr. Irving as a Tragedian," *National Review* I (July, 1883), 680; Dion Boucicault, *The Art of Acting* (New York, 1926), pp. 54-55; Lewis C. Strang, *Plays and Players of the Last Quarter Century*, 2 vols. (Boston, 1903), II, 272; A. B. Walkley, *Playhouse Impressions* (London, n. d.), pp. 257, 261; Frank Rahill, "Melodrama," *Theatre Arts Monthly* VIII (April, 1932), 291; Mortimer Menpes, *Henry Irving* (London, 1906), pp. 32-33.

43. See Newton, *op. cit.*, pp. 13-14; J. Ranken Towse, *op. cit.*, pp. 661-662, and *Sixty Years of the Theatre* (New York, 1916), p. 241; William Winter, *Henry Irving* (New York, 1886), pp. 10-11, and *Shadows of the Stage, 3rd Series* (New York, 1895), pp. 58-60; Frank Archer, *An Actor's Notebooks* (London, n. d.), p. 291; Clapp, *op. cit.*, pp. 210-211; Scott, *op. cit.*, II, 51-53. On Irving's face, see Percy Fitzgerald, "Actor's Faces," *Theatre* (December, 1878), p. 355; Clapp, *op.*

cit., pp. 205-207; Hicks, *Between Ourselves,* pp. 119-120; Mrs. Alec-Tweedie, *Behind the Footlights* (New York, 1916), p. 231; Stoker, *op. cit.,* I, 139-140; Menpes, *op. cit.,* pp. 7-9; Terry, *Memoirs,* p. 269; Martin-Harvey, *op. cit.,* pp. 74, 146-147; G. P. Bancroft, *Stage and Bar* (London, 1939), pp. 54-55; James Agate, *Ego 3* (London, 1938), pp. 121, 278. On his hands, see Stoker, *op. cit.,* II, 63-64; Christopher St. John, *Henry Irving* (London, 1905), p. 6; Hicks, *Me and My Missus,* p. 85; Daniel Frohman, *Daniel Frohman Presents: An Autobiography* (New York, 1935), p. 185.

44. See Clara Morris, "Looking Backward," *McClure's* XXVI (March, 1906), 498-499; Joseph Harker, *Studio and Stage* (London, 1924), pp. 130-131; Craig, *op. cit.,* pp. 52-58.

45. Henry Arthur Jones, *The Shadow of Henry Irving* (London, 1931), pp. 28-35. Irving (Hatton, *op. cit.,* p. 190) called his own Mathias "Dramatically poetic, if you like, but not realistic." On this point, see Georges Bourdon, "Staging in the French and English Theatre," *Fortnightly Review* LXXVII (January, 1902), 165-166.

46. Quoted in Brereton, *Life,* I, 151-152.

47. "The Theatres," *Temple Bar* XXXIX (November, 1873), 548-549.

48. See H. M. Walbrook, *A Playgoer's Wanderings* (London, 1926), pp. 52, 123; Moy Thomas, *Academy* XI (May 26, 1877), 471; Clapp, *op. cit.,* pp. 214-215; Mary Anderson, *A Few Memories* (New York, 1895), p. 133; William Archer, *Henry Irving, Actor and Manager, A Critical Study* (London, 1883), pp. 85-86; Jones, *op. cit.,* pp. 44-46; Walbrook, *Nights at the Play* (London, 1911), pp. 155-157; Agate, *Ego 3,* p. 325.

49. Terry, *Life,* p. 173.

50. See Frederick Wedmore, "Restoration Comedy and Mr. Irving's Last Parts," *Gentleman's* CCXLIV (May, 1878), 594-596; Joseph Knight, *Theatrical Notes* (London, 1893), pp. 211-212; Percy Fitzgerald, *Henry Irving: A Record of Twenty Years at the Lyceum* (London, 1893), pp. 91-94; Dutton Cook, *Nights at the Play,* 2 vols. (London, 1883), II, 177-178; Clapp, *op. cit.,* pp. 212-214; Winter, *Irving,* pp. 27-29; Clement Scott, *Theatre* (August, 1883), pp. 109-110.

51. Joseph Francis Daly, *The Life of Augustin Daly* (New York, 1917), p. 265; cf. Fitzgerald, *Irving: A Record,* p. 316. On Irving and the limelight, see Bram Stoker, "Irving and Stage Lighting," *Nineteenth Century* LXIX (May, 1911), 903-912.

52. Winter, *Irving,* p. 37; Moy Thomas, "Recent Plays," *Academy* XIII (March 30, 1878), 289.

53. Jules Claretie, "A French View of Mr. Irving," *Theatre* (August, 1879), pp. 16-18.

54. *Saturday Review* LV (June 16, 1883), 766; cf. Terry, *Life,* p. 249; Weedon Grossmith, *From Studio to Stage* (London, 1913), pp. 176-179; Justin McCarthy, *Our Book of Memories. Letters of Justin McCarthy to Mrs. Campbell Praed* (Boston, n. d.), p. 152; Henry du Pré Labouchere, "'Amber Heart' and Red Breeches," *Truth* XXIII (May 31, 1882), 942.

55. See Hesketh Pearson, *Gilbert and Sullivan* (New York, 1935), pp. 274-275, for Gilbert's reference to it as a pantomime, and cf. George Francis Savage-Armstrong, *Mephistopheles in Broadcloth. A Satire (a. d. 1888)* (London, 1892), p. 72:

> "travesties of Goethe's lordly rime
> Mixed with tomfooleries of the Pantomime."

See Joseph and Elizabeth R. Pennell, "The Acting in Mr. Irving's 'Faust,'" *Century* XIII (December, 1887), 312-313, for more criticism of the acting, and for a glorification of the spectacle, Joseph Hatton, *The Lyceum "Faust"* (London, 1886).

56. See Clement Scott, *From "The Bells" to "King Arthur"* (London, 1896), p. 294; W. H. Pollock, "Mephistopheles at the Lyceum," *Longman's* X (July, 1887), 294.

57. Towse, *Sixty Years*, pp. 289-291, gave good examples. Coquelin, *op. cit.*, p. 12, attacked Irving for ludicrously excessive manual extravagance.

58. See Charles Frederic Nirdlinger, *Masques and Mummers* (New York, 1899), pp. 268-269; W. L. Courtney, "Mr. Irving's *Faust*," *Fortnightly Review* XLV (January, 1886), 103, 105; William Winter, *Vagrant Memories* (New York, 1915), p. 291.

59. George Moore, "Our Dramatists and their Literature," *Fortnightly Review* LII (November, 1889), 629-630. For a contrary view, see Scott, *From "The Bells,"* p. 312.

60. Sir William Rothenstein, *Men and Memories*, 2 vols. (New York, 1931), I, 184.

61. Thomas Wood Stevens, *The Theatre from Athens to Broadway* (New York, 1932), pp. 167-168.

62. H. D. Traill, *The New Lucian: being a series of dialogues of the dead* (London, 1884), pp. 276-277.

63. Quoted in Stoker, *Reminiscences*, I, 27-28.

64. Terry, *Life*, p. 98.

65. (Archer and Lowe), *The Fashionable Tragedian* (Edinburgh, 1877), p. 5.

66. *Ibid.*, p. 7.

67. *Ibid.*, p. 9.

68. *Ibid.*, pp. 11, 15.

69. *Ibid.*, p. 12; cf. Wilde's comment (Frances Winwar, *Oscar Wilde and the Yellow 'Nineties* [New York, 1940], p. 47): "Irving's legs are limpid and utter. Both are delicately intellectual, but his left leg is a poem."

70. Archer and Lowe, *op. cit.*, pp. 19-20.

71. *Ibid.*, p. 23.

72. Labouchere, "Much Ado about Nothing," *Truth* XII (October 19, 1882), 549-550.

73. Martin-Harvey, *op. cit.*, pp. 332-333; cf. Winter, *Irving*, pp. 8-9.

74. J. Ranken Towse, "Mr. Henry Irving," in Brander Matthews and Laurence Hutton, ed., *Actors and Actresses of Great Britain and the United States. V. The Present Time* (New York, 1886), p. 147.

75. Towse, *Century* XXVII, p. 667.

76. Percy Fitzgerald, *Sir Henry Irving: A Biography* (London, 1906), pp. 302-304.

77. William Archer, *Irving*, pp. 39-54.

78. Clapp, *op. cit.*, pp. 201-204.

79. *Ibid.*, p. 201.

80. Bernard Shaw, *Pen Portraits and Reviews* (London, 1931), pp. 172-173.

81. Craig, *op. cit.*, p. 71; and see pp. 60-63, for a good record of Irvingesque pronunciations, also his "Henry Irving: His Voice," *Mask* XV (October-December, 1929), 134-136.

82. Frederick Wedmore, "Irving in 'Hamlet,'" *Academy* VI (November 7, 1874), 519; cf. Scott, *From "The Bells,"* pp. 62-64.

83. Edward R. Russell, *Irving as Hamlet*, 2d ed. (London, 1875), *passim*.

84. Knight, *op. cit.*, p. 6.

85. Cook, *op. cit.*, II, 45.

86. Russell, *op. cit.*, p. 4.

87. Scott, *From "The Bells,"* p. 61; Terry, *Life*, pp. 126-127.

88. Wedmore, *Academy* VI, p. 519; Terry, *Life*, pp. 130-131.

89. Wedmore, *ibid.*, p. 520.

90. *Ibid.*, p. 519.

91. Frederic Daly (pseudonym of L. F. Austin), *Henry Irving in England and America, 1838-1884* (London, 1884), p. 4; cf. Irving, "An Actor's Notes on Shakespeare. 3. 'Look here, upon this picture, and on this,'" *Nineteenth Century* V (February, 1879), 260-263.

92. Knight, *op. cit.*, p. 5; Scott, *From "The Bells,"* p. 66.

93. See Irving, "An Actor's Notes on Shakespeare. 2. Hamlet and Ophelia," *Nineteenth Century* I (May, 1877), 524-530.

94. Elliott, *op. cit.*, p. 237.

95. George C. D. Odell, *Shakespeare from Betterton to Irving*, 2 vols. (New York, 1920), II, 584.

96. Newton, *op. cit.*, p. 37.

97. "Macbeth at the Lyceum," *Punch* LXIX (October 9, 1875), 138-139.

98. *Figaro*, quoted in Brereton, *Life*, I, 190.

99. Cook, *op. cit.*, II, 105-106.

100. *Ibid.*, II, 106-108.

101. *Ibid.*, II, 319-326; "Othello at the Lyceum," *Saturday Review* LI (May 7, 1881), 593, and (May 14, 1881), 626-627; Labouchere, "Othello," *Truth* IX (May 12, 1881), 639; Scott, *Theatre* (June, 1881), pp. 355-362; Fitzgerald, *Irving: A Record*, pp. 167-170; Mowbray Morris, *Essays in Theatrical Criticism* (London, 1882), pp. 106-112; Theodore Martin, *Essays on the Drama. Second series* (London, 1889), p. 312; Terry, *Life*, pp. 205-206.

102. Cook, "'Othello' at the Lyceum," *Academy* XIX (May 7, 1881), 345; cf. M. Morris, *Essays*, pp. 98-103; Martin, *op. cit.*, 211-212. On Irving's passion for the red cloak, see his "My Four Favorite Parts," *Forum* XIV (September, 1893), 36.

103. Cook, *Nights*, II, 133-136.

104. See the long analysis of his conception, Hatton, *Impressions*, pp. 225-236.

105. J. H. Barnes, *Forty Years on the Stage* (London, 1914), p. 106.

106. See William Winter, *Shakespeare on the Stage. I.* (London, 1912), pp. 179-196, for a most accurate detailed analysis of the Irving method in Shylock.

107. W. Graham Robertson, *Life Was Worth Living* (New York, 1931), pp. 55-56.

108. G. P. Baker, "From a Harvard Diary. Notes Made in the Eighties," *Theatre Arts* XI (July, 1933), 516.

109. See Austin Brereton. *Dramatic Notes 1882-1883* (London, 1883), pp. 12-14; George R. Foss, *What the Author Meant* (London, 1932), pp. 100-101; Odell, *op. cit.*, pp. 378-379. Brander Matthews ("The Art of the Stage Manager," *North American Review* CLXXVIII [February, 1904], 264) complained of ultra-realism.

110. Alec-Tweedie, *op. cit.*, p. 224; cf. Terry, *Life*, p. 298.

111. Walter Herries Pollock, *Impressions of Henry Irving* (London, 1908), p. 34. Cf. Stoker, Reminiscences, I, 96-97, for comments on Irving's ideas and preparations.

112. Jones, *op. cit.*, pp. 49-50.

113. Terry, *Life*, pp. 162-163.

114. Note, *ibid.*, p. 232, Irving's remark when considering *The Tempest:* "I can't do it without three great comedians. I ought not to have attempted 'Twelfth Night' without them." But note also that he made no effort to find them.

115. *Ibid.*, p. 233.

116. J. H. Barnes, "'Irving Days' at the Lyceum," *Nineteenth Century* XCIII (January, 1923), 106; cf. his *Forty Years*, pp. 102-103.

117. See, e.g., Fitzgerald, *Irving: A Biography*, pp. 290-291; Alice M. Diehl, *The True Story of My Life* (London, 1908), pp. 290-291; T. H. Hall Caine, *My Story* (New York, 1909), pp. 241-242.

118. Bernard Shaw, *Dramatic Opinions and Essays*, 2 vols. (New York, 1928), II, 83.

119. Labouchere, "Mr. Henry Irving," *Truth* XI (November 22, 1877), 610.

120. Agate, *Ego 3*, p. 282.

121. "Henry Irving," *Edinburgh Review* CCIX (January, 1909), 39.

122. Terry, *Life*, p. 226; cf. Charles Morgan, "Irving and the Theatre," *New York Times* (February 20, 1938), section 11, p. 3.

The Meininger: An Evaluation

Joel Trapido

MANY students of the theatre have long felt that a certain nineteenth century German theatrical troupe exerted important influences on the development of the theatre from its own time
until today. Indeed, some writers have been so impressed with
the accomplishments of this company that they have asserted
that no important director since its time has worked outside its
influence, that the Western theatre of the twentieth century
has grown out of its accomplishments, that, indeed, the last half
century has produced no theatrical innovation not marked out
by its work.

The company in question is, of course, that of the Duchy of
Saxe-Meiningen. One of the chief reasons for all the enthusiasm
is that André Antoine of the Théâtre Libre and Constantin
Stanislavsky of the Moscow Art Theatre recorded, to the extent
of a few hundred words each, their reactions to the Meininger.
Probably another important reason is that the most extended
and most widely circulated English treatment of the work of
the company, Lee Simonson's chapter in *The Stage Is Set,* is so
enthusiastic and so dogmatic that it leaves the impression that
only a few corroborative details remain to be determined. The
final circumstance is that there is not, even today, any extended,
responsible, well circulated analysis of this unquestionably significant organization.

Let it be understood at the outset that the present paper will
not attempt to offer this final analysis. No analysis will be final
until the German sources, many of which are now unavailable,
are carefully examined and collated. It is, however, possible to
clear the air, even now, by a three-fold attack on the material.

I shall, therefore, report everything said by Antoine and
Stanislavsky on the subject of the Meininger; where I take serious issue with previous reports of their remarks, or with conclusions drawn from those remarks, I shall quote directly. In

addition, I shall make some attempt to deal with errors or mis-conceptions in all important English sources, even where they are secondary. And finally, I shall note pertinent remarks from the most readily available of the important German works on the subject, Max Grube's *Geschichte der Meininger*. Thus, even at the risk of repetition, I hope to define an area of general agreement on the work of the Meininger, and to dispose of some popular exaggerations of their significance in theatrical history.

§1

The history of the Meiningen Company goes back to about the time of the American Revolution. The history which con-cerns us, however, began nearly a century later, in 1866. In that year George II, a talented designer and draughtsman, succeeded to his family's title and became Duke of Saxe-Meiningen. In that year, too, he began to reform his court theatre by making Friedrich von Bodenstedt its director. Bodenstedt, a Bavarian, was professionally a teacher and writer. His qualifications for his new position consisted of a thorough but largely literary knowledge of Shakespeare, very little theatre experience, and two years in Russia. In 1870 his probably unsuccessful tenure of office was terminated by the appointment of Ludwig Kronek as director. Four years later, the Duke sent Kronek and the company on the road.

During the ensuing seventeen seasons, the Meininger gave almost 2600 performances in three dozen European cities. Half these cities were in Germany itself, but the other half were in Russia, Austria, Belgium, Holland, Switzerland, England, Den-mark, and Sweden. Most frequently performed of some forty Meininger plays was *Julius Caesar*, a drama characteristic of a repertory which consisted almost entirely of the romantic drama of Germany and England. In 1890, upon the serious illness of Kronek, the Duke disbanded his company.

Present evidence indicates that the predominant characteristic of the Meininger, and possibly the one which has most influ-enced the theatre of our time, is a characteristic of no profound aesthetic significance, a characteristic of broad and mixed origin, a characteristic, indeed, which was almost a necessary outgrowth of the period and the place in which the Meininger flourished. This characteristic can be perceived in every department of Meininger production. No other quality is so broadly descriptive of the company's work.

Suppose we proceed inductively, examining in the order of their importance the five departments in which the chief Meininger contributions seem to lie—ensemble acting, costuming, method of organization, lighting, and staging. This method of procedure will permit us to clear away some of the debris and to cut through some of the mythology; and perhaps, in the end, it will leave us with a few plain facts.

There can be little doubt that the Meininger achieved greater success in their ensemble play than in any other single aspect of their work. In 1888, a year after the founding of the Théâtre Libre, the company visited Brussels. As is well known, André Antoine, moving spirit of the French organization, did not lose the opportunity to visit Brussels and to see a dozen of the Meininger performances. As is almost equally well known, he wrote, as a result of his Brussels theatre-going, a 2000-word letter to the critic Sarcey detailing his only recorded reactions to the Meininger.[1] With the exception of a sentence here and there, this letter is devoted entirely to Meininger acting, direction, costuming, staging, and lighting. That fully half the letter—more than a thousand words—is spent on all but rhapsodic descriptions of Meininger ensemble play is in itself notable. That Antoine wrote of all other aspects of the Germans' work in highly critical terms—as we shall see later—makes this relatively favorable reaction to ensemble play even more notable. Though the Frenchman does not omit explaining how he would improve upon the Meininger crowds by adding realistic detail to the realistic detail already present, his words stand in marked contrast to the critical terms in which he discusses other aspects of the company's work.

Stanislavsky, whose opinions of the Meininger are somewhat more benign than Antoine's, and perhaps more reasoned, comments favorably on the Meininger mob scenes on a number of occasions, remarking his debt and that of his company to this particular department of their productions.

It may be stated that ensemble work did not originate with the Meininger. On the contrary, the company was preceded by earlier workers in both Germany and England. Though secondary sources show no general agreement as to the origin of the Meininger inspiration, such facts as are available point to a number of sources variously in Germany, England, and Russia, rather than to a single source in any one of these countries, or even to any one of the countries. Efforts to thank Slavophilism in Russia, Keanism in England, or any of a number of earlier German workers for the high and relatively early development of Meininger ensemble play have not yet been successful. In the nature of the case, they are not likely to be.[2]

Evolved during a period when science was affecting every aspect of man's endeavor, Meininger costuming, as might be expected, depended upon the results of scientific research. Thus its principal characteristic was historical accuracy. The importance of this contribution to the development of the theatre need not be enlarged upon if we recall that before the latter half of the nineteenth century costuming was probably the most thoroughly convention-ridden and least lifelike department of the theatre.

Unfortunately, no agreement as to the effect created by the Meininger costumes is to be found. Stanislavsky's chief comment is too oblique to indicate what he thought: "Under the influence of the Meiningen Players we put more hope than necessary . . . on the costumes, the historical truthfulness to the epoch of the play."[3] These words do, however, indicate the Russian's obligation to the Duke's principle of accuracy. On another occasion, in discussing his own costume problems at the time of the founding of the Moscow Art Theatre, Stanislavsky indicates that he took Meininger accuracy for granted. His debt is therefore clear, and his favorable opinion of Meininger execution is implied in the manner in which he speaks of that debt.

Antoine felt otherwise. In the Sarcey letter from which we have already quoted he says: "The costumes, splendid when they are purely historical, and otherwise stupidly rich, are almost always in shockingly bad taste when no documents are to be found and imagination must be relied on."[4] He adds later that the actors sometimes wear their costumes badly, and he notes with apparent disapproval ". . . the marvelous materials which the Duke himself bought"[5] and for which he spent immense sums. This comment, as well as other unfavorable reactions to the technical aspects of Meininger production, should perhaps be read in the light of Antoine's own relatively small resources.

It may be taken as clear, however, that both Antoine and Stanislavsky were aware of the historical accuracy of the Duke's costumes and must to this extent be indebted to him for such principles and such facts as they afterward applied. On the more interesting question whether Meininger costuming tended toward the museum or the theatre, they apparently would not agree. Simonson, lauding the real-life dressmaker, tends toward the opinion that a thoroughly accurate costume will turn out to be theatrically practicable, but does not specifically consider the question of whether the "imaginative" Meininger costumes were good theatre costumes or not.

In either case, the Duke's aim and accomplishment were the replacement of conventional theatrical costumes with period costumes reconstructed from the results of historical research. If this process occasionally brought forth archaeological curiosities rather than creations essentially theatrical, we need not be surprised: a series of accurate details juxtaposed to a creative purpose will often result in a monstrosity. The value of George II's work in costuming lay not so much in his results, as in the research that he himself conducted and in the investigation that his results encouraged.[6]

Since the Duke left many detailed sketches of costumes (and settings, too), it is not difficult to conclude that much of the impetus to research in setting and costume came from him. It is not quite so easy to determine the sources of the tight-knit organization which operated under his name. For, though the Duke was theoretically autocrat-director of his organization, the autocrat-director was actually a triumvirate consisting of the Duke, his wife, and Kronek. The directorial methods, however, did not depend upon which of the three was in charge of a given rehearsal. On the contrary, rehearsals were invariably characterized by three processes: tireless experimentation, direction of every detail of the production, and discipline so rigid that it was often harsh.

If the duties and responsibilities of each member of the directorate were to be classified, the classification might run something like this:

George II—Director and designer.

Kronek—Stage-manager and assistant director; in charge of rehearsals, particularly on tours; the Duke's plenipotentiary on tours.

Ellen Franz (Helene, Freifrau von Heldburg; brought to the company in 1867 by Bodenstedt, the actress-commoner became the Duke's wife in 1873)—In charge of line-reading; perhaps general adviser in matters of acting.

Antoine, strangely, nowhere mentions any of this; his organizational and directorial methods appear to have developed independently of the Meininger. Stanislavsky, on the other hand, lays much of his early autocracy to the profound impression made upon him by the Meininger directorial methods. Though he continued to believe such methods necessary in directing actors of limited talent, he ultimately discarded despotism in handling the more capable members of his company.[7]

There is no important disagreement among secondary sources as to what might be called the tyrannical characteristics of the Meininger directorate. Komisarjevsky notes that the liberalism and socialism of the latter nineteenth century contributed to the critical disfavor with which the directors' dictatorial methods were met. Simonson remarks that the spirit of experiment which pervaded rehearsals prevented any effect of routine. Only Antoine's silence varies the unanimity with which this aspect of the work of the company has been recognized.[8]

In proportion to its importance, stage lighting is ordinarily the subject of relatively less discussion and critical comment than any other department of the theatre. Comment on the

Meininger lighting is not exceptional in this regard—there simply is very little that anyone has taken the trouble to say about it. Stanislavsky is completely silent on the subject. Antoine was not much better pleased by Meininger lighting than he was by Meininger staging:

Their successful lighting effects are most often handled with the greatest naïveté. Thus a beautiful ray from the setting sun comes to illuminate the beautiful white head of an old man dying in an armchair, and suddenly disappears out the window without gradation at the precise moment the old man dies,—simply to create an effect.[9]

Antoine does, thus, admit that the lighting he saw was "successful," which, as we shall see, is rather more than he admits for staging. His only other remark on lighting, quoted below (the use of a projection to create the illusion of rain), indicates a conclusion not unlike that to be derived from the present quotation: Though technically and imaginatively rather advanced, the Meininger lighting left the realistic observer dissatisfied with some detail. A safer conclusion would be that it left Antoine dissatisfied. There is no doubt that in lighting as elsewhere the Frenchman would have been prepared to level the charge of effect without reality, technique without taste. Certain facts are evident, however, through his own testimony: The principles of spotlighting were used by the Meininger and the principles of projection were employed for effects, if not actually for scenery. In view of this it will not be surprising that the delicacy of the Duke's lighting lay in variation in intensity rather than variation in color. Color was not ignored, of course, but it lay in costume and setting rather than in light.

The various second-hand commentators do not add greatly to Antoine's remarks. Komisarjevsky is certainly in error in saying that "all the principles of our illusionistic, natural stage lighting were already shown by the Meininger."[10] Antoine names at least one, gradation, which had not been achieved in 1888, barely two years before the company disbanded. It is in any case certain that the instruments available to the Duke would not have permitted him certain "principles" possible today. Mr. Simonson, ever enthusiastic, feels that the lighting principles in use by the Meininger ". . . were almost apocalyptic revelations of the possibilities of stage-craft at a time when every other stage was filled with a bland radiance and actors singed their trousers at the footlights in order to be seen."[11] Simonson probably exaggerates the extent of the revolution (or "revelation," as he puts it) brought about by the Meininger. Certainly Antoine exhibits no *surprise* at the lighting effects he describes. It is rather Simonson who is surprised. Indeed, just as it was in part the absence of a detail—in this case, gradation—which disturbed the critical Frenchman, so it was the presence of certain other details which marked the Meininger contribution. This was not, be it said again, either revolution or revelation.

In staging, too, we shall find that the company's greatest effort lay in the direction of searching out, discovering, and reproducing realistic detail. In 1870, the year of Kronek's appointment as director, the Duke sent his company a long series of production notes. The following are brief but typical excerpts:

> The actor must never lean against painted scenery. . . .
> Pieces of scenery on which an actor leans or supports himself such as doorposts and tree trunks must . . . be made of some solid material, that is to say be made plastic. . . .
> The simultaneous use of painted and plastic objects on stage must be managed so that the difference of material is not disturbingly apparent.
> There is no more inartistic effect than that of plucking a rose which is the only artificial flower among a lot of painted ones or, in the workshop of the *Violin Maker of Cremona,* seeing on the rear flat among half a dozen painted violins with their painted shadows, the actual violin that has to be used, casting an actual shadow.[12]

This criticism, designed to bring about realistic detail, was not the first of its kind. Indeed, Schlegel had written similarly more than half a century earlier (1808). His remarks, however, were not so specific as the Duke's; and he was a critic—he had no power to give his words immediately tangible results. The Duke, as we know, had this power and lost little time in exerting it.[13]

Mr. Simonson feels that, in doing so, George achieved successes far beyond the aims indicated in his notes:

His [George II's] career inaugurated a new epoch in theatrical production and made the subsequent development of modern stagecraft possible because he eventually convinced every important director in Europe, including Antoine and Stanislavsky, that the fundamental problem to be answered by the scene-designer is not, What will my setting look like and how will the actor look in it? but, What will my setting make the actor do?[14]

The effect of the Duke of Saxe-Meiningen's [staging] methods was to achieve an intensified reality and give remote events the quality of actuality, of being lived for the first time, so that a Frenchman, Antoine, was intensely moved by the assassination of a Swiss tyrant, and a Russian, Stanislavsky, reduced to tears by the degradation of an inconsequential French king.[15]

These enthusiastic statements fairly represent Mr. Simonson's admiration for the achievements of Meininger staging, as well as his aesthetic of those achievements. They also indicate that one of the bases for that aesthetic is to be found in the alleged effect of Meininger settings upon Antoine and Stanislavsky.

In the Sarcey letter already quoted, Antoine writes as follows of Meininger staging:

Their settings, very violent, but oddly arranged, are infinitely less well painted than ours. They abuse set pieces, using them everywhere. . . . Thus also after an extraordinary downpour of rain, obtained by a projection lantern, I was pained to see the rain stop sharply without any transition. Their productions are full of things like that. The same floor-cloth serves for all acts; the rocks of Switzerland are placed on the *costières*. . . .[16]

This is all. Nothing about the relation of actor to setting, nothing about the unity of the two, nothing, indeed, which indicates that Antoine was very much taken with the Meininger settings.

And he was not: the remainder of his letter considers other aspects of the productions—acting, direction, lighting, and costumes.

Yet Simonson, as we have seen, also writes of Antoine's having been "intensely moved by the assassination of a Swiss tyrant." Here he is quite right. Antoine was. But suppose we see what Antoine has to say about his emotion:

And I really believe that if you had seen the arrest of William

Tell and the apple-scene you would have been as enthusiastic as I.

There was in this William Tell another superb thing: the murder of Gessler, stopped on a narrow set-piece forming a kind of curved, hollow path at least twenty-five feet upstage of the footlights, by a beggar and his two children; these three played a long scene of supplication with their backs to the audience, barring the way with their bodies until Tell became aware of Gessler. You would have appreciated what can be done with the back.[17]

Yes, Antoine was moved—there is no doubt of that. There is also no doubt that he was moved by what we call stage direction. It is possible, by "interpretation" of his remarks, to arrive at Simonson's aesthetic of a stage design which is completely integrated to the actor and the play. But I find it very difficult so to "interpret" Antoine's remarks when one recalls his earlier quoted comments on the settings themselves.

What of Stanislavsky, constantly linked with Antoine in this aesthetic? The Russian saw the Meininger in Moscow in 1885 and again in 1890. Though he writes enthusiastically of various aspects of their productions, he has nothing to say of their settings beyond a general reference to historical truth. The reference, made in passing, is so slight as not to repay quoting. This fact, coupled with the knowledge that Stanislavsky had definite technical interests, makes possible only one conclusion: Stanislavsky saw nothing worthy of remark in the Meininger settings.

Again: Simonson alleges that the man who was to assist at the birth of the Moscow Art Theatre was "reduced to tears by the degradation of an inconsequential French king." Here is what Stanislavsky says about that:

The Meiningen Players were able, by using *purely stage direction methods*, without the help of extraordinary stage talents, to show much in the creative works of the great poets. I can never forget a scene from "The Maid of Orleans." A skinny, piteous, forlorn king sits on a tremendous throne; his thin legs hang in the air and do not reach the floor. Around the throne is the confused court, which tries with all its strength to uphold the semblance of kingly ritual. But in the moment of the loss of power the deep bows of etiquette seem out of place. Into this picture of the destruction of a king enter the English ambassadors, tall, stately, decisive, courageous and impudent. It is impossible to bear the scorn and

the despising tone of the conquerors cold-bloodedly. When the unhappy king gives his demeaning order, which insults his own dignity, the courtier who receives the order tries to bow before he
leaves the king's presence. But hardly having begun the bow, he
stops in indecision, straightens up, and stands with lowered eyes.
Then the tears burst from them and he runs in order not to lose
control of himself before the entire court.

With him wept the spectators, and I wept also, for the ingenuity of
the *stage director* created a tremendous mood by itself and went
down to the soul of the play.[18]

The full quotation makes clear what Simonson's quotation with
omissions does not: The Russian is talking about stage direction—with emphasis on *direction*. This is something quite different from staging. The pattern of Stanislavsky's words makes
it difficult to justify Simonson's interpretation. This difficulty
is enhanced by the absence of positive comment about Meininger staging and by the plethora of comment upon direction.

In an analysis of some of the Duke's sketches, Simonson attempts to show, largely by citing and arguing from details in
certain sketches, that the Duke must have planned his settings
with an eye bent very largely toward the movements of the actor
within them.[19] Even though the present writer may not consider the proof satisfactory, he does not quarrel with the argument. He wishes, however, to point out that conclusions drawn
from a study of sketches are not necessarily conclusions reached
by an audience seeing a production, and certainly not the conclusions reached by Antoine and Stanislavsky on seeing the
Duke's productions. It is hardly necessary to add that a sketch is
not a realized setting, that plans are not actual productions.

What then? Unless both Antoine and Stanislavsky were grossly
negligent in omitting even to hint at a momentous obligation
to Meininger staging methods, we must find the ebullient Mr.
Simonson guilty of aiding in the propagation of error. It is possible to argue that the failure of the Russian and the Frenchman to comment specifically upon effect as created by setting is
a point in Mr. Simonson's favor. One cannot help feeling, however, that if the Meininger had really developed the ideally unobtrusive setting of which Fuchs speaks ("The best, like hosts,

are those of which least is said"), two men so thoroughly involved in theatre as Antoine and Stanislavsky would at least have remarked the unobtrusiveness.

The general position taken by Simonson with regard to the Meininger contribution to stage setting, or at least his aesthetic of that contribution, remains generally unsupported not merely by Antoine and Stanislavsky, but by other commentators. Typical of these latter, all writing at second hand, is Tresidder, who cites two English critics who had seen the Meininger in London in 1881 as feeling that the "trappings" (among which they included the settings and the excellence of the crowds) overshadowed the plays and the actors.[20] This certainly does not support Simonson's position. Wiener says merely that the settings were "the results of painstaking studies in libraries and museums, with the purpose of preserving historic truth."[21] He renders no judgment as to the effect of these settings. Komisarjevsky indicates that to painted high lights and shadows the Duke added "three-dimensional details, such as trees, pillars, etc."[22]

We may perhaps conclude that the Meininger represented part of an effort to "unconventionalize" stage setting. This effort proceeded largely by two means: The first brought into the theatre the results of historical research; the second replaced part of the painted setting with three-dimensional set-pieces. In the category of the second means might be included the wide use by the company of levels, later to become one of the characteristic devices of the "modern" theatre; though the Duke hardly discovered the vertical dimension, he does appear to have used it far more often than his predecessor.

There must, however, remain the greatest doubt that the Duke's attempt to free stage settings and make them more "realistic" was successful. Certainly it was not at all successful if we may accept the testimony of Antoine and Stanislavsky.

§2

Agreeing that we cannot here attempt any final analysis of the Meininger as a group, and admitting the often fatal dangers of over-simplification, can we nevertheless put a single phrase which might come close to characterizing every aspect of the company's work? Indeed, is there any such phrase? There is.

The phrase is *attention to detail*.

Nor is the emergence of this phrase in any degree surprising. It is not surprising for its time, a time which brought forth Belasco, master of detail, in the American theatre, Zola in literature, and Darwin in science—and these are merely the brighter lights in a period marked by the birth, or rebirth, of absorption in the significance of the minute. Nor is the phrase surprising for its place, a country whose people remain, even today, more simply and more often characterized by the word *thoroughness* than by any other.

The methodical quality of nearly every aspect of the Duke's efforts and accomplishments is nowhere denied; this is true even of ensemble acting, where it seems most likely that time will reveal the existence of other important qualities. It is not yet possible, however, to describe any other quality which may be considered generally characteristic of the Duke's work. Such other qualities as may be found—archaeological exactness in mounting and a tendency toward realism in the whole production—appear rather to be related to the fondness for detail than to be independent of it.

If, as many commentators seem to feel, the predominant characteristic of modern times is the increasing application of science—or the scientific method, or the scientific approach—to the life, habits, and customs of mankind, then the Meininger may legitimately be considered one of the earliest and most important of the groups which brought science inside the theatre.

NOTES

1. The letter is reproduced in full in André Antoine, *Mes "Souvenirs" sur le Théâtre Libre* (Paris, 1921), pp. 108-113, and in Adolphe Thalasso, *Le Théâtre Libre* (Paris, 1909), pp. 164-170; it is reproduced in part in a number of places. So far as I am aware, there is no complete translation. Partial translations may be found in S. M. Waxman's *Antoine and the Théâtre Libre* (Cambridge, 1926), pp. 95-96, and in B. W. Hewitt's Cornell dissertation, The Theatre and the Graphic Arts, pp. 60-61. For the more creditable translations of portions of the letter quoted in this paper Messrs. Hewitt and Waxman are to be thanked; for the remainder I am responsible.

2. The foregoing remarks on the history of the Meininger and on their con-

tributions to ensemble acting have been here given summarily since a previous article by the present writer [*Quarterly Journal of Speech* XXVI (October, 1940), 380-384] records important facts of both these aspects of the company's work.

3. Constantin Stanislavsky, *My Life in Art*, tr. J. J. Robbins (Boston, 1924), p. 229.

4. Hewitt, *op. cit.*, pp. 60-61. Translated from Antoine, *op. cit.*, p. 111.

5. Antoine, *op. cit.*, p. 112. Translation mine.

6. It may be worthy of note that Grube felt that the Duke had no interest in teaching by means of historical truth. On the contrary, he avers that the Duke ". . . sought truth for its own sake; and because variety of form attracted his painter's eye." Max Grube, *Die Geschichte der Meininger* (Berlin, 1926), p. 60.

7. The quotations from Stanislavsky, reprinting of which would serve no purpose here, may be quickly turned up in Stanislavsky, *op. cit.*, pp. 199 ff. Portions are reprinted in Argus John Tresidder's "The Meininger and Their Influence," *The Quarterly Journal of Speech* XXI (November, 1935), 472-473.

8. Partially anecdotal but rather detailed material on rehearsals, directorial functions, etc. may be found in Grube, *op. cit.*, pp. 44-51.

9. Hewitt, *op. cit.*, p. 61; translated from Antoine, *op. cit.*, p. 111.

10. Theodore Komisarjevsky, *The Theatre and a Changing Civilization* (London, 1936), p. 105.

11. Lee Simonson, *The Stage is Set* (New York, 1932), p. 289. Simonson's final words derive from an anecdote which he himself (p. 282) retells from a letter of Antoine (*op. cit.*, p. 200; Waxman, *op. cit.*, p. 139) written in November, 1890. The story is hardly credible, but its use by Simonson illustrates the exaggeration too often characteristic of writing on the theatre.

12. Lee Simonson, *op. cit.*, pp. 270-271; translated from Grube, *op. cit.*, p. 53. The series of notes from which this portion is translated may be found in Grube, pp. 51-58.

13. Mr. Helmuth Hörmann, working on the Meininger as part of a dissertation at Cornell University, recently brought to my attention statements in the Freedley and Reeves *History of the Theatre* (New York, 1941) which ascribe much of the Meininger design to Israel and Lieberman. I have no other evidence that anyone but the Duke himself did his designs; and Mr. Hörmann tells me his German sources contain no reference to the contribution of either of the men mentioned in the *History*.

14. Simonson, *op. cit.*, p. 272.

15. *Ibid.*, pp. 286-287.

16. Hewitt, *op. cit.*, pp. 60-61; translated from Antoine, *op. cit.*, p. 111.

17. Antoine, *op. cit.*, p. 110. Translation mine.

18. Stanislavsky, *op. cit.*, p. 198. Italics mine. Stage director is used by Stanislavsky (or by Robbins?) in various senses. Only the context of a particular use will indicate the shade of meaning intended.

19. See especially Simonson, *op. cit.*, pp. 287 ff.

20. Tresidder, *op. cit.*, pp. 470-471.

21. Leo Wiener, *The Contemporary Drama of Russia* (Boston, 1924), p. 82.

22. Komisarjevsky, *op. cit.*, p. 104.

The Challenge of Ibsen: A Study in Critical Contradictions

ROSS SCANLAN

THE problem of establishing the functions which may be deemed proper to creative literature is one which has long divided modern critical philosophies. The issue between pleasurable and useful functions does not appear greatly to have troubled critical theorists in antiquity. It is true that the existence of such an issue is suggested when we contrast the second book of Plato's *Laws* with the *Poetics* of Aristotle, for Plato seems to have believed that the wise man could applaud only those poems and dramas which were the deliberate expression of approved moral principles, whereas the extant portions of the *Poetics* frequently refer to pleasure as the natural end of poetry and contain no mention of any function other than pleasure. But, for the most part, on this question literary criticism in antiquity took the view of Horace that a poetic work might, with equal propriety, serve either to teach or to delight and that, other things being equal, the best work was that which effectively combined both functions.

Critical thought in the Renaissance also followed Horace on the question of function. Thus, Sir Philip Sidney commended the poet as the "right Popular Philosopher" whose teaching, thanks to the charm of poetry, was "foode for the tenderest stomacks," and Stanyhurst, in the preface to a translation of Virgil, asserted that "thee chiefe prayse of a wryter consisteth in thee enterlacing of pleasure wyth profit." This was the general view until about the beginning of the seventeenth century when we begin to encounter dogmatic restrictions upon the province of the poet. In his preface to Jean de Schelandre's *Tyr et Sidon*, François Ogier wrote: "Poetry, and especially that which is written for the theatre, is composed only for pleasure and amusement."[1] The Earl of Shaftesbury, 1670-1713, believed that "the Theatre was intended merely for recreation, and . . .

if it have any tendency to improve, the improvement extends only to the art of the poet, and the refinement of taste."[2] In *Émile, ou de l'Éducation* Rousseau declared: "I take [Emile] to the theatre to study taste, not morals; . . . Lay aside precepts and morality, I should say; this is not the place to study them. The stage is not made for truth; its object is to flatter and amuse."[3]

Such statements are examples of a critical doctrine which, once established, maintained itself until, in the nineteenth century, it had become the orthodox creed for critics. Wilde did not exceed the temper of the critical philosophy prevailing in his day when he wrote in the preface to *Dorian Gray:* "The moral life of man forms part of the subject matter of the artist, but the morality of art consists in the perfect use of an imperfect medium. No artist desires to prove anything. . . . No artist has ethical sympathies. An ethical sympathy in an artist is an unpardonable mannerism of style. . . . All art is quite useless." This was a doctrine which thoroughly penetrated the more conventional critical scholarship, journalistic reviews, and the published comments of creative writers themselves.

Its hold upon the critical thought of the period is too well known to need documentation. What has not always been so well understood is the reasoning which the doctrine involved. Orthodox critics of the nineteenth and early twentieth centuries often allowed a measure of instructive or persuasive effect to creative literature, but generally with the stipulation that such effects were accidental by-products and formed no part of the writer's conscious design. Thus the substance of a drama might teach or persuade but only as blind circumstances may do so. From the point of view of the critics the essential consideration was to restrict the writer's deliberate purpose. Some words attributed to Baudelaire assert that "poetry has not truth for its object; it has only itself," and again, "no poem will be so great, so noble, so truly worthy of the name of a poem as that which has been written solely for the pleasure of writing a poem."[4]

The keystone of the critical doctrine was the proposition that between socially useful aims and the essential nature of true art there is a deep-rooted, inevitable, automatic antipathy. To quote again from Baudelaire, "If a poet have pursued a moral aim, it is not impudent to wager that his work will be bad."[5] In line with the doctrine he was advocating, Baudelaire did not find it necessary to qualify that statement by any reference to the natural level of craftsmanship or imaginative power possessed by the offending poet. On the contrary, "bad work" in such cases was deemed to be the direct consequence of "moral aim." A moral or social intention could effectively block artistic achievement regardless of the innate artistic abilities or deficiencies of the writer.

It is this rigid assumption of inherent antipathy which gives a special interest and significance to much of the criticism of Henrik Ibsen's social dramas. German *Tendenzdichtung* or the French *drame au thèse* did not seriously challenge the orthodox critical dogma. Indeed, the works of writers like Augier, Dumas *fils,* and Brieux seemed to offer corroboration for the doctrine. The aims of their plays were deliberate, moral, and social; the artistic quality, demonstrably inferior. From this it seemed to follow that inferior art was a direct result of such aims. Therefore the critic could afford to treat the challenge to his doctrine implied in such plays with a comparatively placid and confident scorn.

It is possible [wrote one] that M. Brieux's plays may exercise some ephemeral reforming influence, just as it is possible that a Socialist *Daily Mail* might bring about a temporary revolution and even probable that a pious *Daily Mail* might create a religious revival. But criticism can have no truck with such factitious effects. The critic, like the dramatist, works by artistic instinct. It is not his part to act as town crier for every municipal councillor with advanced opinions, or to peddle cheap reform from door to door.[6]

From the point of view of orthodox critical philosophy a writer like Brieux was comparatively harmless because of his artistic limitations. But Ibsen, from the very beginning of his social series, presented the critics with a different problem. Here was a dramatist whose themes bit deeply enough into the body of conservative and pseudo-liberal social opinion to cause great pain and outcry, yet one whose technical skill and power of imagination might establish him as an artist of the first magnitude, if hostile criticism could not smother such claims in time. The vehemence of the critics was an involuntary and widespread testimony to the force with which Ibsen had challenged the validity of their most cherished critical doctrine. No doubt a great deal of the vigor and even frenzy of criticism which greeted his plays came from a direct hostility to the nature of his message, but, along with that, the critics consciously or unconsciously recognized the threat to their doctrine.

For a number of reasons, then, these commentaries on Ibsen's social dramas offer the student of critical problems a unique opportunity to study the operations of this doctrine under fire and so to appraise its validity. The essential points to keep in mind are: first, that in Ibsen's day the doctrine had acquired its greatest and most extensive prestige; second, that it was advanced as a universal law of the inherent nature of art and so could admit of no exceptions; and third, that it held the direct and inescapable consequences of deliberate social intention to be unmistakable faults in technique or in the processes of imagination. The effect of a deliberate social aim upon dramatic technique was said to be a poor coordination between speeches carrying the dramatist's message and the elements of situation and character. The effect of such aims on the processes of imagination were held to be either anemia or feverishness, in either case something that was not artistically convincing.

The respect accorded to such critical propositions led, in the case of Ibsen's plays, to an amazing and revealing array of contradictions and evasions. So great was the prestige of this philosophy that Ibsen himself seems to have fallen into its contradictions. He has not left any formal or systematic account of his own philosophy,[7] but, as is well known, his published correspondence contains a number of passages which illuminate this question.

The most noticeable feature of these comments is his frequent denial of any deliberate intention to persuade. He was an agitator, but he prized his standing as an artist, and that led him to be highly sensitive to critical reaction. He wanted his plays to succeed in the theatres, and he went so far at one time as to rewrite, in a most unfortunate manner, the conclusion of *A Doll's House* in order to render it more palatable to the delicate German taste of the period. Undoubtedly he had a considerable practical respect for the power and prestige of orthodox critical views.

One of the more sympathetic yet objective studies of his career disposes of his denials in these words:

We know well enough that Ibsen frequently grew indignant over attempts to get at the "tendency" or idea of his works. He went so far as actually to deny the existence of any definite "tendency"; yet we have had ample opportunity to observe how strenuous he was in support of convictions, with what emphasis, nay vehemence, he staked his very existence upon the cause of light and right. Poets so constituted may say what they please about the absence of ethical motives; we trust our common sense in this matter more than their denials.[8]

Ibsen often denied any direct or immediate responsibility for the thoughts expressed by his characters; yet on at least one occasion his letters indicate a very close connection. In the fourth act of *An Enemy of the People,* Doctor Stockmann, addressing a meeting of the townspeople, says:

What sort of truths does the majority rally round? Truths so stricken in years that they are sinking into decrepitude. When a truth is so old as that, gentlemen, it's in a fair way to become a lie. Yes, yes, you may believe me or not, as you please; but truths are by no means the wiry Methuselahs some people think them. A normally constituted truth lives—let us say—seventeen or eighteen years; at the outside twenty; very seldom more. And truths so patriarchal as that are always shockingly emaciated; yet it's not till then that the majority takes them up. . . . The truths acknowledged by the masses, the multitude, were certain truths to the vanguard in our grandfathers' days. We, the vanguard of today, don't acknowledge them any longer.[9]

Ibsen must have liked what the Doctor said, because in a letter to Brandes he wrote:

I maintain that a fighter in the intellectual vanguard can never collect a majority around him. In ten years the majority will, possibly, occupy the standpoint which Doctor Stockmann held at the public meeting. But during these ten years the Doctor will not have been standing still; he will still be at least ten years ahead of the majority. He can never have the majority with him. As regards myself, at least, I am conscious of incessant progression.[10]

The lines which most clearly indicate Ibsen's internal conflict between adherence to critical orthodoxy and his disposition to put his skill to the service of his moral and social convictions, as well as the solution of that conflict which finally was to govern the composition of his social plays, are to be found in a letter which he wrote from Rome to the vowed dramatic polemist, Björnson:

If I were asked to tell at this moment what has been the chief result of my stay abroad, I should say that it consisted in having driven out of myself the aestheticism which had a great power over me— an isolated aestheticism with a claim to independent existence. Aestheticism of this kind seems to me now as great a curse to poetry as theology is to religion. You have never been troubled with it; you have never gone about looking at things through your hollowed hands. Is it not an inexpressibly great gift to be able to write? But it brings with it great responsibility. . . . If I cannot be myself in what I write, then the whole thing is nothing but lies and humbug.[11]

His critics, on the other hand, did not give up their isolated aestheticism, and the result was confusion and contradiction. The later commentaries have frequently explained these manifestations by saying that Ibsen, following a presumed characteristic of the Norwegian national temperament, shrouded his meaning in enigmatic symbols. It cannot be denied that, whatever the reason, he was fond of an often highly ambiguous symbolism, but this disposition did not prevent the Liberals of Norway or the Conservatives of Norway and the rest of the world from fully appreciating the attack on them and their works which his plays contained. Nor did it effectively conceal the merit of the plays as works of art. It was not symbolism which plunged the critics into contradiction, but the desire to maintain the critical dogma of artistic detachment.

One way to defend the dogma was to admit the polemical

element and deny the art. To Karl Frenzel, writing in the *Deutsche Rundschau*, Ibsen's plays "are essentially editorials and public addresses on Norwegian social questions, cast in dramatic form," and "the dramatic form is chosen, not for the sake of art, but on account of its powerful effect upon the masses."[12] In terms of art the attempt is judged a failure. A play like *A Doll's House* gives Frenzel the impression that he has "wandered by mistake into a court of law"; he is "doubly suspicious of the dramatist who, like Ibsen, steadily seeks to instruct, to compel reflection."[13] He regrets that "in Denmark and Norway the theatre has become a lecture-platform,"[14] and he sadly observes that "when the epic writer leaves the theatre, the rhetorician comes into his own."[15] Because of Ibsen's polemical intention his plays compare very unfavorably with those of such writers as Paul Lindau, Ernst Wichert, and Adolph L'Arronge; their "content is harmless, their fables simple; the impression is pleasing."[16] The critic condemns the polemical playwright because "I cannot surrender myself to him completely and without hesitation," and he concludes, "we would permit his accusations in political debate, but they sound sufficiently strange coming from a work of art."[17]

To another critic of the same period "Ibsen . . . is no personality; he is simply a brain. He never, in a single work, has the physical warmth and pulse-beat of a full and entire being. . . . He is a brain composing literature [*dichtende Gehirnmensch*]; but a brain cannot compose true literature."[18] To a hostile English reviewer, on the other hand, a play like the *Pillars of Society* is "the kind of thing that M. Alexander Dumas *fils*, if he had lost all his brains, kept his facts, and crossed them with a little German sentimentalism, might have written."[19] The aesthetic outlook of this second critic is best revealed by the fact that he can find praise only for Ibsen's attempts at poetic drama. Of *Emperor and Galilean*, he writes: "There is— as in all Ibsen's better work, and especially in his works before he became a social reformer . . . plenty of force and vigor."[20] *Ghosts*, he observes, is "as hopelessly overloaded with *Tendenz* as is the *Doll's House*."[21] He will have none of Edmund Gosse's attempt to protect Ibsen's place as an artist by distinguishing between an inquirer into social problems and a polemist.

[Gosse] defends Ibsen against the disciples . . . by saying that "when they insist that he is preaching them a sermon, he is really working out a problem, watching the evolution of an experiment in character." This is excellent advocacy; but we fear that like the Rake's play, it "will not doe." Mr. Gosse, indeed, catches himself up to tell us that "it would be going too far to deny that, in *The Lady from the Sea,* as in his earlier creations, Ibsen is occupied with didactic ideas." He will pardon us when we say that, if we met Mr. Occupied-With-Didactic-Ideas in the street, we should be very apt to mistake him for Mr. Preaching-A-Sermon.[22]

To such comments as these, we might add many others, all stemming from the challenge which critical orthodoxy felt in these plays. For example, there is Max Nordau's judgment that Ibsen's chief characters are "not human beings of flesh and blood, but abstractions such as are evoked by a morbidly excited brain."

They are attempts at the embodiment of Ibsen's doctrines, *homunculi,* originating not from natural procreation, but through the black art of the poet. . . . Doubtless, Ibsen takes immense pains to rouge and powder into a semblance of life the talking puppets who are to represent his notions. He appends to them all sorts of little peculiarities for the purpose of giving them an individual physiognomy.[23]

For Allan Monkhouse, *A Doll's House, Ghosts,* and *An Enemy of the People* are dramatic failures. The change in Nora, for instance, comes about "under pressure of the necessity for the inevitable didactic issue." In *Ghosts,* Ibsen "has committed the characteristic fault of didactic writers in endeavoring to enforce a principle by extreme, extravagant, impossible instances." In *An Enemy of the People,* with the possible exception of Doctor Stockmann, the characters have "no individual existence whatever, and consist entirely of phrases designed to show the cowardly selfishness of their kind." This reviewer welcomes *The Wild Duck,* for in it "there is no definite contention. The hunter of the social lie seems at best to be following a cold scent. . . . It seems as though the preacher might yet degenerate into a mere tragic poet."[24]

And, finally, from the pen of William Winter: "Mr. Ibsen, as the writer of a number of insipid and sometimes tainted compositions, purporting to be plays, could be borne, although even in that aspect, he is an offense to taste and a burden upon patience. But Mr. Ibsen obtruded as a sound leader of thought or an artist in drama, is a grotesque absurdity."[25]

Here, then, was one way to defend the orthodox principle of artistic detachment: admit the polemic and deny the art. However, the very opposite would serve as well: proclaim the artist and deny or effectively minimize the polemist. Thus, after a long period and much anxiety on the particular question, Georg Brandes comes to the conclusion that "Ibsen is a poet, pure and simple, and has never wanted to be anything else." Ibsen's refusal to join in political and social action as Björnson had done, "has permitted him to keep pre-eminence in his art ever before him as his one idea."[26] Max Beerbohm has much the same view: "Much has been written about Ibsen's 'purpose' in this or that play. 'Purpose' in the sense of wishing to reform this or that evil, he never had. Primarily, he was an artist, pure and simple, actuated by the artist's joy in the reproduction of human character as it appeared to his keen, unwandering eyes." Then the critic adds a somewhat ambiguous analogy: "But he had a joy within a joy: joy in the havoc he wrought. Vesuvius has no 'purpose'; it does but obey some law within itself."[27] Alfred Markowitz agreed that "the primary conscious objectives of the dramatist were purely artistic," admitting, however, that this statement would seem to many to be "an ironical and paradoxical misconstruction of the dramatist's real nature." He defended his position on the ground that Ibsen offered only negative theses, never positive proposals.[28]

This last observation is but one of the many distinctions of theory by which critics who approved of Ibsen, yet were loyal to the orthodox creed, sought to bring his plays under the mantle of artistic detachment. Another was the distinction between objective inquiry into social problems and the deliberate advocacy of a social thesis, a distinction which, as we have seen, aroused the scorn of the anonymous writer in the *Saturday Review*. Edmund Gosse, the target for that scorn, described Ibsen as "always an observer, always a clinical analyst at the bed-side of society, never a prophet, never a propagandist."[29] Elsewhere in the same volume, however, Gosse tells his readers that Ibsen found the patient, society, "excessively distasteful to him." This so-called clinical analyst, "like some ocelot or panther of the rocks, had a paw much heavier than he himself realized, and his play, in both senses, was a very serious affair when he descended to sport with common humanity"; he "roughly but thoroughly awakened the national conscience."[30] This same distinction between the analyst and the advocate is attempted, not more successfully, in a volume by Ibsen's biographer, Henrik Jaeger. According to Jaeger, *Brand, Peer Gynt,* and *The League of Youth* belong to Ibsen's "controversial period," while *Pillars of Society, A Doll's House, Ghosts,* and *An Enemy of the People* are simply described as "dramas of modern life." In this second series, we are told, Ibsen had changed from a writer of polemics to a social "diagnostician."[31]

In this way, orthodox criticism, operating from a common premise, the universal, unfailing incompatibility of art and persuasive intention, involved itself in a double contradiction. One group of critics defended the orthodox philosophy by freely accepting the polemical element and utterly denying the artistic. The other, from the same basic philosophy, proclaimed the artist and denied or tried to minimize the polemical element. Over the aesthetic issue raised by these plays criticism had, indeed, become a house divided.

In our attempt to judge the validity of the critical premise from which both factions operated, this internal, double-edged contradiction is significant. But far more significant for the same purpose is the fact that as time went on, the consensus of criticism tended to show both factions wrong, each on one count. Most of the voices raised against Ibsen's claim as an artist died down before the turn of the century, and in 1906, the year of Ibsen's death, William Dean Howells could truthfully say:

"There can be no doubt that the highest criticism has everywhere recognized his greatness as a dramatist."[32] Yet his polemical purpose was still acknowledged. In the *Quintessence of Ibsenism,* from the perspective of several decades, George Bernard Shaw noted Ibsen's early and not particularly fortunate experiments with poetic drama and continued:

His skill as a playwright and his genius as an artist were thenceforth used only to secure attention and effectiveness for his detailed attack on idealism. No more verse, no more tragedy for the sake of tears or comedy for the sake of laughter, no more seeking to produce specimens of art in order that literary critics might fill the public belly with the east wind. The critics, it is true, soon declared that he had ceased to be an artist, but he ... took no notice of them.[33]

Today, then, these conclusions seem inevitable: first, that Ibsen was a great artist; second, that he was a deliberate polemist. It is certain that no questionable artist ever received the final verdict accorded to Ibsen. It is equally certain that no dramatist who really obeyed the law of complete detachment ever aroused such storms of social excitement.

Blind faith in the sanctity of the law of artistic detachment caused most of the critical confusion and contradiction, and these qualities in that criticism clearly show the inherent weaknesses of the doctrine. If the critics had been willing to admit that at least the exceptional dramatist, possessing a high degree of technical skill and imaginative power, could deliberately use his art as a means for the expression of moral or social views without impairing that art, most of the contradictions and most of the blanket judgments, which criticism itself later reversed, might have been avoided. It then would not have been necessary to deny Ibsen's place either as a polemist or as an artist. Criticism need not then have tried to show that social aims had rendered his imaginative creations anemic in one instance and overblown in another, or that his intention to persuade had resulted in the intrusion of speeches unskillfully coordinated with situation and character.

Present-day critical theory can draw from all these reversed decisions, contradictions, and evasions the important inference that creative literature may serve the deliberate function of instruction or persuasion without loss of artistic quality, if it is in the hands of an artist who has sufficient skill and imagination to carry it through. Although it is a departure from the more conventional critical thought of the modern era, this proposition would not lead to a new or revolutionary philosophy. The worst that can be said of it is that it would constitute a return to the critical wisdom of antiquity and the Renaissance. It is, moreover, a proposition which has had a few eminent professors even in the modern era, and we may conclude this brief analysis of the problem with these lines from Hegel: "Where personal views . . . are not only of superior worth, but are further not expressed in such deliberate separation from the action of the drama as to make the latter appear as a mere means of their exploitation, the claims of true art are not likely to suffer injury."[34]

NOTES

1. Quoted from *European Theories of the Drama*, ed. Barrett Clark (Cincinnati, 1918), p. 119.

2. Quoted from John Styles, *An Essay on the Character and Influence of the Stage* (London, 1820), p. 47.

3. Translated by Barbara Foxley (New York, 1911), p. 309.

4. Quoted from Archibald Henderson, *European Dramatists* (Cincinnati, 1913), p. 21.

5. Quoted from G. L. Raymond, *Essentials of Aesthetics* (New York, 1921), p. 74.

6. Ashley Dukes, *Modern Dramatists* (London, 1911), p. 239.

7. An intelligent and careful reconstruction is to be found in M. Bienenstock's *Henrik Ibsens Kunstanschauung* (Leipzig, 1913).

8. Otto Heller, *Henrik Ibsen: Plays and Problems* (Boston, 1912), p. 280.

9. *The Collected Works of Henrik Ibsen*, ed. William Archer, 13 vols. (New York, 1917), VIII, 135.

10. *Letters of Henrik Ibsen*, trans. J. N. Laurvik and Mary Morison (New York, 1908), p. 370.

11. *Letters*, p. 86 ff.; see also *Collected Works*, XII, 91-92, 185-186.

12. LV (June, 1888), 461. My translation.

13. *Ibid*. XXVI (February, 1881), 306, 308.

14. *Ibid.*, LV (June, 1888), 461.

15. *Ibid.* (March, 1878), 485.

16. *Ibid.*, XXVI (February, 1881), 306.

17. *Ibid.*, LI (June, 1887), 465.

18. Laura Marholm, *Wir Frauen und unsere Dichter* (Berlin, 1896), p. 134. My translation.

19. *The Saturday Review of Politics, Literature, Science, and Art* LXIX (March, 1890), 352, unsigned.

20. *Ibid.*, LXX (December, 1890), 748.

21. *Ibid.*, LXIX (April, 1890), 475.

22. *Ibid.*, LXIX (January, 1890), 15.

23. Max Nordau, *Degeneration,* trans. anon. (New York, 1895 ed.), 342.

24. Allan Monkhouse, *Books and Plays* (London, 1894), pp. 161, 166, 168, 169.

25. William Winter, *Shadows of the Stage,* 3rd series (New York, 1895), p. 334.

26. Georg Brandes, *Ibsen, Björnson; Critical Studies* (New York, 1899), p. 80.

27. *Saturday Review* CI (May, 1906), 651.

28. Alfred Markowitz, *Die Weltanschauung Henrik Ibsens* (Leipsic, 1913), pp. 7, 10. My translation.

29. Edmund Gosse, *Henrik Ibsen* (New York, 1922 ed.), p. 86.

30. *Ibid.*, pp. 80, 152-153, 242.

31. Henrik Jaeger, *The Life of Henrik Ibsen,* trans. William Morton Payne (New York, 1901), 2nd ed., pp. 162, 230, 235.

32. *North American Review* CLXXXIII (July, 1906), 2.

33. George Bernard Shaw, *The Quintessence of Ibsenism* (New York, 1928 ed.), p. 82ff.

34. G. W. F. Hegel, *The Philosophy of Fine Art,* tr. F. P. B. Osmaston, 4 vols. (London, 1920), IV, 277.

Arnold Bennett and the Drama

As THE Edwardian Era recedes, hazy in the battle-glow of the
following decades, the writing of Arnold Bennett, one of the
chief spokesmen of that peaceful period, seems very remote. Yet
the author of *The Old Wives' Tale* and *Clayhanger* should survive the alarms and confusions and, when the tumult dies, take
his place among the great contributors to English letters. He
will be remembered as the penetrating commentator on the
microcòsm of the Five Towns, as the sturdy defender of what
he called "the artistic shapely presentation of truth"—that is,
form—in the English novel, as the honest seeker after beauty
even in the commonplace, proving that all men's lives can be
profoundly meaningful and, in spite of misery and ugliness and
degradation, profoundly beautiful.

It is curious that the thoughtful artist capable of writing
great books should have wasted much of his creative talent in
writing nonsense. Of the thirty-seven novels that Bennett wrote,
eighteen were pot-boilers, twelve were good but by no means
distinguished, and only seven were of the first rank. Another
curious fact is that Bennett, though he was deeply interested in
the theatre and though he wrote many plays, some of which
brought him handsome returns, never wrote a really good play.
Our problem here is to study Bennett's plays in the light of his
own standards. Incidentally, we may discover whether the times
or the themes or Bennett's own personality prevented him from
being a great dramatist or whether there is some fatal antipathy
between writing plays and writing novels which prevents a good
novelist from being a good dramatist and vice versa.

Of all the plays that Bennett wrote during his lifetime, only
sixteen (counting as one the little book of three *Polite Farces*)
are available in book form today. Of these sixteen, three were
written in collaboration with Edward Knoblock. All except
Don Juan de Marana have been produced. The plays in order

of production are as follows: *Polite Farces* (published in 1899); *Cupid and Commonsense,* January 26, 1908; *What the Public Wants,* May 2, 1909; *The Honeymoon,* October 6, 1911; *Milestones* (with Knoblock), March 5, 1912; *The Great Adventure,* March 25, 1913; *Don Juan de Marana* (written in 1914, published in 1923); *The Title,* July 20, 1918; *Judith,* April 7, 1919; *Sacred and Profane Love,* September 15, 1919; *Body and Soul,* 1921; *The Love Match,* January, 1922; *London Life* (with Knoblock), June 3, 1924; *The Bright Island,* February 15, 1925; *Mr. Prohack* (with Knoblock), November 16, 1927; *Flora,* 1927.

Except for *Milestones* and, possibly, *The Great Adventure,* the plays have never caused any great stir in the dramatic world. *Milestones* is the only one remembered today, though several of the others had long runs. They are all competently written, technically well above the average West End and Broadway plays. They are intelligent interpretations of contemporary life, but there is no permanence in them. J. W. Cunliffe devastatingly appraises Bennett as a dramatist in his *Modern English Playwrights:*

His narrative work is uneven, still more his popular philosophies, but never does he sink quite so low as when he has (according to his later view, at a great financial sacrifice) endeavored with the assistance of capable actors to create figures that will take on a semblance of flesh and blood and incidents which will have at least a momentary appearance of probability. From *What the Public Wants* to *Milestones* there has been steady depreciation in his dramatic work until it has ceased to count as a factor in the present, and one must go back to pre-War days for a recollection of the time when it seemed as if he might really do something for the commercial theatre.[1]

Bennett's early biographer, Harvey Darton, a fair judge of the pre-War Bennett, says:

He does not even, in his plays, force an intellectual discussion of the potential problems with which he deals. He does not bring to the theatre what other men could not bring equally well.[2]

One of the later critics has gone so far as to say that though Bennett as a novelist could breathe life into his characters, he lacked a real knowledge of human nature, a lack that is apparent as soon as the characters become live men and women.[3] Most commentators on Bennett mercifully ignore the plays.

Bennett's dramatic work may be divided into four groups: 1. Plays from the novels; 2. Plays with conventional themes; 3. Plays with unconventional themes; 4. Plays written in collaboration with Edward Knoblock. From earlier novels, he made the plays called *Cupid and Commonsense, The Great Adventure,* and *Sacred and Profane Love* (together with *Mr. Prohack,* which was written in collaboration with Knoblock).

Cupid and Commonsense was taken directly from Bennett's excellent early novel, *Anna of the Five Towns* (1902), with a change of ending. The play is essentially expository, telling about an unhappy, browbeaten rich girl, dominated by a miserly father, who forces her to ruin one of her clients. The first act succeeds in condensing a great deal of material into a short space, but so much action is swiftly passed over that the illusion is imperfect. Alice is not so interesting a person as Anna, her counterpart in the novel, for the play does not permit the exhaustive analysis that is the finest quality of the novel. No one in the play, except Mrs. Copestick, a good Five Towns matron, is three-dimensional. The principal characters are all unvital. This play is far from doing what Bennett says *The Second Mrs. Tanqueray* and *Arms and the Man* did to bring a new spirit into English drama, and what he hoped his plays would do. *The Times Literary Supplement,* criticizing the Stage Society's production of *Cupid and Commonsense* at Shaftesbury the year after its original production, calls it a "clever play, neatly and pointedly written, and full of acute observation of small things in small lives," but comments on the barrenness of mere realism, saying that the play is interesting enough neither for the public, nor for the select few.[4]

The Great Adventure was taken from the novel, *Buried Alive* (1908), which it follows quite faithfully. It is a thoroughly amusing story, better for a novel than a play, perhaps, but still delightful even in the condensed form of the play. Bennett himself thought that the book from which the play was taken was one of the funniest he had ever read. There is nothing new in the idea of mistaken identity, but Bennett has very deftly treated the story of a shy, famous painter who takes the place of his dead valet, watches his own great funeral in Westminster Abbey, and finds contentment with a simple wife whom he meets through a matrimonial agency. *The Great Adventure* is probably Bennett's second-best play (if we count *Milestones* as first). It is neatly constructed, amusing in theme, witty, and actable. It still has some vitality in the amateur theatre and has been used several times by moving picture producers as the basis for films.

Sacred and Profane Love shows Bennett struggling with his material in order to condense it satisfactorily. The novel of the same name (or *The Book of Carlotta*, as it was called in America), published in 1905, is a painstaking discussion in the first person of a woman's inner life. Even that falls short of vigorous truth because the woman is neither quite real nor quite interesting enough. Observed from outside herself, she is even less interesting. The story of Carlotta, the eminent woman novelist, who abandons her career to be the savior of a dope-taking pianist, is not sufficiently unified to be dramatically effective. The exposition is very clumsily handled; the scenes are jerky and episodic; and the conclusion, altered from the tragic one in the novel, is insipid. The novel has moments of insight; the play is mostly an imitation of an imitation.

The plays with conventional themes include *Polite Farces for the Drawing Room, What the Public Wants, The Honeymoon, The Title, The Love-Match, Body and Soul,* and *Flora.*

Polite Farces are three one-act plays, all planned for simple sets. Introducing the plays to the reading public, Bennett said,

Dumas *père,* the father of modern drama, once said that all he needed was "four trestles, four boards, two actors, and a passion." For myself, I have dispensed with the trestles, the boards, and the passion, since none of these things is suitable for a drawing-room.[5]

He might with truth have added that he had also dispensed with dramatic inspiration, humor (except for a flabby kind of epigrammatic wit, feebly suggestive of Wilde at his worst), and most qualities of interest. The second of these farces, *A Good*

Woman, holds a stubborn place in several anthologies of one-act plays. It is far superior to the two others, but its situation of a woman about to be married, remembering that she has promised to wait for a former lover, who returns from abroad on that very day, is commonplace. Of the others, the less said, the better. In later years Bennett published a few more one-act plays scattered through out-of-print collections and old theatre magazines, mainly of the curtain-raiser type, which "should be mildly amusing and mildly sentimental, and quite pure, because it has to appeal to the pit and gallery as distinguished from the stalls and dress circle."[6]

What the Public Wants is a spirited attack on the insincerity of contemporary journalism, embodied in Sir Charles Worgan, wealthy proprietor of forty newspapers and journals, who has a different editorial opinion for every paper and is satisfied to be a "muck-merchant" even on Sundays. The play has an ingenious plot and, like many of Bennett's dramatic experiments, a good first act, for his technical handling of exposition is unusually interesting. It may be ranked as Bennett's third best play, considerably ahead of all the other dramatic experiments.

The Honeymoon, presented under the direction of Dion Boucicault, who also took one of the parts, *The Title, The Love Match,* and *Body and Soul* are merely intelligent and clever interpretations of the life of the time, which, if the reviews are to be trusted, were enjoyed by audiences. All of them illustrate more or less of Bennett's pleasant humor, his sense of structure, and his ability to invent interesting plots. *Body and Soul,* however, one of the worst things from his pen, might easily make a reader wonder, as it did one of the critics, "how the author of *Clayhanger* and *The Old Wives' Tale* could write such third-rate stuff." *The Title,* in which appeared Leslie Howard and Nigel Playfair, is an entertaining but unimportant piece, lacking the depth even of Milne's *Wurzel-Flummery,* which remotely resembles it in theme. In it character depends on unindividualized tricks of smartness, and it remains little more than a good frothy story. Like *The Love Match,* it could extend its tenuous life in amateur productions, to which it is well suited.

Flora, the last of Bennett's plays, is of interest only because it deals with a problem of extralegal love that Bennett faced in his own life. Its motive of unrestraint, of doing as one pleases, noteworthy in the character of the later Bennett, is far removed from the motivating forces in the characters of Leonora and Ridware and Sophia Baines, the people of the great novels.

Judith, The Bright Island, and *Don Juan de Marana* are the slightly precious, unconventional plays of Bennett. *Judith* is based on the apocryphal book of *Judith,* but it does not reveal a particularly interesting use of Biblical material. Bennett apparently had to flog his imagination to make the story of Judith and Holofernes dramatically vital. The result is not very satisfactory. Judith's seduction of Holofernes is clumsy, and Holofernes' succumbing to it worse than stupid. Humor is introduced by attendant servants and soldiers, and very heavy, strange humor it is. The play is obviously a poor one, even for Bennett. On the stage it was a complete failure.

The Bright Island, like *Don Juan,* was sumptuously published before production. One wonders at the occasional vagaries of publishers of fine editions. This play is a witty treatment of an H. G. Wellsian subject, not really much of a play, and not very constructively Wellsian, but three acts of reasonably entertaining dialogue among characters with *Commedia dell'Arte* names, who present a satire on politics in England. The element of satire is sincere, and some of the lines are excellent. For the most part, however, Bennett's island of Caspo is a feeble Erewhon, and Bennett runs his good idea into the ground by making the situations either not quite serious or not quite ridiculous enough.

The entry in *The Journal* for the day after the presentation of this play admits that the audience was cold:

The points were not seen by that portion of the audience which applauds. . . . The Press, with the sole exception of *Truth,* who liked it and praised it and said that it ought to be revived before a "more intelligent audience," slanged it like anything. Not partially, but wholly. Some said I ought to be stopped from writing such plays, a great mistake, deplorable, and so on. It was the worst Press any play of mine ever had.[7]

Don Juan de Marana remained a thorn in the side of its author, for though it was one of a meditated series on such large themes as Tannhäuser and the Wandering Jew, it never saw the stage. "Theatre managers have more than once paid money for the right to produce it," said Bennett in the preface to the published version of the play, but nine years after its writing he had to be contented with the beautiful limited edition of 1923. It is the legend of Juan, Duke of Marana, who, Bennett says, lived for an ideal and was not a mere libertine, as was Juan of Tenorio in the Molière and Mozart versions. Bennett, who took some of his words and the character of Juan from a play by Dumas *père*, felt that his hero was a more sympathetic one than Byron's or Mozart's because, as he says in his introduction,

He is not a sensualist; he is an idealist. He is an idealist. He is passionately hungry for perfection, and with him the end justifies the means. As for some of his more startling deeds, it is to be noticed that he did not transgress the code of his age.[8]

The play tells a long story of a thorough scoundrel, thoughtless of everything but his own selfish pleasure, an "unsensual" man who said, "I have lived for an ideal—to defend the rights and honour of my order, and to maintain the supremacy of love." Where the sympathetic hero is, it is hard to say. Juan is gay, brilliant (though his speech is full of epigrammatic clichés), and attractive, but a lustful villain nevertheless. This work is simply a collection of superficialities: an outrageous plot, in which neither coherent writing nor decent purpose appears; an affected style, marked by a rather cheap use of phrases like "an empire on which the sun never sets," as if they were records of first use; utterly unconvincing characters in improbable situations. Artificial, trivial, unworthy of its author, the play is redeemed from sheer mediocrity only by occasional pleasant dialogue.

The remaining plays, *Milestones, London Life,* and *Mr. Prohack,* were all written in collaboration with Edward Knoblock. *Mr. Prohack* was taken from Bennett's novel by the same name and produced by Komisarjevsky, with Charles Laughton in the leading role. Bennett was too skillful a writer to be absolutely dull, and Knoblock had too keen a sense of the theatre to father a dramatic monster. But this is actually more an example of ingenious condensation than a good play. The first act is purely expository. Bennett had a difficult task to bring in all the people of the novel, explain them, and let them forecast the action of the rest of the play without being intolerably artificial. There is, however, in spite of the authors' skill, much clumsy exposition, far too much unnatural hurrying of the situation to fit it into the limits of the dramatic form. Mr. Prohack loses the leisurely contemplativeness that distinguishes him in the novel and simply rushes about, worried, as if he too were concerned with doing all that must be done within three short acts. Mr. Prohack finally discovers that "money never really brings happiness," a cliché that Bennett must have subscribed to with his tongue in his cheek. Prohack lives up to his income, becomes a dandy, makes gestures in what he likes to think of as "the grand manner," and then ends kissing his fat wife, having abandoned his dandyism and his nerves. This is an entirely negligible play, interesting only for the lesson in composition (by contrast with the novel) that it gives. One seldom sees a play bearing more plainly the marks of pen-strokes and authors' sweat.

London Life is a long, bad play about British politics, distantly suggestive of Galsworthy themes, but less pleasing than the Galsworthy plays. There are nine scenes. Six months pass during the first act, eleven years between Act I and Act II, a year between Act II and Act III, and four months in Act III. Twenty-one characters appear, besides an army of supers. When Bennett and Knoblock collaborated, they did not spare properties and casts and complications of plot. The play would make a whole trilogy of Galsworthy's novels. The reader has the impression of a great, bulky mass of people struggling at parties on the terrace of the House of Commons. It is as if the two writers outdid each other in complicating situations, with much resulting triteness and conventional action.

Milestones, Bennett's most successful and best play, is a

marvelous example of construction. It is interesting for its beautiful balance of parts, irony, coherence, dramatically sustained characterization, and meaningfulness. The whole complex story of three generations is told effectively and strongly, bringing out the contrasts in character, time, and social standards. The tendency of Bennett and Knoblock in collaboration was towards heavy snarling of plot, but here the effect is admirably clear. There is perhaps too much condensation in Act I. The events would not have happened so quickly; and there seems to be a brittle, unreal quality about some of the dialogue, as if sometimes the parts written by the two authors did not quite fit together. The peculiar difficulty of a play planned so largely, requiring elaborate exposition at the beginning of each act, is apparent in a certain amount of mechanical awkwardness that is perilously close to artificiality. The development of characters, however, suggests a gentle sympathy and understanding that Bennett shows elsewhere only in his great novels. For once, at least, Bennett wrote a play sincerely, without looking down his nose at theatrical ideals. The closing line is excellent. It is a deliberate aphorism, in Bennett's best manner, quite in key with the rest of the story: "We live and learn." *Milestones* is as near to dramatic greatness as Arnold Bennett ever got.[9]

Here ends the dramatic work of Arnold Bennett. It has added little to his reputation. On the other hand, it has not been entirely discreditable to him, even though, with the exception of *Don Juan*, he did not put great stock in his plays. As in all his writing, including the absurd romances, Bennett gave honest value for time spent, never grudging to exercise his whole skill on what he was doing. It is not unfair to him, however, to say that in his plays he was seldom more than a competent craftsman, giving the public what, in the main, it wanted, never venturing into uncharted territory, uninterested in the revolutionary changes in drama that were going on all about him, contented to be clever, intelligent, and safe in the region of the box office.

In spite of his early pronouncements about managers who would not take original, thoughtful plays, Bennett himself wrote almost no plays that might be included in that category. He did slip away from conventional themes in *Don Juan* and *Judith* and *The Bright Island,* seriously striving towards classical and Biblical ideas and smart satirical fantasy, but his was simply not a dramatic genius. As a student of literary technique, he could learn some of the tricks of exposition and complication of incident, but in employing them he almost inevitably lost vitality, even when he found mechanical efficiency. Characters like Mr. Prohack and Ann Tellwright and even Carlotta Peel, who are real characters in the novels, become flaccid automata in the plays, dully repeating phrases ready made for them by a skilled workman, who sadly lacked the gift of dramatic imagination.

The dates of the plays throw little additional light on the reasons for their inferiority. He wrote *Cupid and Commonsense* in the year that saw the publication of *The Old Wives' Tale.* *Clayhanger* and *Hilda Lessways* were written at about the same time as *What the Public Wants* and *The Honeymoon.* He must have been writing another of his great books, *These Twain,* when *Don Juan* appeared, and *Riceyman Steps* came between *The Love Match* and *London Life.* There is, therefore, no "dramatic period." One fact, however, may be significant. All but one of Bennett's great novels were written before the war. Seven of the plays, including the three best, were produced before 1915. The rest, along with much rubbish in the way of novels and short stories, came after the war. There is some reason to believe, from *The Journal* and the other work of the latter period, that the ideal-annihilating shock of the war had a deep and terrible influence on Bennett as a creative artist.

The same curious inconsistency in Bennett that allowed him to write deliberate pot-boilers along with his serious novels made him see no reason why he should not intimately associate himself with the drama, which he never really understood and secretly despised. During a large part of his life he was a man of the theatre, both as a dramatist and, later, as director of the Lyric Opera House, Hammersmith.[10] He was always interested in the kindred professions of the actor and the playwright, and many of his friends were connected in some way with the theatre. His wife, Marguerite Soulié, was a French actress; Dorothy Cheston, his mistress and inseparable companion in his last years, was an English actress. He had established a friendship with her while she played in his *Body and Soul*, in Liverpool.

In the three volumes of *Things That Have Interested Me* (1921, 1923, 1926), twenty essays are devoted to the theatre. Four of the thirteen stories in the collection, *Elsie and the Child, and Other Stories* (1924), and four of the seventeen stories in *The Night Visitor and Other Stories* (1931) deal with the theatre. The romance, *The Ghost* (1907), is about opera singers. The novelette, *Stroke of Luck* (1932), is about an actress. *The Regent* (1913) is about a London theatre and actors, managers, and producers. Actors and actresses come incidentally into many of the other books. Frequent mention of plays and attendance at the theatre is found in most of the later novels. In both *The Roll-Call* and *Mr. Prohack,* for example, are vivid descriptions of musical comedies, which Bennett himself very much disliked. One can easily imagine Arnold Bennett in Mr. Prohack's place:

The curtain went up, and this simple gesture on the part of the curtain evoked enormous applause. The audience could not control the expression of its delight. A young lady under a sunshade appeared; the mere fact of her existence threw the audience into a new ecstasy. An old man with a red nose appeared; similar demonstrations from the audience. When those two had talked to each other, the applause was tripled, and when the scene changed from Piccadilly Circus at 4 A.M. to the interior of a Spanish palace inhabited by illustrious French actors and actresses who proceeded to play an act of a tragedy by Corneille, the applause was quintupled. At the end of the tragedy the applause was decupled. Then the Spanish palace dissolved into an Abyssinian harem, and Eliza Fiddle in Abyssinian costume was discovered lying upon two thousand cushions of two thousand colours, and the audience rose at Eliza, and Eliza rose at the audience, and the resulting frenzy was the sublimest frenzy that ever shook a theatre. The piece was stopped dead for three minutes while the audience and Eliza protested a mutual and unique passion. From this point onward Mr. Prohack lost his head. He ran to an fro in the bewildering, glittering maze of the piece, seeking for an explanation, for a sign-post, for a clue, for the slightest hint, and found nothing. He had no alternative than to cling to Eliza Fiddle, and he clung to her desperately. She was willing to be clung to. She gave herself, not only to Mr. Prohack, but to every member of the audience separately; she gave herself in the completeness of all her manifestations. The audience was rich in the possession of the whole of her individuality, which was a great deal. She sang, danced, chattered, froze, melted, laughed, cried, flirted, kissed, kicked, cursed, and turned somersaults with the fury of a dervish, the languor of an odalisque, and the inexhaustibility of a hot-spring geyser. . . . And at length Mr. Prohack grew aware of a feeling within himself that was at war with the fresh, fine feeling of physical well-being. "I have never seen a revue before," he said in secret. "Is it possible that I am bored?"[11]

The main reasons for Bennett's lack of inspiration as a dramatist are these three: his attitude of contempt for drama, his rather vulgar commercial motive, and his immaturity as a critic and observer of the theatre.

First, his lack of respect for drama. In his early books on the technique of writing, Bennett had some very curious things to say about playwriting. In the first, *How to Become an Author* (1912), a book of advice to hopeful writers, he seriously listed the points essential in a marketable play:

1. Plenty of contrasting action and business, and at least one big "situation" in each act.
2. Effective curtains to each act.
3. Plenty of comic relief.
4. A luxurious environment.
5. At least one character of great wealth, and a few titled characters if possible.
6. Sentimentality in the love scenes, and generally throughout.
7. A certain amount of epigram in the dialogue.
8. No genuine realism, unless it is immediately made palatable by subsequent sentimentality.
9. A happy ending. Or at any rate a decent ending such as the suicide of a naughty heroine.[12]

Here, surely, is no remarkable idealism, even if his own later plays did not strictly adhere to these artificial specifications. In another book on writing, first issued in 1913, Bennett said in his chapter on playwriting,

The emotional strain of writing a play is not merely less prolonged than that of writing a novel,—it is less severe even while it lasts, lower in degree and of a less purely creative character. . . . The drama does not belong exclusively to literature, because its effect depends on something more than the composition of words. The dramatist is the sole author of a play, but he is not the sole creator of it. . . . A Play is a collaboration of creative faculties. . . . The creative faculties are not only those of the author, the stage-director, and the actors—the audience itself is unconsciously part of the collaboration.[13]

That Bennett was not thinking of artistic harmony in the theatre as was Gordon Craig, saying something similar in *On the Art of the Theatre,* is apparent in another sentence from *The Author's Craft:*

The truth is that no technique is so crude and so simple as the technique of the stage, and that the proper place to learn it is not behind the scenes but in the pit.[14]

Bennett's whole attitude towards drama, outside of a virtuous preface to *Cupid and Commonsense* and an occasional review, was the contemptuous one of a successful novelist, diluting his talent to write for the stage, simply because plays were more profitable than novels. He always believed that fiction is a more respectable form of literature than drama, and that a good novelist, if he would condescend to the lower form, could write passable plays. Professor Baker has pointed out in his book, *Dramatic Technique,* what Bennett never realized:

The fact that drama had had for centuries in England and elsewhere a fecund history before the novel as a form took shape at all would intimate that the drama is a different and independent art from that of the novel or the short story. When the novelists and would-be playwrights recognize that it is, has been, and ought to be an independent art, we shall be spared many bad plays.[15]

To Bennett the drama was always an inferior member of the same branch of literature that included the novel. The result is that his plays are chiefly dramatized novel material.

Bennett never got over his early impression, articulated in *How to Become an Author,* that "the most successful modern plays are a mixture of sweet sentimentality and ingenuous farce,"[16] and rarely did he want to write any other kind. His summary of the divisions of drama in London, though meant only as information for the aspiring writer, reveals his commonplace theatrical standards. He said that the three divisions are musical comedy, melodrama, and comedy. Comedy is the only division with "any sort of an artistic ideal."[17] He was probably aware of a better standard, but his strong tendency to do "what the public wants" inclined him towards popularity and success, contented with an inferior "sort of an artistic ideal." Happily he did not write his best novels according to the same standard.

There were, it is true, occasional utterances by Bennett showing moderate respect for the theatre. In 1912, when he was author of twelve plays, five of which had been sold, but none produced, he was indignant at the decline of the English stage. The fault was chiefly that of the managers and partly that of the public, he believed. Between them they contrived to strangle artistic acting and artistic playwriting. In the preface to *Cupid and Commonsense*, his first play to find production, he said that the art of acting in London

suffers under manifest disadvantages—from the evil of long runs, and, also, at present, from the evil of short runs; from the evil of a far too honeyed press; from the evil of the actor-manager who, with a curious blindness to his own interest, does his best to kill all genuine acting in his immediate vicinity; . . . and from the fatal tendency of the British public to demand from an artist that he shall repeat himself monotonously *ad infinitum*. This last is the bane of all the arts in England. Let a man once act, for instance, a policeman, or paint a policeman, or sing a policeman, or carve a policeman, to the tickling of the public taste, and he stands condemned to act, paint, sing, or carve policemen, and nothing but policemen, to his dying day.[18]

Continuing the manifesto of the preface to *Cupid and Commonsense*, Bennett admitted that, after all, the author may be at the bottom of the theatrical situation, for "since Goldsmith and Sheridan, the literary genius of the English race has turned away from the theatre." The drama had repelled rather than attracted great writers, and an unintelligent public had found pleasure in the "agreeable mediocrity" of the theatre. "Ibsen," he said ironically, "was a foreigner, and therefore to be excused, because he knew no better. But deliberately to encourage new ideas on the stage was outrageous." With such plays as *The Second Mrs. Tanqueray* and *Widowers' Houses,* however, the creative spirit was again approaching the theatre. Nevertheless, producers, unaware of the changing taste of the public, which was getting over the shock of seeing genius once more writing for the stage, were still looking for plays that would have pleased the audiences of twenty years before. Bennett claimed, without much justification, as we have seen, that he was adding his plays to the new group of artistic creations, suited to the improving public taste, but as yet unappreciated by reactionary managers.

His quarrel with managers seems to have been one of long standing. Nine years before the preface to *Cupid and Commonsense,* which stirred up a minor row in London theatrical circles, he had sneered at the affectations and stupidity of most actor-managers in the autobiographical *Truth About an Author.* *A Great Man* (1904) and *The Regent* (1913) contain satirical pictures of managers. In the second series of *Things That Have Interested Me* (1923) he wrote, "The secret of theatrical success is the right choice of plays. Not one manager in ten is fitted to choose a play. If the stage is not absolutely perfect, here is one of the chief explanations."[19] In 1926 he protested again about the short-sighted conservatism of managers: "If they would deign to educate themselves a little, and let themselves be educated, they might, with advantage to themselves and the stage, take risks on original plays instead of on unoriginal plays."[20] It would be unfair to Bennett to attribute to him an entirely personal animus in his attitude towards managers, for after the success of *Milestones* in 1912 he was well treated by managers. Nevertheless, as the history of the theatre has demonstrated, when great plays are written, they somehow find producers. Bennett himself was probably not seriously deceived about the existence of stifled dramatic genius. One excellent reason why he had trouble in having his early plays staged and why he is today little honored as a playwright is that, on the whole, his plays are poor ones.

To the end of his life, Bennett, still an intimate of the theatre, never fully recognized it as the home of a creative art. Infrequently, he saw something that pleased him. For example, he was genuinely interested in the production of such plays as *The Cherry Orchard* and *The Lower Depths,* which were among the fine things looked upon with suspicion by the London managers. In one of the essays in *The Savour of Life* (1931), he sounded a note of patronizing hopefulness for the London stage by saying that it was not necessarily declining, but suffering from several causes: inaudibility of actors, bad acting, bad producing, deterioration of performances during a run, mealy-mouthed dramatic criticism, and poor management. To Arnold Bennett the theatre was the theatre, a place of entertainment, and its product was not to be compared with the serious work of novelists.

The second reason for Bennett's failure as a dramatist was his frankly commercial approach to the theatre. In *The Truth About an Author* (1903) he had said,

My aim in writing plays, whether alone or in collaboration, has always been strictly commercial. I wanted money in heaps, and I wanted advertisement for my books. I have found it easier to compose a commercial play than an artistic novel. How our princes of the dramatic kingdom can continue to spend two years over a single piece, as they say they do, I cannot understand. The average play contains from 18 to 20 thousand words; the average novel contains 80 thousand; after all, writing is a question of words.[21]

The Journal contains many references to plays and playwrights. Yet Bennett's association with the theatre, outside of his duties as a critic and first-nighter, seems always to have been, in his own words, "strictly commercial." In his reviews he rarely touched upon the revolutionary influences that were sweeping through the theatre, though to the individual writer he was kind and, in a purely technical way, helpful. The entries in *The Journal* ignore the problems of dramatic art, but dwell at length upon the box-office receipts. For example, the entry for March 17, 1920, tells that

the first week's receipts of *Sacred and Profane Love* in New York were over 16,600 dollars. This easily bangs *Milestones* and all of my other records. My royalties in that week exceed 350 pounds. My faith in the theatre as a means of artistic expression was, of course, instantly re-established. It would be.

He records with terse smugness the long run of another play: "The 285th and last performance of *The Title* occurred last Saturday at the Royalty. A good house." There was never anything more: no comment on the drama as a social force, no honest criticism of himself or of others. His chief interest was in "a good house."[22]

The third reason for Bennett's failure as a man of the theatre was his immaturity as critic and observer. He set himself up as a literary arbiter and wrote many dogmatic things about all branches of writing. Yet what he had to say about the theatre was more blustering and less convincing than his comments on novel-writing. As a pioneer of the "How to Live by Formula" school, he tried to work out easy rules for every accomplishment, including the art of playwriting. His opinions on the subject remained precociously adolescent. He seems not to have learned anything from his own frequent play-going or even from the experience of writing plays himself and acting as manager of a new theatre. To the end he remained ignorant of the true purpose of drama. His dramatic opinions were as inferior to his other criticisms as his best plays are inferior to his best novels. He could judge plays only by his peculiarly vulgar personal standard, which completely rejected the new art of the theatre. Even his casual criticisms are seldom penetrating. In 1897 he thought that Gabrielle, in Dumas *père's Mademoiselle de Belle-Isle,* "made one forget all the creations of Dumas *fils,* of Donnay, of Ibsen, of Pinero."[23] In 1903 he condemned Ibsen's *Ghosts* as insincere, stagy, too clever.[24] In 1906 he said, "I am pretty well convinced that Ibsen is not a writer of masterpieces. And he is stagy! He who is supposed to have rejuvenated the entire technique of the stage has become stagy in 15 years!"[25] In 1909 he recorded, "Thursday, *What Every Woman Knows,* J. M. Barrie. A despicable piece. He surely must have known what putridity he was turning out."[26] In 1912 he talked with George Moore, who "regarded the theatre generally as a clumsy and infantile art, in which he was quite right."[27] In 1924 he complained that after three performances of Congreve's *Way of the World* he still did not know what the plot was. Of this play, now generally regarded as one of the high points of social comedy, he said,

The last act drags terribly and is enough to kill any play. It seems to me that Congreve had something of the superior and really snobbish artistic negligence of Wilde and Byron. Anyhow his play suffers. It is celebrated; but it cannot hold the stage because of its crude and inexcusable faults of construction.[28]

Later, in 1924, he was bored at a performance of Gilbert and Sullivan's *Gondoliers*. "The whole affair dull, save for the magnif. tunes. I don't want to see any more of G. and S. Fundamentally the whole thing is dead."[29] In 1926 he saw a production of Chekhov's *The Three Sisters*.

Well, I was bored frequently. Did I enjoy myself? No, not on the whole. Was I uplifted as I had been by an even gloomier play, *Rosmersholm?* No. It seemed to me that often the author was wilfully pessimistic. He is certainly very monotonous, and all the plays that I've seen have the same tone.[30]

On the other hand, he thought that Georg Kaiser's *From Morn to Midnight* "showed how all English and French dramatists are in a rut."[31] Though he felt that Barrie, Shaw, Galsworthy, Yeats, Masefield, Ervine, Maugham, Lennox Robinson, and Barker all condescended towards the theatre, "We had a great dramatist, Synge," he said. "He went and died young. It was a greater tragedy than any his pen wrote."[32] In 1912, on the occasion of his first visit to the United States, Bennett felt that "a few minor cases apart, the drama is artistically negligible throughout the world; but if there is a large hope for it in any special country, that country is the United States."[33]

Arnold Bennett will not be remembered for his contributions to the drama, either as playwright or as critic. What he had to say seriously he could not or did not want to say in dramatic form. Whether this lack of depth and originality is to be attributed to Bennett's belief that drama is an inferior branch of literature, chiefly useful in more or less venal exploitation, or to sheer inability to meet the exigent technical demands of plays and still speak significantly, no one can say.

It might be noted that only in *Cupid and Commonsense,* one of his earliest plays, did Bennett use the Five Towns people, who give force and sincerity to his best books. Perhaps he felt that drama must be dynamic and that the grim realities of the Five Towns were not fundamentally dramatic. Here may be part of the answer to the question, "Is there an insuperable barrier between the art of the novelist and the art of the dramatist?" The novelist can tell his story without sharp complication of incident. He need not describe a clash of wills or of forces, as the playwright must. His scenes must move, but not necessarily to a clear-cut climax. Drama is a *doing.* A story can be merely a *telling* of related dramatic or undramatic scenes. Only rarely does a novelist write a story which can be directly converted into a play, as John Steinbeck's *Of Mice and Men* was. Sinclair Lewis, for all his love of the theatre, cannot write a first-rate play, just as G. B. Shaw cannot write a first-rate novel. Thornton Wilder has not yet proved himself as either a novelist or a dramatist. John Galsworthy came the nearest to doing both well.

Bennett knew the rules of drama and tried manfully to observe them. When he did, however, he lost the best of what he had to say. His genius lay in brilliantly focused pictures of simple people. In the concentrated action of a play, his characters become brittle and unconvincing. The writer of *Clayhanger* and *Riceyman Steps* can be dimly heard through the rattling mechanism of *Milestones* and *The Great Adventure,* but in no other plays. Arnold Bennett was a novelist, not a dramatist.

NOTES

1. John W. Cunliffe, *Modern English Playwrights* (New York, 1927), p. 172.
2. Harvey Darton, *Arnold Bennett* (London, 1914), p. 112.
3. Mrs. Belloc Lowndes, "A Letter from London," *Saturday Review of Literature* (January 2, 1932).
4. October 7, 1909.
5. *Polite Farces for the Drawing Room* (London, 1899), prefatory note.
6. Arnold Bennett, *How to Become an Author* (London, 1903), p. 219.
7. *The Journal of Arnold Bennett,* 3 vols. (New York, 1932-33), entry for February 24, 1925.
8. P. xix.
9. The question is sometimes raised about how much credit should be given Edward Knoblock for his share in *Milestones.* It is impossible at this distance to

know just how much each of the collaborators contributed to the whole. Knoblock was a good craftsman, but not an inspired playwright. Certainly he did nothing to rescue *London Life* and *Mr. Prohack* from mediocrity. Bennett's natural gift for plots is evident in nearly everything he wrote. Yet when he and Knoblock got together, they bogged down under too much plot, except in *Milestones*. There they austerely held the plot in control, probably because Bennett's sense of logical composition was dominant.

10. In the preface to *Cupid and Commonsense* he listed his claim to a hearing as critic of the stage. He was "a member of the public, a man of business, a critic, a novelist, a dramatist, a habitué of managerial sanctums, a familiar of the Parisian stage, and a perfect stranger."

11. Pp. 147-48.

12. P. 217.

13. *The Author's Craft* (published serially in *The English Review*, in 1913, in book form in 1914); *The English Review* (July, 1913), p. 564.

14. *Ibid.*, p. 557.

15. G. P. Baker, *Dramatic Technique* (Boston, 1919), p. 5.

16. P. 210.

17. *Ibid.*

18. *Cupid and Commonsense* (London, 1912), p. 18. This idea of the artist forced to repeat himself was one of Bennett's favorite grievances. He had used his phrase about the policeman four years earlier, in *Buried Alive*, to express a painter's hatred of establishing a set style. Perhaps in that opinion may be found an explanation for his own complacent defiance of critics who objected to his Fantasias and other pot-boilers, including his plays, when he was capable of writing *The Old Wives' Tale*. "Why," he probably reasoned, "must I write only Five Towns novels simply because they have met with academic approval? I am a many-sided man, and my books too must be many-sided."

19. "Theatre Managers," p. 30.

20. *Things That Have Interested Me*, Third Series (New York, 1926), "The Play Supply," p. 28.

21. P. 178.

22. Yet, with characteristic inconsistency, he wrote, in 1925, "People say solemnly that the theatre would be better if authors of standing outside the theatre did not turn to the theatre merely as a means of money-making. They don't. The rewards of a successful play are grossly exaggerated in the public mind. No novelist of established prestige and good circulation, in search of money, would leave writing novels for a time in order to write plays—unless he was an ass. . . . If they [novelists] do turn to the stage, it is because they are driven thereto by a powerful instinct, even to their financial disadvantage." *New York Times*, October 18, 1925.

23. *The Journal*, July 12, 1897.

24. *Ibid.*, November 26, 1903.

25. *Ibid.*, May 5, 1906.

26. *Ibid.*, May 13, 1909.

27. *Ibid.*, October 10, 1912.

28. *Ibid.*, February 8, 1924.

29. *Ibid.*, March 19, 1924.

30. *Ibid.*, October 26, 1926.

31. *Ibid.*, March 31, 1920.

32. *Things That Have Interested Me*, Second Series (New York, 1923), pp. 37-39.

33. *Those United States* (Leipzig, 1912), p. 191.

The Dialectal Significance of the Non-phonemic Low-back Vowel Variants Before *R*

Charles K. Thomas

A PHONETIC comparison of *far* with *for*, *farm* with *form*, and *barn* with *born* shows that the vowels distinguish one word of each pair from the other. English has many such pairs in which the vowel is distinctive when *r* is final or immediately followed by a consonant. When, however, a second vowel follows *r* and *rr*, no such distinctive arrangement of pairs is possible, and the main vowel is free to vary in quality without any loss of precision in meaning. Thus the stressed syllables of such words as *forest* and *horrid* sometimes contain the vowel [ɑ] of *far*, sometimes the vowel [ɔ] of *for*, and sometimes the vowel [ɒ], which lies acoustically between [ɑ] and [ɔ].

The use of [ɑ] in *far*, *farm*, and *barn*, and of [ɔ] in *for*, *form*, and *born*, has become standardized in the sense that confusion of meaning may result if the phonemic contrasts between *far* and *for*, *barn* and *born*, and similar pairs are obscured. This confusion actually exists in some forms of American English, but the purpose of the present investigation is to discover whether the phonetically similar, but phonemically non-distinctive, variations which occur in such words as *forest* and *horrid* have any definable regional pattern; to discover, in short, whether the use of [ɑ], or [ɒ], or [ɔ] is more characteristic of one region than of another.

During the past ten years I have been able to make notes on the pronunciation of several thousand persons whose speech has seemed to me to be reasonably characteristic of the localities in which they live. Many of these were Cornell students whom I was able to interview soon after their arrival in Ithaca. For similar contacts at other colleges and universities I have been greatly helped by members of Speech Departments and English Departments who have generously devoted their time and energy on my behalf.[1] In New York State, and to a less extent in Connecticut, Pennsylvania, Vermont, and Colorado, I have interviewed people of all ages and all degrees of education in their homes. Some of my material has been secured in conversation with such people. For statistical purposes, however, it has been necessary for me to rely largely on the reading pronunciation of my subjects; only by having large numbers of people read the same material has it been possible to obtain statistically reliable data on individual words. Necessarily I have more data for some words than for others, and more for some counties, and some states, than for others. In New York and New Jersey I have records from every county; in Vermont and Connecticut, from every county but one; in Massachusetts, from every county but two; in Pennsylvania, from every county but five. In other states my data are somewhat more scattered, but enough information is available to make possible some tentative conclusions.

In this study, the regional units of classification are, with two exceptions, individual states. For dialectal reasons which will become evident with the presentation of the data, I have divided New York and Pennsylvania each into two regions. For New York, the lower area includes fifteen counties: those on Long Island, the rest of New York City, and the Hudson-Valley counties of Columbia, Dutchess, Greene, Orange, Putnam, Rockland, Ulster, and Westchester. For Pennsylvania, the southeastern area includes about a third of the state: the twenty-seven counties south and east of a line drawn along the northern boundaries of Monroe, Carbon, Schuylkill, Columbia, Northumberland, Union, Mifflin, and Huntingdon Counties, and the western boundaries of Huntingdon and Fulton Counties; the north-and-west area includes the rest of the state.

The data available at present for this study are in the four tables which follow. Table I shows the number of speakers recorded for the set of seven words, and their geographical distribution in nineteen states. Table II shows the percentages of those speakers who use one or another of the three vowel types in the words and regions tabulated. Tables III and IV show similar data for seven other words and for speakers in seven northeastern states. Though I have accumulated scattered data from the rest of the forty-eight states, the material is not yet adequate for statistical presentation.

The data suggest several tentative conclusions. First, no two words show quite the same pattern, and several depart noticeably from the characteristic patterns of the others. *Borrow, sorry,* and *tomorrow* show the strongest preference for [ɑ], a preference which is perhaps most noticeable in lower New York, New Jersey, and southeastern Pennsylvania, least noticeable in Vermont and upper New York. This preference agrees fairly closely with Marckwardt's findings for the Great-Lakes area;[2] Marckwardt's suggestion that the preference for the unrounded vowel is associated with "some kind of dissimilation"[3] has much to be said for it. Neither Marckwardt's

TABLE I

	corridor	Florida	forest	horrid	orange	quarry	torrent
Vermont	93	93	102	95	100	92	94
Massachusetts	63	56	82	62	70	56	59
Connecticut	40	34	46	39	41	35	38
Lower New York	177	145	370	259	276	171	247
Upper New York	398	253	860	590	739	264	585
New Jersey	108	101	172	141	144	124	137
S. E. Pennsylvania	100	96	147	94	118	99	110
N. W. Pennsylvania	174	167	222	176	206	162	182
Virginia	63	63	68	65	67	53	64
Florida	59	59	59	59	60	48	60
Tennessee	77	77	78	79	80	61	78
Ohio	68	60	90	69	68	57	66
Illinois	43	41	44	42	41	35	41
Iowa	20	21	22	21	22	19	21
Missouri	24	23	25	24	23	17	23
Arkansas	19	19	20	20	20	17	20
Louisiana	66	67	69	68	70	41	67
Texas	67	66	70	68	68	56	66
Colorado	31	31	31	30	31	14	31
Arizona	56	56	56	57	58	28	57
California	78	71	74	73	76	57	72

data nor mine suggest any important geographical variation between [ɑ] and [ɔ] in these three words.

In the other eleven words we can, however, discern the evidence for regional variation, and can glimpse a dividing line which separates territory in which [ɑ] predominates from territory in which [ɔ] predominates. For some words the line can be traced only in the northeastern part of the country; for others it can be extended further and its direction indicated even when its course cannot be followed with any close accuracy.

For future reference, to provide a definite statement of a hypothe-

TABLE II

	corridor			Florida			forest			horrid			orange			quarry			torrent		
	a	ɒ	c	a	ɒ	c	a	ɒ	c	a	ɒ	c	a	ɒ	c	a	ɒ	c	a	ɒ	c
Vermont	19	9	72	37	16	47	30	21	49	38	25	37	34	31	35	24	29	47	43	23	34
Massachusetts	55	17	28	79	5	16	69	13	18	77	13	10	74	17	9	54	25	21	73	10	17
Connecticut	18	25	57	36	23	41	32	18	50	68	16	16	61	22	17	43	11	46	50	21	29
Lower New York	68	11	21	84	8	8	72	10	18	89	6	5	88	4	8	90	6	4	75	10	15
Upper New York	2	10	88	7	16	77	7	13	80	15	19	66	11	24	65	35	10	55	6	16	78
New Jersey	66	17	17	89	7	4	86	6	8	89	6	5	92	7	1	90	6	4	82	7	11
S. E. Pennsylvania	39	23	38	79	13	8	75	14	11	78	13	9	66	24	10	72	12	16	67	16	17
N. W. Pennsylvania	7	5	88	13	3	84	11	8	81	13	10	77	18	15	67	23	19	58	12	9	79
Virginia	73	17	10	96	2	2	97	3	0	95	5	0	100	0	0	92	4	4	91	8	1
Florida	27	26	47	73	15	12	76	13	11	85	8	7	85	7	8	52	8	40	65	18	17
Tennessee	49	12	29	87	8	5	78	10	12	86	9	5	91	6	3	74	8	18	79	12	9
Ohio	0	5	95	7	15	78	3	15	82	8	15	77	5	20	75	14	18	68	2	21	77
Illinois	3	11	86	2	4	94	2	7	91	2	12	86	3	36	61	17	20	63	3	24	73
Iowa	0	5	95	0	14	86	9	9	82	0	19	81	0	43	57	10	17	73	0	24	76
Missouri	9	12	79	26	39	35	12	40	48	33	21	46	9	55	36	53	29	18	13	26	61
Arkansas	74	16	10	68	5	27	60	20	20	70	20	10	80	5	15	47	6	47	70	10	20
Louisiana	74	18	8	73	20	7	82	14	4	85	13	2	87	11	2	72	14	14	81	12	7
Texas	35	30	35	66	24	10	60	17	23	65	21	14	66	22	12	52	8	40	56	20	24
Colorado	0	7	93	0	13	87	4	12	84	3	40	57	3	42	55	14	0	86	3	26	71
Arizona	2	5	93	2	5	93	3	10	87	2	14	84	5	35	60	29	7	64	0	12	88
California	3	3	94	0	11	89	0	14	86	9	7	84	9	28	63	26	4	70	3	12	85

TABLE III

	authority	borrow	foreign	horrible	sorry	tomorrow	warrant
Vermont	95	96	101	87	95	95	89
Massachusetts	58	78	80	50	67	74	45
Connecticut	32	43	44	28	41	41	28
Lower New York	152	213	180	131	131	170	121
Upper New York	343	607	354	377	432	567	247
New Jersey	112	163	169	92	134	108	82
S. E. Pennsylvania	90	169	198	70	164	156	68
N. W. Pennsylvania	168	233	242	189	223	193	131
Ohio	33	54	58	35	52	55	26

TABLE IV

	authority			borrow			foreign			horrible			sorry			tomorrow			warrant		
	a	b	c	a	b	c	a	b	c	a	b	c	a	b	c	a	b	c	a	b	c
Vermont	27	23	40	15	14	71	28	28	44	45	28	27	58	14	33	64	18	18	14	23	63
Massachusetts	82	10	8	69	17	14	70	13	17	84	10	6	70	15	15	84	13	3	67	13	20
Connecticut	28	28	44	74	13	13	27	27	46	75	4	21	78	2	20	80	10	10	36	25	39
Lower New York	66	13	21	94	2	4	74	8	18	79	7	14	90	3	7	96	2	2	86	6	8
Upper New York	5	22	73	78	3	19	6	16	78	15	21	64	70	6	24	80	5	15	16	17	67
New Jersey	77	11	12	92	7	1	89	6	5	93	7	0	83	15	2	97	3	0	82	8	10
S. E. Pennsylvania	72	14	14	80	14	6	62	22	16	94	4	2	87	10	3	92	7	1	62	10	28
N. W. Pennsylvania	16	10	74	56	20	24	12	13	75	19	9	72	79	10	11	86	10	4	15	9	76
Ohio	6	9	85	76	13	11	8	10	82	17	20	63	65	21	14	87	10	3	8	15	77

To the west of the broken line [ɔ] predominates; to the east, [ɑ].

sis for subsequent testing and possible verification, I should like to indicate the location of this line as it seems to me at present to exist. It enters northern Vermont from Canada, runs south near the western borders of Orleans and Caledonia Counties, swings east to the Connecticut River, and continues south along the eastern border of Orange County. It then swings west again and follows the western boundaries of Windsor and Windham Counties to the Massachusetts line.[4] In Massachusetts the line continues south to the east of Berkshire County. It swings east to the Connecticut River again in Hampden County, crosses into Connecticut, and runs south through the eastern part of Hartford County, continuing south until it is in New Haven County. It then swings west and northwest through northern Fairfield County until it reaches the New York State line. In New York it passes westward through Columbia and Greene Counties, crossing the Hudson in a westerly direction in so doing. Then it turns south again, through the western slopes of the Catskills, roughly along the western boundaries of Greene, Ulster, and Orange Counties, until it comes to the Delaware River, in the neighborhood of Port Jervis. It then follows the Delaware, which forms the northwest boundary of New Jersey at this point, to the neighborhood of the northern boundary of Monroe County, Pennsylvania. From here it follows the generally southwestward trend of the Pennsylvania mountains, along the irregular path described by the northern boundaries of Monroe, Carbon, Schuylkill, Columbia, Northumberland, Union, Mifflin, and Huntingdon Counties, and the western boundaries of Huntingdon and Fulton Counties.[5] It crosses the narrow part of Maryland a few miles east of Cumberland, and then follows the summits of the Alleghenies southwest through Virginia, leaving a narrow strip of Virginia to the northwest of the line.[6] From here it crosses southern West Virginia to the Ohio River, which it follows as far as Cincinnati. From here on it coincides closely with the line by which Baugh[7] indicates the boundary between General American and Southern speech. From Cincinnati the line runs across southern Indiana and southern Illinois. About a quarter of Missouri lies south of the line, and a quarter of Oklahoma lies to the east of it. From the Oklahoma-Texas boundary the line makes a slight arc to the west, and reaches the Gulf of Mexico somewhere below Corpus Christi.

The evidence now at hand seems to indicate that east and south of this critical line is the territory in which [ɑ] predominates, and that west and north of it is the territory in which [ɔ] predominates. By and large, the bibliographical references agree with my data. The New England records of "The Young Rat"[8] agree on [ɑ] in *horror* and *tomorrow*, except for the record from Lancaster, New Hampshire.[9] For New York and New Jersey there is little evidence aside from my own data. Emerson records [ɔ] for Ithaca, New York,[10] Crowningshield [ɔ] for northeastern New York,[11] and there is a record of [ɔ] in St. Lawrence County,[12] but these three localities are so far from the critical line that they give no clue to its location.

In Pennsylvania, the records of "The Young Rat" are from Philadelphia[13] and Lancaster County,[14] both of which are southeast of the critical line, and in [ɑ] territory, as the data and records all show. The equal proportion between [ɑ] and [ɔ] that de Camp[15] reports for Scranton is to be expected, since the city is very close to the critical line.

Further south, my data suggest the possibility of including Virginia entirely within the [ɑ] territory, and of running the line across West Virginia to the Ohio River. Tresidder's findings[16] make it seem likely, however, that the territory west of the Shenandoah Valley and a large part of West Virginia should be included in the [ɔ] territory. Other evidence for Virginia usage includes Shewmake's statement[17] to the effect that Virginians generally identify the vowel of *moral* with that of *hot* rather than with that of *mortal;* this vowel is presumably [ɑ]. Virginia transcriptions of "The Young Rat" show [ɑ] in *horror* and *tomorrow* in Williamsburg[18] and Rockingham County;[19] [ɒ] in Lancaster County;[20] but Ayres and Greet record the last as [ɑ] too.[21]

In the Southeast, McDavid's article on South Carolina[22] is the only one to treat any part of the region statistically. All the words of this class which McDavid includes in his tables show a preference for [ɑ] of nearly 90 per cent, a percentage which accords well with my data for the Southeast with the exception of Florida. The increasingly cosmopolitan makeup of the Florida population is probably the reason for its slight shift toward General American usages. Records of "The Young Rat" show [ɑ] for Charleston, S.C.[23] and Macon, Ga.,[24] and [ɒ] for Charleston[25] and Columbia, S.C.[26] Miss Wheatley's statement that the South always has [ɒ] in words of this class[27] goes counter to McDavid's statistics and my own data.

In Texas, Stanley finds about as much variation as I do.[28] His seeming preference for [ɒ] in the text of the article[29] is offset by a larger number of instances of [ɑ] in his transcriptions.[30] He has few instances of [ɔ], but his field of investigation lay east of the critical line; my own Texas data, moreover, come largely from counties east of the line. Texas records of "The Young Rat" show [ɑ][31] and [ɔ].[32]

According to Kenyon,[33] the prevailing vowel in General American speech is [ɔ]; his opinion coincides completely with my notion of the critical line. Krapp's preference for [ɑ] and [ɒ][34] may be explained partly by his long residence in New York City, south of the critical line, and partly by his early residence in Cincinnati, which is very close to the line. Bloomfield's curious preference for [ɑ] in Central Western speech and his still more curious opinion that [ɔ] may carry a connotation of inferiority in some words[35] are inexplicable; all the factual data point the other way, and Bloomfield's implications about social levels have yet to be verified.

The comparative infrequence of [ɒ] in the data is noteworthy; in no word and in no region is it predominant; most of the time it is used by less than 20 per cent of the speakers. Those who use it evidently use it merely as an approximation of the more definitely realized vowels [ɑ] and [ɔ]. Despite Cable's article,[36] there is no evidence that it is used any more frequently by careful speakers than by careless. Nor is there evidence that any considerable number of speakers have adopted [ɒ] on the recommendation of the "prescriptive" phoneticians.[37] A greater use of [ɒ] can be shown in other classes of words, words of the type of *soft, long,* and *cross,* for example. Some geographical preference for [ɒ] before voiceless fricatives can probably be shown, but not for [ɒ] before [r].

In determining the critical line, therefore, we can disregard [ɒ], and center our attention on [ɑ] and [ɔ]. The location of the line, as I have worked it out in this article, must be taken as the statement of a hypothesis. To prove the hypothesis, to modify it, or to disprove it will require additional investigation; that investigation should be eminently worth making.

NOTES

1. I wish to express special thanks to the following professors and their associates: D. S. Beers, Middlebury College; W. E. Aiken and P. D. Carleton, University of Vermont; H. R. Anderson, Allegheny College; R. T. Oliver, Bucknell University; A. J. Tresidder, Madison College; K. R. Wallace, University of Virginia; J. B. Emperor, University of Tennessee; H. P. Constans, University of Florida; C. M. Wise, Louisiana State University; Elwood Griscom, University of Texas; G. F. Reynolds, University of Colorado; W. A. Cable, University of Arizona; L. S. Hultzén, then at the University of California at Los Angeles; R. K. Immel, University of Southern California; and Virgil Anderson, Stanford University.

2. Albert H. Marckwardt, "Middle English ŏ in American English of the Great Lakes Area," *Papers of the Michigan Academy* XXVI (1941), 561-571.

3. *Ibid.*, p. 567. Marckwardt's data cover *borrow, sorrow,* and *tomorrow;* the present similarity between *sorrow* and *sorry,* and the popular impression that the two are etymologically related, make it likely that recent developments of *sorry* have been by analogy with *sorrow.*

4. Thus far the line coincides almost exactly with the line shown by Kurath for *hoarse-horse* in his article "Mourning and Morning," *Studies for William A. Read,* ed. N. M. Caffee and T. A. Kirby (University, Louisiana, 1940), pp. 166-73. Note especially the map, p. 167. In southern New England, my line runs further west than Kurath's. Since Kurath is dealing with a different type of variation, it is not to be expected that the two lines will coincide for any great distance.

5. This is approximately the Pennsylvania frontier line of 1775, which can be deduced from S. H. Sutherland, *Population Distribution in Colonial America* (New York, 1936), map facing p. 158.

6. The location of the line is still in doubt here. Professor Tresidder suggests the location I have indicated; my own limited data suggest that it should be slightly further to the northwest.

7. A. C. Baugh, *A History of the English Language* (New York, 1935), map on p. 447.

8. Transcribed in *American Speech* V, 340, 348; VI, 398; IX, 140, 141; X, 213, XII, 58.

9. See *American Speech* V, 341; IX, 62.

10. O. F. Emerson, "The Ithaca Dialect," *Dialect Notes* I (1891), 140.

11. Gerald Crowningshield, "Dialect of Northeastern New York," *American Speech* VIII, no. 2, p. 44.

12. Transcribed in *American Speech* V, 346; VIII, no. 2, p. 58.

13. Transcribed in *American Speech* V, 352; VIII, no. 2, p. 57.

14. Transcribed in *American Speech* V, 352; XI, 79.

15. L. S. de Camp, "Scranton Pronunciation," *American Speech* XV, 369.

16. Argus Tresidder, "Notes on Virginia Speech," *American Speech* XVI, 117. Correspondence with Professor Tresidder, and with Professor Harold Wentworth of West Virginia University, has convinced me that my figures, are not high enough to be statistically reliable for this region.

17. E. F. Shewmake, *English Pronunciation in Virginia*, p. 30.

18. *American Speech* VI, 172.

19. *Ibid.,* XII, 289.

20. *Ibid.,* XII, 135-36.

21. *Ibid.,* V, 342.

22. R. I. McDavid, "Low-Back Vowels in the South Carolina Piedmont," *American Speech* XV, 146-47.

23. *American Speech* V, 354.

24. *Ibid.,* V, 345; IX, 297.

25. *Ibid.,* XIV, 124.

26. *Ibid.,* V, 346.

27. Katharine Wheatley, "Southern Standards," *American Speech* IX, 43.

28. Oma Stanley, "The Speech of East Texas," *American Speech* XI, 24.

29. *Ibid.,* XI, 26.

30. *Ibid.,* XI, 333-40.

31. *American Speech* V, 343, 350; XIV, 44.

32. *Ibid.,* V, 350; XIV, 45.

33. J. S. Kenyon, *American Pronunciation,* 8th ed., p. 181.

34. G. P. Krapp, *The Pronunciation of Standard English in America,* p. 58.

35. Leonard Bloomfield, "The Stressed Vowels of American English," *Language* XI, 108-09.

36. W. A. Cable. "The [ɒ] Vowel in American Pronunciation," *Quarterly Journal of Speech* XXV, 433.

37. For a typical recommendation of the prescriptive school see Letitia Raubicheck, *Improving Your Speech,* pp. 110-11.

The Pronunciation of Monosyllabic Form-Words in American English

LEE S. HULTZÉN

IN MOST of the recent English and American works on phonetics, there have been included lists of the "stressed and unstressed forms" or "strong and weak forms" of certain much-used monosyllables. The common characteristic of the words listed is that they have different, obscured, pronunciations when occurring unstressed in normal speech from what they have when stressed. The lists vary greatly in inclusiveness and in the number of variant forms given and especially in the extent to which the use of the various forms is explained.[1] The present essay deals in a comparatively extended manner with this phenomenon of obscured pronunciation.

By *form-words* I mean words which are necessary for building English sentences, without themselves ordinarily contributing any special meaning.[2] Their real function is grammatical and general rather than special, formal rather than meaningful. Many of them have equivalents in inflectional endings or enclitics or are dispensed with in some other languages.[3] All these words may on occasion be significant, some rarely, some often. Thus *a man* may be made to exclude the contrast specificity of *the man* or the abstraction of *man,* but it is very rarely so used. The *a* is usually put before *man* merely because formal English idiom calls for an article there. Pronouns actually have special meaning only when stressed. The word *most* is often significant, but as the form-word of the super-lative it is exactly equivalent to the unstressed suffix *-est,* and in "the most courageous" is ordinarily given no more attention than the last syllable of "the bravest." On the other hand, an unstressed form-word is not utterly devoid of meaning, any more than an unstressed inflectional suffix. The terms *significant* and *meaningful,* as here used, are to be interpreted as referring to a special rather than a general meaning.

It is the good intent of the present essay: 1—to make a tentative list of the frequently used monosyllabic form-words of English; 2—to present the list in two parts, the first part containing those words which are regularly pronounced with full vowels and no extraordinary modification of consonants, and the second part containing those words which are usually or frequently pronounced with obscured vowels or extraordinary modification of consonants, or which call for special comment; 3—to present all the respectable variant pronunciations of the words in the second part of the list; 4—to point out under what conditions each of these variant pronunciations is used; and 5—to give examples of the use of the various pronunciations.

1—The monosyllabic words included in the list are: all articles and a few vague determinatives; all personal pronouns except the *thou* type; all relative pronouns, and other simple connectives; all auxiliary and similar verbs; all common prepositions; a few adverbs, such as those of negation and comparison.[4] Words like *come*, which are often pronounced with obscured vowels but do not fit into any of these classes, are not included.[5]

There are 107 words in the list. All of them are of very frequent occurrence. One hundred of them fall within Thorndike's first 1000, 92 within his first 500.[6] All but two fall within the Faucett and Maki list of "essential" words, and 83 are within their primary list of the first 210.[7] All but 16 are in the list of 1000 words most frequently used in speaking recently compiled by Charles H. Voelker, and 61 are within his first 100, 39 within his first 50, and 22 within his first 25.[8] The least common words are pronouns included for consistency.

2—In the first part of the list, containing 39 words, no pronunciations are given. Nondialectal variations from lexical pronunciation which appear when these words are unstressed are assumed to be such as normally appear in any word spoken without stress. A few comments on individual words are contained in footnotes.

In the second part of the list the variant pronunciations of each word are given in the text, with detailed comment on their occurrence. The arrangement is alphabetical, without regard to orthographic contractions. There are 68 words in this part of the list, 65 of which are in Thorndike's first 500, 63 in Faucett and Maki's first 210, and 53 in Voelker's first 100, 36 in his first 50.[9]

3—The various pronunciations given for the words in the second part are those which occur in good American colloquial speech, formal as well as familiar. This is not to say that they are invariably used, even by the best speakers under the best circumstances of concentration of attention on communication rather than on diction. For the most part, however, they are the pronunciations used under the conditions specified.[10] They are the pronunciations which a foreigner should learn to use if he wishes to speak the language well. While they may not be invariably necessary for good speech, they are never inappropriate.

In indicating pronunciation I have followed in general the practice of *American Speech*. So far as the form-words are concerned, and the significant words as well in the RAT examples,[11] the dialect represented is General American, with the special qualification that |ɒ| is used where GA varies from |a| to |ɔ| with probably a statistical preference for |a|. Eastern American and Southern American dialect variations are tacitly recognized, no attempt being made to show, for example, |ə| where GA has |ɝ|.

I have used the term *full vowel* with reference to form-words with a somewhat specialized meaning. As applied to an unstressed word, i.e., one which would not be marked by a primary or secondary stress mark in ordinary phonetic transcription, it is to be taken as meaning acoustically recognizable as the vowel indicated although not so definite as that vowel under stress. In general it means shorter as well as slightly less definite than the stressed vowel, and specifically: |e| and |o|, so indicated, are without tendency to diphthongization, in contrast to the stressed vowels which may or may not be diphthongized and are indicated by |eɪ| and |ou| in nondialect examples. |i| and |u| are also without tendency to diphthongization, although the same symbols are used under stress where the tendency is often present. |aɪ| has a shorter glide, probably starting from a closer position.

What I call *partially obscured vowels* are |ɪ|, |ʊ|, and |ɝ|, occurring in unstressed syllables. This |ɪ| may vary from a vowel difficult to distinguish from unstressed |i| to one close to retracted |ɛ|.[12] It is to be noted that a final |ɪ| tends to |i| before an initial |ɪ| in the next word, as pointed out only under *the*. |ʊ| represents a similar back vowel of limited occurrence. As I use it, it may be the same as Jones's $|\partial_2|$.[13] $|\eth|$ may result from the obscuration of any centering diphthong as well as $|\eth|$, and may be very hard to distinguish from $|\eth|$ in unstressed syllables.

The *fully obscured vowel,* schwa, $|\partial|$, needs no comment. I include syllabic consonants in the same classification of obscuration, although possibly a distinction should be made. It is often difficult to distinguish $|\partial|$ from $|\Lambda|$ or $|\upsilon|$ in unstressed syllables, but the differentiation should sometimes be made.

A few words, such as *from,* may appear in unstressed position with a restressed vowel, $|\Lambda|$. I have indicated such possibilities without raising the question of the relative frequency of this sound. In a few words, such as *should,* a form may appear with no vowel and no conventional syllabic consonant. It may be that the syllable is lost, or it may be that the syllabic pulse differs from that generally recognized. I mention only the forms.[14]

4—The discussion of the conditions under which each variant pronunciation is most likely to occur is based on a considerable amount of material collected by students and myself over a number of years and over a wide geographical range, as well as on the observations of other phoneticians.[15] In no case is there any unchecked speculation.

Rhythmic stress pattern, as well as qualitative phonetic context, is taken into consideration, and in some cases semantic function. I use the term *stressed* to refer to a syllable which would be marked by a primary or secondary stress mark in ordinary phonetic transcription; *unstressed* to refer to a syllable that would not be so marked, ignoring more subtle distinctions. The terms *initial* and *final* refer to position in the phrase or breath group or intonational group, and when not qualified imply a pause preceding or following. I have in practice paid a great deal of attention to intonational pattern in determining stresses and phrase breaks. Many normal assimilations have been pointed out as well as unusual phonetic modification in form-words.[16]

The terms *easy speech* and *formal speech* are used to indicate variations within the range of good colloquial use, without suggesting either vulgar speech at one extreme or affectation at the other. But forms limited to very easy speech are mentioned only in footnotes. I use the designation *regular* to indicate that I believe the form occurs as indicated almost without exception; whereas *usual*, etc., imply that other forms as well as that indicated frequently occur under the conditions specified. *In set phrases* means in such frequently used patterns of words as "salt and pepper," "I guess so." While I am much less confident of the validity of some of the observations than of others, I have omitted the "It seems to me" and "So far as I have found" qualifications with which the pages should be sprinkled.

5—With a few exceptions, examples of the use of each form of each form-word in the second part of the list are given immediately after the discussion of that word. For a few words many examples are given, including exceptional uses. These examples are for illustration only and are not to be looked upon as evidence submitted to prove that such forms exist. If the validity of an example is to be questioned, the test must be on whether or not the phrase is real speech if so read, not on whether or not such reading is necessary for that succession of words. Sometimes careful attention must be paid to stresses.

Where possible, the first examples given in each case are from the story of "Grip the Rat" as recorded in the series of twenty-one phonograph records of American speech.[17] The records have been checked by three sets of students, with consideration of the published transcriptions where available. The examples as given do not always present typical pronunciations. In most cases I have stated in footnotes the number of uses of each form, all statements being rather tentative because the transcriptions are not perfectly reliable. These records are of reading, not colloquial speech, and it is to be expected they will show many less obscured instead of more obscured forms.[18]

After the examples from the RAT or where there are none, other examples are given, mostly those collected by students.[19] These examples are given in the dialect pattern in which the expressions were heard. I have made no attempt to edit them, and consequently a phrase used to illustrate one form may contain other form-words in exceptional as well as typical uses, and the casual conversational source introduces many form-words under stress.

In the examples the phonetic symbols representing form-words are spaced as individual words even when not syllabic, except where the two parts of a contraction are bound together by some special reciprocal influence. An *r* sound at the end of a word before a vowel is left as |ɚ| even when |ər| was heard.[20] Divisions between phrases are indicated by bars and imply more or less pause. Extra space without a bar indicates an intonational phrase break with practically no pause. Three dots indicate that part of the phrase is not transcribed but that the rhythm of the phrase extends beyond the transcribed part.

THE FORM-WORDS

FULL FORMS: DARE, DOWN, HERE, HERS, HOW, ITS, LEAST, LESS, LET, LIKE, MAY,[21] MIGHT, MINE, MORE, MOST, NEAR, NEED, OFF, ONE'S, OUGHT, OUR,[22] OURS,[22] PAST, ROUND, SINCE, THEIR, THEIRS, THOUGH, THROUGH, TOWARD(S), UP, WHERE,[23] WHICH,[23] WHILE,[23] WHOM, WHOSE, WHY,[23] WITH,[24] YOURS.

OBSCURED AND VARIANT FORMS:

A—|ə| is regular.[25]

  ˈwʌns ðɛɚ wəz ə ˈjʌŋ ˈræt RAT

  ə ˈmæn | ə ˈgʌn | ənd ə ˈfaɪt

AM—The usual position is immediately after *I*, and the form nonsyllabic |m|, i.e., |aɪm|.[26] |əm| or |m̩| is not uncommon after *I*, especially in somewhat formal speech. The same forms occur before *I*, |əm| being most common and |m| least. |əm|, or sometimes |æm|, is usual in the rare cases where there are other words between *I* and *am*. |əm| is usual initially, but all the other forms occur. |æm| is regular finally, and in such expressions as "I am so."[27]

  aɪ m ˈnɒt ˈsɝtn̩ RAT

  aɪ əm ə ˈfrɛʃmən

  aɪ ᵊm ˈnɒt ˈteɪkɪŋ ɪt

  ˈnaʊ m̩ aɪ ˈfɪnɪʃt

  ˈhaʊ m aɪ ˈduɪŋ

  ju ˈnoʊ ðət ˈaɪ əz ˈtʃɛɚmən əm rɪˈspɒnsɪbl̩

  əm aɪ ˈraɪt

  m̩ ˈaɪ tʊ ˈbi ˈðɛɚ

m aɪ ˈvɛrɪ ˈleɪt

aɪ ˈhoʊp ˈaɪ æm

ˈwaɪ aɪ æm ˈtu ə ˈɡʊd ˈtʃɛsˈpleɚ

AN—|ən| is almost always used. |n̩| is occasionally used after alveolar consonants, especially |t|.

. . . ˈθɪŋk fɚ ən ˈɑʊɚ RAT

ɪt s ən ɪntəˈlɛktʃʊəl ˈθɪŋ | nɒt n̩ ɪˈmoʊʃənəl wʌn

AND—The common forms are: |n̩|, |ən|, |n̩d|, |ənd|, and |ænd|, the first two occurring about four times as often as the others.[28] |n̩| seems to occur in all phonetic contexts except after |tʃ| and |dʒ|. |ən| and |ənd| are regular after the affricates, usual initially,[29] and common after nasals and after vowels except in set phrases, where |n̩| prevails. |n̩| and |n̩d| are usual after those alveolars and prepalatals which have not already been mentioned, except in some consonant clusters. |n̩| and |ən| are usual before consonants, especially alveolars and prepalatals. |n̩d| and |ənd| are somewhat more common before vowels, except in set phrases, and common before |h|. It is difficult to decide what the form is before |θ| and |ð|, where the dentalized stop and fricative tend to merge into a composite sound.[30] |m̩| is often used before or after or especially between labials, and |ŋ| similarly next to velars; but many people avoid these assimilations. |ænd|, or sometimes |æn| before alveolars, is occasionally used initially, especially in formal speaking.

ɪt s ˈsoʊ ˈnaɪs n̩ ˈsnʌɡ ˈhɪɚ RAT[31]

. . . ˈrum ən ˈboɚd fɚ ðəm ˈɔl RAT[31]

ðɪ ˈjʌŋ ˈræt ˈkɔft | ən ˈlʊkt ˈwaɪz RAT[31]

ˈhæf ˈɪn | ən ˈhæf ˈɑʊt RAT[31]

ənd ˈɔl ðə ˈræts ˈhɛɚ . . . RAT[31]

ənd (h)i ˈkɔt ˈsaɪt əv ə ˈjʌŋ ˈræt RAT[31]

ŋ ˈkɔt ˈsaɪt . . . RAT[31]

ˈbroʊk n̩ ˈbæk[32]

aɪ v bɪn ˈweɪtɪŋ fɚ ˈtu n̩ ə ˈhæf ˈɑʊɚz

ˈteɪk n ˈɡɪv ɪz ˈhɪz ˈmɒto

wɪ ˈhæv ɪt fɚ ˈlʌntʃ ən ˈdɪnɚ

ˈpro ən ˈkɑn

hɚ ˈvɔɪs wəz ˈkaɪnd ə ˈʃrɪl n̩d ˈhɔɚʃ

n̩d ˈnɑʊ ˈmɒt

ˈdʒɔɚdʒ ənd ˈaɪ ˈwɛnt

ˈsɔlt m̩ ˈpɛpɚ

ˈteɪk ˈðæt wən ˈʌp | m̩ ˈbrɪŋ ðə ˈʌðɚ ˈdaʊn

æn ˈnɑʊ | ˈleɪdiz ənd ˈdʒɛnt̩lmən

ARE—|ɚ| is usual. An r-less |ə| is common after a word ending in |ɚ|,³³ or before |r|, and often occurs not near a dissimilative r. In interrogative construction before a pronoun there may be no sound to represent *are*, especially in easy speech. After *they, we, you*, when not final, the |ɚ| usually combines with the vowel of the pronoun to form a centering diphthong, although it may remain a separate syllable.³⁴ |aɚ| is common initially and regular finally.

əv ˈkoɚs ju ɚ ˈkʌmɪŋ RAT³⁵

huz ɚ ˈðiz

ˈðɛɚ ə æt ˈlist ˈfaɪv

ˈsɪks əv ðəm ə ˈræðɚ ˈsɪlɪ

ə ˈju ˈkɪdz ˈgoɪŋ tə ˈɒɚdɚ

wɛn jə ˈgoʊn tə ðə ˈneɪvi

aɚ ju ˈgoʊɪŋ ˈnɑʊ

ˈhi z nɒt ˈgoɪŋ | bət ˈwi aɚ

ˈhaʊ aɚ ju

haʊ ɚ ˈju

ˈhaʊ ə ˈju

AS—|əz| is usual. |z| is common after the voiced and |s| after the voiceless nonsibilant alveolars in the last part of the *as(so)—as* formula, and infrequently used elsewhere, even after vowels. |æz|, with a somewhat obscured vowel, is often used, especially in somewhat careful speech.

ən ˈlʊkt ˈwaɪz | əz ˈjuʒʊəlɪ RAT³⁶

əz aɪ əv ˈsɛd | ɪt s əz ˈgʊd z ˈnu

ɪt wəz əz ˈflæt s ə ˈpæŋˌkeɪk

æz faɚ əz ˈaɪ ˈnoʊ

AT—|ət| is usual. |æt| is regular finally or before a final obscured pronoun, and common initially, especially when the next syllable is unstressed.

. . . tə ˈlʊk ət ðə ˈlɔft RAT³⁷

æt ˈwʌns ðə ˈtʃif . . . RAT³⁷
ɪt ˈtʊk ˈnou ˈtaɪm ət ˈɔl
æt ʍɑt ˈtaɪm dɪd ɪt ˈkʌm
ˈhum ɚ ju ˈlʊkɪŋ æt
ʃi ˈθru ɪt æt ɪm

BE—|bi| is usual. |bɪ| is often used before a stressed syllable.³⁸
ʍɛɚ ðɛɚ wʊd bi ˈrum ən ˈboɚd . . . RAT³⁹
ʃi ˈwɒnts tə bi ə ˈdænsɚ
ɪt ļ bi ɪnkənˈvinjənt | bət ˈaɪ l bɪ ˈðɛɚ

BEEN—|bɪn| (or |bɛn| in some regions) is the usual American
form in all positions.⁴⁰
ˈʍɑt həv ju bɪn ˈʌp ˈtu
aɪ v bɪn ˈwʌndərɪŋ ʍɛɚ ˈju v bɪn

BUT—|bət| is regular in all positions.⁴¹
bət ˈsɛd ˈnʌθɪŋ RAT⁴²
wi kən du ˈnʌθɪŋ bət ˈhoup
aɪ v sin ˈnou wʌn bət ˈju
bᵊt ɒn ðɪ ˈʌðɚ ˈhænd . . .

BY—|baɪ| is usual. |bə| is often used before a stressed syllable be-
ginning with a consonant, especially in set phrases.
. . . ˈhɒntɪd baɪ ˈræts RAT⁴³
aɪ ˈpʊt ɪt baɪ ðə ˈdoɚ
baɪ ðə ˈweɪ | ʍɑt . . .
ˈtu bə ˈtu ðe ˈpæst

CAN—|kən| is the most common form. |kņ| is common before |t|
and |d|, and sometimes used before other consonants. |kŋ| is often
used before velars. |kæn| is regular finally and not uncommon ini-
tially. The contracted negative is |kænt|.
wi ˈkænt ˈweɪt fɚ ju . . . RAT
ˈhau kən aɪ ˈgɛt wʌn
kən ʃi ˈkʌm
aɪ kņ ˈdu ɪt ˈizɪlɪ
ˈnɒt əf ˈaɪ kņ ˈhɛlp ɪt
ˈhi kŋ ˈgɛt ɪt
du ˈju ˈθɪŋk ʃi kæn
kæn ɪt ˈrɪlɪ bi ˈtru

COULD—|kəd| is usual. It is occasionally reduced to |kd|. |kʊd| is regular finally and sometimes used between unstressed syllables.

ᴍɒt kəd 'aɪ əv 'dʌn

kəd ju 'tɛl mɪ ðə 'taɪm

'ᴍɛ˞ kd aɪ 'gɛt ə'nʌðə˞

'aɪ kᵊd əv 'gɔn ɪf 'ʃi kʊd

hi kʊd əv dʌn 'bɛtə˞ ðn̩ 'ðæt

DID—|dɪd| is usual in any position and regular finally. As an interrogative auxiliary, especially after the stressed interrogative word, the form is often |d| or |d:|⁴⁴ except in formal speech.

dɪd i 'faɪnd ɪt 'ðɛ˞

'ᴍɛ˞ dɪdʒʊ⁴⁵ 'hɪ˞ 'ðæt

hi gɒt 'moə˞ ðən 'aɪ dɪd

'haʊ dʒʊ⁴⁵ 'du ɪt

dʒə⁴⁵ 'ɛvə˞ 'hɪ˞ sʌtʃ 'gɔɪŋz 'an

haʊ d: 'ju 'noʊ

'ᴍaɪ d: 'aɪ 'luz ɪt

DO—|də| is usual before consonants, |dʊ| before vowels. |d| is occasionally used before unstressed *you*, especially in easy speech.⁴⁶ |du| is regular finally and also, more often stressed, in the echo interrogative with unstressed pronoun, but not in the similar contrast construction with stressed pronoun.⁴⁷ The contracted negative forms are: |doʊnt|, |dont|, and rarely |dənt| or even |dn̩t|.

ju 'doʊnt 'θɪŋk ɪt s 'sɛɪf | 'du ju RAT⁴⁸

'aɪ ˌdon 'noʊ RAT⁴⁸

'ᴍɛ˞ də ju 'baɪ 'ðɪs

'haʊ dʊ ɔl əv ðəm 'fɪt

haʊ d ju 'du ɪt

'ju 'ɜn 'moə˞ ðən 'aɪ du

'aɪ dont 'laɪk ɪt | də 'ju

DOES—|dəz| is usual. It is sometimes reduced to |dz|, especially in easy speech, and often to |z| after voiced and |s| after voiceless sounds when following an interrogative. |dʌz| is regular finally, and before the unstressed pronoun of an echo interrogative but usually stressed there.⁴⁹

dəz hi 'meɪk ðəm hɪm'sɛlf

'ᴍɛ˞ dᵊz ɪt 'goʊ

ˈmaɪ dz ɪt ˈhæf tə bi ˈdʌn
ˈhaʊ z ɪt ˈwɝk
ˈmɒt s ɪt ˈmin
aɪ ˈnoʊ ˈʃi dʌz
ɪt ˈdʌz n̩t ˈɔlwɪz ˈstap | ˈdʌz ɪt

FOR—|fɚ| is the most common form. |fə| is probably usual before
|r|, and sometimes used after words ending in |ɚ|, or even next to
a strong stress when there is no nearby *r* sound. |fɔɚ| is common
initially for the adverb, regular finally and whenever *for* comes after
the word it goes with, and usual before a final obscured pronoun.

. . . tə ˈθɪŋk fɚ ən ˈaʊɚ RAT[50]
ˈnoʊ wʌn l ˈɛvɚ ˈkɛɚ fɚ ju | ɪf ju . . . RAT[50]
fɔɚ ʃi ˈkʊd n̩t ˈbɛɚ tə ˈsi . . . RAT[50]
fɚ ˈmɒt ˈrizn̩
ˈmɛɚ də ju ˈgoʊ fə ˈroʊzɪz
ˈðɪz ɚ fə ˈju
ju ˈkænt ˈfɪʃ fə ˈbæs ɪn ˈmaɚtʃ
ˈhi ɪz ˈɔl aɪ ˈæsk foɚ
wɑt ˈaɪ ˈlʊk fɔɚ ɪn ə ˈpleɪ | ɪz ˈplɑt
ˈgɛt maɪ ˈbʊk fɔɚ mi | ˈwɪl jə

FROM—|frəm| is usual, sometimes further reduced to |frm̩|. |frɒm|
(or with restressed vowel |frʌm|) is usual when after the word it
goes with, especially finally, and before a final obscured pronoun.

frəm ˈtaɪm tə ˈtaɪm . . .
aɪ m goɪŋ əˈweɪ frəm ˈhɪɚ . . .
frm̩ ˈnaʊ ˌɒn ɪt l̩ bi ˈdɪfrənt
aɪ ˈnoʊ ˈmɛɚ ɪt s frʌm
ðə ˈbʊk i ˈgɒt ɪt frɒm   ɪz ˈmaɪn
aɪ ˈgɒt ˈɪt frʌm ɪm

HAD—|əd| and |d| are the usual forms, the latter after pronouns,
interrogatives, and relatives ending in a vowel,[51] and sometimes
after other words ending in a vowel. |həd| is usual initially and
occasionally used in other positions. |hæd| is regular finally and is
the more common form initially in even slightly formal speech.[52]

ən ˈsɛd ðe əd ˈfaʊnd . . . RAT[53]
ðə ˈbout əd ˈɔlrɛdɪ ˈseɪld
hi əd ˈgɔn

hi d 'ɔlwɪz hæd 'ðæt

ðe d 'noʊn ə 'mæn hu d 'bɪn 'ðɛ˞

ði 'oʊld 'saʊ d hæd n̩'ʌð˞ 'lɪt˞

həd i 'sin ɪt

hæd aɪ 'bɛt˞ 'goʊ

aɪ 'noʊ wɪ hæd

HAS—|əz| is usual after sibilants, |z| after other voiced sounds, |s| after other voiceless sounds.[54] But |z| is sometimes used after |z|, i.e., the sound is lengthened, or |ʒ|, and |s| after |s| or |ʃ|. |əz| is sometimes used instead of |z| or |s|, but rarely after pronouns. |həz| is usual initially and occasionally used elsewhere. |hæz| is regular finally, and not uncommon initially, especially in formal speech.

ə 'briz əz bɪn 'bloɪŋ 'ʌp

ðə 'sʌn z 'ɔlrɛdɪ 'sɛt

hi z 'dʒʌst 'rɛd ɪt

ðə gə'raʒ z ɔl'rɛdɪ bɪn 'ʃʌt

ðə 'truθ s 'nɛv˞ bɪn 'told

'ðɪs 'brʌʃ s bɪn 'bɜnt 'oʊv˞

həz ʃi 'kʌm 'jɛt

'nid aɪ 'seɪ | ðə 'bɜd həz 'floʊn

aɪ θɪŋk 'ʃi hæz

HAVE—|əv| is usual after consonants, and |v| after vowels, especially after pronouns and interrogatives ending in vowels.[55] |ə| is occasionally used between consonants, especially in easy speech. |həv| is usual initially, but |əv| after a very slight phrase break,[56] and occasionally used elsewhere in slightly formal speech. |hæv| is regular finally, except after could, should, etc., where |əv| is often used, and not uncommon initially.[57]

ðə 'bɔɪz əv hæd 'θri

ju kʊd əv 'traɪd

aɪ dont θɪŋk 'ɛnɪ v 'kʌm

'ʍɛ˞ v ðe 'bɪn

f 'aɪ d faʊnd 'aʊt 'sun˞ | aɪ d ə 'dʌn ɪt

həv ðe 'bɪn 'hɪ˞ 'lɔŋ

'ɔl ðə 'gɜlz ɪn ðə 'ʃoʊ əv gɔn 'hoʊm

'ðeɪ v 'spɛnt 'mo˞ ðən 'wi hæv

dəz hi 'θɪŋk hi 'ʃʊd əv

HE—|i| and |hi| are the principal forms, |hi| being usual initially, even after a very slight phrase break, and regular finally, and |i| perhaps slightly more common medially. |hɪ| is common initially, especially before a stressed vowel, but not with the verb forms |d|, |z|, |l|. |ɪ| is occasionally used medially before a consonant of a stressed syllable.

hi wʊd 'ænsɚ RAT⁵⁸
ənd i wəz nɒt ɪg'zæktlɪ 'aʊt'saɪd ɪt RAT⁵⁸
hɪ 'stʊd 'dʒʌst 'baɪ ɪt RAT⁵⁸
'ʍɛɚ 'ɪz hi
aɪ 'noʊ i 'dɪd
hɪ 'sɛd hi d 'goʊ ɪf i 'kʊd
'ɪz n̩t ɪ 'sɪlɪ

HER—|ɚ| is usual. |hɚ| is regular initially, and sometimes used in other positions, especially between unstressed syllables.⁵⁹

'stæmpɪŋ wɪð ɚ 'fʊt RAT⁶⁰
'gɪv ɚ ɚ 'bʊk
'ʍɛɚ dʒu 'si ɚ
hɚ ɪn'tɛnʃənz wɚ 'gʊd
ðe 'kærɪd hɚ ə'weɪ

HIM—|ɪm| is usual. |hɪm| is not uncommon, especially between unstressed syllables.⁶¹

ʍɛn'ɛvɚ ðɪ 'ʌðɚ 'ræts 'æskt ɪm RAT⁶²
aɪ 'dont 'noʊ ɪm
'gɪv ɪt tʊ hɪm ən 'goʊ ə'weɪ

HIS—|ɪz| is usual medially. |hɪz| is regular initially, and usual finally, and sometimes used medially, especially next to unstressed syllables.

sɛd ɪz 'ænt RAT⁶³
'ðʌs ðə 'ʃɚkɚ hæd hɪz 'du RAT⁶³
'ʍɒt 'hæpənd tə ɪz 'pɛn
hɪz 'dɒtɚ wəz 'dʒʌst 'hɪɚ
. . . 'ðiz ɚ hɪz
ðə dɪs'kʌvərɪ əv hɪz mɪs'fɔɚtʃən . . .

I—|aɪ| is usual. A form without glide, |ɑ| rather than |a|, is often used before the nonsyllabic auxiliary verb forms and sometimes

before other auxiliary verb forms and in set phrases. |ə| is oc-
casionally used in these positions and where *I* occurs the second
time in a phrase.

    aɪ 'θɪŋk a l ˌgoʊ tə'mɒro RAT⁶⁴

    'ʍɑt əm aɪ tə 'du

    ɑ d əv 'dʌn ɪt maɪ'sɛlf | ɪf aɪ d bɪn 'eɪbl̩

    ɑ 'wɪʃ aɪ 'hæd ə'nʌðɚ

    aɪ 'no ə 'wont 'laɪk ɪt

IF—|ɪf| is usual. The vowel may be extremely short, |'f|, and may
be reduced to |ᵊf| except after front vowels, or even to |f| in easy
speech.

    ɪf hi wʊd 'laɪk . . . RAT⁶⁵

    ɪt s 'stɪl 'rɔ ˈf ɪt s 'oʊnlɪ 'kʊkt 'ðæt 'lɔŋ

    'ɑ ᵊf ɪt 'oʊnlɪ 'wʊd

    aɪ l 'si f ɪt 'wɝks

IN—|ɪn| is usual. |n̩| is not uncommon after alveolar consonants,
especially |t| and |d|.

    'steɪ ɪn ɪz 'hoʊl ɪn ðə 'graʊnd | ɔɚ go 'aʊt ɪn ðə 'lɔft RAT⁶⁶

    bət ɪn əz 'mʌtʃ əz ju 'kænt

    'ɔl n̩ 'ɔl | aɪ 'laɪk ɪt

IS—|ɪz| is usual after sibilants, |z| after other voiced sounds, and
|s| after other voiceless sounds.⁶⁷ |z| and |s| are sometimes used after
sibilants except affricates. |ɪz| is usual initially and regular finally
and occasionally used in |z| and |s| positions.⁶⁸

    ɪt s 'soʊ 'naɪs n̩ 'snʌg 'hɪɚ RAT

    'dʒɔrdʒ ɪz 'kʌmɪŋ

    'taɪm z 'ʌp

    ðɪs 'kæp s 'tu 'smɔl

    'hɪz z 'gɔn

    ðə 'skwɒʃ s 'gʊd

    ɪz 'ðɪs 'soʊ

    aɪ 'θɪŋk i ɪz

    'tɑm ɪz ə 'naɪs 'bɔɪ

IT—|ɪt| is usual.⁶⁹ |t| is sometimes used before stressed *is, isn't,*
and before stressed or unstressed, affirmative or negative, forms of
was, will, and *would;* rarely before unstressed *is.*

    ɪt wəz ə 'fɒgɪ 'deɪ RAT⁷⁰

ɪt s ˈnaɪs | bət ʍɑt ˈɪz ɪt

ˈʍaɪ t ˈɪz ɳt ˈɪɔst | ˈæftɚ ˈɔl

JUST—|dʒʌst| and |dʒʌs| are usual, the latter before alveolar and dental and sometimes other consonants. |dʒəst| and |dʒəs| are common when a strong stress follows either immediately or with an intervening unstressed syllable.

ə ˈbɪt   dʒʌs tə ˈmeɪk ˈʌp maɪ ˈmaɪnd RAT[71]

aɪ d dʒʌst bɪˈgʌn ˈɪt

dʒəst ˈweɪt   ən ju ļ ˈsi

ˈɪt wəz dʒəs ˈtɛɚɪbļ

ME—|mi| is used in all positions. |mɪ| is especially common after *give*, whether *to* is used or not and whether medial or final, and often used in similar constructions, and not uncommon in other positions.

ˈbrɪŋ mi ən ˈæpļ

hi ˈdɪd ɳt ˈsi mi

ˈgɪv ɪt tu mɪ

ˈʍɛn dɪd ju ˈsi mɪ ˈlæst

MUST—|məst| is usual before vowels and glide consonants, |məs| before other consonants. |mʌst| is regular finally, if rare. The negative is regularly |mʌsɳt| or |mʌsɳ|, usually stressed.

wi məs ˈliv ˈðɪs ˈpleɪs RAT[72]

ju məst rɪˈgrɛt ɪt ˈdɪplɪ

ˈiðɚ ˈaɪ məs ˈdu ɪt | ɚ ˈju mʌst

MY—|maɪ| is usual. |mə| is occasionally used, especially in easy speech, before consonants, and |mɪ| rarely before vowels.[73]

dʒʌs tə ˈmeɪk ˈʌp maɪ ˈmaɪnd RAT[74]

ˈbrɪŋ mi maɪ ˈhæt

aɪ ˈdont ˈlaɪk mə ˈnu ˈbʊk

hau du ju ˈlaɪk mɪ ˈounlɪ ɑɚˈtɪstɪk əˈtɛmpt

NO—|no| is usual. |nə| is sometimes used before a stress, apparently often in set phrases.[75]

ju hæv no moɚ ˈmaɪnd ðən . . . RAT[76]

ɪt no ˈlɔŋgɚ ˈwɝks

ˈθɪŋk nə ˈmoɚ əv ɪt

NOR—|nɚ| is usual, except that |nɔɚ| is rather more common

initially after a pause and a great many of the occurrences are in that position.

'niðɚ 'ʃi nɚ 'aɪ 'ænsɚd ɪt

'hi 'ɪz ṇt 'gouɪŋ nɚ əm 'aɪ

nɔɚ 'wud aɪ ɪf ə 'kud

NOT—|nɒt| is regular except with auxiliary verbs, but not much used unstressed. In the negative forms of auxiliary verbs ending in a consonant, the regular form is |ṇt|, so: |kudṇt|, |dɪdṇt|, |dʌzṇt|, |hædṇt|, |hæzṇt|, |hævṇt|, |ɪzṇt|, |maɪtṇt|, |mʌsṇt|, |nidṇt|, |ɔtṇt|, |ʃudṇt|, |jusṇt|, |wɒzṇt|, |wudṇt|; but without syllabic value in |kænt|, |ʃænt|, and |wount|. With auxiliaries ending in a vowel the form is nonsyllabic |nt|: |aɚnt|, |dɛɚnt|, |dount|, |meɪnt|, |wɜnt|.[77] The final |t| of the contracted form is sometimes lost before |n| or other alveolar consonants or even other consonants, more with some verbs than with others.[78]

ənd i wəz nɒt ɪg'zæktlɪ 'aut'saɪd ɪt RAT[79]

'aɪ ˌdon 'nou RAT[79]

'ʃi z nat ðə 'bɛst əv ðə 'lat

OF—|əv| is usual. |ə| is used in *o'clock*, etc., and is usual in expressions of quantity, and is not uncommon elsewhere before consonants, especially in easy speech. |ɒv| (or with restressed vowel |ʌv|) is regular finally and common before a final obscured pronoun.

. . . 'bleɪd əv 'græs RAT[80]

ðə 'ræts 'krɔld 'aut ə ðɛɚ 'houlz RAT[80]

ðɪ aɪ'dɪə ɒv ɪt RAT[80]

əv 'hum wɚ ju 'spikɪŋ

aɪ l 'nɛvɚ 'hɪɚ ðə 'læst əv ɪt

. . . ə 'paund ə 'piz

ʍət 'wɜ ju 'θɪŋkɪŋ ɒv

'ðæt s ʍat aɪ 'θɪŋk ɑv ɪm

ON—|ɒn| is almost always used, even in easy speech. |ən| is sometimes used in set phrases, rarely elsewhere.

wɪð 'wʌn 'ɛnd ɒn ðə 'floɚ RAT[81]

ɒn ðɪ 'ʌðɚ 'hænd . . .

. . . 'wʌn ən 'tɔp əv ðɪ 'ʌðɚ

ONE(S)—|wən| is regular after *this* and *that* and common after similar words and stressed adjectives. |wʌn| is usual in other unstressed positions. Similarly |wənz|, rarely |wʌnz|.[82]

ˈnou wʌn ‖ ˈɛvɚ . . . RAT

ju ˈteɪk ˈðɪs wən n̩ ˈaɪ ‖ ˌteɪk ˈðæt wən

aɪ no ˈwʌn əv ðəm | bət nɑt ðɪ ˈʌðɚ wən

aɪ v ˈnɛvɚ ˈsin wʌn

ˈʍaɪt wənz ɚ ˈbɛtɚ

OR—|ɚ| is usual. |ɔɚ| is often used initially, not often elsewhere except in formal speech.[83]

. . . ˈjɛs ɚ ˈnou ˈiðɚ RAT[84]

ɔɚ go ˈaut ɪn ðə ˈlɔft RAT[84]

ˈkʌm ˈnau ɚ ˈɛnɪ ˈtaɪm

ɚ əf ju d ˈræðɚ . . .

ju ˈdu ət | ɔɚ ˈaɪ ˈwɪl

PER—|pɚ| is regular.

wi ˈluz ˈtu pɚ ˈsɛnt pɚ ˈænəm

SHALL—|ʃəl|, or |ʃl̩|, is usual except after *I* or *we,* where |l̩|, or occasionally |əl|, is more usual in any but formal speech.[85] Occasionally |əl| or |l̩| or |l| is used when there are qualifying words between the pronoun and the auxiliary. |ʃæl| is regular finally and occasionally used initially. The contracted negative is |ʃænt|.

aɪ ˈθɪŋk ɑ l ˌgou təˈmɔro RAT

ʃəl wɪ ˈkʌm

ˈʍɛɚ ʃl̩ aɪ ˈfaɪnd ɪt

wi l ˈθɪŋk ɪt ˈouvɚ

wi ˈprɑbəblɪ l ˈkʌm

aɪ ˈθɪŋk ˈaɪ ʃæl

ʃæl wɪ ˈgou ˈnau

SHE—|ʃi| and |ʃɪ| occur with about equal frequency. |ʃi| may be more common between unstressed syllables and with the nonsyllabic forms of auxiliary verbs, and |ʃɪ| more common next to a stressed syllable.

fɔɚ ʃi ˈkud n̩t ˈbɛɚ . . . RAT[86]

ʍɛɚ ˈɪz ʃi

hu ˈɪz ʃɪ

ʃi wəz 'hɪɚ | bət ʃɪ 'wɛnt
ʃi d 'laɪk ɪt . . .

SHOULD—|ʃəd|, occasionally reduced to |ʃd|, is probably the most common form, but |ʃud| seems to be used more than the corresponding form of other auxiliaries. |d| is common after *I* and *we*.[87] |ʃud| is regular finally.

    ʍɛðɚ hi ʃəd 'steɪ ɪn ɪz 'houl RAT[88]

    ʃəd aɪ 'teɪk səm 'moɚ

    aɪ ʃt[89] 'houp 'sou

    ju ʃud 'bi 'moɚ 'kwaɪət

    baɪ 'ðɛn wi d bɪ 'dɛd

    aɪ d 'ræðɚ 'nɑt

    a 'dount 'nou ʍaɪ 'aɪ ʃud

SO—|sə| and |so| are the regular forms, |sə| being more common before a stressed syllable. |so| is regular finally, but rare unstressed.

    . . . 'ræt so 'kould 'blʌdɪd RAT[90]

    aɪ m 'nɒt sə 'ʃuɚ əv 'ðæt

    'waɪ ɪt s so əb'sɝd . . .

    aɪ 'houp so

SOME—|səm|, or |sm̩|, is usual in the meaning "an indefinite number or amount of," except that |sʌm| is regular finally. |sə| is very often used before |m|.[91] |sʌm| is usual, sometimes |səm| before a stress, wherever *some* may occur unstressed with any other meaning, including the partitive use with *of*.

    sə 'mɛn 'keɪm . . . RAT[92]

    aɪ əv səm 'buks ɪn ðə 'kɑɚ

    'hæv sm̩ 'kændɪ

    . . . ɪf ju 'wɒnt sʌm

    aɪ l 'teɪk sə 'mɔɚ 'kæbɪdʒ

    ʃi z ɔl'rɛdɪ 'broukən sʌm əv 'hɪz

SUCH—|sʌtʃ| is used in all positions. |sətʃ| is common before a stressed syllable.

    sʌtʃ ə'trɑsɪtɪz ɚ . . .

    ɪt s sʌtʃ ə 'fɑɚs

    'ʍɛɚ d ju 'gɛt sətʃ 'ɔfḷ 'kʌlɚz

THAN—|ðən| and |ðņ| (with dentalized |n|) are usual. |ən|, |ņ|, and |n| are sometimes used immediately after the comparative, especially in easy speech.

   ... no moɚ 'maɪnd ðən ə 'bleɪd əv 'græs RAT[93]

   ɪt wəz 'bɪgɚ ðən aɪ 'θɔt

   ɪt s 'betɚ ðn̩ ə 'smɔlɚ wʌn

   ɪt wəz 'betɚ ən 'ɛvɚ

   'ju ˌnou 'moɚ n 'aɪ du

THAT—|ðət| is regular.[94]

   so ðət ðə 'pleɪs ... RAT[95]

   ðe 'θɔt ɪt 'ɒd ðət ɪt wəz nɒt 'hɔntɪd ... RAT[95]

   aɪ 'wɪʃ ðət 'sʌm wən wʊd

THE—|ðə| is usual before consonants, and |ðɪ| before vowels. |ðə| is sometimes used before back vowels. |ðɪ| is often used before |j|. |ði| is often used before |ɪ|.[96]

   ɪn ðə 'naɪt ... RAT[97]

   ... ðɪ 'oʊld 'ræt RAT[97]

   ... ðə 'ʌðɚ 'ræts ... RAT[97]

   ... ðɪ 'jʌŋ 'ræt ... RAT[97]

   ði 'ɪndɪən 'læŋgwɪdʒ

THEM—|ðəm|, or |ðm̩|, is regular. |əm|, or often |m̩| after labials, is used for the same meaning, especially in easy speech.[98] |ðem| is unusual, even finally.

   'wʌn əv ðəm 'hæpənd ... RAT[99]

   ... 'jʌŋ 'ræt 'wɒtʃt əm RAT[99]

   aɪ 'dount 'laɪk ðəm

   ɪt s 'izɪ ə'nʌf fɚ ðm̩ tə bɪ 'lɔst

   'θrou əm ə'weɪ

   'kip m̩ fɔɚ mɪ

THERE—|ðɚ| is common medially, and initially before a stressed syllable. |ðɛɚ| is common initially and after an initial unstressed syllable, and often elsewhere, especially between unstressed syllables.[100]

   'wʌns ðɚ wəz ə 'jʌŋ 'ræt RAT[101]

   ʌɛɚ ðɛɚ wʊd bɪ 'rum ... RAT[101]

   aɪ 'nou ðɚ 'ɑɚ

   ðɚ 'ɪz n̩t ˌɛnɪ 'tʃæns 'nɑu

ðɛɚ ʃd bi ə 'lɔ ə'gɛnst ɪt

aɪ 'sɔ ðət ðɛɚ wəz 'nou . . .

THEY—|ðe| is regular. In the contracted form with *are,* the vowel is lowered, monosyllabic |ðɛɚ|.

ən ʍən ðe 'sɛd RAT[102]

fɚ ðe ɚ 'nɑt 'laɪklɪ . . .

aɪ 'nou ðɛɚ 'nɑt

TILL—|tɪl| is usual. |tl̩| is common, especially in easy speech, when not initial.

. . . frm̩ 'nau tɪl 'dumz'deɪ

hi əl 'nɑt bɪ 'hɪɚ tl̩ 'wɛnzdɪ

TO—|tə| and |tu| are the usual forms. As the sign of the infinitive |tə| is much more common before consonants, and |tu| perhaps slightly more common before vowels. As a preposition |tə| is somewhat more common before consonants, and |tu| much more common before vowels; |tu| is usual in the midst of several unstressed syllables. |tu| is usual finally and before a final obscured pronoun.

ɪf hi wud 'laɪk tə ˌkʌm 'aut . . . RAT[103]

tə 'sɝtʃ fɚ ə 'nu 'houm RAT[103]

. . . 'bæk tə maɪ 'houl RAT[103]

hi 'sɛd tu ɪm'sɛlf RAT[103]

ɪt s 'izɪ tə 'lɝn

ɪt s 'taɪm tu 'it

'gɛt tə ðə 'pɔɪnt

ɪt 'kʌmz tu ðə 'seɪm 'θɪŋ

'brɪŋ ɪt tu 'ælɪs

ɪt s 'ʌp tə 'ju tu 'sɪŋk ɚ 'swɪm

'hu ʃəl aɪ 'spik tu

'gɪv ɪt tu mɪ

US—|əs| is usual. |s| is usual in *let us* (*let's*) except in very formal speech. |ʌs| is sometimes used finally.

. . . 'weɪt fɚ ju tə 'dʒɔɪn əs RAT

hi 'ænsɚd əs wɪð ə 'smaɪl

'lɛt s 'gou

. . . ðe dɪs'kʌvɚd ʌs

USED (*to*)—|jus| or |jus| is usual; rarely |just|. The contracted negative, not at all common, is |jusn̩t| or |jusn̩|.

ˈwi jʊs tə ˈbɔɪl əm

ˈtam jus tə ˈhæv wʌn

WAS—|wəz|, occasionally reduced to |wz|, is usual. |wɒz| (or with restressed vowel |wʌz|) is usual finally. The contracted negative is often |wəzn̩t| when unstressed.[104]

ˈwʌns ðɛɚ wəz ə ˈjʌŋ ˈræt RAT[105]

ɪt wz ə ˈvɛrɪ ˈdrɪrɪ . . . RAT[105]

wəz ʃi ˈgoɪŋ

ˈmat wz ˈðæt

ˈmɒt ˈmeɪks ju ˈθɪŋk ɪt wɒz

aɪ wəz n̩t ˈpeɪɪŋ əˈtɛnʃən

WE—|wi| and |wɪ| are common in all positions, including that before the nonsyllabic verb forms, except that the contracted form with *are* is monosyllabic |wɪɚ|. |wɪ| may be somewhat more common between stressed syllables.

wi məs ˈliv ðɪs ˈpleɪs RAT

ˈmɛɚ ˈaɚ wi

wi l ˈdu ɪt   ɪf wɪ ˈkæn

ˈdɪd wɪ ˈwɪn

wɪ d əv ˈgɔn   ɪf wɪ d ˈnoun

aɪ ˈnou wɪɚ ˈgouɪŋ

WERE—|wɚ| is usual. |wɝ| is common finally. The contracted negative is often |wɚnt| when unstressed.

. . . ˈræftɚz wɚ ˈɔl ˈrɒtn̩ RAT

wɚ jə ˈgouɪŋ

aɪ ˈdɪd n̩t ˈnou ˈmɛɚ ðe wɝ

wɪ wɚ nt ˈplænɪŋ tə ˈgou

WHAT—|mət| or |wət| and |mɒt| or |wɒt| are the forms, with the former perhaps somewhat more common after a stressed syllable and the latter before a strong contrast stress.[106]

aɪ ˈdɪd n̩t ˈhiɚ mət jə ˈsɛd

aɪ ˈnou wət l̩ hæpən ˈnau

mat ˈaɪ wɑnt ɪz əv ˈnou ɪmˈpɔɚtn̩s

ˈtɛl mɪ wɒt ˈju min

WHEN—|mɛn| or |wɛn| is probably somewhat more common than |mən| or |wən|, especially initially, the usual position.

ən mən ðe ˈsɛd RAT[107]

ɑ l 'tɛl ju | ʍɛn ə 'faɪnd 'aʊt
ðe l 'kʌm   wɛn ðe 'fil 'laɪk ɪt
aɪ dont 'noʊ ʍən ʃɪ l 'kʌm
ɪt l̩ 'snoʊ wən ðə 'wɪnd 'tɜnz

WHO—The word is almost always initial in the phrase. |hu| is the usual form, especially after a pause. |hʊ| is common when there is no phrase break, or an exceptionally slight one. |u| and |ʊ| are used infrequently.

. . . 'jʌŋ 'ræt | hu 'kʊd n̩t . . . RAT[108]
ʃi z ðɪ 'oʊnlɪ wʌn   hu kən 'du ɪt
'aɪ no hʊ jə 'min

WILL—Syllabic |l̩| is usual after consonants, and nonsyllabic |l| after vowels. |əl| is regular after the affricates and is often used in any position. |wəl| is not uncommon, and |wl̩| rarely used. |wɪl| is usual initially and regular finally, and sometimes used medially, especially in formal speech. The contracted negative is |woʊnt| or |wont|, with considerable variation in the vowel.

'noʊ wʌn wəl 'ɛvɚ 'kɛɚ . . . RAT[109]
'ðɪs wont 'du RAT[109]
'tu 'drɑps l̩ bi ɪ'nʌf
'mɛɚ l wɪ 'goʊ
ðə 'tɛnɪs 'mætʃ əl bɪ 'pleɪd tə'deɪ
'hi əl bɪ 'leɪt
wɪl 'ju bi 'ðɛɚ
aɪ 'noʊ 'ju wɪl

WOULD—|əd| is usual after consonants. |d| is usual after vowels, especially after you, he, she, they,[110] but |əd| is sometimes used. |wəd| is common initially before a stressed syllable, and before a strong stress such as not, and sometimes used elsewhere. |wʊd| is regular finally, and common initially before an unstressed syllable, and occasionally used elsewhere, especially in formal speech.

hi d 'ɔlwɪz 'ʃɜk . . . RAT[111]
hi wəd 'nɒt 'seɪ . . . RAT[111]
wʊd ju 'laɪk tə 'stɒp . . . RAT[111]
'ðɪs 'pis əd 'fɪt
ðə 'skaɪ d bɪ 'dɑɚk bə 'ðɛn

ðe d hæv ə 'haɚd 'taɪm
hɪz 'pleɪ əd bi 'vɛrɪ 'pɑpjʊlɚ
wəd 'ʃi laɪk ɪt
wʊd i 'rɛkəgnaɪz ɪt
'hi d 'gou ɪf 'ʃi wʊd

YOU—|jʊ| is common in any position. |ju| is much used, especially when not next to a stressed syllable. |jə| is occasionally used, especially next to a stressed syllable. |jɪ| is used, but rarely.[112] When, as frequently, a form-word, or some other word in easy speech, ending in |d| or |t| immediately precedes one of these forms, there is a strong tendency for the stop and |j| to assimilate to |dʒ| or |tʃ|, often even in rather formal speech. The contracted form with *are* is monosyllabic |jʊɚ|, occasionally |jɚ|.

ɪf jʊ 'kærɪ 'ɒn . . . RAT[113]
'nou wʌn l̩ 'ɛvɚ 'kɛɚ fɚ ju RAT[113]
'ʍaɪ ˌdountʃu 'spik RAT[113]
əv 'koɚs jʊɚ 'kʌmɪŋ RAT[113]
hi hæz ə 'bʊk fɔɚ ju
ju dɪd 'vɛrɪ 'wɛl
'hau də jə 'gɛt 'ðiz
a l go 'aut 'wɪð jɪ
'ʍɛɚ dʒə 'gou
aɪ 'nou jɚ 'nɑt

YOUR—|jʊɚ| is common in any position. |jɚ| is almost as common, especially next to a stressed syllable. There is assimilation with a preceding |d| or |t| as in *you* forms, but not so common.

'aɪ hæv jʊɚ 'ʌðɚ 'bʊk
'hau z jɚ 'mʌðɚ
hi 'nouz mʌtʃɚ 'neɪm ɪz

NOTES

1. For example, J. S. Kenyon's list is somewhat better annotated for use in the Introduction to the Merriam *Webster's New International Dictionary* (2d ed., 1934) than it is in his *American Pronunciation* (6th ed., 1935). Daniel Jones's notes are the best I have seen, especially as giving consideration to rhythmic patterns, but they are scattered, some of them far away from his list of weak forms. *Outline of English Phonetics* (3d ed., 1932), pp. 115-26 and *passim* pp. 242-53. Brigance and Henderson's *Drill Manual for Improving Speech* (1939) has comment on the influence of phonetic context. Other lists, with more or less

comment, are to be found in many recent books, such as Gray and Wise, *The Bases of Speech* (1934).

2. An alternative term, *function words*, has the advantages claimed for it by Professor Charles C. Fries (*American English Grammar*, New York, 1940, p. 109n.); and *tool words*, as used by Hayes A. Newby (*Quarterly Journal of Speech* XXVI [1940], 396-400), is simple and vivid. Yet I prefer *form-words*, with the backing of Henry Sweet's usage (*New English Grammar*, Oxford, 1892, Part 1, pp. 22-24). The meaning of *forms*, as used in the first paragraph, is of course quite different; one may speak of "various forms of a form-word" without confusion.

3. In Latin, for instance, the subject pronoun is usually taken care of by a verb ending; the enclitic -*que* may be used for the meaning *and;* and there are no articles.

4. It must be noted that some form-words are identical with meaningful words. Thus *am* is a form-word in "I am going," "I am happy," "I am John Doe," and "I am a man," although the use is not exactly the same in any two of these sentences; but is a meaningful verb in "I think; therefore I am." And *have* is a form-word in "I have spent a dollar," but not in "I have a dollar." In the discussion of individual words no mention is regularly made of the meaningful uses of the word, nor are the pronunciations of such uses regularly noted.

5. The list may be too short. It is subject to criticism on semanto-grammatical grounds as to the propriety of including certain categories and also as to the specific words belonging to these categories. Fries does not include articles and determinatives or personal pronouns in his lists of function words (*American English Grammar*, pp. 111, 129-30, 199, 206-7), and he omits more than a dozen other words included here; on the other hand he lists *get, keep, then,* and *yet,* all of which, questionable or not, I would have added if my collection of pronunciations had not been completed before Fries's list appeared.

6. E. L. Thorndike, *Teachers Word Book of the Twenty Thousand Words Found Most Frequently . . .* , rev. ed. (1932).

7. Lawrence Faucett and Itsu Maki, *A Study of English Word-Values Statistically Determined from the Latest Extensive Word-Counts* (Tokyo, 1932).

8. "The One-Thousand Most Frequent Spoken Words," *Quarterly Journal of Speech* XXVIII (1942), 189-97.

9. Cf. footnotes 6, 7, 8, and also 17.

10. The use of full instead of appropriate obscured pronunciations usually accompanies, if it does not indicate, a sort of absent-mindedness, such as preoccupation with what is about to be said or overcareful attention to diction.

11. Cf. *infra*, sec. 5.

12. Whether the vowel in unstressed *been*, etc., should be classified with the vowel of that word stressed in GA, or should be classed with the vowel which may result from the partial obscuration of any front vowel, is a point not worth raising while we use the same symbol for both. On this point and the whole distinction between partially and fully obscured vowels, see the author's "Vowel Quality in Unstressed Syllables in American English," *Quarterly Journal of Speech* XXIX (1943), 451-57.

13. *Outline*, p. 89.

14. Jones and Kenyon record one of these forms. *Outline*, p. 121. *American Pronunciation*, p. 106.

15. Cf. note 1 on the published material. I have not made references to these or other published works in discussing the forms. I am most grateful to Professors J. S. Kenyon of Hiram College, Albert H. Marckwardt of the University of Michigan, William Matthews of the University of California at Los Angeles, C. K. Thomas of Cornell University, and C. M. Wise of Louisiana State

University for comments which they have made on the manuscript in its earlier stages.

16. One other matter, not of the same order, may need comment. In final phrases of preposition and pronoun, if a less obscured form is used in one, a more obscured form is generally used in the other. In noting this detail with prepositions, "before a final obscured pronoun" is to be taken as meaning "before a final pronoun having a more obscured rather than a less obscured form."

17. Prepared under the direction of Professors Cabell Greet and H. M. Ayres. Linguaphone Records No. 65-75A. No. 75B is of Goose Creek Gullah and not included. Transcriptions of sixteen of these records are available in *Phonetic Transcriptions from "American Speech,"* edited by Jane Dorsey Zimmerman, rev. ed. (1939) as well as in the numbers of *American Speech* in which they first appeared. Fifty-four of the 68 form-words in the second part of the list make up 276 of the 556 words in the RAT, counting contractions as two words. Eight form-words from the first part of the list account for 12 more words in the RAT text.

18. These examples are all marked RAT and references to the text of the story and to the records are made with RAT as a short title. Where RAT appears after an example without footnote index, it is to be understood that there was substantial agreement among all transcribers that the form shown appears on almost all the records.

19. Misses Jean Condie and Ethel Blaney of the University of California at Los Angeles and Helen Means of the University of Missouri did an extraordinary amount of work in assembling examples and putting them in usable form.

20. Other comments on transcription appear in sec. 3, *supra.*

21. This word may belong in the second part of the list, where I formerly had it. My present impression is that the form with obscured vowel is rare and limited to very easy, but not substandard, speech.

22. The triphthong is often simplified, but not according to any pattern of stress or position.

23. The initial consonant is often voiced, but I have not found any consistent correlation between lack of stress and voicing.

24. The final consonant may be voiced or voiceless, regardless of the conditions of stress and position.

25. The stressed form is extremely rare in good speaking or reading, but often heard in artificial elocution, whether on the platform or in conversation. Its occasional use by the best orators is probably as a time-filling device when it is not due to momentary absent-mindedness.

26. Often spelled *I'm.* Cf. *I* for variation in the vowel.

27. The negative has the same forms, the contracted negatives not being generally acceptable in American English.

28. This is the most difficult form-word to deal with, the phonetic proprieties calling for simple patterns which actual use does not consistently agree with.

29. When there is only a slight pause or none in the break between phrases, the preceding sound may be as influential as the initial position. On the other hand there may be the equivalent of a break within the phrase, as when the word after *and* has a slight extra stress, and an initial form.

30. Both these sounds are frequently lost in dialects, where a lengthened dentalized |n| is the only consonant heard. It is also often difficult to decide whether the |d| is pronounced or not before |l| and |n|.

31. The word *and* occurs 15 times in the RAT, giving 313 pronunciations in the 21 records, the word being omitted twice. Twelve occurrences are initial in the phrase and show some 200 forms beginning with a vowel against fewer than

50 beginning with |n|. In the noninitial position the ratios are 6 to 1 after *room*, 1 to 2 after *beams,* and less than 1 to 4 after *nice.* There is one occurrence before a stable vowel, with 11 forms ending in |n| to 10 ending in |d|. Before alveolar consonants the ratio of forms ending in |n| to those ending in |d| is 25 to 1; before stable |h| 5 to 2; before *he* 2 to 1; before other consonants 5 to 1. The syllabic velar nasal shown in the last example here appears in only one record, where *he* was omitted.

32. This pun, *broke and back* interpreted as *broken back,* was heard on the Fibber McGee and Molly radio program 4 March 1941.

33. This dissimilation occurs with strong *r* speakers, occasionally with those who carefully use a full vowel under all circumstances.

34. Often spelled *they're, we're, you're.* The modification of the vowel of the pronoun in forming these diphthongs is noted and examples given under *they, we, you.*

35. This is the prevailing form on the records, many without *r* coloring. Six records have the contracted form.

36. The obscured vowel appears in more than two thirds of the records.

37. *At* occurs five times, twice initially before a stressed syllable. There are not more than two pronunciations with full vowel in noninitial position, and about an equal number of full and obscured vowels initially.

38. The British tendency to use this form in all unstressed positions except finally is not at all common in America.

39. The partially obscured vowel appears in about four records.

40. Stressed or unstressed. The British limitation of this form to the unstressed position, with |bin| when stressed, is rare in America, where most of those who use |bin| at all use it unstressed as well as stressed.

41. *But* is probably the most frequently misstressed of the form-words in speaking, i.e., where its stressing obviously indicates a lack of co-ordination between idea and speech. Stressed *but* is used by orators as a time-filler or attention-directing device in adversative transitions.

42. In the three occurrences of *but,* all initial, there are only two or three full vowels on all records.

43. Five or six records have the form with schwa.

44. My attention was called to this form, in which there is an unusually long closure between the stop and plosion of the consonant, by Professor A. H. Marckwardt. I have not found a pattern for the occurrence of this form; it may be only before a stress.

45. The assimilations shown in these forms are not of importance here and are discussed under *you.*

46. But not so much used as the same form for *did* and not regularly subject to affrication with the initial consonant of *you.* Compare the fifth example here with the corresponding example under *did.*

47. As in "The Smiths don't go there, do they?" and "They don't have to go; do I?" There are equivalent patterns with the contracted negative in the echo.

48. There is no unstressed *do* in the RAT. *I don't know* occurs four times, showing all possibilities in the vowel of *don't,* the form shown being slightly more common than any other.

49. Cf. note under *do.*

50. The first example shows only one full vowel. In the second example two or three records have an *r*-less schwa where there is an *r* sound in the preceding word; the full vowel does not occur and is not to be expected, as the final pronoun, though unstressed, has a full vowel. In the third example the full vowel appears in about two thirds of the records.

51. Often spelled *'d*. This form may even occur after *it* in very easy speech, and possibly after *that* and *what*.

52. The obscured forms of *had, has,* and *have* are not uncommon, if less usual, for the verb meaning "to own" when unstressed. They are not used for the meaning "be obliged to." The past participle for these meanings always has the full vowel, although the |h| is sometimes lost.

53. Only two records show a definite |h|, and six or more seem to have only |d|.

54. Often spelled *'s*, especially after pronouns.

55. Often spelled *'ve*.

56. A compound or many-worded subject seems to give a short phrase break so that this form may follow after a vowel.

57. The usual form in the meaning "be obliged to" has the full vowel and an unvoiced final consonant, but the regular auxiliary never has this form.

58. The first example shows only one or two partially obscured vowels. The second example shows more forms without |h|, fewer than half the records, than any other occurrence of *he,* although all medial positions show some. In the third example about half the records have this form, the others |hi|. Note that *stood* need not be stressed.

59. The possibility of a full vowel in unstressed *her* had better not be suggested until some means is found for checking such delicate shades of difference in vowel quality.

60. About half the records have this form without |h|.

61. The possibility of a further reduction of the vowel to schwa is to be considered in this word and some others, but such pronunciations are probably at the moment to be regarded as exceptional.

62. *Him* occurs three times in the RAT, once in *himself*. More than half of the pronunciations are without |h|.

63. *His* occurs six times, all medially, in the RAT. There are more pronunciations with |h| than without. In the first example given about half the records are without |h|; whereas in the second, after two unstressed syllables and in the rather formal closing line, there are only two or three pronunciations without |h|.

64. In this and the similar phrase which comes shortly after it, there are more reductions of the diphthong, in the second *I,* than elsewhere, some to schwa.

65. *If* occurs twice in the RAT and shows one or two pronunciations each of the forms with schwa and without vowel.

66. The first *in* shows no pronunciation without vowel, the second and third show several. The six other occurrences show only five or six pronunciations without vowel.

67. Often spelled *'s*, especially after pronouns. The forms without vowel are, of course, indistinguishable from those of *has*.

68. There seems to be no difference between the forms for the auxiliary use of *is* and those for its use as a copula.

69. Schwa is heard rather often in *it,* but it seems to be an individual or dialect variant, unrelated to phonetic context. In some parts of the United States, Western so far as I know, a strongly stressed *it* is used where *that* would be the literary word; several examples appear under other form-words.

70. *It* occurs nine times and shows no variants except ten or twelve forms with schwa, several of which are on one record.

71. *Just* occurs three times, stressed on most of the records. The example given is read with *just* unstressed on about seven records, of which three are with schwa. About two thirds of the pronunciations, all before consonants, are without |t|, stressed or unstressed.

72. Not more than three records show final |t|, and more than half have this form with schwa.

73. The use of the last form in all unstressed positions is very rare in America except in stage speech which imitates the British pattern.

74. Three or four records show a form with schwa. The other occurrence of *my* shows fewer schwa forms.

75. The adjective is usually stressed and the adverb meaning "not so" regularly stressed.

76. Only a few of the records show this form and only one has a schwa, with stressed *more*. *No* is usually stressed in this and other occurrences in the RAT.

77. Where these negatives involve modification of the form of the simple verb or have special unstressed forms, those facts are commented on under the verb entry. Otherwise no comments are made and, inasmuch as the words are usually stressed, illustrations of use are not regularly given.

78. The idea of *not* may be conveyed by stress and intonation alone, without any speech sounds. Note in the last example here that the stress on *she,* with no stress on *not,* calls for a special intonation.

79. The form in the first example shows on only six records, the others having the contracted form. In the four occurrences of the phrase in the second example, considerably more than half the pronunciations are without |t| and many with the consequent doubled |nn| simplified to |n|.

80. The first of these examples shows the schwa form without consonant on only three or four records; the second has it on more than half. The third example shows no instance of this form with schwa only and shows six or more forms with full vowel.

81. In the three occurrences of *on* there is no record that shows an obvious schwa form and in only four or five instances is there a suggestion of reduction in the vowel.

82. The forms without the |w|, common in England, seem to be rare in this country. The form in syllabic *n* is probably restricted to very easy speech.

83. The comparatively large number of occurrences in initial position makes for a considerable use of the less obscured form, although not so much so as with *nor.* Professor C. K. Thomas suggests that *r*-less speech has a higher ratio of use of the full vowel in *or.*

84. The first of these examples shows the more obscured form in more than two thirds of the records; the second shows the fuller form in about three fourths of them.

85. That this contracted form is from *will* is beside the point. Certainly people who are careful to observe all the grammatical proprieties and never say *I will,* do use the form *I'll;* and as a matter of current usage *I'll* is the contracted form equivalent to *I shall,* as noted in the recent *Thorndike Century Senior Dictionary.*

86. Three of the records show the other form.

87. This form may be limited by some syntactical or semantic pattern. It does not, for instance, appear in the phrase *I should think so* indicating casual agreement, but it may appear in the same phrase indicating more deliberate agreement, as with *too* added. Cf. the note on *shall.*

88. A few more records show this form than show the full vowel. There are several occurrences of |d|, but they are probably for *would* (a misreading?), which appears in full form on two records.

89. This assimilation before the voiceless consonant is common in set phrases such as this and *I should think so.*

90. Four or five records have the form with schwa. Elsewhere in the RAT *so* has full form because of rhythm or is stressed.

91. This is, of course, a normal assimilation, but it is of such frequent occurrence in *some more*, etc., and the syllabic division so clearly appears to be after the schwa, that it seems advisable to recognize the separate form. Kenyon's note, *American Pronunciation*, p. 106, deals with the meanings of *some*.

92. This form appears on only four or five records. The word is stressed on several records, and has the full vowel unstressed on some.

93. Six or seven records have the full vowel.

94. Forms without the first consonant, or without the second consonant, or without the vowel, are probably used only in very easy or substandard speech. The demonstrative has full vowel and is usually stressed.

95. One or two records show a full vowel in the first example, and one transcriber heard several in the second.

96. Professor Kenyon makes this point, and adds that the form is sometimes used before other front vowels. Professors Marckwardt and Thomas separately call my attention to the Southern American tendency to use the form in schwa before front as well as back vowels.

97. *The* occurs 29 times before consonants other than |j| in the RAT and in 97 per cent of the pronunciations the form with schwa is used. It occurs 6 times before vowels, with no schwa forms except in the third example here where there are 4 or 5 before *other*. It occurs 4 times in *the young rat*, with about one third schwa forms. The full vowel appears several times before vowels and |j|, but not more than 5 or 6 times out of 609 possibilities before other consonants.

98. The fact that this form is from *hem* rather than from *them* is beside the point. The forms are exact extensional equivalents. The spelling *'em* is common in dialect stories.

99. *Them* occurs four times, mostly with the form as in the first example. The shorter form appears on nearly half the records in the second example, and on some of the records for each occurrence. There is a considerable number of pronunciations with full vowel.

100. The adverb of place is usually stressed.

101. The first of these examples shows the obscured vowel in nearly half the records, the second in somewhat fewer.

102. The other occurrences of *they* show a considerable number of full, diphthongized, vowels; this one a few.

103. The first of these examples has the schwa form on all records; the second on a few more than half. In the nine occurrences of *to* as the sign of the infinitive, all before consonants, the schwa appears eight times as often as a less obscured vowel. The third example has the schwa form in about three fifths of the records; the fourth has it in not more than six.

104. There is an unstressed form of *was* without the first consonant, but probably rarely used outside very easy or substandard speech.

105. *Was* occurs ten times. The first of these examples is the only one that appears unstressed on all records with no instance of the reduced form without schwa; the second example has six or more such reduced forms. There are only two full vowels except where the word is stressed as part of the contracted negative.

106. I have been unable to find any correlation between the voicing of the initial consonant in this and similar words and the obscuration of the vowel. Forms of *what* with restressed vowel are not uncommon, but probably only in very easy or substandard speech.

107. Forms with schwa appear on about half the records. The six forms with voiced initial |w| are equally distributed between the full vowel and schwa.

108. Three or four records have the partially obscured vowel, one without the consonant.

109. The *will* in the first example seems very difficult to interpret from the records. One or more transcribers heard each of the forms listed on at least two records, with very little agreement among transcribers. The most common forms seem to be the one noted, that without initial consonant, and syllabic *l*. The negative form shown is definite on three or four records; the others show several variations, many under stress.

110. Even after *it*, but probably mostly in very easy speech.

111. *He would* occurs five times. In the first example given the form shown appears on well over half the records; it is nearly as frequent in other occurrences except in the second example shown, where it appears but once. The third example is uniformly as shown but for assimilation with the following pronoun on some records.

112. This form is often interpreted as a sign of rustic, but is not limited to substandard, speech. Its relation to *ye* is beside the point.

113. *You* occurs ten times in the RAT. Every occurrence except possibly one shows on one or more records each of the three grades of full, partially obscured, and fully obscured vowel. Each of the examples given shows a preponderance of the form shown, except that the contracted form of the fourth example appears in only six records.

The Meaning of *Dispositio*

RUSSELL H. WAGNER

THE five main divisions of ancient rhetoric—invention, *dispositio,* memory, style, and delivery—have been of varying influence and significance. Memory is slighted today, but style and delivery retain much of their earlier meaning and importance. Invention is well understood by most students of rhetoric today, and, in the larger English dictionaries, is usually defined in its special rhetorical sense. But *dispositio* is, and for long has been, misunderstood; and, consequently, its cardinal principles have been neglected.

Dispositio, almost always, is translated "arrangement," which suggests to most persons the order of points, and nothing more. To those familiar with modern text-books on public address, it may suggest the parts of a speech—usually introduction, discussion, conclusion—and, possibly, some elementary and meagre theories, or rules, of planning.

The older rhetorics in English are of little aid to us on this point. Wilson, in *The Arte of Rhetorique,* 1553, apparently devotes only a few pages to *dispositio,*[1] and does not even include, under it, the parts of a speech, since he had already dealt with them under invention. Campbell's *Philosophy of Rhetoric* ignores *dispositio* altogether. Blair, in his *Lectures on Rhetoric and Belles Lettres,* calls it, suggestively, "Conduct of a Discourse," but, for the most part, is content to name and describe the divisions of a speech, using the Latin terminology.[2] Whately, in his *Elements of Rhetoric,* reduces "arrangement" to the ordering of logical arguments, chiefly from the point of view of logic, except for brief remarks on the kinds and functions of different types of introductions and conclusions.[3]

Current treatises, with one exception, which attempt to summarize or interpret ancient rhetoric, maintain the traditional limitation. Thus, D. L. Clark, in *Rhetoric and Poetry in the Renaissance*[4] points out that *inventio* included all of what we call "working up the case," and that *dispositio* is the art of arranging the material; and he confines his discussion of the latter to the parts of a speech—*exordium, narratio,* etc. W. P. Sandford, in his *English Theories of Public Address, 1530-1828,*[5] gives much the same impression. Not uncommon is the limitation found in a recent digest of rhetorical theory; *dispositio* is here characterized as ". . . the arrangement of material for delivery."[6] C. S. Baldwin is the first and apparently the only modern scholar to point out the inadequacy of "arrangement" as the word for *dispositio.* He says: *"Dispositio (collocatio)* refers not to the arrangement of details, but to the plan of the whole. . . . *Compositio* does not mean, though it is often translated, 'composition' in the wide sense now current. For the latter the term is *dispositio.*"[7] It is unfortunate that Baldwin does not amplify these emendations, for they are suggestive rather than definitive. "Plan of the whole" and " 'composition' in the wide sense now current" may mean organization as befits subject matter, or as suits the taste of writer or speaker, or as the persuasive problem requires, or the like. It is small wonder that this brief and obscure correction has borne no fruit in rhetorical scholarship.

To determine what *dispositio* really meant to the ancients let us look at the definitions they give and the principles they teach under that name. For the doctrine in its widest and fullest application, let us turn to Cicero, and to his matured views of the work of the orator, as found in the *De Oratore* and in the *Partitiones Oratoriae.*

The first definition, or characterization, is to be found in *De Oratore* (I, 31) where invention and *dispositio* are distinguished:

. . . since all the business and the art of the orator is divided into five parts, he ought first to find out what he should say; next to dispose and arrange his matter, not only in a certain order, but according to the weight of the matter and the judgment of the speaker.[8]

The distinction here is fully clarified elsewhere in this work and in the *Orator.* We are told that invention begins with a systematic search for arguments by means of running through all the topics, not only (though chiefly) the logical "places of argument" but also those of ethos and emotion; it ends with the analysis of the case; it includes the acquiring of a minute and thorough knowledge of the case—the considering of all the circumstances and all the potentialities of strength and weakness involved in the case (*De Oratore* II, 34; *Orator* XIV, XV). In short, invention is the ascertaining of all that one can say and the least that one must say—the minimum case in view of the issues involved.

The next step, says Cicero, is to "dispose and arrange his matter, not only in a certain order, but according to the weight of the matter and the judgment of the speaker." What does this mean, beyond ordering the points and dividing the speech into parts? The answer is plainly made in the words of Antonius, in the *De Oratore* (II, 76-77):

I now return, therefore, to that point, Catulus, on which you a little while ago accorded me praise; the order and arrangement of facts and topics of argument. On this head, two methods may be observed; one, which the nature of causes dictates; the other, which is suggested by the orator's judgment and prudence. For, to premise something before we come to the main point; then to explain the matter in question; then to support it by strengthening our own arguments, and refuting those on the other side; next to sum up, and come to the peroration; is a mode of speaking that nature herself prescribes. But to determine how we should arrange the particulars that are to be advanced in order to prove, to inform, to persuade, more peculiarly belongs to the orator's discretion. For many arguments occur to him; many, that seem likely to be of service to his pleading; but some of them are so trifling as to be utterly contemptible; some, if they are of any assistance at all, are sometimes of such a nature, that there is some defect inherent in them; while that which appears to be advantageous is not of such import that it need be advanced in conjunction with anything prejudicial. And as to those arguments which are to the purpose, and deserving of trust, if they are (as it often happens) very numerous, I think that such of them as are of the least weight, or as are of the same tendency with others of greater force, ought to be set aside, and excluded altogether from our pleading. I myself, indeed, in collecting proofs, make it a practice rather to weigh than to count them. . . . Since, too, as I have often observed, we bring over people in general to our opinions by three methods, by instructing their understandings, conciliating their benevolence, or exciting their passions, one only of these three methods is to be professed by us, so that we may appear to desire nothing else but to instruct; the other two, like blood throughout the body, ought to be diffused through the whole of our pleading.[9]

This distinction between the finding and the selecting and adapting of materials according to need is found in other writings of Cicero. In the *Partitiones Oratoriae* (III) Cicero replies to the question of Cicero *filius*, "What comes next after invention?" as follows:

When you have discovered your arguments, to arrange them properly; and in an extensive inquiry [e.g., the propounding and arguing of an abstract thesis] the order of topics is very nearly that which I have set forth; but in a definite one [e.g., a speech to secure action, as in the defense of an accused person] we must use those topics also which relate to exciting the required feeling in the minds of the hearers. . . . I have general precepts for producing belief and exciting feelings. Since belief is a firm opinion but feelings are an excitement of the mind either to pleasure, or to vexation, or to fear, or to desire, . . . *I adapt all my arrangement to the object of the inquiry.*[10]

A moment later, Cicero *filius* asks: "Can we, then, always preserve the order of arrangement which we wish to adopt?" and the answer is: "Surely not, for the ears of the hearers are guides to the wise and prudent orator, and whatever is unpleasing to them must be altered or modified."[11]

In the *De Oratore*, following the definitions by explication and by division cited in the long quotation from it above, Cicero continues for some nine chapters to sketch the nature and work of *dispositio* (II, 77-86) in such a way as to amplify these highly suggestive but over-concise statements in the *Partitiones Oratoriae*. He points out that the choice of topics, order, coloring, proportion of logical, ethical, and emotional arguments, depend much on speaker, hearers, and kind of speech; and he stresses the variety of methods to be employed, referring especially to differences between speaking to the senate and to the people, between panegyrical and deliberative speeches.

Dispositio, then, according to Cicero, is the adapting of the product of *inventio* to the particular situation at hand. It is of two kinds—or, rather, there are two main parts of the process, two divisions of the work. One is grouping the ideas invented in the natural order—the familiar exordium, narration, proof, and peroration. To Cicero this is a mere skeleton, offering useful broad divisions, or first steps, but of little significance in the work of organizing a real speech to be given to a real audience. The major work of *dispositio* is the "exercising of prudence and judgment"; in brief it is building the speech— *each* speech—to meet the particular persuasive problem involved.

Judging from Cicero's account of *dispositio,* it involves these tasks:

1. A careful and final selection of invented materials, especially of emotional and ethical proofs, applicable to particular problems. This involves elimination of some ideas tentatively selected, and the construction of others.

2. Ordering and arranging. This means determining order, not by the nature of the subject alone, nor by the traditional roles of the parts of a speech (though these may aid in forming a rough general plan), but according to *need.*

3. Massing and shaping, expanding, contracting, proportioning, and emphasizing, coloring and toning, according to the special circumstances of the speech.

These tasks—selection, arrangement, and proportionment— are all, separately and as a whole, governed by consideration of the speech situation and by the variable conditions it involves.

The *need* or *situation* is really a sum of five factors or conditions to be considered—not a simple but a compound set of criteria, all of which, says Cicero, must be met. They are:

1. The purpose of the speech.
2. The cause, or subject.
3. The kind of speech—judicial, panegyric, deliberative.
4. The audience: age, function, composition, mood.
5. The speaker—his age, reputation, personality, limitations, capabilities.

All that has been said of Cicero's view applies equally well to Quintilian's in his *Institutio Oratoria.* His first explanation of *dispositio* is: "For not only what we say and how we say it is of importance, but also the circumstances under which we say it.

It is here that the need of arrangement comes in" (III, 3, 2).[12] This statement is abundantly clarified in the long and eloquent defense (II, 13, 1-9) of his refusal to write a book of rules on rhetoric—laying down immutable laws and prescriptions on exordium and narration and other parts of a speech would be as absurd as requiring a general to dispose his troops according to fixed rules instead of allowing him to marshal them according to terrain, nature of the enemy's forces, and his own strength. The circumstances make the organization. In war and in speech-making, says Quintilian, disposition is determined by the special circumstances which exist in each engagement.

With Quintilian, too, the work of disposition includes selection, elimination, ordering, massing or proportioning, and coloring—all from the point of view of the necessities imposed by circumstances of time, place, speaker, purpose, audience. It is true that in his long book (VII) entitled *dispositio,* devoted largely to legal case-making, he stresses other features of *dispositio,* such as tactics or planning of the case.[13] Elsewhere he treats fully all the features of Ciceronian selection and adaptation.[14]

Aristotle does not define τάξις, the Greek *dispositio,* in the third book of the *Rhetoric.* His conception must be inferred from his discussion of the subject. In essence, he says the parts of a speech are not the essential features of arrangement, for only the statement of thesis and the proof of it are vital. He seems, at first glance, to reverse this judgment in developing the subject, for he treats in turn the four parts of the speech— proem, statement, argument, and epilogue. But after he is fairly launched into the subject, which is to say, near the beginning of his remarks on "statement," the discussion consists almost wholly of principles of adaptation. For example, the nature of the narration depends on the kind of speech to be made; and that in turn on the function of the hearers—whether they are judges in forensic dispute, legislators who are to vote, or critics of epideictic oratory. Its length, too, depends not on traditional standards or the dicta of critics; instead, one is to say ". . . just so much as will make matters plain—enough to make your hearer believe."[15] He goes on to give advice on how to select, order, and adapt materials of a speech according to the function and character of the audience, the subject, the speaker, the opponent, and the changing course of the debate; he touches on such matters as the formulation of a case, the varying uses to be made of one's ethos and of emotional persuasion; he tells what may be included and what omitted, and when and where to use interrogation and other special methods, but, more important, what the criteria of selection and adaptation are. In general, then, Aristotle in this section attempts to state and illustrate the criteria of the selection, adaptation, and arrangement of the materials of speeches.

It must be admitted that this broad conception of disposition is not equally maintained at all times, even in Cicero's mature writings;[16] and that the priority of invention, both in the sense of its importance and of its natural right to be dealt with first, leads to the inclusion in it of much of *dispositio,* even the parts of the speech, in Quintilian's *Institutio.*[17] And in the minor an-cient rhetorics the conception is usually narrowed to arrange-ment or distribution according to arbitrary rules. But in the greatest of the ancient rhetorics—by implication in Aristotle's, and by explicit and repeated statement of scope and nature in the others—*dispositio* was conceived as planned adaptation.

To reconstruct fully and in detail the body of principles logically included under this concept is another task than that attempted here. It would involve, first of all, the establishment of sound definitions of the nature and scope of *inventio, dis-positio,* and *elocutio.* It would also mean the reassembling of working principles; some would have to be subtracted from *inventio,* as, for example, those which are clearly concerned with selecting arguments for the benefit of particular audiences; some would be found by cross-reference—for many of the topics of *inventio* are also topics of *dispositio,* as, for example, the principles of emotional persuasion as applied to both general and particular audiences. The re-discovery of these principles would not be easy, but it is feasible, and it would be highly serviceable.

Finally, what English term should we use for this amplified

conception of *dispositio?* "Arrangement" conveys only a fraction of its scope. "Planning" is also inadequate. "Composition" or "speech construction" does not coincide at all with the matching of material to needs created by real situations, which is the heart of *dispositio.* But "adaptation" also covers the area incompletely. Of modern terms, "organization" comes nearest to being a satisfactory equivalent. But it most commonly means a rather elementary process of achieving substantive, logical form—the making of an outline—and, in its broadest usage, is far from an adequate equivalent.

The same problem once confronted translators and rhetoricians in the case of *inventio.* We have no English word which conveys its full meaning. The problem was solved in this case by settling on "invention," and giving it a special rhetorical meaning—the meaning of *inventio.* Why not follow the same procedure in the case of *dispositio?* There is ample warrant for serving notice, by using "disposition," that here, as in the case of "invention," the full meaning must be sought in the rhetorical classics. We should also have a warrant for its use in the fact that Wilson, in the first complete work on rhetoric in English, used "disposition" as well as "invention," and this in spite of his concern to avoid coining words in English from the Latin. In fact, the first and second definitions in our unabridged English dictionaries warrant its use in this sense far better than all but the special rhetorical dictionary definitions of "invention."

The service which will be rendered by a return to "disposition" in rendering *dispositio* and in referring to its classical doctrines, will be nugatory indeed, if we do not restore the full meaning behind the term. Just as it is not enough to know that rhetorical invention does not mean inventing in the popular sense, so it is not enough to know that disposition means more than arrangement. To begin with, we must add other negations: for example, disposition is not concerned with setting up rules for unity and coherence, length or proportion, which derive from tradition or from a devotion to such ideals as symmetry or harmony *per se,* or from personal, subjective preferences unrelated to consideration of particular situations, audiences, or persuasive problems. It *is* concerned with the principles of disposing (in the sense of using) the materials invented for a speech, in the best possible manner, for the purpose of effecting the end intended by the speaker in any given situation. The discussion of disposition usually begins by describing the typical form of the speech—the parts or divisions—or it may be altogether organized under those conventional heads. But always, in the best writers, the principle of adaptation to need is uppermost, and the distinction between conventional organization and functional use of material is insistently made. It is this meaning—the functional selection and use of materials for a particular purpose—which must supplant "arrangement" and which, as "disposition," may well be added to our rhetorical terminology in English.

NOTES

1. Pp. 156-160 in the edition of G. P. Mair (Oxford, 1909). It is to be noted that Book II, in which are treated the parts of a speech and the methods of amplification, including, in Wilson's organization, the emotional appeals, constitutes a discussion of *dispositio*, much of it in the best classical sense, although Wilson does not label it "disposition."

2. Lectures XXXI and XXXII.

3. Pt. I, Chap. III, Secs. 5, 6, and 9 esp., and Chap. IV. The brief remarks on "Conclusions," found in a footnote in Sec. 2 of Chap. IV were not expanded and placed in the text until the seventh and last edition, 1846.

4. (New York, 1922), p. 27.

5. (Columbus, Ohio, 1931), pp. 16, 19.

6. H. D. Rix, "Rhetoric in Spencer's Poetry," *Pennsylvania State College Studies*, No. 7 (State College, 1940), p. 7.

7. *Ancient Rhetoric and Poetic* (New York, 1924), p. 67.

8. *Cicero on Oratory and Orators*, trans. J. S. Watson (London, 1891), p. 178, has been used here save for the last thirteen words. Watson's "with a sort of power and judgment" is inaccurate for Cicero's "momento quodam atque iudicio." The translation of Sutton and Rackham, *Cicero de Oratore*, 2 vols. (London, 1942), I, 99: "with a discriminating eye for the exact weight as it were of each argument" is apparently sound but somewhat free. For the difficulties involved in translating this passage and the reasons for rejecting Watson's rendering, see *Ciceronis de Oratore Liber I*, ed. A. S. Wilkins (Oxford, 1888), p. 144, note 6.

9. Trans. J. S. Watson, *op. cit.*, pp. 313-314.

10. *Orations of Marcus Tullius Cicero*, trans. C. D. Yonge (London, 1919), III; italics mine.

11. *Ibid.*, p. 490. Cf. *Orator*, XV.

12. Trans. H. Butler (London and New York, 1920), I, 385.

13. In his summary of *dispositio* at the end of the book, however, he stresses the Ciceronian conception in a memorable passage, from which the following excerpts may be cited: "For the most effective, and what is justly styled most

economical disposition [oeconomica . . . dispositio] of the case as a whole, is that which cannot be determined except when we have the specific facts before us. It consists in the power to determine when the exordium is necessary and when it should be omitted . . . ; in what cases we should prefix questions to the exordium . . . ; whether we should reserve emotional appeals for the peroration or distribute them throughout the whole speech." (VII, 10, 11-12, trans. Butler, *op. cit.*, III, 169). But see VII, 10, 4-17 for a full exposition of this conception.

14. II, 13; III, 8; IV; VI; X, 4, 6, 7, 8; XII, 8.

15. *Rhetoric*, 3, 16, trans. Lane Cooper (New York, 1932), p. 229.

16. See, e.g., *De Partitione Oratoria*, I, 3: ". . . but arrangement . . . nevertheless is applied to invention." (Trans. H. Rackham, *op. cit.*, II, 313); and note the apparent fusion of invention and *dispositio* in *Orator*, XIV, XV.

17. This is not to overlook other causes of variation, confusion, and inconsistency in the ancient treatment of *dispositio*. A definitive account of the causes would be highly useful.

The Decay of Eloquence at Rome in the First Century

HARRY CAPLAN

§1

WITH the death of the Roman republic "a hush fell upon eloquence."[1] Political oratory was restricted virtually to the emperor, who wielded absolute authority, and when he addressed
the Senate his aim was rather to impose his will than to persuade. The Emperor himself presided over the Senate, and its
duties were largely administrative. Speech there was not really
free, and especially not when Caligula, Nero, and Domitian
occupied the throne. The popular assemblies, certainly by the
time of Tiberius, lost their importance altogether. Forensic
oratory was confined largely to the Centumviral courts, which
were charged with civil cases such as arose out of rules of in-
heritance, and with like cases of no great import. Secundus in
Tacitus' *Dialogue on Orators* ruefully observes that the lawyers
are reduced to trying cases of theft, or winning an interdict for
a client (37). *Causes célèbres* carrying political implications,
such as Tacitus and Pliny did indeed handle against provincial
governors, are rare. Jurisprudence, to be sure, is making great
strides, but pleading, in so far as it followed the rules of rhetoric,
seems not to have had a great effect upon the theory of juristic
interpretation; so at any rate most modern students of Roman
law contend. Epideictic speaking, in the form of the funeral
oration and especially the panegyric, continued, and enjoyed
a history of progressive degradation for several centuries. For
oratory the first century is a time of decadence.

Yet eloquence was still the most popular and most conspicuous of the arts. It had lost its power, but not its prestige.[2] If
the issues were not great, there were yet brilliant speakers. The
younger Pliny thinks Tacitus the best orator of his day, and
ventures the hope that he himself occupies the second place

(*Epist.* 7. 20). Fragments of speeches from several other orators have been collected;[3] many speeches were too strictly legal for preservation. We know a good deal about Pliny's career at the bar, and especially how carefully he revised his speeches after delivery, tried them on his friends, and recited them before large audiences he had invited to hear him. From him and others we learn that the public was deeply interested in the speeches delivered in court. Quintilian thinks that the law-courts of his day can boast a glorious wealth of talent, the best speakers being serious rivals of the ancient great (10. 1. 122). Several of the emperors were accomplished speakers. That Seneca was on occasion "ghost-writer" for Nero was a scandal; after listening to Nero's panegyric on Claudius "the older men in the audience remarked that he was the first emperor to be in need of borrowed eloquence" (Tacitus, *Ann.* 13. 3). There *were* brilliant speakers, and, unfortunately, among the most effective of these were the public informers.[4]

But in greatest part the activity was shunted off and confined to the schools of rhetoric. The lecture-halls were often crowded to the doors by the public come to hear distinguished professors. Many a Roman and many an inhabitant of the provinces (Gaul especially was later a lively centre of rhetorical studies) continued rhetorical exercises long after their school-days were over. Juvenal, for one, practiced exercises until he was forty.

The type of oratory that predominated in the schools, and was there pursued with consummate ardor, was *declamatio*.[5] Introduced probably from Rhodes soon after the beginning of the first century B.C. or earlier (and it is fair to remember that declamation was inherited from the time of the republic), it underwent a change in nature. Early rhetorical fare was comprised of narratives, eulogies of famous men, commonplaces such as invectives against some vice, general *theses* (for example, Is the lawyer's life preferable to the warrior's?), deliberative questions (Should one marry?), or specific *causae* resembling actual cases at law. In each the reference to real life was close. But now we have the *suasoriae* and the *controversiae*. Several of the rhetors published collections of their declamations, and works such as those of the elder Seneca and of Ps.-Quintilian give us a clear picture of what these declamations were like.

Seneca's third *suasoria* is typical: Agamemnon deliberates whether to sacrifice Iphigenia. Here the source is Greek legend, but Greek or Roman history might supply the subject. The *controversiae*, harder to treat, belonged to the judicial type, but the situations were almost invariably subtle, complicated, unreal, and sensational, and the "laws" involved were often vague, imaginary, or borrowed from the Greeks. Seneca, *Contr.* 9. 4, will serve to illustrate a less extreme type: The "law" reads, "He who has beaten his father shall have his hands cut off." A tyrant has summoned to his citadel a father and his two sons. He orders the sons to beat their father. One son throws himself down from the height. The other beats his father, and when he is thereafter accepted as a friend by the tyrant, kills him. The penalty—that he have his hands cut off—is demanded of him. His father defends him. We may select Musa to represent for us the twelve declaimers who speak in the father's role, and one *sententia* to represent Musa's style. "Cut off the hands of the tyrannicide," he exclaims, "when the tyrant in his tomb possesses all his limbs!"

Tyrants, pirates (there had been none in the Mediterranean since the time of Pompey), disinherited children, poisonings, adultery, seduction—these comprised much of the little-varied diet fed the youngster at school. Variety was sought rather by introducing novel, striking, and intricate complications. Emphasis was placed on ingenuity, not solid argument, and on abundance, bizarre extravagance, mannerism, dazzling ornament in *sententia* and *color*. The imagination had free rein, and historical truth was often distorted and falsified—a privilege which, as Atticus in Cicero's *Brutus* (42) smilingly admits, is accorded to rhetoricians when they wish to achieve "point" (*dicere argutius*). Pollio says that declamation is not persuasion but playing with words (Seneca, *Suas.* 2. 10), and Montanus that its aim is not victory but entertainment (Seneca, *Contr.* 9, *Praef.* 1). In Seneca, *Contr.* 9. 6. 10, Montanus laughs at those rhetors who treat as though she were a baby the girl accused of poisoning her half-brother, and especially at Cestius who represents the mother as saying to her daughter: "Give your brother poison," and receiving the reply: "Mother, what is poison?" Triarius, outdoing Cestius, has the daughter say: "Give me some, too." Cestius at least admitted the ineptitude of his dialogue, but maintained in extenuation that many of the things he said were intended to please his audience. Again, it was a fiction preserved in the school that a certain Popillius was the murderer of Cicero, and that once when charged with parricide, he had been successfully defended by the great orator. Inevitably one of the rhetors (Sabidius Paulus, Seneca, *Contr.* 7. 2. 14), describing the moment when Popillius is about to behead Cicero, makes the orator recite to his slayer the very speech he had given during the trial.

The elder Seneca himself of course has a high opinion of declamatory eloquence. To his son Mela he says: "It equips also those whom it does not train for its own purposes" (*Contr.* 2, *Praef.* 3). But always a man of sense and an excellent critic, he can be critical of it too (e.g., Montanus in *Contr.* 9, *Praef.* 1). In *Contr.* 3, *Praef.* 12–13, he quotes Cassius Severus on the bad side of this discipline: "In the school-exercises what is not superfluous, since they are themselves superfluous?" "Declaimers are like hot-house plants that cannot stand up in the open air."

The schools, then, were sealed, as it were, from public life and had no contact with reality. The younger Seneca cries: "We educate ourselves for the class-room, not for life" (*Epist.* 106. 12). Latro, in the first rank of *ex tempore* declaimers, yet funked appearance in the forum when called upon to plead a case (Quintilian 10. 5. 18).

The declaimers occasionally gave utterance to ideals of political liberty. Albucius dared in Milan to invoke Marcus Brutus, whose statue was in sight, as "the founder and defender of our laws and our liberty," and for that "narrowly escaped punishment" (Suetonius, *De Rhet.* 6). In the two Senecan *suasoriae* dealing with Cicero (6 and 7), the attacks on Antony and on the proscriptions by which Cicero lost his life may have borne implications that Octavian shared in the responsibility as a member of the triumvirate. Julius Caesar is never eulogized in the declamations. But most of the rhetors did not touch on politics. It is precisely because Seneca's son Mela finds civic duties and ambition repugnant to his spirit that he is urged by his father to indulge his sole passion—declamation (*Contr.* 2, *Praef.* 3). Furthermore, since the declaimers were trained to take either side of a question, we must in the case of some who expressed republican sentiments beware of exaggerating their sincerity, just as we must not overrate the influence they wielded in the realm of political action. For example, Haterius could say to Cicero (in retrospect, of course): "I would urge you to hold your life dear, if liberty still had its abode in our State, and eloquence its abode in liberty," and could utter noble words on Cato (Seneca, *Suas.* 7 and 6), yet Tacitus paints an abject picture of him in his relations with Tiberius (*Ann.* 1. 13).

The contentions of modern apologists for *declamatio* must have a hearing. Certain benefits did indeed accrue from it: it often showed respect for things of the spirit, provided an outlet for some criticism of society, satisfied the desire for "romance," insured the students facility and stylistic finish. It is likewise only just to remind ourselves that some of the contemporary critics who attacked declamation (when is education not a target for criticism?) themselves practiced it; that the declaimers preserved eloquence when otherwise it would virtually have died; and, finally, that most of the great writers of the Silver Age underwent this training. Indeed it is astonishing that at a time when oratory itself was in such sore straits, rhetoric was making inroads into all the fields of literary activity, of prose and of poetry, and especially history and the epic, exercising a potent influence upon them, and in a sense taking them over as her own. And we must further agree that it was not education which corrupted the national taste, but rather that this training was itself a reflection and manifestation of the decline in taste.

As will soon be clear, *declamatio* was almost universally criticized; yet its popularity continued. As it differed from the oratory of the forum in subject matter, kind of audience, and even language, so it was a very different system of education from the *tirocinium fori* of republican times. Then the young speaker had been under the patronage of a leading statesman. He would attend at his patron's home where current topics were discussed, assist in the trying of cases, exchange opinions on the speeches delivered by other orators. He learned to fight, as Messalla in Tacitus' *Dialogus* says (34), on the firing-line, and won experience, self-possession, and sound judgment. But oratory now, during the Empire, is deprived of the inspiration that comes from reality, since the forum is no longer the centre of public life.

§2

The elder Seneca, who died *c.* A.D. 37, reproduces for us the *declamatio* of the earlier period, its brilliant products as well as inept. That the themes continued unreal and melodramatic, and the style pompous and grandiloquent, all the witnesses[6] of the first century agree, expressing their dislike and disgust in varying tones—the humorous satirist Petronius, the philosopher Seneca, the historian-critic Tacitus, the lawyer-epistolographer Pliny, the bitter castigator of Roman society Juvenal. In the time of Nero, Petronius (1-2) thus condemns the schools:

I believe that our young men become utter simpletons in the schools, because they neither hear nor see anything of actual life there. It is rather pirates standing on the shore with chains in hand, tyrants writing edicts which order sons to cut off their fathers' heads, oracles in time of pestilence calling for the sacrifice of three virgins or more, rounded phrases, honey-sweet, every word and act besprinkled as it were with poppy-seed and sesame. Persons who are nourished on this diet can no more be intelligent than persons who live in the kitchen can be sweet-scented. With your good leave I must tell you that it is primarily you teachers who have ruined eloquence. Your light and empty tones produce absurd effects, and as a result the *substance* of your speech withers and fades. In the days when Sophocles or Euripides found the indispensable word to use, young men were not yet confined to declamations. When Pindar and the nine lyric poets humbly refrained from using Homer's lines, no pedant in his study had yet ruined the talents of the young. I certainly do not find that either Plato or Demosthenes resorted to training of this kind. Great style, and that is also, if I may say it, modest style, is neither spotty nor swollen, but rises up by virtue of its natural beauty. Your puffed-up and extravagant verbosity is a recent immigrant to Athens from Asia. Like a pestilential planet it paralyzed the minds of young men who aspired to great achievements, and when the old standards were once corrupted, eloquence came to a standstill and lost the power of speech.

A letter (108.6-7) of the younger Seneca (his letters were written in A.D. 63-65, during the reign of Nero) describes and censures the levity of the students, their apathy towards ideas, and their passion for the sound of empty words:

To a large part of the listeners the philosopher's class-room is a retreat for their leisure. Their purpose is not to receive a rule of life there, but to enjoy thoroughly the pleasures of the ear. Some appear even with writing-tablets, not to take down the matter, but only the words, that they may repeat them to another, providing him with no more advantage than they themselves received in hearing them. The right kind of hearer is rapt and stirred by the beauty of the subject matter, not by the thunder of hollow words.

If we accept the argument of some scholars that Tacitus' *Dialogue on Orators* was composed probably in A.D. 80/81, then Messalla's words in that book speak for the time of Titus. They express a judgment no different from that of Petronius above:

The exercises in which the schools engage largely run counter to their own purposes. Ye gods! what stuff the *controversiae* are made of, and how unnaturally they are contrived! And furthermore, in addition to the matter that is so at variance with real life, there is the declamatory style in which it is delivered. And so it comes that themes like "the reward for the tyrannicide," or "the options left to the ravished maiden," or "a remedy for the plague," or "the unchaste matron," and all the other topics that are daily treated in the school, but seldom or never in the forum, they set forth in grandiose style (35).

At the end of the century, Pliny the Younger in a letter (2. 14) to a friend describes in painful detail how the declamatory method has invaded and come to dominate the ancient tribunal of the *Centumviri*:

Your supposition is correct: I am kept busy by cases in the Centumviral court, and they bring me more toil than pleasure. They are generally paltry and meagre, and it is very seldom that one of significance comes up. Furthermore, there are very few counsel with whom I care to plead; the rest are a bold lot, and the majority in fact obscure youngsters who have come over from the schools to practice declamation, and do so without reverence or consideration. In the old days young men, even of the best families, were not admitted to the bar unless introduced by some person of consular rank; so great was the respect with which our ancestors honored this noblest of professions. But now that everything is opened wide to everybody, the young men are not introduced; rather they break their way in.

The hearers are worthy of such pleaders, having been hired and bought; the dole is paid out to them in the middle of the court-house as openly as if it were a dining-room, and for the like fee they go from one court to another! Just yesterday two of my nomenclators, scarcely old enough to wear the toga, were bribed to applaud at the price of three denarii [about thirty-six cents] each—that is how much it costs if you wish a reputation as "The Most Eloquent." At this price we fill crowded benches, and at this price endless shouts are raised when the chorus-leader gives the signal. Indeed these claqueurs need a signal, for they understand nothing of what is said, and do not even listen to it. If at any time you should pass by the court-house, and should like to find out how well any of the speakers is doing, you can be sure that that speaker who receives the loudest praise is the worst.

I am ashamed to tell you with what a mincing utterance they deliver their speeches; this sing-song oratory lacks only hand-clapping, or rather cymbals and drums.

Up to now, only the interests of my friends and the consideration of my youth have kept me in this court; but I attend less often than I used to, and so am preparing a gradual retirement.

Finally Juvenal, writing perhaps in A.D. 118, after observing Roman life for many years, bears satiric witness to the persistence of theme and method in the schools:

O Vettius, of iron must your bowels be when your mob of pupils butchers the cruel tyrant in a chorus. The cabbage, so served up repeatedly, is death to the unhappy teacher! "It is made out to be the teacher's fault that the dull Arcadian youngster feels no flutter in his left breast when dinning my unhappy ears on every sixth day of the week with his 'Hannibal the dire,' whatever be the question which he is deliberating." If the teacher of rhetoric takes my advice, he will give himself a gladiator's discharge, and enter upon some other walk of life (7.150 ff.).

The actual tyrant on the Palatine did not always ignore the "academic" habit, inherited from the Greeks, of inveighing against tyranny; Caligula banished Carrinas Secundus, and Domitian put a certain Maternus out of the way, for delivering such speeches as rhetorical exercises.[7]

These Roman critics make amply plain what the nature and inspiration of public discourse in their times were. The final expression of the spirit of *declamatio,* however, we find in a Greek satirist of the next century. The following excerpts from Lucian's dialogue, "The Professor of Public Speaking," show that the meretricious methods employed by the teachers in the first century persisted in the next, despite the fact that Quintilian's *Training of an Orator,* which represented a return to the rhetoric of Cicero, was published before the second century opened. But the influence of this great work, strong for a time, was thereafter impeded by Fronto and the archaizers. I should remind the reader that Lucian was himself a rhetorician, and that he pleaded in court, but enjoyed much more his wide travels in many countries as a lecturer before educated audiences; further, that the aim of his satire was amusement. Lucian makes the same points as his Roman predecessors: the successful speaker needs none of the old type of training, no study of good authors, no command of fact and logic, no wealth of ideas, but only a loud and assertive manner, and a style of purple patches all compact. The young man ambitious to become a public speaker is encouraged to join the great company of nonentities who by the power of speech have gained a reputation for respectability, wealth, and even gentle birth. To the summit where sits Rhetoric, attended by Wealth, Fame, and Might, two roads lead. The narrow, steep, and thorny track must be avoided, for it promises thirst and sweat, and the poet who said that the Good is got by toil was wrong. The guide of this rough road must not be heeded. Pointing out the footprints of Demosthenes and Plato, "this quack and old fossil will expect you to unearth long-buried speeches as if they were a treasure, forgetting that we are now at peace, with no aggressor Philip to make the speeches of a sword-maker's son

[Demosthenes] perhaps seem useful." But the young man is to take, at a leisurely pace, the other road, which, pleasant and short, leads through flowery meadows. At this road he will meet a man of honeyed voice who will modestly speak as follows:

My good man, surely not Apollo sent you to me? Ah, you will find that my voice overcomes all others, as the trumpet the flute, as the cicada the bee, as the choir the master who gives the key-note of the tune. You could not learn to be a speaker with so much ease from anyone but me. Have no scruples and be not disturbed that you have not passed through all the weary rites of initiation which the ordinary system of preparatory teaching sets in the path of silly fools. Sail right in, even if—a by no means uncommon thing—you do not know how to write. Speaking is something else again! I will first list all the equipment for your journey, then add some advice, and before sunset, I shall make you known as a better speaker than all the others, as good indeed as myself, without doubt the first, middle-most, and last of all the speaker-profession.

Bring then, first of all, ignorance, and then self-assurance, effrontery, and shamelessness. Modesty, fairness, moderation, and shame? Leave them at home; they are useless and cumbrous. Then too, a very loud voice, and an impudent sing-song delivery. Further, have a company of attendants, and always a book in your hand.

You must take special care of your appearance. Next, pick out from some source or other fifteen old Attic words—or twenty at the outside, exercise yourself in their use carefully and have them at the tip of your tongue; for example: *sundry, upon which, surely not, in some wise, Good my Sir;* these are the seasoning which you will apply in every speech, and you are not to concern yourself about any dissimilarity, incompatibility, or discord between them and the rest. Go after esoteric, unfamiliar words only rarely used by the ancients, and have ready an accumulation of them to discharge at your hearers. Thereby you will draw the attention of all the crowd, and they will consider you marvelous, if, for example, you do not say "earnest"-but "caution"-money. You may also now and then create monstrous neologisms of your own, and ordain, for example, that a "sage" shall be called a "sapient."

If you commit a solecism or barbarism, let your one remedy be boldness: be ready to cite as your authority the name of some poet or historian who does not now exist and never did exist. As for reading the ancient classics, that is not for you to do—whether that silly Isocrates, that insipid Demosthenes, or that spiritless Plato. Study rather the speeches of the last generation, and the exercises which they call declamations; these will supply you with a store of provisions on which you can draw at need.

When the time comes for you to speak and the hearers have proposed themes and starting-points for discussion, find fault with all the difficult ones; disparage them as offering no challenge, any of them, to a he-man. Do not hesitate, but say whatever comes into your head. Have no care that the first thing shall be said first because it actually is first, or that your second and third shall be in the proper order. Just say first what comes first to you. But press on, keep going, and only do not stop. For all occasions have Marathon in readiness; you cannot do without it. And always have a fleet crossing Mount Athos in ships, and an army the Hellespont on foot, the sun eclipsed by the arrows of the Medes, Xerxes in flight, and Leonidas receiving acclaim. And in everything let those few words of your selection, your seasoning-condiment, abound and flourish—apply *sundry* and *doubtless* constantly, even if you do not need them; they are lovely words, even when used haphazardly. Exclaim "Ah, woe unto me" often, smite your thigh, bellow, punctuate what you say with clearings of the throat, and sway your hips as you pace about.

That they may admire the copiousness of your speeches start with the Trojan war, and bring your narrative down to today. Perspicacious people are rare; any comment they may make will be laid to jealousy. Never write anything out, nor think a subject through before you come forward to speak; that will certainly give you away.

Be sure to have a chorus of your own, one that sings in unison, and as you go home afterwards, analyzing what you have said, let them attend you as a bodyguard. And if you meet anyone on the way, talk vaingloriously about yourself. Ask him: "Who is Demosthenes compared to me?"

But the most important and most cogent means of winning repute I had almost left out: ridicule all the other speakers. If one of them speaks well, the charms he displays are borrowed; if mild exception is taken to his speech, all of it is censurable. In general smile faintly; make it clear that you do not accept what is being said.

Learn these instructions thoroughly, my boy, and I confidently promise that you shall very soon become a first-rate speaker, like myself. And now I have given you my advice, so help you the Goddess of Venery.

§3

For the effects which the changed political conditions brought about in the position held by public utterance in the Roman State, we must turn to Tacitus in his capacity of historian. In the *Annals* 1. 2 (about A.D. 115) he describes the effect upon character wrought by the change from Republic to Empire, and in the *Histories* 1. 1 (A.D. 104-9) the effect upon the writing of history:

> There was no opposition, since the most courageous had fallen on the fields of battle or by proscription; while the rest of the nobility found that the readiness to accept servitude brought them elevation to wealth and office, and having flourished on revolution, they preferred now the new order with its security to the old with its perils.

> Many historians, so long as they were treating of the Roman republic, wrote with equal eloquence and freedom. But after the battle of Actium [31 B.C.], when in the interests of peace all power was placed in the hands of one man, historians of like great talent passed out of existence. And at the same time the truth was falsified in many ways: first, because historians were ignorant of politics as though politics were not their business, later because of their inordinate desire to flatter; or again, because of their hatred of their rulers. If my life lasts long enough, I have saved for my old age the history of the deified Nerva's reign and of Trajan's rule, a richer and safer subject, thanks to the rare good fortune of an era in which you may feel what you wish and may say what you feel.

The prosecutions for seditious utterance under Domitian moved Tacitus, breathing the freer air of a more enlightened reign, to write some of his most eloquent lines (*Agricola* 2-3; A.D. 98):

> The records tell us that when Rusticus Arulenus praised Thrasea Paetus, and when Herennius Senecio praised Helvidius Priscus,[8] their praise constituted a capital crime, so that vengeance was wreaked not only on the authors themselves but also on their books; to the public hangman[9] was delegated the task of burning in the Comitium and Forum the memorials of these noblest of characters.

> No doubt they believed that in those flames were being effaced the voice of the Roman people, the liberty of the Senate, the conscience of mankind; especially when in addition the professors of philosophy were expelled, and thereby all worthy accomplishments banished, in order that nowhere might anything that is honorable occur.

> Surely we have given abundant proof of our tameness of spirit; and just as men of former times saw the extremes of liberty, so have we seen the extremes of slavery, the public informers having robbed us even of the intercourse of conversation. We should have lost memory itself as well as voice, if only we had found it as easy to forget as to be silent.

Now at last spirit is returning to us; from the very beginning of the dawn of this happiest of eras Nerva has joined two things formerly irreconcilable, Empire and liberty; and Trajan is daily increasing the happiness of our times.

During a period of fifteen years [the reign of Domitian, A.D. 81-96], a large space in human life, many of us have died from natural causes; the most courageous have perished by the Emperor's cruelty; while the few of us who survive have survived not only our friends but also, so to speak, ourselves; since from the prime of life have been effaced fifteen years, during which those of us who were young reached old age, and those who were old reached the very limits of a completed life, and all in enforced silence.

When in the *Annals* (4. 34) Tacitus dealt with the famous prosecution of Cremutius Cordus, he seized the opportunity to present his own views on freedom of speech:

During the consulship of Cornelius Cossus and Asinius Agrippa [A.D. 25] there took place the prosecution of Cremutius Cordus, upon the novel and up to then unheard-of charge that in a history which he had published he had eulogized Brutus, and termed Cassius the last of the Romans. That the accusers were dependents of Sejanus was of fatal consequence to Cordus, and so also was the grim countenance of Tiberius as he listened to the defence. Cremutius began the defence as follows: "It is my words, Conscript Fathers, that are under accusation—so true is it that I am guiltless of deeds. Nor are they even words directed against the emperor or his parent, the only persons embraced by the law of treason. I am said to have praised Brutus and Cassius, whose exploits ever so many writers have recorded, and none has mentioned except with respect. Livy [who eulogized Pompey without forfeiting Augustus' friendship] nowhere refers to Brutus and Cassius by the now popular appellations of brigand and parricide, but again and again as distinguished men. Cicero's book lauded Cato [of Utica] to the skies, and how did the dictator Caesar reply to it? Only in the form of a written speech,[10] as though he were presenting his case before jurors. The letters of Antony, the speeches of Brutus, the poems of Bibaculus and Catullus contain invectives and insults against the Caesars, yet the deified Julius and the deified Augustus tolerated these works and left them alone—whether with the motive of forbearance or of wisdom it would not be easy to say. For the things you spurn soon pass from memory, while your anger is taken as an admission that they are true.

I do not mention the Greeks. Among them not only liberty but even license went unpunished; or if a man paid heed, he avenged words by means of words. But especially free from punishment and immune from detraction was the publishing of opinions on those whom death had removed beyond the bounds of hate or of partiality. Are Brutus and Cassius now upon the plains of Philippi, armed for battle, and am I upon the hustings, inflaming the people to civil war?

If my condemnation is upon me, there will not be lacking those who will remember not only Brutus and Cassius, but me as well!

Cordus then left the Senate, and ended his life by starvation. The fathers ordered that his books be burned by the aediles; but there remained hidden copies, which were later published—and that fact disposes me the more to deride the senselessness of those who believe that by the use of power in the present there can be blotted out also the memory of a subsequent age. On the contrary, if genius is punished, it grows in influence; nor have alien kings or such men as have adopted their cruel practices thereby begotten anything but ignominy for themselves and glory for their victims.

§4

A number of authors in the first century were deeply conscious of the decadence in oratory and the other arts, and were interested in its causes. I shall let them in most part speak for themselves, and by way of preface shall merely call attention to two considerations. The reader of these passages must make allowance for what Ps.-Longinus (44. 6) calls the human tendency to find fault with one's own era, realizing also that an age which produces great satirists and other writers who are alive to the faults of their civilization is on that very account itself praiseworthy. We can doubtless find in every period of history, whether it be of a high or a low state of culture, some reputable observer who looks upon his day as one of decline. Aper in Tacitus' *Dialogue* says: "You must lay it to the fault of human malignity that the old is always held in high esteem, the modern in scorn" (18).[11] And especially in the first century it was a pious convention among Romans to glorify the good old times. Secondly, the question of the decline of eloquence has been treated by some scholars as one which arose only at this special time, a burning literary question of the day, comparable, for example, to the Battle of the Books in the time of Bentley and Swift.[12] Such issues, it is maintained, are always hotly fought for a time, and at the end neither side wins the victory. "'Tis best to dismiss the question, and to let things go as they please," says Orestes in Euripides' *Electra* (379), and these words are used by Longinus as an epilogue to his discussion of decay. In any event, the attitude to be observed at this period is obviously different from that of Cicero's *Brutus*, in which, as Rand has said, the course of oratory is onward and upward, "with a precious little autobiography at the end."[13] Yet in *Tusc. Disp.* (2. 1. 5) Cicero wrote: "And in oratory the renown of Rome has from a humble beginning reached its acme, so that now, as is the law of nature in virtually everything, it is in its decline and seems destined soon to come to nothing," and these words should be borne in mind when we read Velleius below.

It was possible to be conscious of a decline, and to find the causes in the private morality of the citizens, rather than in the shaping influence of political institutions. Thus Livy in the Preface to his work, which was begun about 27 B.C., looks upon his own time as one of debased morality "when we can endure neither our vices nor their cure," and yet this ethical critic of history sees in the establishment and enlargement of the Empire the realization of the qualities he hoped to instill by means of his history. He was aristocratic and republican in sympathy, but under Augustus a sentimental regard for the brave days of old (*prisca illa*) was not incompatible with loyalty to the emperor, whose respect for tradition and whose moral reforms Livy must have warmly approved, and whose intimate friendship he enjoyed. Augustus could overlook the *licentia* of Livy's question whether the birth of Julius Caesar had brought more harm or good to the State (Seneca, *Nat. Quaest.* 5. 18. 4), even as when, instead of punishing his nephew for reading a book by Cicero, he said of the orator: "A learned man, my child, a learned man, and a great patriot" (Plutarch, *Cicero* 49. 3). Livy attributes the cause of decline to wealth, bringing avarice in its train, and to the physical pleasures, bringing licentiousness and through it personal and universal ruin. Eumolpus in Petronius' *Satyricon* (88), discoursing on the fine arts, likewise traces the decline to the root of all evil:

Love of money brought these changes about. For in former ages, when virtue was still loved for herself alone, the liberal arts flourished. But we, immersed in wine and women, attack the past, and teach and learn nothing but vices. Where is dialectic now, or astronomy? Who has ever come to a temple and made an offering in the hope of attaining to eloquence? They do not even ask for good sense or good health, but one promises an offering if he may bury his rich neighbor, another if he may dig up a treasure, another if he may make thirty millions in safety. So do not wonder that painting is decadent, when all the gods and men think a mass of gold more beautiful than anything ever done by those crazy Greeklings, Apelles and Phidias.

Pliny the Elder, in a digression from a study of viticulture (*Nat. Hist.* 14. 1; about A.D. 77), offers some scholarly comments in explanation of the "accidie" of his day. He essentially concurs with Petronius, but goes beyond the satirist in tracing the cause of moral decadence to the complexity of the Empire:

Who would not admit that now, when the sovereignty of the Roman Empire has united all the world, civilization has advanced, through the exchange of goods and the common fellowship in the joys of peace. Yet the ancient writers have handed down to us much which, I swear, no one now knows. So much more fruitful was their research, or so much more fortunate their industry. We of today must inquire not only into the discoveries of modern times, but also into those of the ancients, discoveries which our slothfulness has let fall into utter oblivion. The causes of this lethargy—shall we not find them to be the same as those which operate generally throughout the world? New fashions, no doubt, have now sprung up; new interests engage the minds of men; and the only arts that are now cultivated are those of avarice.

In former times, when the sway of nations was circumscribed by their own narrow limits, and consequently so also circumscribed was the genius of their people, what I may call the niggardliness of fortune forced them to exercise the faculties of the intellect. Innumerable kings received the homage of the arts, and when displaying their resources gave special prominence to these arts, believing that through them immortality would be secured. Hence rewards as well as the works of civilization multiplied. To succeeding ages an expanded world and the grandeur of our Empire have been injurious. Ever since senators began to be chosen according to their wealth, judges appointed according to their wealth, and it became usual to think that nothing confers greater honor upon magistrates and generals than their wealth, ever since legacy-hunting became the most remunerative of occupations, and it became usual to think that there are no pleasures except those of possession; ever since that time, all the rewards of life have gone to ruin, and all those arts which we call liberal, from liberty, that greatest good, now deserve the opposite name, and indeed only servility is profitable. And so, I swear, pleasure has begun to live, and life itself is now no more.

Compare with Pliny, and with each other, two authors of the next century: Appian extols with high praise the spread of the Roman Empire and the unification of the world (*Roman History*, Preface 7); the philosopher Epictetus minifies the achievement, wishing to indicate the limitations of the Caesar's power to provide peace as against the power of philosophy to do so in a more vital sense (3. 13. 9 ff.).

At the end of the first century Quintilian wrote a treatise, now lost, on the Causes of Corrupt Prose Composition; evidence indicates that the point of view was purely technical. He wrote his great work, *The Training of an Orator* (before A.D. 96), because he thought the time ripe for a rebirth of eloquence. When we talk about decay in this century, we must yet always be mindful that this great work belongs to the period. More than once Quintilian refers to the decline of eloquence, but again his observations are technical and not historical. The teachers are to blame for the extravagance and ignorance of our declaimers, and therefore for the decline in oratory (2. 10. 3 ff.). He is aware of the unreality of declamation and its extravagance in the choice of words (8. 3. 23). But Quintilian is a constructive teacher. He thinks eloquence an accomplishment transcending even success in navigation and astronomy (12. 11. 10). The idea of declamation is basically sound. Only choose subjects modeled on the pleadings for which it is devised as training. Have the young man write out speeches of his own dealing with cases which he has actually heard pleaded, and argue them from both sides. Make utility again the aim of eloquence. Choose cases that are longer to deliver and more complicated, use more humor, use words drawn from the speech of every day. Go back to the old practice of declaiming commonplaces. *Occa-*

sional magnificence, *occasional* unreality are not too harmful, if these are limited to the exercises in the schools and do not appear in actual practice. The danger of engaging the young too long in false semblances of reality is that they will shrink with terror from the real perils of public life, like men dazzled by unfamiliar sunlight. Seek virility of style instead of the effeminate quality now popular. Emphasize careful preparation; some declaimers are led by a perverse ambition to speak the moment the theme has been given them, and even ask for a word with which to start—an affectation which is in the worst and most theatrical taste.[14] It is significant of the times that Quintilian bases his treatment of deliberative oratory almost entirely on the *suasoriae*.

The historian Velleius Paterculus (1. 16 ff.), writing in A.D. 30, does not explain the phenomenon of decline by defective education or by the growth of luxury and avarice, however stimulated, but by a natural "law" of reaction:

I cannot refrain from making note of a subject which I have often revolved in my mind, but have never clearly reasoned through. Who can wonder enough that the most eminent geniuses in each art come together within the same narrow space of time? A single epoch gave lustre to tragedy through three men of divine inspiration—Aeschylus, Sophocles, and Euripides; a single epoch to the old and new Comedy. The philosopher-geniuses, too, inspired by Socrates, how long did they flourish after the death of Plato and of Aristotle? And as in Greece, so in Rome. Oratory burgeoned forth under Cicero, so that there are very few before his time who can give you pleasure, and none whom you can admire unless he had seen Cicero or had been seen by Cicero.

Though I often search for the reasons why men of like genius are confined to certain periods, I can never find any of whose truth I am sure. Yet I do find some reasons which are perhaps plausible, and among them the following: Genius is nourished by emulation, and it is sometimes envy, sometimes esteem which enkindles imitation; and it is natural that that which is cultivated with greatest zeal rises to the highest point of perfection. Yet to stay at the point of perfection is difficult, and naturally that which cannot go forward recedes. When we have given up hope of being able to surpass or equal those whom we regard as our superiors, our zeal declines with our hope; it ceases to follow what it cannot catch up with, and abandoning the subject as though it were in another's possession, it seeks a new one.

The greatest obstacle to perfection in any work is our fickle habit of deserting to something else.

Seneca the Elder (*Contr.* 1, *Praef.* 6 ff.), writing in A.D. 37, finds a possible explanation in the same "law" of nature, and applies the "law" in the same way as Velleius:

Whatever quality Roman eloquence has which can vie with or surpass insolent Greece flourished about the time of Cicero. All the talents which gave lustre to our studies were born then. Since his day the art has daily deteriorated, whether through the luxury of our time (for nothing is so deadly to talent as luxury); or whether, when the reward accorded to this most beautiful art vanished, all efforts were turned toward base practices abounding in glory or profit; or whether by some fate whose spiteful and constant law in all things decrees that what has risen to the greatest heights slips back again to the lowest depth, and more quickly than it ascended.

To this same "law," it must be noted, Blass[15] has recourse in his endeavor to explain the decay of eloquence in Greece after Alexander, and Cucheval[16] makes it the primary factor in the decay at Rome. True, thinks Cucheval, liberty was lost. True that the education was defective. But the most important consideration in his eyes is the validity of Velleius' "law": decay would have come in any event. So far as Velleius himself is concerned, one cannot help remembering at this juncture that he was not ordinarily of a philosophical bent and in practice was unable to discern the great movements in history.

In wistful retrospect Pliny the Younger describes (*Epist.* 8. 14) the sounder method on which in other days the training for public life was based, and from the security of Trajan's reign he looks back with repugnance upon the dark days of Domitian, in whose insolent and repressive tyranny he finds the true causes of the decline. This letter, published about A.D. 109, in special gives a picture of the wretched degradation into which the Senate had sunk:

Our subjection under a former reign covered with a blanket of oblivion and ignorance all the arts of culture; for who is so tame-spirited as to desire to learn an art which he will be unable to put in practice? And so liberty when restored on Nerva's accession [in A.D. 96] found us wanting in skill and experience.

It was our rule in the olden days that we should learn from our

elders both by precept and example the principles which we ourselves should one day put in practice, and in our turn hand down
to the younger generation. So when our elders became candidates
for office, they used to stand at the doors of the Senate-house, and
were spectators before they were colleagues in this body. Thus they
were taught by the most unfailing method of instruction, example,
all the Senatorial practice.

[During Domitian's reign] I paid a visit to the Senate, but a Senate
that was frightened and speechless; since it was dangerous if you
said what you felt, and detestable if you said what you did not feel.
What could be learned, what pleasure was there in learning, when
the Senate was convened either for utter idleness or for business of
utter sinfulness, was kept in session either for ridiculous or grievous
ends, and passed resolutions that were never serious, but often sad-
dening? On becoming a Senator, and hence a sharer in these evils,
I witnessed and suffered them for many years, and as a result my
spirits were dulled, broken, and crushed even for a time thereafter.

And in an earlier letter (3. 18; A.D. 101), in which Pliny reports that his panegyric of Trajan was listened to for three
days, he states briefly but emphatically the main prerequisite
for a healthy epideictic: "The reason is not that we write with
more eloquence, but with more freedom than formerly, and
as a result with greater enjoyment. It will redound to the
further glory of our present Emperor [Trajan] that discourses
of this kind, once as detested as they were false, are now as
pleasing as they are sincere."

A word about the recluse Persius (A.D. 34-62) and the realist
Juvenal[17] (A.D. ?60-?138). Both satirists seem unconscious of the
main cause of the decline, and their silence under the despot-
isms of their day is of course understandable. Persius explains
the weakness of poetry and oratory by the decay of morality,
which he does not connect with the loss of freedom. But even
when you think that he may really discuss the qualifications of
the Statesman in Satire 4, or when he discourses on human
freedom in Satire 5, you find no recognition of the state of
political subjection in which the Romans now found themselves. The discourse on freedom is a typical Stoic treatment
of the subject—How can one master one's own soul?; political
considerations are entirely absent. Juvenal had lived through
the terrible latter years of Nero's reign and through Domitian's.

He believes deeply in the virtues of the past, admires the heroes of the republican time, and cites them as models; he criticizes Roman life caustically, but Roman *private* life. The degeneracy which he brilliantly describes he relates but seldom to the despotic character of the government. Only a few verses emerge from his silence: "But Rome was free when she called Cicero parent and father of his country" (*Sat.* 8. 243-4, and see also 1. 151 ff.). Contrast with Persius and Juvenal the words of Lucan (A.D. 39-65) on Pharsalus (*Civil War* 7. 639 ff.):

> More was lost there than mere life and safety; we were overthrown for all the future ages of the world; all the generations, which shall ever live in slavery, were conquered by those swords. For what crime of their own commission were the sons and grandsons of those who fought at Pharsalus born to servitude? If to us born after that battle, thou, Fortune, gavest a master, thou shouldst have given us also the chance of fighting for our freedom.

But Lucan's revolutionary enthusiasm and audacious championship, during Nero's reign, of the defenders of the ancient republican system are subjects that cannot be enlarged upon here. Nor, on the other hand, may I discuss the contradiction offered us by his oily flattery of Nero (1. 33-66); all the horrors of the Civil War were not too high a price to pay if the Fates could not otherwise have willed the coming of Nero: "When your watch on this earth has come to an end, and you seek the stars at last, the sky will rejoice. But to me you are already a god." For Lucan believed that Fate had ordained the monarchy.[18]

Ps.-Longinus and Tacitus I have saved for the last, because more specifically than all the other observers they see that the main issue is between political freedom and autocracy. The one permits an insight into the truth to show through his protective coloration; the other comes perhaps as closely to grips with the question as was in the conditions of his time possible. We must of course read both in the light of these conditions.

In the last chapter of his essay *On the Sublime,* Ps.-Longinus brings up a question "lately raised by a certain philosopher," who speaks as follows:

> I wonder, as no doubt do many others, too, how it is that in the

present age there are men who are gifted with the powers of persuasion and statesmanship in the highest degree, and are keen and
versatile, and especially expert in the charms of style, yet truly lofty
and sublime natures are no longer produced, or only quite exception-
ally. So great and universal is the dearth of eloquence that has its hold
upon our age! Must we really believe that oft-repeated observation
that democracy is the kind foster-mother of greatness, and that literary
excellence may be said to flourish only with democracy, and with
democracy to die? For freedom, it is said, has power to nourish the
imagination of the high-minded and to kindle hope, and where it
prevails there spreads abroad the zeal of mutual rivalry and the
ambitious struggle for pre-eminence. Moreover by reason of the rewards which are open to all in free states, the mental powers of the
speaker are continually sharpened by exercise, and as it were rubbed
to brightness, and shine forth, as is natural, with the same freedom
as animates the State. But today we seem to be trained to righteous
servitude in our childhood, being all but swathed in its customs and
practices when our minds are still tender, and never tasting of that
most lovely and most abundant fountain of eloquence, I mean
liberty. And so we turn out to be nothing but sublime flatterers. One
has aptly represented all servitude, even if it be most righteous, as
the cage of the soul and a public dungeon.

Longinus' formal answer to the question posed by the philosopher is far from satisfactory. What enslaves us, he says, is
rather love of money and pleasure: "No, for such as we are it
is perhaps better to be held in subjection than to be free, since
our appetites, if let loose altogether upon our neighbors like
beasts from a den, would set the civilized world on fire with
evil deeds." Gibbon comments: "Longinus was forced to ener-
vate [his noble ideas on liberty] not only by the term 'most
righteous,' which he takes care to apply twice to the present
despotism, but by employing the stale pretence of putting his
own thoughts into the mouth of a nameless philosopher."[19]
In Tacitus' distinguished little book of criticism, *The Dialogue on Orators,* Maternus bids Messalla to discuss the decline
of eloquence and in doing so to avail himself of the old-fashioned freedom of speech "from which we have degenerated
even more than we have from eloquence" (27). Maternus had
said: "The mercenary eloquence of the present day is a recent
innovation, born of a degenerate state of society" (12). Messalla

discusses the laxity of the training at home, the carelessness of parents, the ignorance of teachers, the decline in old-fashioned virtue, and especially the vices characteristic of the city Rome— the passion for play-actors and the interest in the contests of gladiators and of horses. The past is not solidly learned, nor as in Cicero's day is universal knowledge sought, but now the essential thing is declamation, the training of tongue and voice in imaginary debates which have no relation with real life. He prefers the rough home-spun of Gracchus and Crassus, and bewails the practice of some speakers of today, who boast that their speeches can be sung and danced to (25-26, 28-32).

But of special significance are the utterances of two other interlocutors in the *Dialogue,* Secundus and Maternus. Secundus argues that the unsettled political conditions which prevailed during the republic, the dissensions and feuds of those days of unrest and unrestraint, when there was no single ruler to apply a strong hand, and freedom of speech was untrammeled, tore the State apart. But it is in such an environment that eloquence thrives. "Great oratory, like a flame, needs fuel to sustain it, movement to excite it, and it brightens in the burning." Eloquence was then an indispensable passport to success in public life, and great issues and trials brought it immense rewards. Cicero's reputation would never have been great if there were no Catiline, no Milo, no Verres, no Antony (36 ff.).

Maternus admits that the turbulent days of the republic encouraged greater oratory, but insists that the blessings of peace and the tranquillity of the present more than compensate for the superior oratory of the past:

The art we are discussing is not a quiet and peaceable art. Truly great and distinguished oratory is rather a foster-child of license, which foolish men call liberty,[20] an associate of sedition, a goad for the unbridled multitude; and it does not grow in a well-regulated civic order. Do we hear of the existence of any oratory at Sparta or in Crete, states whose constitution and laws were the most rigorous ever recorded? Eloquence was unknown in Macedonia certainly, and in Persia [all these states were either militaristic or autocratic], and in fact in all states that were content with an undisputed government. There were some orators at Rhodes, at Athens a great many; in both states the populace could do everything, the ignorant multitude could do everything, everybody, so to speak, could do everything. Likewise in our own State, so long as it swayed hither and thither, so long as it spent itself in partisan struggles and dissensions and disagreements, so long as there was no peace in the forum, no harmony in the Senate, no self-control on the part of the speakers in the law-courts, no obedience to authority, no sense of restraint on the part of the magistrates, such turbulent times produced an eloquence that was no doubt more vigorous. But the eloquence of the Gracchi was not so beneficial to the country that it should endure their laws as well, and ingloriously did Cicero pay for his fame in oratory by such a death. . . . Just as the art of medicine is least needed and is consequently of least advantage amongst peoples who enjoy great good health and sound constitutions, so oratory has less value and repute where people are well-behaved and ready to obey their sovereign. What need is there of long arguments in the Senate, when gentlemen agree so quickly? What need of a long succession of speeches before the public assembly, when it is not the ignorant multitude that deliberates upon the common welfare, but *one man,* and he the all-wisest? (40-41).

I refrain from putting any of the emperors of the first century to the test of the appraisal in this last sentence, even as I omit to draw modern analogies.

It may seem that Maternus is bluntly taking issue with Cicero, who in a number of places[21] expresses himself to the following effect: "The ambition to speak does not arise among men who are shackled and bound fast by the tyranny of kings. Eloquence is an associate of peace and an ally of tranquillity and is, so to speak, a foster-child of a well-regulated civic order." "This one art has constantly flourished above all others in every free nation, and especially in those states which have acquired peace and tranquillity." But Cicero's thought is not necessarily in conflict with that of Tacitus' interlocutor. Cicero is thinking of freedom from foreign wars, and his "well-regulated civic order" is opposed not to a state torn by dissensions, but to one whose institutions have not yet been firmly established. Quintilian, on the other hand, stresses the part played by oratory in the establishing of stable governments: Denouncers of eloquence say that it "stirs up not only sedition and popular tumult, but wars that can never be expiated." But "never, I believe, would the founders of cities have brought it about that the nomadic multitudes should join into communities if these had not been persuaded by learned utterance; nor without the consummate power of oratory would the great law-givers have prevailed upon humankind to yield to the servitude of Law" (2. 16. 1 ff.). More directly opposed to Maternus would be J. A. Symonds, discoursing on an art allied to eloquence. A comparison of the drama of different peoples proves to him that one of the two conditions necessary for the creation of great drama is that a nation must be free: "It requires a *free* and *active* race, in which young and turbulent blood is flowing, to produce a drama."[22]

§5

It is likely that some of the authors I have cited avoided for reasons of prudence a discussion of political causes. Ps.-Longinus, for example, may indeed have written with timidity. We are not even sure that the treatises by Ps.-Longinus and Tacitus were intended for other than private circulation.[23] From passages in different works of Tacitus we are led to assume that he realized the past could not be recalled; he felt that the inevitable must be accepted, and that even under the Empire prudence and moderation could assure one honor and dignity.[24] In the *Dialogue* Maternus says: "Let everyone enjoy the advantages of his own era without disparaging any other age" (41). Seneca the Elder acquiesced in the new order (e.g., *Contr.* 2. 4. 13). Velleius accepted it with enthusiasm—its peace, stability, public works, the generosity of its princes—and we read his rhapsodical eulogies of the emperor Tiberius (e.g., 12. 111) with disapproval. Yet he said of Cicero that when he "was beheaded by the crime of Antony, the voice of the people was cut off" (2. 66). Quintilian held a chair of rhetoric under the Caesars, and wrote fulsomely of Domitian—"a prince pre-eminent in eloquence as in all other virtues" (4, *Praef.* 3, and see also 10. 1. 91-2).

Eloquence is, of course, traditionally connected with democracy. According to Aristotle[25] it was democracy which first gave birth to rhetoric in the revolutions of Sicily. When the Sicilian tyrants were expelled in 465 B.C., democracies came into being, and numerous lawsuits were instituted to recover the property which the tyrants had illegally confiscated. Corax wished to influence the people by speech and to that end wrote an art of rhetoric. The Greeks considered that the only kind of agreement desirable among rational men is that got from free discussion, and *parrhesia*, the right of the citizen to speak his mind, was staunchly prized. And if we wish to find a clear outline of the role discussion plays in a democracy we had better go, as for so many other touchstones, to the funeral speech Thucydides puts into the mouth of Pericles: "Those of our countrymen who are occupied chiefly with business yet do not lack a knowledge of public affairs. For we alone regard a man who takes no part in these public duties not as one who only minds his own business, but as a useless person; and we at least decide for ourselves, or reflect rightly upon, public questions, believing that it is not discussion that is a stumbling-block to action, but rather not to be instructed by discussion before entering upon action" (2. 40. 2). Rhetoric was forbidden in militaristic and bureaucratic Sparta.

Political bias is bound to affect our criticism of eloquence. Consider the varied fate of Demosthenes in recent times. If you believe in democratic principles, you are likely to read Demosthenes sympathetically, as the spokesman of democracy against Macedonian autocracy. But if your ideal is the empire of the Caesars, you will feel only contempt for the mean little State that had to yield to efficient Macedon, and feel only scorn for her provincial lawyer-spokesman who swam against the current without realizing that it was the wave of the future. It was in this spirit that, in 1916, the scholar Drerup made an appeal to banish the Greek orator from the schools of Germany.[26]

Want of space forbids us to compare the decline of eloquence in Greece after Alexander. Hellenistic scholars may have discussed the question. And at the beginning of Chapter 36 in Tacitus' *Dialogue* we read: "In our State, *too*, the eloquence of our fathers was promoted by the same conditions." A lacuna is properly thought to belong here, representing a discussion of Attic oratory, in which the same political-historical causes which brought about a high state of eloquence in Rome were set forth as bringing about like results in democratic Athens. Blass[27] thinks that the main cause of decay at Athens was the loss of free speech, and the resultant debasement of the character of the people. Thus we have the servile spectacle of the Athenians erecting 300 statues to one governor, Demetrius of Phalerum, and giving divine honors to his successor who overthrew him. Jebb[28] accepts the political explanation for the decay of deliberative and forensic oratory, but for the decline in the oratory of display, a fine art, he assigns another cause. The decay of citizen-life of the Greek republics brought about a change in the nature of Greek art. That art had been popular, fixing its attention on the essential and typical, and suppressing the accidental, trivial, and transient. When the moral unity of the city-state was broken, and men lived life apart from the city, the artist worked for a few, and caste and coterie make capricious judges. "In this sense, it may justly be said that nothing is so democratic as taste." If, by the way, we use this criterion for a comparison of Cicero and Pliny, we are forced to place Pliny in an age of decadence. Cicero repeatedly says that the opinion of a real ordinary Roman audience supplies the best test of good speaking;[29] whereas Pliny shows disdain for an audience other than intellectual.

In contrast to the situation in Greece, in the Roman Empire epideictic flourished, so far as popularity is concerned, for centuries. It became more and more debased. Compare Cicero's eulogy of Pompey (66 B.C.), Pliny's panegyric of the emperor Trajan (A.D. 100), and the panegyrics of the third and fourth centuries. Cicero's speech contains overmuch adulation, but is after all a *free* man's speech. Pliny's, except for a few passages, shows decency in the relations of orator and imperial patron. But Mamertinus' oration addressed to Maximian in A.D. 289 represents the extreme of unhealthy servility: "When our enemies would have invaded our provinces, O Emperor, what need was there of a multitude, since you in person contended?"

"Yes, you were so carried away through all the battle as a mighty stream, enhanced by winter snows and showers, is wont to invade the field on every side." "He who would enumerate your exploits, Emperor, must hope to have innumerable years, ay, centuries—indeed a life as long as *you* deserve."[30] Seyss-Inquart in Vienna on March 15, 1938: "My Fuehrer, wherever the way may lead we follow. Hail, my Fuehrer."

While we are in this general way considering the relation between the democratic civic order and eloquence, let us briefly glance back at an earlier day in our own democracy, and review the essay by Edward T. Channing, entitled "The Orator and His Times."[31] It was first published in 1819 and was reprinted by him in 1852. I report in condensed form, yet mostly in his own words, certain points of his argument:

Public Speaking cannot have now the importance and power it had in Greece and Rome. The ancients had a false estimate of national grandeur; the spirit of their governments was utterly warlike, their love of freedom was another name for ferocious lawlessness, and their love of country cloaked a boundless ambition for power. Society seemed to be a combination for extending power rather than for setting up a prosperous security. The population was ignorant and inflammable, and in the courts of justice the speaker was allowed to go beyond the law. Today [1819, 1852] we have a stable foundation and the ample protection of government. In free countries we are now disposed to make the security of individuals and of the State rest on laws and institutions, and not on the popular caprice, or on the power of any one man. That helps to explain what is reproachfully called the *temperate* and *inefficient* character of modern eloquence. [Recall that Channing's career spanned the time of Clay, Calhoun, Webster, and Wendell Phillips!] In Greece and Rome individuals seem to create great changes; but we think it one of the happiest, and we trust most permanent, distinctions that today we do not need the great man to take the place of our laws and institutions. The great man's sole power is restrained; he is perpetually taught that we can do without him. The orator is fortunately less able to do harm, and less needed to do good. The diffusion of knowledge helps us to help ourselves and to do without the orator's instruction. The orator in ancient times controlled his audience; today the audience controls him. Modern eloquence aims at making men think patiently and earnestly; it has only to secure a lodgment for truth in the mind, and then by and by the truth will quietly prevail. It seems as if the effect of our increased knowledge has been to make men more contemplative, and it is indeed true that the imagination and passions do not predominate—they are not our turbulent masters. It is the general effect of our improved society to give an influence to purity, firmness, and stability.

One might wish to defend the ancients against some of the accusations made by Channing, but would find it even more tempting to study how far the conditions which he describes for his day hold in 1944.

Hume in his essay on eloquence also thinks the modern world inferior to the ancient in eloquence. "It would be easy to find a Philip in modern times, but where shall we find a Demosthenes?" And De Quincy in his essay on rhetoric believes that the complexity of modern business will ever prevent the resurrection of rhetors.

The causes then, direct or contributory, to which the decay in the first century is assigned by our ancient theorists are the complexity of the Empire, degraded morality, debased education, general factors of cultural development (a natural law of reaction), and the loss of political liberty. The truth may well be that all these causes operated in a complex, but certainly the loss of political liberty is the major and ultimate consideration. The subject deserves profounder study than it has had. "Maturism," for example, is a favorite theory in the observation of human institutions—that they finish growing, become ripe and ready to fall after passing, as do individuals, through a process of youth and flowering.[32] Livy's figure is akin; he likens the downward plunge of morals in Roman life to a falling edifice (*Praef.* 9). De Quincey, deeply impressed by Velleius' reflections on the tendency of intellectual power to gather in clusters, endeavors to show that the observation founded by the Roman author's review of two literatures "we may now countersign by an experience of eight or nine"; his illustrations of the phenomenon in Greek and English literature in the essay on style must be known to all my readers. Further, symptom must be distinguished from cause. The education of the period cannot

be divorced from the society of which it was a manifestation
and accompaniment. The younger Seneca in *Epist.* 114 takes
the position that the style of speaking reproduces the general
character of the time. He thus replies to the question set him
by Lucilius, "why during certain periods a corrupt style of
speech comes to the fore, and how it happens that men's natural
capacities have declined into certain vices." And Persius in
Sat. 1 takes a comparable stand. The schools, as modern critics
say, were not responsible for the decadence. Nor can the character of the times and of the people be separated from the
political conditions of which they were largely the result. I
have here not attempted such a study as I think to be needed,
nor even emphasized the part played by Stoic thought in this
period—in particular by Stoic opposition to the worship of the
Caesars, and adherence to the tradition of *Cosmopolis* and the
brotherhood of man. I have not in detail discussed the decline
of the arts in their broadest form or of civilization in general,
nor the philosophy of history maintained by the historians, nor
the attitude to Fate held by the poets. My aim has been simply
to review what observers in the first century said on the decline
of oratory in particular, and we learn that some of these clearly
realized that eloquence flourishes best on soil dedicated to free
institutions.

NOTES

1. Secundus in Tacitus, *Dialogus de Oratoribus,* ch. 38.
2. See Gaston Boissier, *Tacitus,* tr. W. G. Hutchison (New York, 1906), pp.
180 ff.
3. Heinrich Meyer, *Oratorum Romanorum Fragmenta,* 2nd ed., Zürich, 1842,
and ed. H. Malcovati, Paravia, 1930.
4. See Victor Cucheval, *Histoire de l'éloquence romaine depuis la mort de.
Cicéron jusqu'à l'avènement de l'empereur Hadrien,* Paris, 1893, ch. 13.
5. See Cucheval, *op. cit.,* 1. 217-293; Henri Bornecque, *Les déclamations et
les déclamateurs d'après Sénèque le Père,* Lille, 1902; Boissier, *op. cit.,* pp. 163-
194; Bornecque, *Sénèque le rhéteur, controverses et suasoires,* 2 vols. Paris, no
date; W. A. Edward, *The Suasoriae of Seneca the Elder,* Cambridge, 1928; J.
Wight Duff, *A Literary History of Rome in the Silver Age,* New York, 1927,
pp. 1-64; Caplan, "The Latin Panegyrics of the Empire," *Quarterly Journal
of Speech* x (1924), 41-52; Wilhelm Kroll, art. "Rhetorik" in Pauly-Wissowa, coll. 80
ff.; Werner Hofrichter, *Studien zur Entwicklungsgeschichte der Deklamation
von der griechischen Sophistik bis zur römischen Kaiserzeit,* diss. Breslau, 1935.
6. The texts in this paper are for reasons of space often presented with omissions.

7. Dio Cassius 59. 20, 67. 12.

8. Thrasea was an outspoken opponent of Nero; his son-in-law Helvidius opposed Vespasian. Rusticus Arulenus in his biography of Thrasea spoke of him and of Helvidius as *sanctissimi viri*. Rusticus Arulenus was executed in A.D. 94, Herennius Senecio in A.D. 93.

9. *Triumviri capitales*. These minor officials superintended the prisons. The insult was greater in that the burning of books was usually performed by the aediles.

10. Caesar replied to Cicero's *Laus Catonis* with *Anticatones*, in two books.

11. On the popularity of the commonplace see Alfred Gudeman's Boston edition (1894), pp. 201-2.

12. See Gudeman, *op. cit.*, pp. xxxii ff.

13. E. K. Rand, *The Building of Eternal Rome* (Cambridge, 1943), p. 160.

14. See 2. 1. 9; 5. 12. 17ff.; 10. 5. 17ff.; 10. 7. 21.

15. Friedrich Blass, *Die griechische Beredsamkeit in dem Zeitraum von Alexander bis auf Augustus* (Berlin, 1865), pp. 12-13.

16. *Op. cit.*, 2. 369.

17. For this section see G. G. Ramsay, *Juvenal and Persius*, Loeb ed., 1920, Introd.

18. See, e.g., 3. 393.

19. *Journal*, Oct. 25, 1762; W. Rhys Roberts, *Longinus On the Sublime* (Cambridge, 1907), p. 13, n. 2; and cf. Ulrich von Wilamowitz-Moellendorf, *Der Glaube der Hellenen* (Berlin, 1932), 2. 547.

20. Cf. Plato, *Rep.* 572 d on the democratic man turned into the tyrannical: "complete lawlessness, called by his seducers 'perfect freedom' "; Ps.-Plutarch, "On Listening to Lectures":[1] "anarchy, which some of our young men, lacking an education, think to be freedom."

21. *Brutus* 45, *De Oratore* 1. 30; see also *De Oratore* 1. 14, 2. 33, *Orator* 141, and cf. *De Inv.* 1. 1 and *De Oratore* 1. 38.

22. *The Greek Poets* (New York, 1882), 2. 11.

23. See Roberts, *op. cit.*, p. 15.

24. For pertinent passages see *Annuals* 1. 9, 1. 74, 4. 33, 14. 12; *Agricola* 42; *Hist.* 1. 1, 1. 16, 4. 5; Gudeman, *op. cit.*, p. xxxvii.

25. In Cicero, *Brutus* 46; see art. "Korax" in Pauly-Wissowa.

26. Engelbert Drerup, *Aus einer alten Advokatenrepublik*, Paderborn, 1916.

27. *Op. cit.*, p. 12.

28. R. C. Jebb, *Attic Orators from Antiphon to Isaeos* (London, 1876), 2. 433 ff.

29. E.g., *Brutus* 184.

30. See Caplan, *art. cit.*

31. *Lectures*, Boston, 1856, pp. 1-25.

32. The cyclical view of history is very prevalent today; cf., e.g., the plan of A. J. Toynbee's *A Study of History* (London, 1934, 1939), which includes a treatment of the Genesis, Growth, Breakdown, and Disintegration of Civilizations.

Compendium Rhetorices by Erasmus:

A TRANSLATION

Hoyt H. Hudson

Publication of the tenth volume of the Oxford edition of Erasmus's letters[1] makes available a slight addition to the rhetorical work of the great humanist, his *Compendium Rhetorices,* reprinted from the unique extant copy of the first and only edition, Louvain, 1544. The circumstances of its publication by Rutger Rescius, a humanist-printer, set forth in the Oxford editors' introduction (and, for the most part in the prefatory epistle translated below), need not be recounted here. We may rather address ourselves to an estimate of the value and interest of the work.

A glance will show that what we have is a bare set of notes such as a college teacher might use, and perhaps write on the blackboard, covering a large part of the field of classical rhetoric as it flourished in the best Roman period. Erasmus bases his outline upon *Rhetorica ad Herennium,* Cicero's *De Inventione* and *Topica,* and Quintilian's *Institutio Oratoria.* His notes are such as will mean much to the man who made them but will appear somewhat cryptic to anyone else. "Nothing about the book," say the Oxford editors, "is interesting except that it was put together by Erasmus." This judgment may be disputed, however, in view of the great number of students who of late have given close attention to rhetorical history and theory. For them the work of Erasmus will provide a useful conspectus, something between a "cram-book" and an elaborated system, with fragmentary illustrative material which reflects the keen insight of the author. Readers not familiar with the classical system may still find the *Compendium* clear enough to provide a convenient introduction. And any teacher will appreciate the difficulties of William Bernaerts, who reveals himself in his introduction as a somewhat pedantic and fussy pedagogue, in finding a suitable textbook for an accelerated course. On the other hand, no modern student is likely to share Bernaerts' transport over a treasure-trove; and his wishful plea that the *Compendium* would become a widely used manual proved to be vain.

It will be noticed that Erasmus did not fill out his entire plan, but left untouched the subjects of disposition, elocution (style), memory, and delivery. He may have considered his *De Copia* a sufficient treatment of elocution,[2] and probably he shared with other scholars a negligent attitude towards memory and delivery. After his preliminary analysis he begins going through the outline of a speech, part by part. Upon reaching the Proof, he first treats proofs in forensic speaking (much forensic material had also been included in handling the Division), then proofs in deliberative speaking, and finally in epideictic. But he does not go on to treat of the Refutation and the Conclusion. The whole, then, is a truncated treatise *De Inventione*.

The translator has not retained the typographical display of the original volume (presumably followed by the Oxford reprint), except when it seemed necessary to show relation of parts. He has attempted to make those relations clearer by the use of small capitals and italics. Here and there the original grouping or subordination of headings appears to be erroneous. Any lecturer will testify that entries made in the margins of his notes should not necessarily so appear in a printed edition. The principal difficulties of interpretation arise in the section on *status*, a circumstance which will not surprise any student of the subject or anyone who has but tried to read the third book of Quintilian. The use of "position" as the most satisfactory English eqivalent of *status* has been adopted from Professor W. S. Howell.[3] No attempt has been made to indicate what particular author or authors Erasmus follows under any given heading. The few references in footnotes are for the sake of directing the reader to a clarification of what may be "blind" in Erasmus's shorthand; and while reference might have been made to *Rhetorica ad Herennium* (though not so often as the Oxford editors would indicate), Cicero and Quintilian have been favored as being more readily available. There are no marks of

parenthesis in the original of the text; they have been introduced to set out illustrative hints. Material insertions by the
translator appear in square brackets. The translation follows.

THE COMPENDIUM OF RHETORIC
OF DESIDERIUS ERASMUS OF ROTTERDAM

To Damian a Goes, Knight of Lusitania

To the most famous and learned Damian a Goes, Knight of
Lusitania, William Bernaerts of Thielt sends greetings:

When I had decided, most noble and learned Damian, to
lecture on rhetoric to the pupils whom Master John Maevius,
Moderator of the College of the Castle[4]—a man singularly zeal-
ous in promoting the liberal disciplines—had consigned to me
for instruction in dialectics, and brevity of time did not allow
any extended presentation of the former art (since, according
to the custom of colleges offering a philosophical education,
young men destined for that field are committed in the first
instance to the care of but a single master until, when they have
acquired the rudiments of dialectics under him, it is judged
that they are ready for the wholly admirable instruction in the
philosophy of Aristotle), I diligently looked about to find which
of all the writers whose precepts concerning rhetoric are extant
might be pre-eminently suitable for my course. Cicero, Fabius
Quintilian, and, older than these, Aristotle came to mind, as
well as Hermogenes, Trapezuntius, and some others. Although
these men wrote eruditely upon rhetoric, they are so difficult and
prolix that they ought not to be placed before beginners. I was
not unaware that in our very fortunate age men of great and
famed learning have published manuals in which they explain
the art clearly, and that without prolixity. Indeed, as should be
frankly stated, their books are such that no others, so far as the
liberal arts are concerned, would be more suitable for schools
in which youths of tender age are trained, were it not that these
authors stuff all their writings, in which they teach sound disciplines supremely well, with inappropriate examples. How
great a havoc they wreak upon letters by this course the complaints of many eager students abundantly testify.

So neither these modern writers (though in other respects they would serve our purpose not at all badly) on account of their examples, nor those ancients, because they were too heavy and prolix for beginners, seemed to be suitable for the end I had in mind; for my aim was to give to my pupils, so far as could be done, at least a taste, if nothing more, of rhetoric. But now the total lack of any suitable manual had turned my mind away from lecturing on the subject, even though I perceived that it would be to the advantage of my young students to combine it with the dialectics. There the matter stood until Rutger Rescius, a man of most liberal spirit united with versatility of talent and a singular modesty in respect to his learning, taking me into his library, showed me many letters of learned and famous men, not yet put into type, addressed to you—a most pleasant sight to me. Moreover he brought out a book written by the hand[5] of the great Erasmus, wherein, besides various of his letters to you, there were included a number of pages upon the art of rhetoric, composed some time ago for your sole use. When, casually reading the headings of these pages, I saw their conciseness, to which the order of the treatment lent a wonderful clarity, transported, as it were, by finding a treasure, I began straightway to urge Rescius to publication, and to tell him that it was intolerable so useful a work by such an author should any longer be suppressed, to the great disadvantage of the studious— especially at this time when there is available no guide to rhetoric which is well adapted to the use of schools and can safely be made the basis of lectures.

Wherefore I advised that he should issue the work, unless he wished to appear hostile to those who were aspiring to mastery of the liberal arts; that he should obtain permission from you, so that under your good auspices the manual would be printed for the general advantage of students. Rescius said that if he knew as well as he thought he did the inclination of your mind toward aiding and propagating sound learning, there would be no trouble about making this request of you; for you, of deepest learning yourself, had abundantly witnessed your devotion to good disciplines by the many books you had published. He said, however, that a certain letter of Erasmus stood in the way, wherein he forbade publication of these notes. For Erasmus wrote that treatises of this sort could not be issued except to the disgrace of his wide reputation, even saying that if some one were a mortal enemy, he could not do anything more unfriendly.[6] But truly, most renowned sir, I am sensible of these considerations—that much of the fame and esteem belonging to this author is the product of books published for general reading; how great will be the utility which will accrue from this work to students of honorable arts; and even that the universal splendor of the author's name ought to be taken into account in connection with giving general circulation, for the public good, to his lucubrations.

Accordingly I do not see that it will be to the disgrace of the Erasmian fame that these papers will come forth into the light, because just by so doing will they be profitable[7] to all who take rhetoric seriously. For how substantial the utility which the works of a conscientious and diligent teacher may provide, by way of aiding the ignorant, I shall not say. And for the others, indeed, who have already learned this art in one way or another from long and comprehensive instruction—I think there is no person who will deny that these precepts are useful, unless, perchance, he does not realize how valuable it is, with respect to any art, for one who wishes quickly to store it in his memory to have the main points, out of the vast multitude of precepts, noted down in a sort of tabular form. Yet, as certainly should be said, it would be ridiculous to account as useless to the generality of students something which a man like Erasmus thought would be profitable to you, at a time when you already were cultivated in the humanities. Hence to the end that this profit, whatever it may be (and it is not slight), may no longer be withheld from the public, with the kindly assistance of Rescius I have seen to it that these pages have been printed for the general use of all men, and this under grace of the great Erasmus and with your kind permission; so that a work which up to this time has been dedicated to your private studies shall now be publicly given over to the study of all men. Since it may be a benefit and convenience for all, anyone who seeks a knowledge of rhetoric you shall hold obliged to you, as most deserving of thanks, for this great benefaction.

Farewell. From the College of the Castle, Louvain, August 8, 1544.

COMPENDIUM OF RHETORIC
by Desiderius Erasmus of Rotterdam

THE ART—THE ARTIFICER—THE WORK

Matters of *the art:* the judicial or forensic kind; the deliberative or suasory kind; the epideictic or laudatory kind.

Tasks of *the artificer:* invention of materials; disposition, or ordering; elocution; memory; pronunciation, or action.

His faculty arises from: nature, art, imitation, and practice.

Parts of *the work:* the Exordium prepares the hearer; the Narration explains the case; the Division shows the position taken in the case, and forecasts [how it is to be argued], and so on; the Proof; the Refutation; the Conclusion, or Peroration.

EXORDIUM

A beginning—direct
An insinuation—oblique

The exordium brings it about that the hearer will be: well-disposed, so that he will give favorable attention; attentive, in respect to details; teachable, in respect to difficult matters.

The bad exordium: equally appropriate to either side; inappropriate; vulgar [or commonplace]; long; vehement;[8] verbose, etc.

The best exordium: one which is drawn from the bowels of the case.

NARRATION [or] EXPOSITION

Brief, clear, appropriate to the case.

This part of the speech does not argue, but contains the planted seeds of the arguments.

DIVISION is the doorway to the argument

It sometimes has two parts. In the first it makes manifest the position and the chief issue of the case. In the second it announces how many points the speaker will present, and in what order; or, if that is not convenient, what things will be talked about.

THE POSITION

The position, or *status*, is the chief point of the whole controversy, a matter that should have been first of all sought out by the speaker, lest in carrying on his argument he should discuss matters foreign to the case, useless, or even harmful to it. One should aim at the throat.

The position	Conjectural, or negative[9] (Whether poison was given; whether it was given by this man)
	Legal, when there is no agreement concerning the meaning of a law or document
Conjectural	Juridical, or Qualitative (He killed, but with right)
Definition[10]	From disagreeing laws; contradiction of laws;
Nature	one and the same law contradicts itself (the man
Precedent	who raped two women[11])
	From Ambiguity
	From Definition (He admits the theft; he denies the sacrilege[12])
	From Procedure: when the plaintiff is changed, or the judge, the place, or time, etc.
	Ratiocination [or Syllogism[13]]
	The twofold position; the shifting position
	Comparison[14]
	Showing good cause; "Heaven as furnishing a precedent" (Orestes)[15]

ARGUMENT or PROOF

Inartistic, which is looked for from the cause: prejudices, rumors, tortures, documents [or public records, contracts, etc.]

Artistic, which the orator must produce from his own resources: sworn asseveration, witnesses, oracles [prophecies, holy writ]

Artistic: signs, arguments, examples.

Signs[16] appear almost as inartistic

Necessary: those which do not call for any other support.

Not necessary: which have validity when used in connection with other proofs.

They are drawn from three times [past, present, and future]. (She bore a child; therefore she had cohabited with a man. When questioned, he grew pale; he spoke hesitantly.)

"*An argument* is a means of producing assurance concerning a doubtful matter."[17]

More regard should be paid to the advice of the old, because they are wise through great experience of affairs.

Conjectures are drawn from circumstances	Of things:	cause time place	opportunity means manner
	Of persons:	descent race	rank habit of mind
Whether he would have desired [the deed], would have had the ability, would have acted		native land sex age	studies eager desire previous actions
		education bodily condition fortune	agitation plan reputation

Whether a thing exists, what exists, of what sort it is.

Lines of *Argument*

1. Definition, description, and etymology
2. Genus (virtue)
3. Species (justice)
4. Peculiar property (speech in man [speech is the peculiar property of man])

5. Differentia (rational [a differentia of man])

6. Division, or Partition (the four forms of a commonwealth; the classes of a commonwealth—senate, aristocracy, and people)

7. Either the whole is false or one [argument] is proved, etc.[18]

Dilemma, or two contrary propositions, either of which may be turned against the adversary

Turning of tables, or using the opponent's own weapon against him

What is like—what is unlike—artful induction

8. Things incompatible: contraries (wise, foolish)

                                  negatives (blind, seeing)

                                  contradictions (learned, not learned)

                                  relatives (father, son; producer, director)

9. Consequences (He who intentionally caused pain was not a friend)

10. Causes [and] effects (If you seek glory, you must expect envy)

11. Events (He conquered; therefore he had the better cause)

12. Authority

Examples

These differ very little from comparisons or similes. They are drawn from authenticated facts. Thus: Just as there is no shadow unless you are in the light, so you are not the object of envy if you are unknown. That is a comparison. Great respect is due to virgins; Flaminius was expelled from the Senate because he embraced his wife, who was frightened by thunder, when his daughter was present. That is an example.

Examples are handled in the same manner as comparisons: from what is equal, what is less, what is greater.

Fiction has a place in all of these.

DELIBERATIVE or SUASORY Kind

Three things are to be kept in view: what it is that is being deliberated upon; who they are that deliberate; who he is that persuades.

Also: whether a certain thing can be done; whether it ought to be done.

Points in deliberating

1. What is right *per se*. Here belong all kinds of virtues.

2. What is honorable or laudable, having reference to that glory which is often a stronger motive than virtue itself. So also with infamy.

3. What is useful depends upon other circumstances. Comparison whether more useful or more honorable.[19]

4. What is necessary.

5. What is possible.

6. What is easy.

7. What is safe.

8. What is pleasant. What is seemly.

What has been done. Banished persons who entered the city limits have freed the city from siege.

In dissuading, we use the contraries of these.

Advantages are to be artfully exaggerated; disadvantages are to be minimized.

The reverse is done in dissuading.

Ladder of propositions[20]

Conjecture	Antony does not do this that he may protect Cicero, but that he may utterly wipe him out, his philippics having been burned.
From what is honorable	Although he puts the stipulation out of his mind, it is base for Cicero to owe his life to Antony, especially now that it is forfeited.
Comparison	Even if you are young, let not your life be purchased at the cost of your fame. For the life of the body is short; fame, which is the true life of a man, is eternal.
Impossible	As you despise these things, you will not be able to endure Antony as a master; you will voluntarily depart from life in disgust.

Another example

It is not profitable to marry.

Even if it is profitable, it is not so for a philosopher.

Even if it was profitable, it was not so for Socrates.

Or it is not suitable at this particular age.

Even if age does not dissuade, or any other consideration, certainly this particular wife should not be taken.

Concerning the EPIDEICTIC Kind

External goods—Goods of Body—Goods of Mind.

External: native country, descent, wealth, honors, buildings, wife and children, etc.

Of body: age, beauty, dignity, powers, health, quality of voice, a clear-sounding harp, etc.[21]

Of mind: learning ability, versatility of talent, a strong memory, mental health, piety, fortitude, prudence, temperance, justice, friendliness, etc.

Since external goods do not really belong as matters of praise [since they cannot be attributed to the praised person's own efforts], they must be fitted into the eulogy by art. If the man, for instance, made an illustrious fatherland more illustrious by his virtue, or made famous an obscure one. The same should be spoken concerning family. If he gained his wealth without fraud, or if, having inherited it from his forebears or having received it by good luck, he made good use of it. If he selected his own wife and lived with her in kindly fashion. If he educated his sons scrupulously. If he was fortunate in the interests of his country rather than in his own interest.

The same should be done in regard to bodily goods. In adolescence, sobriety; in the handsome person, modesty. If dignity, or gravity of mind, shows in the face. Care and sobriety of life beget and augment strength and health of body.

Goods of the mind ought to be treated through the steps of all periods of life: what the boy had accomplished, what the youth, what the man, what the old man. How he acted toward his native land, toward his parents, his wife, his children, his friends, his fellow-citizens, his enemies.

Just as in vituperation we deprave the virtues into the vices nearest them, so in praising we extenuate vices, giving them the names of virtues, designating parsimony as frugality, cruelty as austerity, shrewdness as prudence, etc.

There is a kind of eulogy by comparison. As when we praise a certain one we compare him to some one who is most highly glorified in the general judgment, or with several such, and show that he is either equal or superior; as, for instance, if some one compared the Emperor Charles with Alexander the Great.

Commonplaces

When we extol some virtue or exaggerate some vice, to the advantage of our case. As, if you are to praise some one for the study of philosophy, it will be a commonplace how great profit a knowledge of philosophy brings to mankind.

Sententiae should be sprinkled in—the windows, as it were, of a speech. They are of various kinds.

Simple: Nothing is so popular as kindness.

With a reason suggested: In every contest, he who is richer, even if he receives injury, seems to inflict it.

Double: as, Flattery begets friends; truth, hatred.

From distinctions: Not death, but the approach to death, is sad.

Moral: A miser lacks what he has as much as what he does not have.

Figured: Is it sad, indeed, even to die?[22]

Transferred to a person: I could save—do you ask whether I can destroy?[23]

Epiphonema is added to a matter that has been narrated or proved.[24]

Noema, not expressed but understood: You who had clean hands were worthy.

From the unexpected: Who has permitted you thus to fear?

From contraries: I hold him whom I flee from; whom I follow I do not hold. Also: He is pitiable who does not know how to speak yet cannot keep silent.

Methods of exaggerating and discounting

From change of a word, as when for *killing* you say *murder;* or for *a dishonest man* you say *a bandit;* on the other hand, for *he struck* you might say *he touched.*

From augmented comparison: We bring to your judgment not a thief but a kidnapper, not an adulterer but a violator of chastity, not a committer of sacrilege but an enemy of all things sacred and all religions, not an assassin but a most cruel butcher of citizens and associates.

By ascent, when as if by a ladder it reaches the highest point or even goes beyond the highest: It is a misdeed to bind a Roman citizen; it is a crime to flog him; it is parricide to kill him. What shall I say it is to crucify him?

From an invented comparison, when with less important matters magnified, what we uphold rises high in importance: If this had happened with you at dinner, who would not have counted it shameful? But conducting the public business of the Roman people at a party—you, the master of the cavalry! It is done also without invention.

From reasoning, when from certain circumstances which seem to be foreign to the matter is gathered how great is that which we are upholding: You, with those jaws, with those flanks, that gladiatorial strength of the whole body—you drank so much wine at the wedding of Hippias that the next day you were forced to vomit in full sight of the Roman people.

A heaping up, when we press the same point with now one, now another phrase: Janitor of a jail, the praetor's hangman, the death and terror of associates and citizens of Rome, Sextus the Lictor.

Richness of style

These things make for copiousness: a variety of propositions, of methods, of proofs, comparisons, contrasts, and examples; some of them ancient, some more modern, some poetical, etc.

Figures

Some figures make for pleasingness of speech, some for emphasis, some for clearness and openness. Among them all the meta-

phor is king, with its related figures such as comparison, charac-
ter-sketch, word-picture, etc.

There remain the Emotions, Moral Appeals, and Excitations.

The End

NOTES

1. *Opus Epistolarum Des. Erasmi Roterodami* (ed. P. S. Allen), Tom. X, 1532-1534 (ed. H. M. Allen and H. W. Garrod), Oxford, 1941. *Compendium Rhetorices* appears in Appendix XXII, pp. 396-405.

2. Although on p. 396 the Oxford editors suggest that the *Compendium* repre-sents notes made at an early period in Erasmus's life, pressed into service later for the use of Damian a Goes, on an earlier page (251) they say: "It was doubtless on this visit [in 1534] that Erasmus composed . . . *Compendium Rhetorices*." If the suggestion of earlier composition is correct, however, we might still con-jecture that upon reaching the subject of elocution Erasmus allowed his notes to expand, and the result was *De Copia*.

3. *The Rhetoric of Alcuin and Charlemagne*, translated with Introduction and Notes, by W. S. Howell, Princeton, 1941. Professor Howell's clear exposition of the doctrine of *status*, and his reasons for translating the word as *position*, will be found at pp. 34-44.

4. Of the University of Louvain.

5. *manu descriptum*; perhaps *ascribed to the hand*.

6. Sc., than to publish this book. The passage to which Rescius referred is in Epistle 2987 (not yet published in the Oxford edition, but quoted from, X, 396), addressed to Damian himself, and may be translated: "If you were my mortal enemy, you could not do anything more hostile than if you were to allow the notes I made for you alone to be printed."

7. Reading *profuturae* for the Oxford edition's *profutura*.

8. *concitatum*; perhaps *hurried*, in contrast to the preceding *prolixum*. An exordium, however, is also supposed to be calm.

9. For the identification of the conjectural with the negative position, see Quintilian, III, 6, 32.

10. *Finis* is Erasmus's word; it may mean *purpose*, perhaps here *motive*, but in rhetorical writings it is sometimes used to mean *definition*.

11. The law, according to a well-known classical controversy (Seneca Rhetor, *Controversiae*, I, v) allowed a woman who had suffered rape to demand either that her attacker should marry her or that he should be put to death. In this case, a man had raped two women, one of whom demanded death and the other marriage.

12. In this case a man had stolen a privately owned sacred object; he is willing to plead guilty to theft, but he pleads not guilty to sacrilege, which is the charge pressed by the plaintiff and for which the punishment is much more severe. Cf. Cicero, *De Inventione*, I, viii, 11.

13. For the syllogistic position see *De Inv.*, I, 31, 34; Quintilian, III, 6, 43 *et passim.*

14. A defensive comparison of a crime with a good deed, on account of which the crime was committed; cf. *De. Inv.*, I, 11, 15; II, 24, 72.

15. The word translated as "showing good cause" is *ratio;* in this sense, re-sembling the modern appeal "to the unwritten law," it is used by Cicero, *De. Inv.*, I, 13, 18, and Quintilian, III, 11, 4, and both cite the act of Orestes as an illustration.

16. *Signa;* some translators English the word as *indications;* the modern "circumstantial evidence."

17. Cicero, *Topica,* II, 7, slightly misquoted. The following statement seems to be introduced as a brief specimen of argument.

18. That is, unless you accept this argument you must reject as false a whole corpus of presumably accepted argument.

19. This sentence, which appears in the Oxford edition as an unattached entry on a line with point 5, has been put where it seems to belong.

20. The four propositions under this heading seem to be drawn, though not quoted, from the sixth *Suasoria* of Seneca Rhetor, the subject of which is: "Cicero considers whether he should beg Antony for life."

21. *Plectrum articulatum,* apparently a eulogist's metaphor, in praise either of the *vocalitas* or the *salubritas* (the typography does not make clear which) of his subject; or perhaps it summarizes all bodily goods.

22. The figure here is interrogation, rhetorical question.

23. That is, a general sentence ("he that has power to save has power to destroy") is implied by this question concerning a specific person.

24. Epiphonema or acclamation may be defined as an aphoristic summary or comment placed as a kind of moral at the end of an extended passage of narrative or argument.

The Listener on Eloquence, 1750-1800

HAROLD F. HARDING

IN ENGLAND during the years 1750-1800 there appeared some two score schoolbooks, text-essays, lectures, and treatises on rhetoric. From them the student of rhetorical theory can derive what the professional rhetorician—he who systematizes his thoughts on the art of speaking—considered the proper standards, principles, and canons of oratory. The last half of the eighteenth century also witnessed the activities, often spectacular, of Burke and Sheridan, Pitt and Fox, Windham and Elliot. From a study of the speeches of such men, the historian of rhetorical theory can often discover what the expert thought to be the principles that guided his efforts. Taking the principles that the historian has discovered and set before him, the critic of public address can proceed to interpret and evaluate discourse. The critic of oratory is of course concerned, among other things, with the reception of the speech by those who heard it. But since he is interested in all aspects of the speaker-audience relationship, the critic should also consider whether the orator has tried to adapt not only his message to the intellectual and emotional nature of his hearers, but also his performance to their standard of taste. And if the speaker made this attempt, did the audience judge that he succeeded? Did his content and manner of presentation conform to their stereotype of a good speaker? Had they indeed such a stereotype, and can it be reconstructed from their own comments on the speakers they heard, rather than inferred from the recorded speeches now available? These questions are not without interest: to concern for the vote or other practical effect of a speech, they add concern for the auditors' conscious response to the speech as a work of art, and thus round out the account of the relation between the speaker's performance and his influence.

The object of this paper, accordingly, is to suggest, on a somewhat limited scale, what the audience of 1750-1800 thought about public speaking. For the most part, the audience dealt with is that gathered in the House of Commons, and, for the purpose of studying its views on public address it is divided into two main groups: the layman or popular observer, in the galleries and on the floor, who is relatively unskilled and inexperienced in speaking; and the expert or skilled speaker. We shall report what both of these groups had to say about the speakers they heard, and then from the rhetorical categories mentioned and implied in their comments, we shall try to describe the listener's conception of oratory. In order to limit the scope of the paper, the contemporary comment on speakers cannot be all-inclusive; it is drawn from the chief diaries, letters, and memorials of the period, and excludes newspaper reports; it offers comment on specific speakers only, and omits generalized observations both about speaking at large and about types of oratory.

The testimony of observers who, although interested in speaking, themselves had little or no experience in public address is mainly concerned with Burke and Sheridan; comment is less extensive on speakers like Lord North, John Courtenay, and Sir Joshua Reynolds.

Burke's oratory at the Hastings trial, of course, impressed the spectators. Sir Nathaniel Wraxall, civil servant and politician whose *Memoirs* often comment on contemporary speakers, recorded the general effect that Burke's speech of February 17, 1788, made upon him. The oration, he believed, was "unequaled . . . either in antiquity or in any modern period of time,"[1] and he observed that even Burke's opponents could not avoid appreciating "the magnificent structure of ideas, the prodigious grasp of his mind which could arrange and his memory which could retain, such a magnitude of transactions."[2]

Frances Burney and Hannah More, like most women who crowded the galleries at the trial, were keenly sensitive to Burke's ability to make his delivery fit his ideas, and to stir his listeners emotionally. Miss Burney's is the longer report:

When he narrated, he was easy, flowing, and natural; when he declaimed, energetic, warm, and brilliant. The sentiments he interspersed were as nobly conceived as they were highly coloured; . . . his allusions . . . were apt and ingenious . . . his language fluent, forcible, and varied. . . . But though frequently he made me tremble by his strong and horrible representations, his own violence recovered me, by stigmatizing his assertions with personal ill-will and designing illiberality. Yet at times, I confess, with all that I felt, wished, and thought concerning Mr. Hastings, the whirlwind of his eloquence nearly drew me into its vortex.[3]

To Miss Burney, Burke was especially effective in narration: "And when he came to his two narratives, . . . when he related the particulars of those dreadful murders, he interested, he engaged, he at last overpowered me; I felt my cause lost. I could hardly keep my seat."[4] Upon hearing one of Burke's speeches at the Hastings trial, Hannah More, who knew Garrick and many of Dr. Johnson's friends, wrote to her sister:

Such a splendid and powerful oration I never heard, but it was abusive and vehement beyond all conception. . . . I think I never felt such indignation as when Burke, with Sheridan standing on one side and Fox on the other said, "Vice incapacitates a man from all public duty; it withers the powers of his understanding, and makes his mind paralytic." I looked at his two neighbors, and saw that they were quite free from any symptoms of palsy.[5]

It is evident that both Miss Burney and Mrs. More felt the impact of Burke's emotional thrusts, though the partisanship of the first and the moral righteousness of the second seem not to have dulled the capacity for criticism. But other women in the audience, if we may accept Wraxall's observation, responded less critically:

It would be difficult to convey an idea of the agitation, distress, and horror excited among the female part of the audience by his statement of the atrocities, and in many instances of the deeds of blood, perpetrated, as he asserted, by Hastings' connivance or by his express commands.[6]

Indeed, it would seem that Burke's pathos, to which his wit and ridicule were at times an intellectual foil, was most impressive to the gallery observer:

Every power of oratory was wielded by him in turn, for he could be during the same evening, often within the space of a few minutes, pathetic and humorous, acrimonious and conciliating, now giving loose to his indignation or severity, and then, almost in the same breath, calling to his assistance wit and ridicule.[7]

One observer thought that Burke's ridicule was handled with *"taste* and *learning,"*[8] and another seems to have approved of Burke's taste in his use of satire, for it revealed "a poignancy of wit that made it as entertaining as it was penetrating."[9] Yet another observer, a Mr. Maltby, was disappointed in Burke's speeches in the House of Commons, because he made use of "the most vulgar expressions, such as 'three nips of a straw,' 'three skips of a louse,' " and because he once introduced, as an illustration, "a most indelicate story about a French king, who asked his physician why his natural children were so much finer than his legitimate."[10] Upon Burke's delivery, we find Wraxall saying:

> His enunciation was vehement, rapid, and never checked by any embarrassment; for his ideas outran his powers of utterance, and he drew from an exhaustless source. But his Irish accent, which was as strong as if he had never quitted the banks of the Shannon, diminished to the ear the enchanting effect of his eloquence on the mind.[11]

Concerning Sheridan, the gallery onlooker also had something to say. While still a young man, Samuel Rogers, the poet, heard Sheridan's Begum speech at Hastings' impeachment, and recorded that the orator was listened to "with such attention that you could hear a pin drop."[12] Wraxall, too, testified as to the general impression made by Sheridan in this speech:

> It occupied considerably more than five hours in the delivery, attracted the most intense attention, and was succeeded at its close by a general involuntary pause or hum of admiration, which lasted several minutes; . . . he led captive his audience, of whom a large proportion was very incapable of discriminating truth from misrepresentation or exaggeration.[13]

But Wraxall, a more mature judge than Rogers, was also attracted by the variety of materials that Sheridan drew upon and by his manner of handling them:

> Sheridan's invocations, allusions, and exclamations the most pa-

thetic, though clothed with all the garb of nature or of passion, were not less the fruit of consummate art and mature reflection. He neither lost his temper, his memory, nor his judgment throughout the whole performance, blending the legal accuracy of the bar when stating facts or depositions of witnesses with the most impassioned appeals to justice, pity, and humanity. [He availed] himself with dexterity of the ample materials which the subject offered him, presenting objects to the imagination under forms the most picturesque, appealing, and impressive.[14]

Charles Butler, the Roman Catholic barrister, thought that Sheridan displayed "a happy vein of ridicule."[15]

On the speaking of Fox and Pitt, comments from the general audience are few. The youthful Rogers, in reference to Fox's rebuttal speech at the great trial, declared that "never in my life did I hear anything equal to Fox's speeches in reply, they were wonderful."[16] Rogers does not record the general impresson that Pitt's oratory made upon him; he mentions only Pitt's voice that "sounded as if he had worsted in his mouth."[17] Richard Porson, the Greek scholar, was sufficiently interested in the manner in which Pitt and Fox constructed sentences to register that "Pitt carefully considered his sentences before he uttered them; but that Fox threw himself in the middle of his, and left it to God Almighty to get him out again."[18]

Other speakers of George III's England, whose reputations today are not what they were yesterday, received passing notice from their contemporaries. Wraxall recorded that John Courtenay used irony "on every subject, even the most serious," and that Lord North often employed humor.[19] Boswell was most impressed with North's "calmness, perspicuity, and sufficient elegance."[20]

Although diaries and memoirs afford considerable contemporary observation on the forensic drama of the period and include, to some extent, testimony on parliamentary speaking, they are for the most part silent as to the speaking that took place outside the theatre of the Lords and Commons. Dr. Johnson seems to have been generally pleased with some of Sir Joshua Reynolds' *Discourses*,[21] but neither he nor anyone else among the journal keepers was sufficiently impressed with Reynolds' delivery to make note of it. Sir Gilbert Elliot, more interested in speaking than most observers, tells of Pitt's attendance at a boisterous dinner in his honor at Merchant Taylors' Hall, London, in 1802, but says nothing of the actual speaking.[22] Again, Horace Walpole speaks of a magnificent dinner for Pitt and Lord Temple given by the Lord Mayor of London in November, 1761, but omits any mention of the after-dinner speeches.[23] In short, the student in search of observations on speaking in the reign of George III meets with small reward outside of the colorful and historic occasions furnished by the House of Commons. Nor does one often meet with observations on preachers, although in some sources, largely outside the scope of this paper, one encounters general criticism of sermons.[24]

Thus far the observations on the later eighteenth-century speakers represent the reactions of those unskilled as speechmakers. Memorials and letters, in addition, often record the comment, both kind and caustic, that the experienced speaker directed at his fellow experts of the craft. To include such comment here not only makes accessible the testimony of craftsmen on craftsmen, but also reveals the response of the learned and judicious hearer to the performance of his fellows.

Burke is the orator about whom there is most comment, as a comprehensive study[25] already in print shows. After Burke, Sheridan receives most attention, and much of the comment upon him is from Sir Gilbert Elliot, himself an able parliamentary speaker. Concerning Sheridan's speech of June 5, 1788, Elliot thought that "it was a very great exertion of talent, understanding, and skill in composition, and was the work of a man of very extraordinary genius."[26] After Sheridan's Hastings speech eight days later, Elliot spoke of its pathos: "I believe there were few dry eyes in the assembly; and as for myself, I never remember to have cried so heartily and so copiously on any public occasion."[27] Again, it was the pathos of the Begum speech that made a deep impression upon Elliot and excited the entire assembly:

The bone rose repeatedly in my throat, and the tears in my eyes—not of grief, but merely of strongly excited sensibility; so they were in Dudley Long's, who is not, I should think, particularly tearful. The conclusion, in which the whole force of the case was collected, and where the whole powers were employed to the utmost pitch, worked the House up into such a paroxysm of passionate enthusiasm on the subject, and of admiration for him, that the moment he sat down there was a universal shout, nay, even clapping, for half-a-second; every man was on the floor, and all his friends throwing themselves on his neck in raptures of joy and exultation.[28]

But Elliot, as an expert observer, was keenly aware of other qualities in Sheridan's speaking. Although he regarded Sheridan's style and delivery as generally excellent, he felt that the orator's fine and surprising exertions unduly caught attention and reminded the audience of the speaker's performance.[29] Likewise, mismanagement of voice, the use of words too far removed from those of ordinary speech, and rapidity of utterance, led Elliot to complain of the theatrical and artificial nature of Sheridan's speaking.[30] A much later speech of Sheridan's, that in the Commons on May 15, 1802, held Elliot by its wit; indeed, the speech seems to have entertained and pleased everyone.[31]

Other commentators on Sheridan were attracted principally by the Begum speech. Burke, Fox, and Pitt, amazed at Sheridan's prodigious memory,[32] were most lavish in their praise of the oration as a whole, and Burke in particular remarked on the performance as "the most astonishing effort of eloquence, argument, and wit united, of which there was any record or tradition."[33]

On Charles James Fox, both Horace Walpole and Sir Gilbert Elliot offer general observations that perhaps indicate the taste of the judicious observer. Elliot believed that Fox's speaking "excels all other men's," and pointed out that its peculiarity was to be found in its "nature and simplicity."[34] Walpole also seems to refer to Fox's natural simplicity when he preferred Fox's " 'native wood notes' to Burke's feigned voice, though it goes to the highest pitch of the gamut of wit."[35]

Upon Pitt, Walpole looked with particular favor, and went so far as to declare that he surpassed Cicero and Demosthenes.[36] Perhaps he most admired Pitt's versatility, especially his ability in debate where he showed to advantage his skill at rebuttal and repartee,[37] and his facile irony, ridicule, and satire. Pitt's parody of Burgoyne's talk with the Indians was "the *chef d'oeuvre* of wit, humour, and satire, and almost suffocated Lord North himself with laughter."[38] To Walpole, in short, Pitt seemed to have "an universal armoury—I knew he had a Gorgon's head, composed of bayonets and pistols, but little thought that he could tickle to death with a feather."[39]

The observations on other speakers are less extensive, although all show the concern of the expert over the abilities of another. Burke thought that Elliot's maiden speech in Parliament, December 12, 1787, bore "the substantial points which go to character,"[40] thus perhaps testifying to the speaker's ability in sound analysis and selection of arguments, and to the qualities of discourse that reveal the orator's own character. It was Burke, also, who remarked on the ability shown by Sir Philip Francis when in the Commons he sketched the history of his contentions with Warren Hastings in India:

He [Mr. Francis] was clear, precise, forcible, and eloquent to a high degree. . . . He was two hours and a half on his legs, and he never lost attention for a moment. Indeed, I believe very few could have crowded so much matter into so small a space.[41]

When William Windham spoke on Fyzoola Khan, in March, 1787, Elliot recorded that "both his ideas and language are remarkable for a terse, accurate, logical, and scholarlike character."[42] Walpole heard Wesley in 1766, and after writing to his friend, John Chute, that he had been to Mr. Wesley's "opera," he made these observations on the speaker's appearance, his delivery, and his audience:

Wesley is a lean, elderly man, fresh-coloured, his hair smooth combed, but with a soupçon of curl at the ends. Wondrous clean, but as evidently an actor as Garrick. He spoke his sermon, but so fast, and with so little accent, that I am sure he has often uttered it, for it was like a lesson. There were parts and eloquence in it; but towards the end he exhalted his voice, and acted very ugly enthusiasm; decried learning and told stories, like Latimer, of the fool of his college, who said, "I *thanks* God for everything." Except a few from curiosity, and some honourable women, the congregation was very mean.[43]

If such observations on the orators of the period are representative, they reveal, partly through the terminology employed and partly through the qualities of discourse that are singled out for comment, the listeners' conception of public address.

Perhaps the most interesting inference to be drawn from the remarks of both layman and specialist is that the listener makes small use of the language of the professors of eloquence and pays little heed to systematic criticism. In the vivid phraseology of the listener, there is little evidence of the textbook terminology of Lawson and Ward, Blair and Campbell. Although some of the observers use the terms "style" and "delivery," they ignore the rhetoricians' technical labels of "invention," "disposition," "logical proof," and "fallacies," of "pathetic appeal" and "ethical proof," of "topics," "lines of argument," and "commonplaces," of "tropes," "figures," and "ornamentation." The professors are remote and the panoply of the textbook mostly absent, because the listener was not concerned with systematic criticism and orderly analysis. Indeed, with the exception of the lay observer, Wraxall, and the expert, Elliot, few of the critics show respect for balanced and developed judgments; rather, they are impressed with the most striking qualities of the speech—with the way the oration made them feel, with its wit and humor, and with the speaker's skill in statement and his powers of memory.

Another striking aspect of the commentators' testimony is that the criticism, unsystematic and disproportioned as it is, is often directed to the speech as a performance. Reference to the speaker's astonishing genius, his ability to use varied means of amplification and to fit voice and expression to a variety of sentiments and ideas, his powers of memory, his precision of statement, his humor and satire, his ability in argument and reply, and his success in moving his hearers both to emotional heights and to overt demonstrations of applause—all suggest that the listener considered a speech as a triumph of skill. To the eighteenth-century audience, then, a speech is a tangible production in which the artist's touch is plainly evident.

Further indication that the listener thought of a speech as an artistic product may be found in the occasional references to the speaker's taste and judgment. The violence of his feelings, the intensity of his emotional appeals, and the impropriety of his illustration and diction, when mentioned, indicate that the artist offended the sensibilities of his audience; the speaker did not measure up to the listeners' notion of what a good speaker ought to do in similar situations. Perhaps Walpole, in making a general reference to the speaking of the day, intimates the kind if not the quality of judgment that the listener habitually made concerning the taste and propriety of an orator's efforts. "Eloquence," he said, "has advanced with us to such masculine superiority, even in the youngest men, that studied flowers and affected pathos, composed by the pen, are in my eyes quite puerile."[44] The point of view of George III's listener is that of Hamlet in cautioning his players not to abuse their art, or of Hugh Blair in lecturing on taste and *belles-lettres*.

Still further evidence that the listener was judging an artist may be found in the remarks of the commentators on the immediate effect of the speech. An oration, they observed, held the closest interest, compelled overpowering emotion, delighted by its wit, amused by apt rejoinder, humor, and ridicule, and excited applause and spontaneous congratulation. The effect of a speech, then, lay in its capacity to hold attention and to evoke bodily response, rather than in its capacity to attain the real ends with which discourse is most directly concerned. No observer reports whether the efforts of Burke, Fox, and Sheridan had appreciable effect upon the Lords who alone could declare Hastings innocent or guilty. What appeared to be most telling in the arguments of the prosecutors? Was the case as a whole convincing? Was the selection of arguments and evidence such as to secure weight and conviction? What, in short, led the judges to make their decision? These questions, pointing directly to a functional view of discourse as opposed to the artistic view, both lay and expert observers seem to be unaware of. Even the judicious Wraxall, in mentioning that Sheridan availed himself of the "ample materials" which the subject afforded him, is more interested in the speaker's "dexterity" than in his persuasiveness. Elliot, it is true, remarks on Sheridan's "understanding," and on Windham's "logical" ideas; Burke alludes in one word to Sheridan's "argument," and to Elliot's "substantial points which go to character;" but the context of these observations, without the benefit of more explicit exposition, leaves their meaning in doubt. To the listener, then, choice of material and the logical requirements of a case or a proposal seem to have weighed no more seriously than they did with the fourth Earl of Chesterfield who, in 1751, advised his son:

When you come into the House of Commons, if you imagine that speaking plain and unadorned sense and reason will do your business, you will find yourself most grossly mistaken. As a speaker, you will be ranked only according to your eloquence and by no means according to your matter; everybody knows the matter alike, but few can adorn it.[45]

The final observation on the commentators' testimony must concern delivery. Yet it is this aspect of speech-making on which, in the face of the record, it is most difficult to generalize. A number of observers were clearly conscious of qualities of voice and of accent; they were aware of pronunciation and enunciation; they remarked on the speaker's pace and tempo. The student is tempted, therefore, to observe that the listener, unconcerned with the canons and rules of the professors of elocution, was attracted by the obvious qualities of delivery. But it is hard to reconcile this judgment with the omission of any reference to gesture, and with the scant attention that was given to the speaker's appearance. Only Walpole saw fit to describe the visual picture presented by Wesley. Accordingly, the testimony suggests that to the listener of the period a speaker's proper medium of communication is the audible symbol, rather than the visual.

If an audience's conception of public speaking may be distilled from the nature of its criticism and the rhetorical categories it uses or implies, we may conclude that the listener in George III's England viewed oratory as a performance designed to reveal the speaker's powers. His skill, so the audience thought, lay in moving their feelings and holding their attention by telling and entertaining strokes, whether by choice of ideas, by effective language, or by impressive utterance; and in these terms principally they judged him. But they also expected the speaker to conform to current standards of taste, which required him to avoid jarring or repulsive ideas and images as well as unclear voice and strange accent. And always the listeners thought of the oration as an artistic effort that augmented or diminished the stature of the orator.

NOTES

1. *The Historical and Posthumous Memoirs of Sir Nathaniel William Wraxall* (*1772-1784*), ed. Henry B. Wheatley, 5 vols. (London, 1884), V, 66. This work is hereinafter referred to as Wraxall.

2. *Ibid.*, II, 35.

3. *Diary and Letters of Madame d'Arblay*, ed. Charlotte Barrett, 6 vols. (London, 1904-05), III, 448-449.

4. *Ibid.*, III, 472.

5. *Memoirs of the Life and Correspondence of Mrs. Hannah More*, ed. William Roberts, 2 vols. (New York, 1855), I, 287.

6. Wraxall, V, 66.

7. *Ibid.*, III, 31.

8. *Ibid.*, IV, 431.

9. *Diary and Letters of Madame d'Arblay*, ed. Charlotte Barrett, 6 vols. (London, 1904-05), III, 448.

10. *Recollections of the Table-Talk of Samuel Rogers*, ed. Alexander Dyce (New York, 1856), p. 78. This work is hereinafter referred to as Rogers.

11. Wraxall, V, 66. At the trial, also, was Samuel Rogers; he too thought that Burke's "manner was hurried, and he always seemed to be in a passion." (Rogers, p. 78.)

12. Rogers, pp. 65-66.

13. Wraxall, III, 386.

14. *Ibid.*

15. L. C. Sanders, *Life of R. B. Sheridan* (New York, 1891), p. 109.

16. Rogers, p. 78.

17. *Ibid.*

18. *Ibid.*, p. 79.

19. Wraxall, III, 452-453.

20. *Private Papers of James Boswell from Malahide Castle*, ed. Geoffrey Scott and F. A. Pottle, 19 vols. (London, 1928-36), VI, 82-83. Boswell here refers to a speech on April 5, 1773.

21. James Boswell, *Life of Samuel Johnson*, ed. G. B. Hill, 6 vols. (Oxford, 1887), III, 369-370.

22. *The Life and Letters of Sir Gilbert Elliot*, ed. Countess Minto, 3 vols. (London, 1874), III, 250. This work is hereinafter referred to as Elliot.

23. *The Letters of Horace Walpole*, ed. Mrs. Paget Toynbee, 16 vols. (Oxford, 1903-05), IV, 141-142. This work is hereinafter referred to as Walpole.

24. Some of the more accessible sources are Swift's *Letter to a Young Clergyman*, Goldsmith's *Of Eloquence* and *On the English Clergy and Popular Preachers*, John Mason's essays on elocution and on action, Sheridan's *Lectures*, William Cockin's *Art of Delivering Written Language*, Priestley's *Course of Lectures on*

Oratory and Criticism, Wesley's *Directions,* and Jerningham's *Essay on the Eloquence of the Pulpit in England.*

25. D. C. Bryant, "The Contemporary Reception of Edmund Burke's Speaking," in *Studies in Honor of Frederick W. Shipley* (St. Louis, Washington University Studies, 1942), pp. 245-264.

26. Elliot, I, 210.

27. *Ibid.,* I, 218.

28. *Ibid.,* I, 124-125.

29. *Ibid.,* I, 210.

30. *Ibid.,* I, 123-125, 208, 214, 215.

31. *Ibid.,* III, 249.

32. W. F. Rae, *Sheridan, A Biography,* 2 vols. (London, 1896), II, 59 ff.

33. Elliot, III, 125 note.

34. *Ibid.,* I, 215.

35. Walpole, X, 187.

36. *Ibid.,* III, 369.

37. *Ibid.,* III, 375-376.

38. *Ibid.,* X, 187-188.

39. *Ibid.,* III, 375-376.

40. Elliot, III, 176.

41. *The Francis Letters,* ed. Beata Francis and Eliza Keary, 2 vols. (New York [?]), II, 371-372. The editors took the quotation from Burke's *Correspondence* (1844), III, 56. For Burke's observations on other speakers, see D. C. Bryant, "Edmund Burke's Opinions of some Orators of his Day," *Quarterly Journal of Speech* XX (April, 1934), 241-254.

42. Elliot, III, 137.

43. Walpole, VII, 49-50.

44. *Ibid.,* XIV, 36.

45. *The Letters of Philip Dormer Stanhope,* ed. Bonamy Dobree (London, 1932), p. 1700. Cf. *Letters of Philip Dormer Stanhope,* ed. Lord Mahon, 5 vols. (London, 1845-1853), I, 357, 359, 372, 375-376; IV, 179.

Edmund Burke's Conversation

Donald C. Bryant

FROM Boswell's journals it is apparent that, excepting Johnson's only, there was no conversation Boswell was more eager to record than Burke's. Furthermore, Boswell frequently indicated disappointment when he was unable to recall for his notebook things he had heard Burke say. Such a preference on his part must have been determined by good reasons; and there is, in fact, ample evidence, in the forms both of testimony and of recorded conversations, to show that Burke, if not as great a talker as Johnson, was a close rival.

Johnson himself is a major witness to the excellence of Burke's conversation. He "delighted in the conversation of Mr. Burke," wrote Arthur Murphy, who reported also that on the day after Johnson had first met Burke, then under thirty, Johnson exclaimed, "I suppose, Murphy, you are proud of your countryman. *Cum talis sit, utinam noster esset.*" At this first meeting Johnson had been so much pleased with Burke's conversation that he had allowed Burke to contradict him with impunity.[1] Later Johnson said that he loved Burke's "knowledge, his genius, his diffusion, and affluence of conversation."[2] "Burke *is* an extraordinary man," he declared again. "His stream of mind is perpetual."[3] "That fellow calls forth all my powers," he once asserted; and one day when he was out of spirits he confessed, "Were I to see Burke now, 't would kill me."[4] Johnson declared that he admired Burke because he was "never what we call humdrum; never unwilling to begin to talk, nor in haste to leave off."[5] Burke, he insisted, was "the only man whose common conversation corresponds with the general fame which he has in the world. Take up whatever topic you please, he is ready to meet you."[6] True, Johnson recognized faults in Burke's conversation, one of which he described in 1778 by saying that Burke was "not so agreeable as the variety of his knowledge would otherwise make him" because he talked "partly from ostentation";[7] but by 1783 he had come to realize that "Burke's talk is the ebullition of his mind; he does not talk from a desire of distinction, but because his mind is full."[8]

Like Johnson's, Boswell's admiration for Burke's conversation, as I have already suggested, is repeatedly manifest. There is, for example, his elaborate defense of Burke's wit in a footnote to the *Hebrides*,[9] and his reiteration of that defense in brief in the *Life*.[10] He, like Johnson, was impressed with the abundance and variety of knowledge which Burke displayed in conversation. After recording what he could of Burke's talk at Reynolds' on October 29, 1787, Boswell wrote, "I felt my own emptiness sadly while I heard him talk a variety of knowledge ten times more than I have recollected."[11] The next April, when he had Burke at his own house to dinner, he wrote, "I regret that I did not attend better and record more of Burke."[12] Another judgment of Boswell's, familiar to readers of the *Life of Johnson*, follows his account of Bennet Langton's report of hearing Burke and Johnson dispute the comparative merits of Homer and Virgil. Boswell observes, "It may well be supposed to have been one of the ablest and most brilliant contests that ever was exhibited. How much we must regret that it has not been preserved."[13]

Fanny Burney may be taken as a witness who, though somewhat idolatrous with respect to Burke, possessed discernment and taste, and represented the point of view not of the giants of the Club, but of the women. In one of her long accounts of her first meeting with Burke, at a dinner party at Sir Joshua Reynolds', where Gibbon, Bishop Shipley and his daughter, and Dr. Burney were also present, she wrote of Burke:

He is tall, his figure is noble, his air commanding, his address graceful; his voice is clear, penetrating, sonorous, and powerful; his language is copious, various, and eloquent; his manners are attractive, his conversation is delightful. . . . Since we lost Garrick I have seen nobody so enchanting. . . . The conversation was not suivi, Mr. Burke darting from subject to subject with as much rapidity as entertainment. Neither is the charm of his discourse more in the matter than the manner; all, therefore, that is related from him loses half its effect in not being related by him.[14]

In summary she wrote, "I think Dr. Johnson the first Discourser, and Mr. Burke the first Converser of the British Empire."[15]

Miss Burney's accounts of this dinner party and of a later one at Mrs. Crewe's should be reread in connection with her comments, for they are the most artistic representations we have of Burke in the throes of conversation, and they illustrate vividly the qualities which Fanny observed in him. Though Miss Burney found occasion in the years that followed to take offense at Burke's political behavior, she apparently never lost or even modified her first enthusiasm for his conversation. In her old age, when she was composing the memoir of her father in that caricature of Johnsonian pomposity which was her later style, she wrote that she and her father sometimes had encountered Burke at Miss Monckton's assemblies where he was sure to find "many chosen friends with whom he could coalesce or combat upon literary or general topics," and that "he commonly entered the grand saloon with a spirited yet gentle air, that shewed him full fraught with generous purpose to receive as well as to dispense social pleasure, untinged with one bitter drop of political rancour, and clarified from all acidity of party sarcasm."[16]

That Fanny Burney was not alone among the women in her admiration for Burke's conversation is abundantly witnessed in the correspondence of the bluestockings themselves, though records of his conversations at their assemblies are lacking. He was early a frequenter of the conversation parties of Mrs. Montagu and Mrs. Vesey, where he continued to appear off and on until the last years of his life.[17] In her *Bas Bleu*, in which she described the bluestocking gatherings, Hannah More included Burke (Hortensius) as one of those who "lov'd to sit" in Mrs. Vesey's circle, though in 1787 when the piece was written, politics, lamentably, had made him "apostate . . . from social wit." Even so, as late as April, 1790, she found him at Mrs. Montagu's "a sufficiently pleasant party of himself."[18] In 1772, as she wrote to her Irish friend, Mrs. Montagu imagined the scene in Mrs. Vesey's blue room. Though Garrick sat in one corner, Lord Lyttelton close to the fire, and Mrs. Carter on the sofa, Burke was, characteristically, "in the midst of your circle."[19] At Mrs.

Vesey's Burke apparently took full advantage of the freedom allowed by the hostess, for Fanny Burney says that when at any time he stopped in and found no one he wished to talk to, he would sit down with a book and read aloud to himself. Fanny says he read "incomparably" and not seldom so.[20] Burke would also appear at the salon of Mrs. Chapone where, says Wraxall, he "sometimes unbent his faculties among persons adapted by nature to unfold the powers of delighting and instructing with which genius and study had enriched him. His presence was, however, more coveted than enjoyed."[21] Johnson reenforces this impression of the value set upon Burke's social conversation. In 1780 he wrote to Mrs. Thrale:

But [Fanny Burney] and you have had, with all your adulation, nothing finer said of you than was said last Saturday night of Burke and me. We were at the Bishop of [St. Asaph's] . . . and towards twelve we fell into talk, to which the ladies listened just as they do to you; and said, as I heard, *there is no rising unless somebody will cry fire.*[22]

This remark, of course, may indicate desperation rather than absorption.

Others of Burke's acquaintances and friends were not less laudatory. Andrew Dalzel, the classical scholar and historian of Edinburgh University, wrote of him, "—the most agreeable and entertaining man in conversation I ever knew. . . . We got a vast deal of political anecdotes from him, and fine pictures of political characters both dead and living. Whether they were impartially drawn, that is questionable, but they were admirably drawn."[23]

Next only to his painting, Sir Joshua Reynolds, the perennial and perpetual host, prized good conversation at his dinner table. For this reason among others no one was more welcome there, or indeed in the painter's studio, than Burke. Northcote, who disliked Burke, insisted that to get Burke to his table, Reynolds sacrificed his interest, "for associating with men like Burke . . . did him no good at Court."[24] Reynolds and Burke, nevertheless, were the best of friends, and Reynolds once told Boswell that he had frequently heard Burke say in the course of an evening ten good things each of which would have served a noted wit, whom he named, for a twelvemonth.[25] Many of the fullest and best of Boswell's accounts of Burke's conversation derive from dinners at Sir Joshua's.

Goldsmith's description of Burke's conversation is well known. "Is he [Johnson]," said Goldsmith to Boswell, "like Burke, who winds into a subject like a serpent?"[26] And Langton, who later had cause to complain about Burke, once told Boswell that there had been Club meetings where he had wished Burke had talked more and Johnson less.[27] Mrs. Thrale, who was not usually lenient in her judgment of Burke, described (in verse) his conversation as striking one blind;[28] and she once told Johnson that there was no one whose conversation diffused more knowledge than Mrs. Montagu's except his own and Burke's.[29]

Dissenting voices are not wanting, however, nor is the same mind always to be found in those who praised Burke. The complaints and attacks usually centered in one or more of three major objections: Burke, his detractors asserted, monopolized conversation, he demonstrated the utmost lack of consideration and courtesy, and he wallowed in puerile wit.

One of the earliest of these dissenters was Johnson's friend, that "most unclubbable" man, Sir John Hawkins, to whom, as the descendant of Elizabeth's famous sea dog, Burke apparently paid too little deference. It is notorious that Burke and Hawkins never got on well; and in preference to Hawkins' own rather transparent excuse-making, we may readily accept Boswell's story that the extreme violence of Hawkins' attacks on Burke led to his being "frozen out" of the Club.[30] Burke's biographer Bisset says that the final dispute was over Fielding's novels, which Burke defended and Hawkins attacked.[31] Be that as it may, Hawkins' daughter, Letitia Matilda, took up the cudgels for her father. She described her father's contempt for "the Burkes" as Irish adventurers who had to talk their way to position, and she continued, not without some justice on her side:

I suspect that he [Sir John] was disgusted with Mr. Burke's overbearing manners, and the monopoly of conversation which he as-

sumed, reducing the other members—Johnson excepted—to silence.
... That Johnson was aware of the Burkes' obtrusiveness was shown
by the language he used regarding them in conversation with my
father.[32]

She did, however, admit that Edmund was the best of the
Burkes. That Johnson "was aware of the Burkes' obtrusiveness,"
was also shown by his remark to Boswell: "No: I cannot say he
is good at that [listening]. So desirous is he to talk, that if one
is speaking at this end of the table, he'll speak to somebody at
the other end."[33] Langton is reported by H. D. Best to have said
that "Burke was rude and violent in dispute," instancing,

if anyone asserted that the United States were in the wrong in their
quarrel with the mother country, or that England had a right to
tax America, Burke, instead of answering his arguments, would, if
seated next to him, turn away in such a manner as to throw the
end of his own tail [pigtail] into the face of the arguer.[34]

According to Farington, Malone, always a friend and admirer
of Burke, thought that Burke would not do as one to take Sir
Joshua Reynolds' place as a host, for "by his eloquence and
habitual exertions in company, he would keep his guests too
much under."[35] Earlier Farington had noted, also apparently
quoting Malone,

[Burke's] manner in conversation, were it not for the great superiority of his talents and knowledge, would be disagreeable. He seldom
appears to pay any attention to what is said by the person or persons
with whom he is conversing, but disregarding their remarks, urges
on whatever rises in his mind with an ardour peculiar to himself.[36]

The best known attack on Burke's conversation, however,
came from the otherwise laudatory Johnson. His denial that
Burke had wit must be familiar to readers of Boswell. Boswell
quotes him as early as 1763 as saying of Burke, "He is, indeed,
continually attempting wit, but he fails."[37] And on September
15, 1773, during the tour of the Hebrides, Johnson again is
shown demolishing at some length Burke's pretensions to wit.
"No, Sir," said Johnson, "he never succeeds there. 'Tis low, 'tis
conceit. I used to say, Burke never once made a good joke." "No,

Sir, he's not the hawk there. He's the beetle in the mire." Boswell protested, "But he soars as the hawk." "Yes, Sir," shouted Johnson, "but he catches nothing."[38] This conversation when it appeared in print gave Boswell the opportunity of composing, with Malone's help, that preposterously long note in defense of Burke which covers nearly two pages in Hill's edition. Even as late as 1784 Johnson could still assert: "When Burke does not descend to be merry, his conversation is very superior indeed. There is no proportion between the powers which he shows in serious talk and in jocularity."[39] Burke seems not in the least to have resented Johnson's strictures; and while thanking Boswell and Malone for the notes in the *Hebrides,* he took pains to assure them that he was perfectly willing to abide by Johnson's judgment.[40] Two others who agreed with Johnson were Langton and Walpole. Langton said he could not laugh at Burke's wit, that "Burke hammered his wit upon an anvil, and the iron was cold. There were no sparks flashing and flying all about."[41] Walpole spoke of Burke's "pursuit of wit even to puerility" and added, "Burke himself always aimed at wit, but was not equally happy in public and private. In the former, nothing was so luminous, so striking, so abundant, in private it was forced, unnatural, and bombast."[42]

There were, however, many competent and talented persons whose reactions to Burke's pleasantries were far different. The most obvious example is Boswell, whose long vindication of Burke's wit has already been mentioned. A sentence or two from that note will suffice to illustrate its tone:

Surely, Mr. Burke, with his other remarkable qualities is also distinguished for his wit, and for wit of all kinds too; not merely that power of language which Pope chooses to denominate wit:— . . . but surprising allusions, brilliant sallies of vivacity, and pleasant conceits. His speeches in Parliament are strewn with them . . . and his conversation abounds in wit.[43]

The assiduous relish with which Boswell in his journals recorded examples of Burke's wit, attempted similar sallies in Burke's presence, and complimented himself when he had achieved a good pun,[44] is ample evidence of his regard for

Burke's talent. Perhaps also it shows a penchant in himself which would make him more likely than some others to enjoy Burke's specialty. Translating a passage from Sir George Mackenzie's *Characteres Advocatorum*, Boswell applied to Burke the following sentences: "He often indulged himself in every species of pleasantry and wit. Like a hawk, having soared with a lofty flight which the eye could not reach, he was wont to swoop upon his quarry with wonderful rapidity."[45]

Malone thought Burke witty, and, as we know, supplemented Boswell's printed defense of Burke's wit.[46] William Windham thought "that Mr. Burke was often very happy in his merriment";[47] and Barnard, Bishop of Killaloe, countered one of Langton's complaints with: "I don't think the iron is cold, but Burke is not so much a smith as he is a chymist, he analyzes a word, he decomposes it, and brings out all its different senses."[48]

This quality in Burke's conversation, which aroused such contrary responses can, perhaps, be analyzed and defined. Johnson called it "low"—"conceit"—and others agreed with him. Such samples as have been preserved, and there are now a great many, indicate that in conversation Burke boasted, or suffered from, an irrepressible addiction to punning, in Latin and in English. The illustrations of Burke's wit which Boswell adduces in the note in the *Hebrides* are chiefly puns or plays on words, and Boswell's journals are prolific of other examples:

Burke there, pleasant. I told of Liberty and necessity to be tried at law. HE. "I should be for necessity, as necessity has no law."[49]

Murphy flattered Burke much, and in particular said he was the best punster of the age; and after censuring Shakespeare, said, "You never pun out of place." Said Burke, "I pun *now—out of place.*" [Burke was not then in office.] Said Courtenay, "I believe you like better to pun *in* place." "Ay," said Burke. "Dulce est desipere in loco"; then he played himself as if sipping wine, saying "Desippere, or rather, in place decipere, with a c."[50]

Seated beside a ham he would refer to himself as "Ham—Burke";[51] or mentioning the Dean of Ferns, he would call his a "barren title";[52] hanging he termed a "scurvy cure" for scurvy;[53] as a motto for Boswell's visit to the Isle of Man, he suggested,

"The proper study of mankind is Man";[54] he punned on "Lee" and "lees," "succedaneum" and "succeed any of 'em," "Titan" and "a tight one," "syllabus" (on brewing) and "syllabub."[55] The whole conversation in which Burke and Boswell participated preceding Burke's installation at Glasgow in 1784 is studded with plain and elaborate puns.[56] This quality in Burke's conversation will be sufficiently illustrated in one more scene from Boswell's journal. The place is Reynolds' dinner table:

I was in delightful spirits. Burke was playful. "Will you have some of the sounds of the cod?" "No, I thank you." "You're all for the sense?" "O, I did not think the sound had been an echo of the sense." . . . [Burke's] definition of a good Manor: "*Est Modus in Rebus* (a Modus in the tithes), *certi denique fines* (and certain fines)." . . . I said cookery was a proof of reason. Burke, "If it be cooking eggs, there is reason in roasting of eggs." He was merely sportive to-day.[57]

The puns unquestionably constitute the ingredient of Burke's wit which would be most quickly identified by an observer, most easily recorded by a scribe, and longest remembered by anyone. They are, in all likelihood, what Johnson, Walpole, Langton, and others objected to at the same time that Boswell, Reynolds, and Murphy found them amusing. Though perhaps for those persons who found Burke's wit tedious, the puns and word play gave it its distinctive color and obscured its other qualities, in the face of some of the testimony one can hardly suppose that there was no other factor present.[58] The term wit, we know, has enjoyed a loose and ambiguous usage for several centuries, and should not be understood in too narrow a sense. Even should one consider only his puns, still Burke must be credited with some capacity for what commonly passes for wit, for the Latin pun, at which he often proved himself adept, is not without witty quality. We have, however, definite testimony that Burke showed other kinds of pleasantry, if not of what Johnson might choose to call "wit." Boswell, it will be recalled, declared that Burke was capable of all kinds of wit, not merely the brilliance of apt and appropriate language, but "surprising allusions, brilliant sallies of vivacity, and pleasant conceits."

Though Burke, unlike Johnson, has never been featured as the master of retort and repartee, his ability to sustain pleasantry in conversation and to turn an ingenious compliment cannot be doubted by one who studies the extant samples of his conversation, especially those preserved and reconstructed by Fanny Burney. The puns and word play, good and bad, are there in abundance, but there also we encounter the brilliant figure of speech and the incisive illustration which may without great violence be included in the idea of wit. Young French Laurence, Burke's friend and admirer in the later years, gave it as his opinion on this moot point that Burke's play of mind was not so much wit or humor as a certain "sportive vivacity."[59] Perhaps one need labor the point no further.

Apparently Burke seldom managed to steer a middle course between trivial frothiness and the serious, energetic, thought-laden, vivid talk which was so much admired. That Burke did have in his conversation the range, depth, variety, and amplitude for which he is praised is plentifully evident in the chief contemporary records where his talk is reproduced at some length: Boswell's *Life* and his journals, Fanny Burney's *Diary and Letters*, and Mrs. Crewe's notes on his table-talk as printed in the *Miscellanies of the Philobiblon Society*.[60] In those accounts one sees, as one would expect, that his interests and his knowledge were as wide as life. From daily events to religion, to politics, to history; from canine statuary to economics, to travel and philology; from personal tastes to literature, to biography, to morals; from theology to farming, rural economics, and conjugal felicity—Burke's talk would dart or roll, usually giving a listener the feeling that the speaker could go on vitally and informatively on any subject as long as his companions would follow, and perhaps much longer.

In this discussion one cannot avoid, even if one would, the implicit question, Was Burke equipped in learning and in knowledge of literature to meet Johnson on something like equal terms? The answer must be inferential, for there is not adequate reporting of their actual conversations to serve as convincing direct evidence. The evidence of witnesses, not the least of them Johnson himself, however, and the records we have of the subject matter and the scope of Burke's conversation point to a confident affirmative. Though Burke's profession, unlike Johnson's, was hardly conversation, most of the extant testimony and illustration confirm Johnson's own assertion that no matter what topic you took up, Burke was ready to meet you.

Apparently it was not in Johnson's presence only that Burke's reservoirs were readily opened, though the bouts with Johnson were probably the most astounding. Langton and Boswell both testify to the superlative quality of these displays, and displays at times they doubtless were. George Steevens once observed to Johnson that a question had been agitated between him and Burke with rather too much warmth. "It may be so, Sir," replied Johnson, "for Burke and I should have been of one opinion, if we had had no audience."[61] Boswell observed to Tom Davies, "Burke keeps to Johnson." "Yes," replied Davies, "like a man fishing salmon with a single hair: lets him flounce, then draws."[62] It is probably true that Burke, like Johnson, was, especially in his latter years, often violent and inconsiderate in conversation. His own excuse for Johnson, however, will be applied, except by his foes, to Burke himself: "It is well, if when a man comes to die, he has nothing heavier upon his conscience than having been a little rough in conversation."[63]

From the foregoing pages some general conclusions may be drawn concerning the nature and worth of Burke's conversation. It is an axiom that in the literary circles where Burke moved no accomplishment was prized more highly than conversational ability. Now, conversational ability, if it is to manifest itself in something more than entertaining chitchat, must be grounded upon knowledge, not of a special kind, but knowledge of a great variety of subjects. This kind of knowledge Burke possessed to a remarkable extent; and he communicated it with a clarity, a vivacity, and a brilliance which were the continual astonishment and delight of his friends. Again and again those persons whose business was learning and literature—Johnson, Boswell, Fanny Burney, Hannah Moore, Dalzel—in attempting to characterize Burke's chief excellence use almost the same terms: they speak of the great store and variety of his knowledge, the prodigality with which he diffused it, and the vast range of objects and conceptions from which he illustrated and illuminated his ideas and opinions. So learned a scholar as Dr. Parr, even, could think him the greatest man that ever lived, and James Mackintosh could compare him only to Cicero and Bacon for the powers of his mind.

This prodigality, however, was the basis for the complaints of such persons as Hawkins and Langton, who felt themselves excluded from conversation when Burke was present. It is inevitable, I suspect, that a person like Burke, who takes conversation seriously, and who knows more about almost any subject than the persons with whom he converses, will often be found lecturing or haranguing. Burke was by no means free of this fault, and it is not to be wondered that there were those who resented this behavior. Most of us at times would have been impatient. Most of his friends, nevertheless, even those who themselves had much of worth to say, realized that one could be worse employed than in giving Burke his cues and listening to him.

The other charges against Burke—lack of wit and lack of taste—derive from his great knowledge, his extreme sensitiveness to language, and the energy and nervousness with which he talked. His special form of wit was clearly the pun, and obviously he made many bad ones. On the other hand, as Dean Barnard said, the intricacy and agility of Burke's mind made him see and expose relations, facets, and nuances of meaning in a word which to other persons were initially imperceptible. As for his monopolizing conversation and his lack of consideration, the seriousness of that crime is at all times relative. Burke's apparently firm conviction that what he had to say was worth saying and could not wait (and he was probably right most of the time) may be offered as explanation though not as excuse for a fault which obviously cannot be denied. His alleged want of taste seems to have shown itself chiefly in his readiness to draw upon any kind of knowledge and any class of object in literature or in life for illustrations and figures. This habit undoubtedly produced some strange and perhaps revolting juxtapositions in his conversation. "How many maggots have crawled out of that great body!"[34] he said in speaking of the books about Johnson. This fault, if fault it be, must also be admitted. Even for Hannah More, however, to whom the figure of the maggots was presented, such elements seem not to have detracted seriously from enjoyment of the fascination and brilliance of Burke's conversation.

NOTES

1. Arthur Murphy, "An Essay on the Life and Genius of Samuel Johnson, LL.D.," *The Works of Samuel Johnson*, ed. R. Lynam, 6 vols. (London, 1825), I, liii.

2. James Boswell, *Life of Samuel Johnson*, ed. G. B. Hill, 6 vols. (Oxford, 1887), II, 181. This edition is hereinafter referred to as Boswell.

3. Boswell, II, 450.

4. *Boswelliana*, ed. Charles Rogers (London, 1874), p. 273.

5. "Burke, Sir," he continued, "is such a man that if you met him for the first time in the street where you were stopped by a drove of oxen, and you and he stepped aside to take shelter but for five minutes, he'd talk to you in such a manner, that, when you parted you would say, this is an extraordinary man." Boswell, V, 34. Boswell originally wrote and then erased ". . . where there was a shower of cannon bullets and you and he ran up a stair." *The Private Papers of James Boswell*, ed. Geoffrey Scott and Frederick A. Pottle, 19 vols. (Privately printed, 1928-1936), VI, 72. This work is hereinafter referred to as *Boswell Papers*.

6. Boswell, IV, 20. In the last year of his life he responded to Boswell's assertion that Burke had a "constant stream of conversation," with "Yes, Sir; if a man were to go by chance at the same time with Burke under a shed, to shun a shower, he would say—'this is an extraordinary man.' If Burke should go into a stable to see his horse drest, the ostler would say—'we have had an extraordinary man here.' " *Ibid.*, IV, 275-276.

7. *Ibid.*, III, 247.

8. *Ibid.*, IV, 167. These remarks of Johnson's will, of course, be familiar to readers of Boswell's *Life*, and are reproduced here mainly to refresh the memory.

9. *Ibid.*, V, 32-34.

10. *Ibid.*, IV, 276.

11. *Boswell Papers*, XVII, 51.

12. *Ibid.*, XVII, 100. Here and there through the journals there are other phrases and sentences of similar import: "Burke as usual was full of talk. . . . I am sorry my record is so imperfect." *Ibid.*, XVII, 89-90. "The earnest animation with which he talked . . . made me wonder and feel my own languor." *Ibid.*, XVII, 9. "Walked with him to the Adelphi. Great." *Ibid.*, XI, 269. And referring to Burke's talk about poetry on one occasion, Boswell noted "run on fine." *Ibid.*, XI, 281.

13. Boswell, III, 193, n. 3; *ibid.*, V, 79, n. 2.

14. *Diary and Letters of Madame d'Arblay*, ed. Austin Dobson, 6 vols. (London, 1906), II, 91. See also *Memoirs of Dr. Burney*, by Madame d'Arblay, 3 vols. (London, 1832), II, 227-228. In her other published account of this same dinner she exclaimed: "How proud should I be to give you a sample of the conversation of Mr. Burke: But the subjects were in general, so fleeting, his ideas so full of

variety, of gaiety, and of matter, and he darted from one of them to another with such rapidity, that the manner, the eye, the air with which all was pronounced, ought to be separately delineated to do any justice to the effect that every sentence, nay every word produced upon his admiring hearers and beholders." *Memoirs of Dr. Burney,* II, 228-229.

15. *Memoirs of Dr. Burney,* II, 237-238. In a spontaneous effusion penned at this time to Mrs. Thrale, Fanny wrote of Burke, "—such Spirit, such Intelligence, —so much energy when serious, so much pleasantry when sportive,—so manly in his address, so animated in his conversation,—so eloquent in Argument, so exhilarating in trifling—!" *London Times Literary Supplement,* July 23, 1938, p. 493.

16. *Memoirs of Dr. Burney,* II, 278.

17. See, for example, E. Climenson, *Elizabeth Montagu, Queen of the Bluestockings, Her Correspondence, 1720-1761,* 2 vols. (New York, 1906), II, 100-101, 108, 144, 156, 159-160, 169-171, 173; R. Blunt, *Mrs. Montagu, "Queen of the Blues,"* 2 vols. [1932?], I, 4, 41, 49-53, 89, 168, 179, 219, 224, 243, 245-246, 246-247, 249, 253, 263, 276, 306, 365; *ibid.,* II, 23, 34, 35, 42, 64, 118, 252; H. Roberts, *Memoirs of Hannah More,* 2 vols. (New York, 1835) I, 126, 204, 235, 349, 409.

18. *Memoirs of Hannah More,* I, 349.

19. Blunt, *op. cit.,* I, 263. How valuable an addition to her circle Mrs. Vesey considered Burke may be seen in a sentence of Hannah More's, written in 1786: "When I sent word last night to poor Mrs. Vesey that I was coming to her, she was so afraid she should not make it agreeable that she immediately sent for Mr. Burke to meet me." Burke could not come, but sent his son who turned out to be "an amiable young man, but not an adequate substitute for such a father." *Memoirs of Hannah More,* I, 236.

20. *Memoirs of Dr. Burney,* II, 267.

21. N. W. Wraxall, *Historical and Posthumous Memoirs,* ed. H. B. Wheatley, 5 vols. (London, 1884), I, 111.

22. *Johnson's Letters,* ed. G. B. Hill, 2 vols. (Oxford, 1892), II, 157.

23. *History of the University of Edinburgh,* I, 42, quoted by John Rae, *Life of Adam Smith* (London, 1895), p. 361.

24. William Hazlitt, "Conversations of Northcote," *Complete Works of William Hazlitt,* ed. P. P. Howe, XI (1932), 304.

25. Boswell, V, 32, n. 3.

26. *Ibid.,* II, 260.

27. *Ibid.,* IV, 26-27.

28. Leslie and Taylor, *The Life and Times of Sir Joshua Reynolds,* 2 vols. (London, 1865), II, 49.

29. *Diary and Letters of Madame d'Arblay,* I, 116.

30. See Boswell, I, 479-480; Sir John Hawkins, *Life of Johnson,* 2d ed. (1787), p. 425, n.

31. Robert Bisset, *The Life of Edmund Burke,* 2d ed. (London, 1800), I, 77. Burke's most recent biographer, Sir Philip Magnus, Bart., asserts, though with apparent independence of additional evidence, that Hawkins attacked Burke "on the subject of his stock-jobbing." *Edmund Burke* (London, 1939), p. 56.

32. F. H. Skrine, *Gossip about Dr. Johnson and Others,* pp. 57-58.

33. Boswell, V, 34.

34. *Johnsonian Miscellanies,* ed. G. B. Hill, 2 vols. (Oxford, 1897), II, 23, n: 4.

35. *The Farington Diary,* ed. James Greig, 8 vols. (London, 1922-1928), I, 136.

36. *Ibid.,* I, 103.

37. Boswell, I, 453.

38. *Ibid.*, V, 32-34. See also F. A. Pottle and C. H. Bennett's full text of Boswell's *Hebrides* (New York, 1936), pp. 171-172.

39. Boswell, IV, 276. Boswell could report, however, that Johnson approved of two of Burke's later puns, and actually laughed at one of them. *Ibid.*, III, 322-323.

40. *A Catalogue of Papers Relating to Boswell, Johnson, and Sir William Forbes, found at Fettercairn House,* ed. Claude Colleer Abbott (Oxford, 1936), Item 121, p. 25.

41. *Boswelliana*, p. 327.

42. Boswell, IV, 276, n. 2. Hill is quoting from the *Journal of the Reign of George III*.

43. Boswell, V, 32, n. 3.

44. See, for example, *Boswell Papers*, XIV, 174; *ibid.*, XV, 188-189, 206, 213; *ibid.*, XVII, 9-10; *ibid.*, XVIII, 24; Boswell, IV, 73.

45. Pottle and Bennett's edition of Boswell's *Hebrides*, pp. 171-172. In an *Ode to Edmond Malone*, attributed by Pottle to Boswell, occur the following lines:

> No Burke pours out a stream of wit,
> No Boswell joys o'er wine.

Frederick A. Pottle, *The Literary Career of James Boswell* (Oxford, 1929), p. 230.

46. Malone said once to Farington that Burke's conversation became frequently enlivened by appropriate sallies of wit and humour; and at another time reported that Burke joked and punned as usual. *The Farington Diary*, I, 201, 187.

47. Boswell, IV, 276.

48. *Boswelliana*, p. 328.

49. *Boswell Papers*, IX, 263.

50. *Ibid.*, XVII, 9-10.

51. *Ibid.*, XVII, 66.

52. *Ibid.*, XIV, 174.

53. *Ibid.*, XIII, 213.

54. *Ibid.*, XIII, 281.

55. *Ibid.*, XI, 263-264; *ibid.*, X, 184-185; *ibid.*, VI, 139.

56. *Ibid.*, XVI, 48-51.

57. *Ibid.*, XIV, 179-181. For further illustration see *ibid.*, VI, 130; XIII, 213, 220-222; XV, 188-189, 210-212; XVI, 115.

58. See, for example, the accounts of the meeting of the Club in *Boswell Papers*, XIV, 176-178, and of the dinner conversation at Sir Joshua Reynolds' in the *Diary and Letters of Madame d'Arblay*, II, 87-92.

59. *Boswell Papers*, XVII, 55.

60. (London, 1862-1863), Vol. VII, Sec. 5.

61. Boswell, IV, 324.

62. *Boswell Papers*, IX, 256.

63. Boswell, IV, 280.

64. This particular image, possibly, Burke drew from his memory of Lucretius, with whom he was well acquainted. Cf. *De Rerum Natura*, III, 713 ff., where Lucretius lightly inquires about the relation of the seeds of the departed spirit to the worms which infest the corpse.

God's Dramatist

C. HAROLD KING

§1

MOST of the great orators who have attracted the interest of scholars have left speeches valued as literature. George Whitefield, though without any claim to literary distinction, yet merits study, for he was the leading revivalist in eighteenth-century Britain and America. As the central figure in the Great Awakening in America, he stimulated the first popular movement on this continent; by initiating field preaching, he enabled a fledgling Methodist Movement to reach the masses and thus to become a prime factor in saving England from a French Revolution. In a career of thirty-four years he travelled forty thousand miles and preached eighteen thousand sermons. For him, on occasion, as many as twenty-five thousand auditors stood in the open air. He had a voice so powerful that his preaching could be heard a mile away and so melodious that Garrick is reported to have said, "I would give a hundred guineas if I could say 'O' like Mr. Whitefield."[1]

Nothing is more striking than the incongruity between George Whitefield's prominence among contemporaries and the obscurity that has clouded his name recently. In the seventeen-forties he was commonly referred to as the leader of the Methodists. One hundred and fifty-four out of two hundred anti-Methodist publications between 1739 and 1749 were levelled at him as the source of evil.[2] Today good Methodists think of him as a kind of assistant to Wesley. Yet Wesley was dragged unwillingly into field preaching after Whitefield had inaugurated it. Whitefield was first among the Methodists to achieve conversion, without which the fervor of the Methodist Movement might have risen little higher than the earnest piety of the religious societies that had existed for thirty years. Whitefield was first to get in touch with these older societies, although it was Wesley whose societies came to form the sinews of an organization that could endure. Whitefield was first to sponsor

Methodist journalism with the *Weekly History;*[3] yet it is Wesley's host of publications which is remembered. Although Methodism all over the world is thought of as the shadow of John Wesley, Whitefield first became head of a corporate Methodist body, the Welsh Calvinists. The monuments to Wesley are legion, including a likeness of his horse; there is one statue of Whitefield—on the campus of the University of Pennsylvania. Nor did it take two hundred years to dull his prestige. An historian of Gloucester, writing a generation after the evangelist's death, lamented, "Whitefield is . . . forgotten in his native place."[4]

The reasons for the decline of Whitefield's reputation would make an interesting study in themselves. More important, however, is the attempt to explain his indubitable success in his own day, for Lecky has expressed the verdict of sober history, that Whitefield "as a popular preacher indeed . . . appears never to have been equalled in England."[5] And the absence of all after-fame makes Whitefield a better witness on the age-old question, "In what does eloquence consist?"

The phenomenon of Whitefield can be explained not by one, but by several factors. His ideas must be examined, of course, and his mode of composition, as well as his manner of delivery. But that is not enough. The audience matters a great deal. In Whitefield's case, it might almost be said that the audience matters more than all other factors combined. It is as if the audience and the speaker met half way and worked out the technique of revivalism between them.[6]

The story of how Whitefield and his audience met tells much about them both. He was prepared for the meeting more by his conversion than by his speech training. A normal boy in most respects, the intensity of his passions was above the average. The turmoil of his adolescence thus became especially acute, and he was driven to look for some remedy that would mitigate his discomfort. The religious works he read told him not only that romances and plays, of which he was fond, were wicked, but that his flesh was naturally sinful. Unable to explain to himself his mysterious torment, he found it more and more probable that he was, as the books said, hopelessly depraved. Trouble at home deepened his melancholy. His going to Oxford was partly the result of a natural desire to better himself and partly an urge to escape from conditions that had become unpleasant. At Oxford he made the acquaintance of a little group of pious students whom the other students had dubbed "Methodists" because they were so methodical in their good works. Whitefield was so plunged in despair by this time that the confident piety of the Methodists attracted him. Doing good by schedule, however, did not bring him peace of mind, and so he branched out on experiments of his own. He tried "quietism": he refused to attend church, to visit the poor, or to associate with others for fear that he would be puffed up with pride at his own goodness. Although he soon ceased this nihilistic pursuit of inner grace, he continued such ascetic practices as fasting and neglecting his dress. When emotional strain had almost made him a nervous wreck, he found relief in conversion. Familiar as this phenomenon is in religious history, it was out of fashion then. The Methodists had no idea what was happening to Whitefield. He had left them behind—and had set for them an example which they were to follow before their movement could pass beyond small waters.

Whitefield's early experience did not include a great deal that can be set down as training for platform or pulpit. Doubtless it was helpful to observe, at the Bell Inn, different types of people in various moods. Doubtless the plays and romances he read stimulated his imagination. At St. Mary de Crypt, his teacher composed skits in which Whitefield and other boys appeared. In one of these productions, George played a female part and dressed in girl's clothes.[7] "The remembrance of this," he wrote later, "has often covered me with confusion of face, and I hope, will do so to the end of my life." He condemned school dramatics and, indeed, all theatricals, as calculated "to debauch the mind, to raise ill passions, and to stuff the memory with things as contrary to the Gospel of Jesus Christ as light to darkness, Heaven to Hell." But to the same master he was always grateful for teaching him "to speak and write correctly"; and apparently the boy showed a spark of talent, as he was selected "for making speeches before the corporation, at their annual visitation."

But most of Whitefield's training came from practice. The year 1737 was important in the young evangelist's development. While waiting twelve months for a ship to America, he was without special assignment in England. Full of the new spirit that had recently come to him, he was eager to tell others about the New Birth. He was officially licensed to preach in churches, and the promise he had already displayed brought him invitations. He made good immediately. The invitations increased and the audiences grew until he was able to write, "I began to grow a little popular."[8]

Whitefield learned a great deal about popular preaching in this year of "rehearsal." He found that he could preach extempore when necessary, a practice scorned in the eighteenth century. He learned to his surprise that he could agree on fundamentals of doctrine with a Baptist minister, a tolerance questionable in an Anglican clergyman. He discovered at Bath that fashionable people listened to him flatteringly, a compliment to which the erstwhile barkeeper was not indifferent. He saw and capitalized the possibilities of a farewell sermon when his ship was about to sail. As he made the long voyage to America, the young man had an ample store of pulpit experiences on which he could reflect; and he had some right to think that his apprenticeship was over.

§2

Whitefield arrived at full stature as an orator only after his venture into field-preaching. The circumstances leading up to this innovation provide us with facts useful in understanding the preacher and his audience. Whitefield's exploits showed resourcefulness—and also a tendency toward irregularity. He always thought of himself as orthodox in doctrine and practice. He revered tradition, but tradition in him was lightly traced, and when confronted by an unprecedented situation, he would do what he called "a new thing." Hence substantial citizens detected in him a constant threat of the unexpected, and they became uneasy. Irregularity in the eighteenth century was no light sin. The preceding century had been turbulent with religious and political strife. Only after the Glorious Revolution and with the accession of the House of Hanover had an established order seemed guaranteed. And now in the seventeen-thirties the Right Thinking People resented anything that appeared to threaten their tranquillity.

When Whitefield returned from America in 1738, his doctrine and practice were seen to be more unconventional than ever. He had become distressingly Calvinistic and thus altogether too suggestive of the Puritans and the Scotch. He continued his irregular practices with zeal—and with success. He had been known to consort with dissenters. He filled respectable sanctuaries with the rabble, and the rabble was indecorous. Accordingly his meetings often were marked by emotional extravagance. Clearly this man was a disturber of the peace. It remained only to find an indictment to fit the offense, and for the greatest of eighteenth-century crimes there was a name. George Whitefield was definitely charged with Enthusiasm. One could today add together "radical," "demagogue," and "communist" and still hardly approximate the venom contained in the epithet "Enthusiast." So it came to pass that the Right Thinking People cried in unison, "Away with him from the Church of England." One Anglican church after another was denied him. Nor could the dissenters suffer his presence without risk; they had to keep within the good graces of the bishops in order to enjoy the benefits of the Toleration Act. At last the Warden of Bristol Prison, certain that his thieves and murderers would be corrupted by an Enthusiast, forbade Whitefield's preaching to the inmates.

Not far from Bristol was a district known as Kingswood. Once a hunting ground for kings, it now was a grimy region where colliers burrowed for coal. On February 17, 1739, Whitefield stood on Kingswood Hill and preached to a small congregation of miners. He watched for some indication that his audience listened. At last the sign came, and it was authentic.

White channels began to appear on the coal-blackened faces. Even colliers had tears to shed, and Whitefield was convinced that their souls could be saved. There came to him a sense of relief which he expressed at the end of the day, "Blessed be God I have now broken the ice."[9]

George Whitefield was not the first outdoor preacher. The Mediterranean world had held its assemblies in the open air. In England, the fourteenth-century John Wycliffe had inspired his preachers to appear in outdoor settings. The Scotch Covenanters had been familiar with "field conventicles." Hence Whitefield was not original in an absolute sense. In a relative sense, however, he was both original and daring, because in eighteenth-century England field-preaching was virtually unthinkable. How unthinkable it was can be inferred from the attitude of John Wesley, who had everything to gain from espousing it, but who was, nevertheless, a good eighteenth-century man: "I could scarcely reconcile myself at first to this strange way of preaching in the fields, of which he [Whitefield] set me an example on Sunday; having been all my life (till very recently) so tenacious of every point relating to decency and order; that I should have thought the saving of souls almost a sin if it had not been done in a church."[10] Once the venture was demonstrated as practical, however, Wesley "submitted to be more vile"[11] by commencing his field-preaching under the auspices of Whitefield.

The inauguration of field-preaching brought Whitefield and his audience into full collaboration. Accordingly, one may inquire next: What was the nature of the audience in cooperation with which Whitefield developed his technique of evangelism? One should note first the size. Although he was extremely versatile and could charm one, ten, or a hundred as readily as thousands, it was the multitude that brought his talents into full play. Franklin, in one of his ingenious experiments, estimated that it was possible for Whitefield to be heard "by more than thirty thousand."[12] A painstaking calculation by an enterprising reporter for *The Gentleman's Magazine* offered good evidence that one of Whitefield's large audiences numbered 25,443.[13]

These large numbers do more than establish impressive records; they indicate the presence of factors that would make mob psychology completely operative.

The tendency of these large audiences to let themselves go was aided by the unconventional settings in which they found themselves. Whitefield continued throughout his career to preach in churches when allowed; and after the general exclusion of all Methodist preachers in February, 1739, churches were presently opened to him again, as well as to others. Nevertheless the out-of-doors became his habitual auditorium, sometimes because of exclusion, but more often because churches would not hold the crowds. Frequently one reads of the back window of a church being removed so that the overflow might hear.[14] A barn or public house would do sometimes. An open field, a common, or a market place would do better. His outdoor pulpits came to be any slight elevations from which he might be seen and heard: a table, a horseblock, a market cross, or a balcony. In one case he used a stage set up for wrestlers. At Hackney he competed successfully with a horserace, and at the Moorfields with mountebanks. In such situations a large audience is less inhibited by conventional restraints.

The interest of Whitefield's large public was sustained by reports of his interesting adventures when on tour. Not only were the climaxes dramatic, as when he ventured into field preaching for the first time, but the habitual routine was striking. Choosing almost at random one journey from Wales to Plymouth in 1744, we note the following experiences: preaching in an allegedly haunted house, the owner hopeful that Whitefield would "pray the devil out of it"; watching a man hung in chains at Hampton Common and then delivering a sermon near the site; the next day preaching at "Gloucester-Ham," near the gallows of a lesser felon, not dignified with chains. At Larn Ferry, one ship fired several guns in tribute and others hoisted their flags. When he arrived at Plymouth, he was assaulted in his rooms by a stranger with a gold-headed cane.[15] Such adventures were all in the day's work for Whitefield, but they excited the curiosity of others. One issue of the *New York*

Gazette, during the high tide of the Great Awakening, was filled almost entirely with accounts of him and his work.[16] Tall tales were whispered admiringly or in exasperation. People wrote letters about him to their friends. Whitefield made no conscious effort to seek this publicity. Yet in advance of his arrival at a new rendezvous, rumor had made vivid his image, and before he opened his mouth the people were disposed to listen. Moreover, he had the capacity to live up to advance notices. Josiah Smith, for instance, wrote that the expectations of the Boston ministers were "all answered, and exceeded."[17]

Since this gray mass we call the public or the audience was made up of people, we may ask: What kind of people was fascinated by the orator's presence and the traveler's adventures? Wesley, at Whitefield's death, testified to his colleague's appeal "to persons of every rank and condition, high and low, rich and poor."[18] Negroes listened in the Bermudas. Apprentices crowded the Moorfields outside London. Merchants heard him talk metaphorically of goods bought and sold. Soldiers and sailors attended him in the shadow of the Rock of Gibraltar, where several ships were drawn up within hearing distance. Judges adjourned their sittings when he was in town. Governors accompanied him on his journeys. Shuter, the comedian, and Chesterfield came to the "Soul Trap," one of his tabernacles. Franklin stood in Market Street while the evangelist preached from the courthouse steps. "Brilliant assemblies" gathered at the Countess of Huntingdon's mansion, while in her chapel at Bath princes of the Church sat discreetly hidden by curtains.[19] Hume said of one of Whitefield's passages, "This address . . . surpassed anything I ever saw or heard in any other preacher."[20]

Nevertheless, this catholic picture must be qualified. In spite of the knowledge that every now and then "a fine gentleman was touched," in spite of flattering praise from men of great names, we know that, on the whole, the aristocracy of brains and rank remained to praise but not to be converted. We are forced to conclude that although the quality and the intelligentsia came to enjoy a good show, they did not, as a rule, submit themselves as candidates for conversion. The most responsive elements in Whitefield's audience were from the lower classes. His assemblies might sparkle with isolated gems from the more ornamental and more substantial strata of eighteenth-century society, but the "have nots" became his regular clientele, those who lacked material and spiritual confidence and would gaze hungrily at Utopia.

Whitefield discovered his clientele after a short period of groping. On his second pulpit mission he was depressed by the stupidity of Dummer peasants; yet his career was scarcely launched before he noticed that the greatest response came from people "at the dock." Once the lowly had made known their eagerness, he became their champion. He approved Paul for saying, "God hath chosen the weak things of the world, to confound the things which are mighty: and the base things of the world, and things which are despised hath God chosen, yea and things that are not, to bring to nought the things that are."[21]

The masses of eighteenth-century England were particularly susceptible to the agitator's plea. The Right Thinking People fondly believed that reason was king, and to his judgment bar were brought all things in heaven and earth. The have-nots, however, were unaware that this was the age of common sense. Had they been analytical, they would have understood the disruptive effects of the Industrial Revolution upon their rhythms of life.[22] Had they been critical, they would have denounced the absurdity of putting their fellows in jail for debt where their solvency was reduced to zero. Had they been observant, they would have noticed how many of their friends had gone to America, where at least was hope and a fighting chance. Had they been class conscious, they might have rebelled against those who had the power but not the desire to help them.

The depressed classes of England, however, were not class conscious; neither were they critical, nor observant, but, like dumb animals in pain, sought relief that was convenient and within their means. Hogarth's picture of Gin Lane is hardly an exaggeration. An advertisement, appearing in London in 1727, promised "a mad bull to be dressed up with fireworks to be baited."[23] In the stupor of drink or in sadistic whoops over the sufferings of animals a little lower than themselves, the masses of England found relief from misery.

And how did the Church, classic haven for the oppressed, respond to this challenge? It had no answer for the challenge, for the Church had become rational. Bishop Butler, after much labor, had established religion upon a firm basis of probability.[24] The Anglican divines and the comfortable parishioners who so languidly adorned the pews, were satisfied that they at last had made Christianity reasonable. But were there no country-wide enthusiasms through which popular discontent might be drained off? The Right Thinking People had made Enthusiasm a crime and had seen to it that no palpitation of popular ardor should disturb the existing status. The long, bleak age of Walpole seemed to have effected permanent inoculation against the dread disease, and the popular frenzy over the small War of Jenkins' Ear in 1739 did not warn the statesmen that there must be words other than *prudence* in their vocabularies.

Here was the material for revolution: the masses dogged by misery, unloved and ignored by those in robes of office or in vestments, plunged in sordid debauchery and lacking adequate illusions of escape. But misery alone does not cause revolution. Those who revolt must not only be unjustly treated; they must think themselves the victims of injustice. Discontent must be focused and turned into action. Revolutions, in short, do not happen without leaders.

George Whitefield made himself leader of the people, but not of revolution. He gave them a stimulus, aroused their hopes, reformed their ways, and all without stirring them to resentment against the more fortunate, and without organizing political action of any kind. He offered them a Promised Land and dramatized its features.

§3

For the common people Whitefield had a message. His message was refracted through Calvinistic dogma and then focused for popular consumption. The principal tenets of his doctrine were Original Sin, Justification by Faith, and Election. According to the doctrine of Original Sin, man's nature was depraved because of the indiscretion of Adam and Eve. "Remember, I beseech you to remember, that you are fallen creatures, that you are by Nature lost and estranged from God."[25] Those who drank gin to excess, those who indulged in light pleasures, those whom the world thought good but who could not be sure that they had been converted, were alike fallen creatures. If one were inwardly distressed for reasons he himself could not fathom, Original Sin would explain his unhappiness. If one were well born and rich, but unconverted, his situation was dangerous because he was apt to allow his worldly blessings to obscure his consciousness of innate depravity. If one were happy, yet unconverted, he was in greater danger still, for his sense of well-being made him indisposed to think of himself as essentially foul. In this picture, the common man came out best. In sin he was the equal of the privileged; in capacity to realize his sin he was undoubtedly superior.

If all men were equally vicious, they must be cured by the same remedy: Justification by Faith, leading to Conversion. A man achieved Conversion, not by performing faithfully the offices of the Church nor by doing good acts, but by throwing himself upon the mercy of God. Thus again the humble man found himself on terms of equality with any on this earth; and in Heaven he would be especially blessed.

Whitefield's doctrine of Election seemed incongruous with the general pattern of his persuasions. According to the doctrine, God had determined who should be saved and who should be damned. Whitefield was always in controversy over this matter. His opponents claimed that it seemed nonsense to urge people to undergo the severe discipline of a good life if their fate were sealed in advance. Whitefield's answer was:

It is the doctrine of election that mostly presses me to abound in good works. I am made willing to suffer all things for election's sake; this makes me preach with comfort, because I know that salvation does not depend on *man's* free will but *the Lord* makes me willing on that day of power and can make use of me to bring some of his elect home when and where he pleases.[26]

The position was that good works in themselves would not bring salvation but would follow the all-important requisite of salvation: justification by faith. In any case the elect had already been chosen and the pattern they would follow already determined. To the average man this kind of fatalism may account for resignation or serenity but does not readily explain Whitefield's energetic admonitions to reform while yet there was time. Actually Calvinists have not been particularly noted for resignation. Many of them have labored strenuously to change the hard course of events. But the attempt to reform the world according to one's wishes often proves discouraging. And so those who by temperament were Calvinists have sought to assure themselves by Predestination that the universe is actually well ordered and that God has always known how it will come out.

Although Whitefield upheld Predestination staunchly in paper controversy and thought that he did so on all occasions, often his remarks in sermons would bear another construction. For instance, he said, "When we are all convinced of our need and helplessness, and of Jesus being a Redeemer, that is mighty and willing to save, a poor soul then throws himself upon this Jesus, receives this Jesus, ventures upon this Jesus, believes the word and by venturing on this promise, receives the thing promised."[27] The thing promised was salvation. This passage may be interpreted to support Predestination if one tries hard enough. Whitefield was talking to an audience, however, whose members almost certainly would prefer the obvious interpretation. It looked very much to the average man as if he were being offered a reward in fulfillment of certain conditions. The academic precedence of justification by faith over good works in the hierarchy of theological values mattered little to him. Theoretical determinism mattered less. A panacea for all his ills was offered to him. Some of his friends took advantage of the offer; some did not. To his way of thinking that involved choice. The evangelist who must consider the common man's way of thinking has to assume freedom of choice even if it does not exist. As time passed, Whitefield was less and less insistent upon predestination and came to offer what, to his auditors, looked like free grace. Evidently the audience qualified their leader's theology.

It is easy to see that Whitefield's program would appeal to the hopelessly frustrated. The people to whom he was talking had very substantial motives for wanting a New Deal. He developed their vague and gnawing discontent to a point of tragic hopelessness until they should be forced to cry, "What shall we do to be saved?" The solution he offered was easy and cheap. It was as if he said: "Be convinced of your innate sinfulness, confess your sins, and you will receive a salvation that will solve all your difficulties. If you accept this offer you will be eligible for a place hereafter where all life's inequalities will be compensated for. If burdened by debt, riches will be waiting; if clothed in rags, fine raiment will be yours; if blighted by man's contempt, you will be God's elect. Earthly troubles are as nothing when you are destined for royal favor." Whitefield's emphasis was adapted to what his listeners wanted to hear, and so the audience was not without influence upon his total message. At the same time, his teaching was one from which the established order had nothing to fear.

§4

Whitefield's message, potentially appealing to those poor in the goods and privileges of this world, was cast in a fashion that would attract the lowly:

I would further observe, that if any here do expect fine preaching from me this day, they will, in all probability, go away disappointed. For I am not here to shout over people's heads; but, if the Lord shall be pleased to bless me, to reach their hearts. Accordingly, I shall cloath my ideas in such plain language that the meanest negro or servant ... may understand me; for I am certain, if the poor and unlearned can comprehend, the learned and rich must.[28]

Adaptable as Whitefield was, he allowed the audience to influence his style.

The manner in which the orator wove his spell can be learned partly from his sermons. He won the attention of his unlearned subjects by making himself clear, vivid, and dramatic, and in all cases, by translating what he had to say into terms of their experience. His ability to make himself intelligible to the uncultured is apparent in his interpretation of scriptural texts.

For instance, we all know the Biblical statement that it is harder for the rich man to win God's favor than for a camel to pass through the eye of a needle. Whitefield was aware that his listeners knew little about camels. But they knew something about cable ropes, and the attempt to thread a needle with one would illustrate the rich man's difficulty very well. So he interpolates thus: "It is easier for a camel (or a cable rope) to go through the eye of a needle, than for a rich man to enter the kingdom of God."[29] Again he paraphrases Biblical phraseology into everyday language. Esau's rumination within himself is rendered as follows: "The days of mourning for my father will soon come and what then? Why though I have some compassion for the old man, and therefore will not lay violent hands upon my brother while my father is still alive, yet I am resolved to kill him before my father is cold in the grave."[30]

Whitefield was not merely comprehensible; he was vivid. He sensed that the nearer an audience approaches the primitive, the more it is inclined to "think" in images. Whitefield had, of course, great sources of imagery in the Bible. Accordingly he needed only to accentuate a few details of his Biblical images to produce a simple but clear picture. In discussing Jacob's ladder experience he says, "God was at the top of the ladder; pray, mind that. He appears not sitting, as he is often represented in heaven, but standing. . . ."[31] The mixture of Biblical and colloquial is sometimes incongruous: "Methinks I see the heavens opened, the Judge sitting upon the throne, the sea boiling like a pot, and the Lord coming to judge the world."[32] The humble listener could visualize a sea boiling like a pot and would not resent the incongruity.

Whitefield's pictures were not all brought down to a reassuring colloquial level. At times his clientele wanted him to lift them up. That he was capable of what must have seemed the grand manner to his followers is shown by the following comment upon his style:

You may be sure . . . that when he treated upon the sufferings of our Saviour, it was not without great pathos. . . . As though Gethsemane were within sight, he would say, stretching out his hand, . . . "Look yonder. What is that I see? It is my agonizing Lord." And as though it were no difficult matter to catch the sound of the Saviour praying, he would exclaim, "Hark! Hark! Do you hear him?" You may suppose that, as this occurred frequently, the efficacy of it was destroyed: but no, though we often knew what was coming, it was as new to us as though we had never heard it before.[33]

Whitefield's capacity for the pictorial reminds us of the old Arabian proverb, "He is the best orator who can turn men's ears into eyes."

Whitefield was not merely clear and vivid; he always saw the dramatic possibilities of his material. Although the Gethsemane incident may not please us, it thrilled those who listened. He summoned characters who acted much as his audience supposed they should. In many cases he suggests the character by drawing attention to some significant physical attitude. The Pharisee is represented: "Our Lord first takes notice of his posture; the Pharisee stood. . . . Perhaps he pointed at the poor man [the publican] that others might treat him with contempt."[34] Whitefield is also capable of a comparatively full-length portrait, as when he reveals Abraham's character by cumulation of such items as Abraham's "holy familiarity with God," his anguish of soul as he walks with his son to the sacrifice, and the nature of the last farewell.[35] Whitefield made dialogue for his characters. If stage directions, necessary to orient Whitefield's audience, are omitted, we have a simple, natural conversation between the vacillating Eve and the confident, insinuating serpent:

[Serpent] Yea hath God said, Ye shall not eat of every tree of the garden? What! hath God planted a garden, and placed you in the midst of it, only to teaze and perplex you? Hath he planted a garden, and yet forbid you making use of any of the trees of it at all? . . .

[Eve] We may eat of the fruit of the trees of the garden; God has not forbid us eating of every tree of the garden. No; we may eat of the trees of the garden; . . . there is only one tree in the midst of the garden, of which God hath said, ye shall not eat of it, neither shall ye touch it, lest ye die. . . .

[Serpent] Ye shall not surely die. Surely God will not be so cruel as to damn you only for eating an apple; it cannot be; . . . it is all a delusion, a mere bugbear to keep you in servile subjection; . . . God doth know that in the day ye eat thereof, ye shall be as gods."[36]

The attention of "the meanest negro or servant" may be captured for the moment by having heretofore abstruse matters reduced to terms of his experience; he may be fascinated for the time by vivid scenes or thrilled by dramatic fragments; but his attention is sustained by some coherent art of composition. Whitefield knew how to tell a story. Cornelius Winter, who heard the evangelist as often as anyone, said, "He abounded in anecdotes which, though not always recited verbatim, were very just as to the matter of them."[37] His most constant source of narrative was the Bible, and when reproducing Bible stories, he was at his best. The most effective sermons were based on scriptural drama: "The Seed of the Woman and the Seed of the Serpent" [the story of Adam and Eve], "Saul's Conversion," "Peter's Denial of his Lord," "Jacob's Ladder," "The Resurrection of Lazarus," and especially "Abraham's Offering up his Son."

These stories have dramatic possibilities. In them is simple yet definite conflict between good and evil. In "Abraham's Offering up his Son" there is conflict between Abraham's love for his son and his allegiance to God. In "Saul's Conversion" true righteousness triumphs over false, but only after tense and exciting struggle. In "The Seed of the Woman and the Seed of the Serpent" there is the tragedy of the Fall of Man. Whitefield indeed produced dramas of the gravest import.

The plots of the Biblical dramas were within the comprehension of the humblest, and the essential drama of the plot was heightened by capitalizing on every moment of suspense, such as when Whitefield tantalized the listener with the possibility of Isaac resisting as he was bound for the sacrifice, by dramatic irony such as Abraham's walking behind Isaac in order to contemplate lovingly the son he was about to kill, by making the most of the climax when the knife was about to descend. Whitefield accentuated the drama also by skillful portrayal of character, as has already been suggested. He said at the end of the drama, "I see your hearts affected, I see your eyes weep."[38]

Of course, Whitefield had a utilitarian motive in dramatizing these stories. The heroes who conquered and the villains who departed in gloom did so to further the evangelist's message.

The negro or servant unconsciously approved Abraham for his faith and condemned Eve for her lack of it, thus partly committing himself on the great issue to which Whitefield was leading.

This identification of his listeners with the progress of the story was necessary for the focusing of their attention. The catastrophe of Adam and Eve was a threat to the self-preservation of mankind and to the individual who felt himself identified with it. The continual emphasis on Abraham's yearning for his son appealed to the universal love of parent for child. In "Christ the Best Husband or an Earnest Invitation to Young Women to Come to see Christ," the preacher appealed to the sex urge when he said, "Do you desire one that can love you? None can love you like Christ: his love, my dear sisters, is incomprehensible; his love passeth all other loves."[39] By deprecating the snobbishness of the Pharisee and exalting the humility of the publican, we may be sure that he released sympathetic reactions in his lower-class hearers whose desire for status and prestige was necessarily unfulfilled. It does not seem, at first thought, that the prospect of persecution, as in the sermon "Persecution Every Christian's Lot," would appeal to the average person, scarcely capable of the higher reaches of sainthood. But since Whitefield suggested that privation is riches, and ignominy glory, he enhanced the prestige of his humble listeners. Through dramatization, then, Whitefield stirred the fundamental urges.

Once the evangelist had released the passions of men, he was not less skillful in directing them toward immediate action. If he stimulated the instinct of self-preservation by the story of Adam and Eve's fall, he indicated that eternal life may be assured by surrendering to God; if he touched the parent love by depicting Abraham's pain at the thought of losing his son, he proffered that which was insurance against domestic tragedy, absolute faith in God; if he aroused sex passion in young women, he did not hesitate to suggest that gratification would result from marriage to Christ; if he aroused the smoldering resentment of social outcasts against the self-righteousness of the Pharisee, he claimed that Christ would raise up the humble; if he built a formidable picture of the hardships of the Christian life, he revealed that hardship, the stock in trade of the lowly, was especially pleasing to God. Even though, as Winter said, ". . . the description upon paper, wanting the reality, as exemplified by him with voice and motion, conveys but a faint idea,"[40] it is possible to see that there is art, if not literature, in the sermons of Whitefield.

§5

Whitefield's powers of delivery must have been tremendous. No discussion can reconstruct them. The fallacy of embalming some isolated gesture as the secret of success is shown by the dissatisfaction Whitefield and his friends expressed at a picture of him in the act of holding up his hands as if rendering a benediction. Winter observed, "It is necessary to remark, that the attitude was very transient, and always accompanied by some expressions which would justify it."[41] One contemporary wrote, "Every accent of his Voice, every Motion of his Body *speaks*, and both are natural and unaffected. If his delivery is the Product of Art, 'tis certainly the Perfection of it, for it is entirely concealed."[42]

In conjunction with expressive action Whitefield made full use of a magnificent voice. One of his Philadelphia listeners recorded that when the orator preached from the gallery of the courthouse in Market Street, three blocks from the Delaware River, he could be heard on the Jersey shore and every word distinctly understood on board a shallop at Market Street Wharf.[43] Franklin testified that Whitefield's voice was loud and clear, that he "articulated his words and sentences so perfectly, that he might be heard and understood at a great distance. . . ." With respect to vocal quality and flexibility, Franklin continued, "Every accent, every emphasis, every modulation of voice, was so perfectly well turned and well plac'd, that, without being interested in the subject, one could not help being pleas'd with the discourse; a pleasure of much the same kind with that receiv'd from an excellent piece of musick."[44]

If delivery comes from the whole man, then we must take into account Whitefield's tremendous earnestness and his dramatic instinct. Whatever sincerity means, it meant in his case going all out for his cause. So intense was he at times that he "exceedingly wept, stamped loudly and passionately, and was frequently so overcome that for a few seconds you would suspect that he never would recover."[45] And yet, extravagant as such conduct was, we have the assurance of Franklin and others that whatever Whitefield did seemed appropriate to the occasion.

This propriety in extravaganza was made possible by Whitefield's most useful trait, his dramatic sense. This it was that determined the symmetry of the total phenomenon. We have already seen this trait at work in the treatment of his sermons. How his sense of drama helped him in the selection of material and in his sensationally vivid presentation may be followed in one example. We find him at a trial "observing the formality of the judge putting on his black cap to pronounce sentence"[46] and then later coming up with this in a sermon: "I am going to put on my condemning cap. Sinner, I must do it: I must pronounce sentence upon you!" And then, says the reporter, in a tremendous stream of eloquence describing the eternal punishment of the wicked, he recited the words of Christ, "Depart from me, ye cursed, into everlasting fire, prepared for the Devil and his angels."[47]

Whitefield's ability to dramatize a situation is again shown in two excerpts from *The Gentleman's Magazine* of 1760. The first act went as follows: "Ended the Sessions of Old Bailey which began the 16th when Robert Tilling for robbing the house of Mr. Lloyd, his Master, received the Sentence of Death."[48] Later the final act developed:

This Evening there was a prodigeous Concourse of People to hear Mr. Whitefield speak at Bunhill-fields, at the Grave of Robert Tilling. There was no burial office read; but after the Corpse had been laid in the Ground sometime, Mr. Whitefield came into the Burying Ground, and, in a declamatory Way, showed that the Wages of Sin is Death; gave some Account of the Malefactor's Penitence; exhorted all in general to turn from their Vices and come to Christ; and pressed all Servants in particular to take Warning from the Criminal's Execution, and show all Fidelity to their Masters.[49]

The authentic quality of Whitefield's dramatic genius was often tested in extempore situations. Gillies, a contemporary and the evangelist's first biographer, tells of an impromptu adjustment to a thunderstorm that came up during a sermon. He likened the lightning's flash to the angry glance of Jehovah and the thunder to the voice of the Lord in his anger. When the fury of the storm was at its height, he knelt in the pulpit and covered his face with his hands. After the storm was spent, a rainbow appeared in the sky. Whitefield arose and said: "Look upon the rainbow, and praise him who made it. Very beautiful it is in the brightness thereof. It compasseth the heavens with glory: and the hands of the Most High have bended it."[50]

§6

Such was George Whitefield, perhaps the greatest evangelist in the history of the English-speaking world. Rarely has there been a better example of rapport between speaker and audience, between listeners who craved much and a speaker who was superbly equipped to give his listeners what they craved. The crowds who gathered paid him tributes of unrestrained fulsomeness. Nor did his influence vanish when the crowd scattered. Franklin said of his effect in Philadelphia in 1739: "It was wonderful to see the change soon made in the manner of our inhabitants. From being thoughtless or indifferent about religion, it seem'd as if all the world were growing religious, so one could not walk thro' the town in an evening without hearing psalms sung in different families of every street."[51]

In power to consolidate his labors, however, Whitefield was sadly lacking. It would be untrue to say that he never tried to organize anything. He formed societies at haphazard intervals. He built a few churches which were carelessly administered. He was surrounded by assistants who were indifferently supervised. He accepted unwillingly the moderatorship of the Welsh Calvinists and then gave it up at the first opportunity. He founded a minor orphanage whose financial demands kept him on the rack for thirty years. A more characteristic picture was Whitefield itinerating from place to place, reaching for the crowd intoxication again and again, passing from one immediate triumph to another. This, of course, suited his dramatic temperament better than the mechanics of administration.

Nevertheless, his converts had received too powerful a stimulus to slide back casually into the life they had renounced. Societies were often formed in his wake through the spontaneous initiative of laymen; when he came again, he blessed them and passed on. Without leadership, these converts found their way, with some wastage, into other congregations. Whitefield was content to spur the revival in Scotland to its highest pitch; the Presbyterian kirks benefited by his presence. As champion orator amongst a race of eloquent men, he was the rallying point for Welsh Calvinism, a movement that was taken over by the Countess of Huntingdon. In America fifty thousand converts found their way into Congregational, Presbyterian, and other churches.[52] He was the great international crusader, too cosmopolitan to be restricted to provincial boundaries. He spoke of himself as a "Presbyter at Large."[53]

Thus his followers lost their identity. Since the character of his movement was effaced in the presence of other more clearly defined organizations, notably Wesley's, Whitefield's fame was at the mercy of the winds of oblivion. He was prophetic without regret when he wrote: "You judge right when you say I do not want to make a sect, or set myself at the head of a party. No; let the name of Whitefield die, so that the cause of Jesus Christ may live."[54] Franklin's testimony at Whitefield's death is worth noting: "I knew him upwards of thirty years. His integrity, disinterestness, and indefatiguable zeal in prosecuting every good work, I have never seen equalled, and shall never see excelled."[55]

If Whitefield was a poor organizer, he was nevertheless a great artist—a great artist to the end. His exit was as if carefully staged. When he came to America in 1769, he was ill and felt as if his end were near. There ensued a sort of Indian summer of peace from his enemies and renewed power with his audiences. On September 29, 1770, he was scheduled to speak in the fields near Exeter. Just before the sermon he was taken ill again. Advised not to preach he said, "If I have not yet finished my course, let me go and speak for Thee once more in the fields, seal thy Truth, and come home and die!"[56]

A hogshead served for a pulpit. All the collaborating factors were there which had made him great: the hundreds of people whom none could satisfy but him; the fervor of what was to him a divine message couched in terms the humblest could understand; the dramatic talent which had enthralled the rich and the poor, the lowly and the proud; the "solemnity of the approaching evening"; the consciousness of his listeners that this would be his last message. When he began, it seemed that he could not continue. His sentences and phrases were disjointed, his message incoherent. Then suddenly his lion-like voice soared to the edge of the crowd, electrifying all with the old magic. His illness was forgotten. The anxiety of his friends was swallowed up in the hypnotic Whitefield spell.

When the sermon ended, crowds followed him to the house of the Reverend Jonathan Parsons, with whom he was to stay at Newburyport. They waited outside while he was having his supper and then pushed into the house. Upon seeing them, Whitefield said to another clergyman, "Brother, you must speak to those dear people; I cannot say a word." But on the way to the stairs he was obliged to pass the suppliants. Part way up the staircase he stopped, turned and looked at his audience, his last audience. Habit was strong and he began to speak to them. He had delivered his final sermon in the afternoon; everyone seemed to know that this was his final exhortation. He carried in his hand a lighted candle. As he continued speaking, the candle slowly consumed itself. Just as he finished, the candle went out in the socket.[57] He died that night.

NOTES

1. E. S. Ninde, *George Whitefield, Prophet-Preacher* (New York and Cincinnati, 1924), p. 132.

2. Richard Green, *Anti-Methodist Publications Issued During the Eighteenth Century* (London, 1902). Between 1732 and 1771, Whitefield was the target for 178 out of 446 attacks.

3. *The Weekly History; or, an Account of the Most remarkable Particulars relating to the present Progress of the Gospel.* London: printed by J. Lewis. Price one Penny. The first number appeared April 11, 1741. In No. 4 the editor says, "The Rev. Mr. Whitefield intends to supply me with fresh matter every week."

4. *A History of Gloucester* (Gloucester, 1812), p. 172.

5. W. E. H. Lecky, *A History of England in the Eighteenth Century*, 8 vols. (London, 1879), II, 567-568.

6. Whitefield, as chief character in this speaker-audience relationship, deserves a short biographical summary. He was born in the Bell Inn, Gloucester, December 27 (N.S.), 1714. He attended St. Mary de Crypt Grammar School between 1726 and 1728 and again in 1730-32. He entered Pembroke College, Oxford, in 1732, and there, in May, 1735, he was converted. His religious activity in college

and out attracted the attention of Bishop Benson of Gloucester, and he was ordained a deacon in June, 1736. Returning to Oxford almost immediately, he received the degree of Bachelor of Arts in early July. He planned to remain at Oxford to convert students who in turn would go out and convert others, but was shortly called out of what he termed his "sweet retirement" to supply, first in London and then in the village of Dummer. While at Dummer he decided, partly through the influence of the Wesleys, to go as a missionary to Georgia, where he spent the summer of 1738. Ordained a priest in January, 1739, Whitefield remained in England, field-preaching, until August, 1739. Then came his second visit to America where, until January, 1741, he toured the northern, middle, and southern colonies, bringing to high tide the various revivals which collectively became known as the Great Awakening. From 1741 to 1744 he was in Great Britain, adding momentum to the Methodist Movement and to the revivals which had sprung up in Scotland and Wales. From October, 1744, to June, 1748, he was in America again, but there he found that enthusiasm for the Great Awakening was giving way to concern over the immediate emergency created by the French and the Indians. Thereafter he crossed and recrossed the Atlantic eight times. He died at Newburyport, Mass., September 30, 1770, and was buried in a crypt under the pulpit of the Federal Street Church.

7. The foregoing interpretation of Whitefield's conversion and the following account of his speech training are based on an autobiographical fragment, *A Short Account of God's Dealings with the Reverend Mr. George Whitefield*, London, 1740.

8. The Rev. L. Tyerman, *The Life of the Rev. George Whitefield*, 2 vols. (London, 1876-77), I, 73.

9. *Whitefield's Journals*, ed. William Wale (London, 1905), p. 76.

10. *The Journal of the Rev. John Wesley*, ed. Nehemiah Curnock, 8 vols. (London, 1909-1916), II, 167.

11. *Ibid.*, II, 172.

12. *The Life of Benjamin Franklin*, ed. John Bigelow, 2d ed., 3 vols. (Philadelphia, 1879), I, 271.

13. Vol. IX (1739), pp. 416-417. "Having heard several object against the calculation of Mr. *Whitefield's* Hearers in your last Magazine," the reporter replies (IX, 472) with a detailed explanation of how he arrived at his estimate. There were no further criticisms. *The Gentleman's Magazine*, IX, 162, also cited a crowd that covered three acres and was estimated to number 20,000.

14. For instance, *New York Gazette* (Bradford's), No. 733.

15. Tyerman, *op. cit.*, II, 36-101.

16. The issue of Nov. 26—Dec. 3, 1739.

17. Letter, October 1, 1740, from the collection, published by the Rev. Josiah Smith in *South Carolina Gazette*, quoted by John Gillies, *Memoirs of the Life of the Reverend George Whitefield* (London, 1772), p. 52.

18. John Wesley, *A Sermon on the Death of the Rev. Mr. George Whitefield* (London, 1770), p. 20.

19. Called "Nicodemus' Corner." See *The Life and Times of the Countess of Huntingdon*, by a Member of the Houses of Shirley and Hastings, 2 vols. (London, 1844), I, 477.

20. James Paterson Gledstone, *George Whitefield, Field Preacher* (London, 1900), p. 247.

21. John Bunyan, *The Work of the Eminent Servant of Christ, Mr. John Bunyan. . . . With a Recommendatory Preface by the Rev. George Whitefield*, 2 vols. (London, 1767-68), Preface.

22. See J. L. and Barbara Hammond, *The Village Labourer, 1760-1832* (London, 1913) and *The Town Labourer, 1760-1832* (London, 1917).

23. Abram Lipsky, *John Wesley* (New York, 1928), p. 4.

24. Joseph Butler, *The Analogy of Religion, Natural and Revealed, to the Constitution and Course of Nature* (London, 1736).

25. George Whitefield, *Works*, 6 vols. (London, 1771-72), I, 64.

26. Quoted by R. Elliot, *Grace and Truth, or A Summary of Gospel Doctrine, Considered in a Funeral Discourse Preached on the Death of the Rev. George Whitefield* (London, 1770), p. 33.

27. John Gillies, *Memoirs of the Rev. George Whitefield, Revised and Corrected with Large Additions and Improvements, to which is appended an extensive Collection of his Sermons and other Writings* (Middleton, 1837), p. 522. Subsequent citations from Gillies will refer to this edition.

28. *Works*, V, 174.

29. Gillies, *op. cit.*, p. 403.

30. *Ibid.*, p. 529.

31. *Ibid.*, pp. 534-535.

32. *Ibid.*, p. 514.

33. William Jay, *Memoirs of the Life and Character of the Late Rev. Cornelius Winter*, 1st American ed. (New York, 1811), p. 20.

34. Gillies, *op. cit.*, pp. 381-383.

35. George Whitefield, *Sermons on Important Subjects* (London, 1861), pp. 59-68.

36. *Ibid.*, pp. 35-36.

37. Jay, *op. cit.*, p. 22.

38. Whitefield, *Sermons on Important Subjects*, p. 65.

39. *Ibid.*, p. 84.

40. Jay, *op. cit.*, p. 23.

41. *Ibid.*, p. 21.

42. *New York Gazette* (Bradford's), Nov. 19—Nov. 26, 1739.

43. Gillies, *op. cit.*, p. 43, footnote.

44. Franklin, *op. cit.*, I, 271-272.

45. Jay, *op. cit.*, p. 22.

46. Jay, *op. cit.*, p. 18; Gillies, *op. cit.*, p. 282.

47. Jay, *op. cit.*, p. 18; Gillies, *op. cit.*, p. 264.

48. Vol. XXX (1760), 200.

49. *Ibid.*, pp. 245-246.

50. Gillies, *op. cit.*, pp. 266-268.

51. Franklin, *op. cit.*, I, 267.

52. Joseph Tracy, *The Great Awakening* (Boston, 1842), pp. 388 *et seq.* Osgood thinks this estimate a good guess and substantially true. Herbert L. Osgood, *The American Colonies in the Eighteenth Century*, 4 vols. (New York, 1924), III, 447.

53. "To be a presbyter at large is the station which, I think, divine providence hath called me to for near these thirty years past." G. Whitefield, A.M., *A Letter to his Excellency Governor Wright* (London, 1768), p. 9. Right after resigning the Moderatorship of the Welsh Calvinists he wrote, "I have given over the immediate care of my Societies to Mr. Harris; so that now I am a preacher at large." Tyerman, *op. cit.*, II, 234.

54. Letter to Hervey, April 5, 1749, Tyerman, *op. cit.*, II, 223.

55. Letter to Robert Morris and Thomas Leach, March 5, 1771, *The Writings of Benjamin Franklin*, ed. Albert Henry Smith, 10 vols. (New York and London, 1905-07), V, 308.

56. Tyerman, *op. cit.*, II, 596.

57. The story of this last scene is based upon the account by the daughter of Mr. Parsons, in whose house the scene occurred. Abel Stevens, *The History of the Religious Movement in the Eighteenth Century called Methodism*, 30th ed., 3 vols. (New York and Cincinnati, 1858, 1859, 1861), I, 466.

The Style of Robert G. Ingersoll

WAYLAND MAXFIELD PARRISH

"INGERSOLL's style," said Herman E. Kittredge, "is utterly unique. Should one of his marvelous pages, separated from its context, be found in the sands of Sahara, its author would be instantly recognizable."[1]

Though such uncritical praise from a devoted admirer needs to be heavily discounted, yet a careful student of Ingersoll's reported addresses will find that his style does have a distinctive flavor and an undeniable effectiveness that amply justify an attempt at its analysis. Notable also is an infectious quality in it that leads many of his admirers both consciously and unconsciously to imitate it. Since Ingersoll died before the development of the phonograph and the news-reel, and since descriptions of his delivery are regrettably few, all that remains to us of his genius is the pattern of his spoken words as recorded in print. They do not, of course, tell the whole story of his power as an orator, but they are an important element in it. His sentences when read today, whether aloud or silently, have a conciseness, clarity, beauty, and power that make them worthy of study by any serious student of rhetoric. Kittredge's further statement that "the whole of rhetoric was rejuvenated by his genius" is also too extravagant, but there can be little doubt that present-day addresses such as are published in *Vital Speeches* would be much more vital if their authors would study the style of Ingersoll.

In analyzing the texts of speeches we can seldom be sure that we are dealing with the speaker's words as uttered. The text we study may represent what the speaker intended to say, what he wished afterward that people would believe he had said, what some hearer remembers of what he said, or even what some reporter thinks he ought to have said. In Ingersoll's published works[2] we probably have all these forms of representation, and several others besides. The texts of some are taken from newspaper reports; of others, from notes found among his manuscripts after his death. This is partly because he had no uniform method of preparing his speeches. "Sometimes," he once told a reporter, "and frequently, I deliver a lecture several times before it is written. I have it taken by a shorthand writer, and afterward written out. At other times I have dictated a lecture, and sometimes I deliver lectures without any notes—this, again, depending much on how I happen to feel at the time."[3] When in 1879 he published "Some Mistakes of Moses," he stated in his preface: "The lecture was never written and consequently never delivered twice the same. On several occasions it was reported and published without consent, and without revision."[4] Fortunately Ingersoll was "good copy" for the newspapers, and some of them published complete stenographic reports of his speeches. These, when compared with the texts in his published *Works*, while they reveal great variation in the plan and substance of his addresses, yet show no important variations in style. Fortunately, also, Ingersoll had a remarkable memory and, whether he spoke with or without a manuscript, would repeat what he doubtless considered his finest and most important passages with scarcely the variation of a word. In this study I shall depend mainly upon the text of the *Works*, with occasional reference to newspaper reports. However imperfect our text, we can still find in it a characteristic Ingersollian manner that distinguishes the author from other authors.

That this characteristic manner derives chiefly from the personality of the man is, of course, obvious. His clarity and simplicity of mind, his forthright honesty, his horror of cruelty, his love of freedom, his tremendous earnestness—all are important conditioners of his style, but they do not *completely* explain it. Buffon's statement that style is of the man himself is only a part of the truth. Style has, as Wackernagel taught, an objective, as well as a subjective, side. It is, he said, "the mode of representation in language, conditioned partly by the psychological peculiarities of the one who represents, partly by the matter and purpose of what is represented." Ingersoll the legal advocate struggling for countless days through the thousandfold minutiae of the Star Route cases, was the same Ingersoll who as evangelist stumped the country against what he conceived to be the super-stitions and stupidities of orthodox theology, but the style of his legal pleas seldom approaches that of his lectures. Their pur-pose is different. They aim not to free the world from fear, but to win a jury verdict in an immediate case. They concern often an abstract point of law, not the happiness of mankind. Inger-soll at his typical best is revealed in his lectures, and it is there that he is best studied.

Gladstone justly observed concerning Ingersoll's letter to Dr. Field: "Colonel Ingersoll writes with a rare and enviable bril-liancy, but also with an impetus which he seems unable to con-trol. . . . The paper, noteworthy as it is, leaves on my mind the impression of a battlefield where every man strikes at every man, and all is noise, hurry and confusion."[5] This tumultuous bril-liancy is even more evident in Ingersoll's speeches than in the essay to which Gladstone referred. His style is a medley of vehement assertion, popular anecdote, genial wit, cutting satire, withering sarcasm, pungent metaphor, close reasoning, lucid exposition, brilliant narrative and description, poetic fancy, rhetorical questions, and dramatic dialogue. His tone ranges from the flippant and vulgar colloquial to the height of the sub-lime. But through it all runs a characteristic quality that derives from his unique personality, his purpose and his material.

Since no standard rubrics are generally accepted for the ana-lysis of style, one may feel free to use whatever analysis seems most fitting for the study of a given writer or speaker. The qualities of Ingersoll's style most likely to strike the attention of a reader are, I believe, its vitality, its conversational direct-ness, and its poetic quality. Under these three heads the various aspects of his style will be considered.

The striking vitality of Ingersoll's style derives from his vital personality, from what Emerson called "great volumes of ani-mal heat." His habits of public address were formed in the rough forensic and political debates of the Illinois prairie, and he was the perfect exemplar of those qualities which Emerson said the stump orator requires—presence of mind, heat, spunk, continuity. Probably because he lacked formal schooling, he escaped the Ciceronian tradition that descends through Burke and Webster. His sentences reveal nothing of Latin influence, and such smooth-rolling sonorities as characterize the closing paragraphs of Webster's reply to Hayne were utterly foreign to his genius. He was, however, a very well-read man. As a prosperous lawyer in Peoria he was a steady customer at the local book store. His astonishing and capacious memory retained a wealth of fact, allusion, example, anecdote, and detail which poured forth in his speeches in a tumultuous and irresistible flood. His periods were invariably short and hence produced the effect of bluntness and monotony, but they struck with the abrupt force of bullets.

Here is a typical passage from his lecture "A Thanksgiving Sermon":

Back of all that is—back of all events—Christians put an infinite Juggler who with a wish creates, preserves, destroys. The world is his stage and mankind his puppets. He fills them with wants and desires, with appetites and ambitions— with hopes and fears, with love and hate. He touches the springs. He pulls the strings—baits the hooks, sets the traps and digs the pits. . . .

He withholds the rains and his puppets starve. He opens the earth and they are devoured. He sends the flood and they are drowned. He empties the volcano and they perish in fire. He sends the cyclone and they are torn and mangled. With quick lightnings they are dashed to death. He fills the air and water with the invisible enemies of life—the messengers of pain, and watches the puppets as they breathe and drink. He creates cancers to feed upon their flesh—their quivering nerves—serpents to fill their veins with venom,—beasts to crunch their bones—to lap their blood. . . .

What have the worldly done?

They have investigated the phenomena of nature. They have invented ways to use the forces of the world, the weight of falling water—of moving air. They have changed water to steam, invented engines—the tireless giants that work for man. They have made lightning a messenger and slave. They invented movable type, taught us the art of printing and made it possible to save and transmit the intellectual wealth of the world. They connected continents with cables, cities and towns with the telegraph—brought the world into one family—made intelligence independent of distance. They taught us how to build homes, to obtain food, to weave cloth. They covered the seas with iron ships and the lands with roads and steeds of steel. They gave us the tools of all the trades—the implements of labor. They chiseled statues, painted pictures and "witched the world" with form and color. They have found the cause of and the cure for many maladies that afflict the flesh and minds of men. They have given us the instruments of music and the great composers and performers have changed the common air to tones and harmonies that intoxicate, exalt and purify the soul.[6]

This bit of exposition is, for Ingersoll, relatively unemotional, but it reveals some of the mechanics of his characteristic style. He achieves energy by a series of short hammer strokes, uninterrupted by dependent clauses or modifying phrases. The units of thought are brief, and the economy of wording gives an effect of great condensation, of conciseness, and of hurry. The sense of hurry and of onward drive is accentuated by the lack of connective words—by the fact that his sentences are merely added together, laid one after the other, with no variety in their relationship to each other.

In this passage the sentences are uniformly short. It must not be supposed, however, that Ingersoll avoided long sentences. His style reveals the futility of trying to discover much that is significant about style by merely counting the number of words per sentence. It is not the length of a sentence that determines its clarity and simplicity (and Ingersoll is always clear and simple in his utterance), but rather the length of the units that compose it and the nature of their relation to each other. The final sentence in "Some Mistakes of Moses" covers more than five pages, but it is made up of brief clauses all of which bear the same relationship to each other and to the main clause, and the structure is not periodic. It begins: "Let us admit what we know to be true: that Moses was mistaken about a thousand things; that the story of creation is not true"; and runs on through ninety-seven clauses beginning with "that." Since there was little attempt to vary the inner structure of the component clauses, the effect is monotonous, but it is the effect of powerful and well-directed axe strokes, which never strike twice in the same place, and each of which cuts away its chip of wood.

Sometimes his axe seemed double-edged, for he was much given to linking words in pairs, often expressing contrast, and sometimes with alliteration, as in this passage from his lecture "Superstition": "We know that superstition has given us delusions and illusions, dreams and visions, ceremonies and cruelties, faith and fanaticism, beggars and bigots, persecutions and prayers, theology and torture, piety and poverty, saints and slaves, miracles and mummeries, disease and death."

Sometimes his strokes consist of clauses arranged in contrasting pairs, as in this passage from the same lecture: "By the same book they proved that nearly everybody is to be lost, and that all are to be saved; that slavery is a divine institution, and that all men should be free; that polygamy is right, and that no man should have more than one wife; that the powers that be are ordained of God, and that the people have a right to overturn and destroy the powers that be"; and so on through two pages.

But though he was very fond of these ladders of development, he seldom seemed interested in building them into effective climaxes. He lays down the rungs of his ladder in a merely historical or haphazard order, and the reader is often disappointed in finding no cumulation of intensity, no satisfying copestone for the structure. Somewhat exceptional is his soliloquy at the tomb of Napoleon, which ends with a strong assertion of his preference for the life of an unknown peasant over that of the "Imperial impersonation of force and murder, known as Napoleon the Great."

The peaks of Ingersoll's intensity are generally found in the passionate assertion of his indignation and hatred for the doctrines of orthodox theology, and especially the doctrine of hell:

This frightful dogma [he says in "Why I Am an Agnostic"], this infinite lie, made me the implacable enemy of Christianity. . . . Like a venomous serpent it crawls and coils and hisses in every orthodox creed. It makes man an eternal victim and God an eternal fiend. It is the one infinite horror. Every church in which it is taught is a public curse. Every preacher who preaches it is an enemy of mankind. Below this Christian dogma, savagery cannot go. It is the infinite of malice, hatred, and revenge. Nothing could add to the horror of Hell except the presence of its creator, God. While I have life, as long as I draw breath, I shall deny with all my strength, and hate with every drop of my blood this infinite lie. . . .

In a few years the Christians will become—let us hope—humane and sensible enough to deny the dogma that fills the endless years with pain. They ought to know now that their belief in Hell gives to the Holy Ghost—the Dove—the beak of a vulture, and fills the mouth of the Lamb of God with the fangs of a viper.

This surely is strong language. The elements of its strength seem to lie partly in the emotional heat of the speaker, partly in the abrupt brevity of his clauses, the simplicity and concreteness of his wording, the power of his flashing metaphors, and partly also in his shocking irreverence toward things commonly regarded as sacred.

Part of his strength is due also to his variety, for he never continues long in one vein. Daring assertion, hilarious humor, rhetorical question, flippancy, sarcasm, poetry, lucid exposition, and cheap colloquialisms follow each other through his speeches in bewildering succession. Here, for instance, in a newspaper report of a lecture on "Talmagian Theology," is a quick succession of humor, sentiment, sarcasm, and indignant assertion. He has just called forth peals of laughter with the story of the preacher who prayed by mistake, "O, Thou great and unscrupulous God," and he proceeds:

This Presbyterian believes that billions of years before that baby in the cradle—that little dimpled child, basking in the light of a mother's smile—was born, God had made up his mind to damn it: and when Talmage looks at one of those children who will probably be damned he is cheerful about it. That is Presbyterianism—that God made man and damned him for his own glory. If there is such a God, I hate him with every drop of my blood. [Applause.][7]

In utterance of such intensity there could be little room for delicacy of phrase or subtlety of expression. But Ingersoll was not always so intense, and many passages in his speeches show that he exercised great care in composition. His frequent poetic flights will be considered later. But through all his changing moods runs a vital earnestness derived from his clarity of mind, simplicity of expression, and warmth of feeling.

Hamlin Garland recalled this quality of his style forty years after hearing the orator lecture in Boston. He said:

As I studied him I came to the conclusion that a large part of his power lay in the fact that he vitalized every word, every syllable. He thought every sentence out at the moment he gave it utterance. He was alive to the tip of his tongue. . . . As I go over [his addresses] today I find them as I remember them, well written and vibrant. Only last summer I read one of them to an audience of young people of literary training, and its English, crisp and clear and vital as when I first heard it more than forty years ago, aroused the applause of my auditors.[8]

There is another quality which Garland noted in Ingersoll's delivery which is also plainly apparent in, and which strongly affected, his style; this is his directness, his constant awareness of an audience.

He began to speak [says Garland] almost before he left the wings, addressing himself to us with colloquial, unaffected directness. I say "to us," for that was precisely the effect he produced. He appeared to be speaking to each one of us individually. His tone was confidential, friendly, and yet authoritative. . . .
He was a master of colloquial speech. Unlike Lowell, he eyed us, and laughed at us and with us. He bantered us, challenged us, electrified us. At times his eloquence held us silent as images and then some witty turn, some humorous phrase, brought roars of applause. At times we cheered almost every sentence like delegates at a political convention. At other moments we rose in our seats and yelled. There was something hypnotic in his rhythm as well as in his marvelous lines like a Saxon minstrel. His power over his auditors was absolute. . . . As he spoke, all barriers between his mind and mine vanished. His effect on his hearers was magical, but the magic lay in his choice of words, rather than in beautiful enunciation.

There can be no doubt that Ingersoll greatly enjoyed such bouts of rollicking joviality as Garland describes—enjoyed the laughter and applause of his audience—was carried away by their response and, in his attempt to achieve a "folksy" good fellowship with them, sometimes descended to the cheapest colloquialisms, sacrificing grammar, diction and dignity. The following passage from a newspaper report shows the quality of his showmanship. He reads the promise of Christ that His disciples will be able to cast out devils, speak with new tongues, take up serpents and drink poisons without suffering injury. Then he cries :

Bring on your believer.—Applause and laughter.—Let him cast out a devil. I don't claim a large one.—Laughter.—Just a little one for a cent.—Renewed laughter.—Let him take up serpents.—A Voice: "Copperheads."—If he drink any deadly thing it shall not hurt him. Let me mix up a dose for an average believer—laughter—and if it doesn't "hurt" him I will join a church.—Laughter and applause.[9]

But whatever the level of his style—whether sublime or vulgar—it has always the pervading quality of colloquy. It is meant to be spoken and meant to be heard. His arguments are addressed directly to the reason of his hearers, his emotional passages are direct appeals to their feelings, his frequent capitalization of his own *ethos* is designed to challenge their admiration and approval. But Ingersoll knew that attention quickly wavers, that audiences cannot follow long chains of reasoning, and that no emotion can be long sustained. These factors doubtless contributed to his style some of its most characteristic qualities—its constant variety, its simplicity of structure, its concreteness in diction, and its unvarying lucidity.

His urgent directness shows itself also in his frequent use of questions. "The sharp, nervous rhetorical question," says Charles D. Adams, " is particularly adapted to . . . vigorous style. The sleepy hearer is aroused, the indifferent is challenged, even the stupid man is tempted to think, when the sudden question is thrown in his face."[10] Ingersoll's questions often alternate with dialogue and with daring assertions of his own feelings and beliefs, as in this passage from his lecture on Orthodoxy:

No man can control his belief. If I hear certain evidence I will believe a certain thing. If I fail to hear it I may never believe it. If it is adapted to my mind I may accept it; if it is not, I reject it. And what am I to go by? My brain. That is the only light I have from Nature, and if there be a God it is the only torch that this God has given me to find my way through the darkness and night called life. I do not depend on hearsay for that. I do not have to take the word of any other man or get upon my knees before a book. Here in the temple of the mind I consult the God, that is to say my reason, and the oracle speaks to me and I obey the oracle. What should I obey? Another man's oracle? Shall I take another man's word—not what he thinks, but what he says some God has said to him?

I would not know a god if I should see one. I have said before and I say again, the brain thinks in spite of me, and I am not responsible for my thoughts. I cannot control the beating of my heart. I cannot stop the blood that flows through the rivers of my veins. And yet I am held responsible for my belief. Then why does not God give me the evidence? They say he has. In what? In an inspired book. But I do not understand it as they do. Must I be false to my understanding? They say: "When you come to die you will be sorry if you do not." Will I be sorry when I come to die that I did not live a hypocrite? Will I be sorry that I did not say I was a Christian when I was not? Will the fact that I was honest put a thorn in the pillow of death? Cannot God forgive me for being honest? They say that when he was in Jerusalem he forgave his murderers, but now he will not forgive an honest man for differing from him on the subject of the Trinity.

They say that God says to me, "Forgive your enemies." I say, "I do"; but he says, "I will damn mine." God should be consistent. If he wants me to forgive my enemies he should forgive his. I am asked to forgive enemies who can hurt me. God is asked to forgive enemies who cannot hurt him. He certainly ought to be as generous as he asks us to be.[11]

Here one notes the sharp staccato of dramatic dialogue, the challenge of rhetorical questions, the homely simplicity of vocabulary, with long successions of monosyllables, the cutting brevity of clauses pared to the quick, the blunt thud of daring assertion—all thrown in the faces of the audience with inescapable directness. Ingersoll's hearers were constantly stimulated to response, and they *did* respond—with enthusiastic applause, with shouts of laughter and approval, and exclamations of delight. Their attention was never allowed to relax, and no one who reads his printed addresses today can feel that he is merely looking over the shoulder of a man who is writing an essay. He envisions from the printed words an earnest man in heated talk, feels himself directly addressed, and is moved by the impact of his challenging words. Ingersoll's is pre-eminently a style of direct address.

The passage above illustrates another distinctive element in

Ingersoll's style, and one that has been much admired—his poetic imagination. Reason he likens to a torch that lights his way through the darkness and night called life; he will not get upon his knees before a book; in the temple of his mind he consults the God; blood flows through the rivers of his veins; honesty puts a thorn in the pillow of death. All of Ingersoll's speeches are studded with such metaphors. For the most part they are fresh, unhackneyed, and apt. Though some of them show the marks of the file, they generally seem to rise unbidden from his heated imagination. James Redpath, who knew Ingersoll intimately, is reported to have said:

Ingersoll's talk is fully equal to his oratory, and sometimes it is vastly better, except in his great passages, greater in pathos, in rare insight, in poetical imagery, and in delicate fancies. He has often an Oriental style of rhetoric in his most familiar conversations. . . . His talk is full of phrases that would be considered gems in anybody's writings.[12]

Some of Ingersoll's metaphors are very brief, his image being crystallized in a single word or phrase. He says, for instance: "God cannot clothe with fire the man who has clothed the naked here." "Is it good to teach that the serpent of regret will not hiss in the ear of memory?" "Upon Love's breast the church has placed the eternal asp." The liberty to read the Bible is liberty to "read by the glare of hell." "Imagination, the artist of the mind, on the canvas of the future deftly paints the things to be." Or he says that when reason is denied, "the brain, swept by the sirocco of God's curse, becomes a desert."

But some of his figures are more extended, more elaborated, and more consciously designed. Such passages as the following could hardly arise spontaneously even in the speech of one who had "an Oriental style of rhetoric in his most familiar conversations."

We do not know, we cannot say, whether death is a wall or a door; the beginning or end of a day; the spreading of pinions to soar, or the folding forever of wings; the rise or the set of a sun, or an endless life that brings the rapture of love to every one.

Take our dear old merciful Puritan fathers. What did Christianity do for them? On the door of life they hung the crape of death.

They muffled all the bells of gladness. They made cradles by putting rockers on coffins. In the Puritan year there were twelve Decembers.

Compared with Shakespeare's "book and volume of the brain," the "sacred" Bible shrinks and seems as feebly impotent and vain as would the pipes of Pan, when some great organ, voiced with every tone, from the hoarse thunder of the sea to the winged warble of a muted bird, floods and fills cathedral aisles with all the wealth of sound.

Here there is evidence of a conscious play with words and phrases and images. But this is not, we may safely say, a mere rhetoric of display. From this he is saved by the cogency of his thought and the genuineness of his feeling. He is saved also by the fact that his scrollwork of exornation is never long continued. He rises quickly from the earth, but may descend as quickly to earth again. Note, for instance, how in the following passage he soars suddenly from a rather crude jocosity to a height that is truly sublime:

Give me a good cool grave rather than the furnace of Jehovah's wrath. I pray the angel of the resurrection to let me sleep. Gabriel, do not blow! Let me alone! If, when the grave bursts, I am not to meet the faces that have been my sunshine in this life, let me sleep. Rather than that this doctrine of endless punishment should be true, I would gladly see the fabric of our civilization crumbling fall to unmeaning chaos and to formless dust, where oblivion broods and even memory forgets. I would rather that the blind Samson of some imprisoned force, released by chance, should so wreck and strand the mighty world that man in stress and strain of want and fear should shudderingly crawl back to savage and barbaric night. I would rather that every planet should in its orbit wheel a barren star!"[13]

Or note the highly wrought, perhaps overwrought, apostrophe to liberty which forms the peroration of his "Myth and Miracle." It follows immediately after a rough frontier anecdote concerning a cannibal's reply to a missionary who objected to being eaten, used to ridicule the argument that one should follow the religion of his mother. "My mother," said the cannibal, "was good enough for me. Her religion is my religion. The last time I saw her she was sitting, propped up against a tree, eating cold missionary." Twelve lines later comes the apostrophe:

O Liberty, thou art the god of my idolatry! Thou art the only deity that hateth bended knees. In thy vast and unwalled temple, beneath the roofless dome, star-gemmed and luminous with suns, thy worshippers stand erect! They do not cringe or crawl, or bend their foreheads to the earth. The dust has never borne the impress of their lips. Upon thy altars mothers do not sacrifice their babes, nor men their rights. Thou askest naught from man except the things that good men hate—the whip, the chain, the dungeon key. Thou hast no popes, no priests, who stand between their fellow-men and thee. Thou carest not for foolish forms, or selfish prayers. At thy sacred shrine hypocrisy does not bow, virtue does not tremble, superstition's feeble tapers do not burn, but Reason holds aloft her inextinguishable torch whose holy light will one day flood the world.

That this alternation of the sublime with the ridiculous was not accidental, but rather the result of conscious method, is apparent from some comments that he once made to a reporter on how to be an orator. As this interview throws considerable light upon his theories of style, and describes his own practice in speaking, it is worth quoting at some length:

The great column of [the orator's] argument should be unbroken. He can adorn it with vines and flowers, but they should not be in such profusion as to hide the column. He should give variety of episode by illustrations, but they should be used only for the purpose of adding strength to the argument. The man who wishes to become an orator should study language. He should know the deeper meaning of words. He should understand the vigor and velocity of verbs and the color of adjectives. He should know how to sketch a scene, to paint a picture, to give life and action. He should be a poet and a dramatist, a painter and an actor. He should cultivate the imagination. He should become familiar with the great poetry and fiction, with splendid and heroic deeds. He should be a student of Shakespeare. He should read and devour the great plays. From Shakespeare he could learn the art of expression, of compression, and all the secrets of the head and heart.

The great orator is full of variety—of surprises. Like a juggler he keeps the colored balls in the air. He expresses himself in pictures. His speech is a panorama. By continued change he holds the attention. The interest does not flag. . . .

The great orator is full of episode. He convinces and charms by indirection. He leaves the road, visits the fields, wanders in the woods, listens to the murmurs of springs, the songs of birds. He gathers flowers, scales the crags, and comes back to the highway refreshed and invigorated. He does not move in a straight line. He wanders and winds like a stream. . . .

He must be a reasoner, a logician. He must have a keen sense of humor—of the laughable. He must have wit, sharp and quick. He must have sympathy. His smiles should be the neighbors of his tears. He must have imagination. He should give eagles to the air, and painted moths should flutter in the sunlight.[14]

It should be noted that even in this informal interview, presumably dictated to a reporter, there are evidences of an "oriental style" of expression. Also noteworthy is the fact that Ingersoll twice states the need for imagination in oratory. The vividness and compression of his imagery have already been illustrated, but a word needs to be said concerning the range of his imagination. He was powerfully influenced by the scientific discoveries of the nineteenth century as he found them in the writings of Darwin, Spencer, Haeckel, and others. The history of the universe, the evolution of man, the development of civilization, excited his wonder and stimulated his imagination to the long descriptive recitals that appear in many of his lectures. But he was sensitive also to the common sounds and sights of everyday life—forests, fields, flowers, sunsets, strains of music, childish laughter, home life—and he penetrated to the heart of them with his imaginative insight. In reading through his works one finds a too frequent reference to "fang and faggot," "slimy snakes," and "dimpled babes," but in general his imagery is highly varied. And every topic his mind touches upon was, in Aristotle's phrase, set vividly before the eyes.

Another point to be noted in the interview above is his recommendation of the study of Shakespeare. It is likely that his study of the great dramatist was one of the important influences in forming his style. He could recite from memory many passages from the plays, but he rarely quotes Shakespeare in his speeches. The poet's influence is seen rather in the quality of his imagery, in the sweep of his imagination, and in occasional passages of continuous blank verse.

It is a natural tendency for strong, but controlled, emotion to express itself in rhythm, and perhaps a gifted writer of prose who, if such a thing were possible, had never read formal poetry, would find his thoughts of highest tensity flowing naturally into conventional metre. But when a writer is known to have treasured many pages of Shakespeare in his memory, when his more impassioned utterances flow constantly into regular iambics, and when his phrase units are often successions of pentameters, one may presume at least that Shakespeare had some influence upon his style. In the illustrative passages that follow, a reader may or may not find a Shakespearean influence or a Shakespearean quality, but he can hardly fail to find authentic poetry of a very high order, often expressed in long runs of iambic metre. Wherever these passages are capable of being scanned as iambic pentameters, they are set as blank verse. The first four are from the lecture "Myth and Miracle," first delivered in 1885, when Ingersoll was fifty-two years old and his oratorical and intellectual powers had reached full maturity.

In all these myths and legends of the past we find philosophies and dreams and efforts, stained with tears, of great and tender souls who tried to pierce the mysteries of life and death, to answer the question of the whence and whither, and who vainly
Sought with bits of shattered glass to make
A mirror that would in very truth reflect
The face and form of Nature's perfect self.
These myths were born of hopes and fears, of tears
And smiles, and they were touched and colored by
All there is of joy and grief between
The rosy dawn of birth and death's sad night.

They clothed even the stars with passion, and gave to gods the faults and frailties of the sons of men. In them the winds and waves were music, and all
The springs, the mountains, woods and perfumed dells
Were haunted by a thousand fairy forms.
They thrilled the veins of Spring with tremulous
Desire, made tawny Summer's billowy breast
The throne and home of love, filled Autumn's arms
With sun-kissed grapes and gathered sheaves
And pictured Winter as a weak old king,
Who felt, like Lear, upon his withered face,
Cordelia's tears.

Give me the Sixth Symphony—this sound-wrought picture of the fields and woods, of flowering hedge and happy home, where thrushes build and swallows fly, and mothers sing to babes; this echo of the babbled lullaby of brooks that, dallying, wind and fall where meadows bare their daisied bosoms to the sun; this joyous mimicry of summer rain, the laugh of children, and the rhythmic rustle of the whispering leaves; this strophe of peasant life; this perfect poem of content and love.

The rise

And set of sun, the birth and death of day,
The dawns of silver and the dusks of gold,
The wonders of the rain and snow, the shroud
Of Winter
And the many colored robe of Spring,
The lonely moon with nightly loss or gain,
The serpent lightning and the thunder's voice,
The tempest's fury and the zephyr's sigh,
The threat of storm and promise of the bow, . . .
The snow-crowned mountains with their tongues of flame, . . .

and over all

The silent and immeasurable dome.
These were the warp and woof, and at the loom
Sat Love and Fancy, Hope and Fear, and wove
The wondrous tapestries whereon we find
Pictures of gods and fairy lands and all
The legends that were told when Nature rocked
The cradle of the infant world.

Nothing was created, nothing has happened for, or with reference to man. If not a human being lived—if all were in their graves, the sun would continue to shine,
The wheeling world would still pursue its flight,
Violets would spread their velvet bosoms to the day,
The spendthrift roses give their perfume to the air,
The climbing vines would hide with leaf and flower the fallen and dead,
The changing seasons would come and go,
Time would repeat the poem of the year,
Storms would wreck and whispering rains repair,
Spring with deft and unseen hands would weave her countless robes of green,
Life with countless lips would seek fair Summer's swelling breasts,
Autumn would reap the wealth of leaf and fruit and seed,
Winter, the artist, would etch in frost the pines and ferns,

While Wind and Wave and Fire, old architects,
With ceaseless toil would still destroy and build,
Still wreck and change, and from the dust of death
Produce again the throb and breath of life.

The last of these passages does not break readily into pentameters, but the iambic metre is remarkably constant, and in all will be found genuine poetic feeling of high seriousness and a continuous play of the imagination. It will be found, too, that images are not employed merely as decorative detail; all are used to carry forward the thought. A few of the images are conventional, but all are true and accurate, and all are stated with simplicity and brevity. It is notable that in three descriptions of the seasons Ingersoll only once repeats an image—that is, in his reference to Summer's breast. In an earlier lecture, "Ghosts," he has another description of the seasons containing a remarkably true picture of Autumn:

Let the monsters fade away—the world remains, with its hills and seas and plains, its seasons of smiles and frowns, its Springs of leaf and bud, its Summer of shade and flower, its Autumn with the laden boughs, when

The withered banners of the corn are still,
And gathered fields are growing strangely wan,
While Death, poetic Death, with hands that color
Whate'er they touch, weaves in the Autumn wood
Her tapestries of gold and brown.

One paragraph from his lecture on Burns is notable, not so much for its imagery as for the regularity of its blank verse:

The house in which his spirit lived was not large. It enclosed only space enough for common needs, built near the barren land of want;

But through the open door the sunlight streamed,
And from its windows all the stars were seen,
While in the garden grew the common flowers—
The flowers that all the ages through have been
The messengers of honest love; and in
The fields were heard the rustling corn,
And reaper's songs, telling
Of well-requited toil; and there were trees
Whose branches rose and fell and swayed while birds
Filled all the air with music born of joy.

And here is an intensely vivid, but not a beautiful series of pictures from his last lecture, "What is Religion?" written in 1899.

The dungeons against whose dripping walls
The brave and generous have sighed their souls away,
The scaffolds stained and glorified with noble blood,
The hopeless slaves with scarred and bleeding backs,
The writhing martyrs clothed in flame,
The virtuous stretched on racks, their joints and muscles torn apart,
The flayed and bleeding bodies of the just,
The extinguished eyes of those who sought for truth,
The countless patriots who fought and died in vain,
The burdened, beaten, weeping wives,
The shriveled faces of neglected babes,
The murdered millions of the vanished years, . . .
These frightful facts deny
That any God exists who has the will
And power to guard and bless the human race.[15]

In such passages as these we have perhaps as happy a marriage of oratory with poetry as can be found in English literature. But in none of them does poetry usurp the place of oratory, for, as the contexts would reveal, each is integral with the speaker's argumentative or persuasive purpose. There were indeed occasions on which Ingersoll seems to have yielded to the temptation to win applause by introducing a merely decorative *ecphrasis,* but they were rare. His feeling was too deep and his purpose too genuine to permit descent to mere sophistical display. His development of a thought proceeded, as these excerpts show, from fertility of mind, not from virtuosity in dilation of a theme. It is this copiousness of intellect, combined with great fecundity of imagination and unusual emotional intensity, that largely conditioned the poetic quality of his oratory, as it conditioned also its vitality, its onward rushing movement.

Faults of style Ingersoll certainly had. He was frequently irreverent, and often coarse and vulgar. Even the poetic passages just quoted would not by many critics be called elegant or finely finished. One can well imagine the shock of horror with which Samuel Johnson would have heard such utterance—and such sentiments. He would have been disturbed by its tumultuous intensity, affronted by its direct assault upon his mind and heart, cloyed by the lushness and profusion of its ornamentation. But one can imagine that in another age the keen critical insight of Aristotle would have approved its clarity, its idiomatic purity, its rhythm, and its metaphors that "set things before the eyes." And Lord Brougham might well have applied to Ingersoll the words he spoke of Demosthenes in his *Dissertation on the Eloquence of the Ancients:*

All is at each instant moving forward, regardless of every obstacle. The mighty flood of speech rolls on in a channel ever full, but which never overflows. Whether it rushes in a torrent of allusions, or moves along in a majestic exposition of enlarged principles—descends hoarse and headlong in overwhelming invective—or glides melodious in narrative and description, or spreads itself out shining in illustration—its course is ever onward and ever entire;—never scattered—never stagnant—never sluggish. At each point manifest progress has been made, and with all that art can do to charm, to strike, and to please.

NOTES

1. "Ingersoll as an Idealist," *The Arena*, XXXI (March, 1904), 245.
2. *The Works of Robert G. Ingersoll*, 12 vols. (New York, 1900).
3. *Works*, VIII, 542.
4. *Works*, II, vi.
5. *Works*, VIII, 223, 224.
6. *Works*, IV, 180-81, 199-200.
7. *Chicago Tribune*, Nov. 13, 1882.
8. *Roadside Meetings* (New York, 1930), p. 44.
9. *Chicago Tribune*, Sept. 20, 1880.
10. *Demosthenes and His Influence* (New York, 1927), pp. 81-82.
11. *Works*, II, 406-08.
12. Reprinted from the *San Francisco Chronicle* in *Complete Lectures of Col. R. G. Ingersoll* (printed for the trade. No place, date or paging).
13. *Works*, II, 422.
14. *Works*, VIII, 594-99.
15. Other illustrations might be added—his soliloquy at the tomb of Napoleon, his vision of war, his vision of the future, his rhapsody over a child's laughter, his tender words of comfort spoken at a child's grave—most of which have become somewhat familiar through frequent inclusion in collections of declamations and in textbooks on public speaking. It is regrettable that the unpopularity of Ingersoll's favorite theme has not permitted the inclusion in such works of other examples of his eloquence, and that his splendid talents were not more frequently employed on less objectionable subjects.

On Analogy:
Re-definition and Some Implications

Karl R. Wallace

MAY the hen who sits on a nest of china eggs be said to show analogical behavior? Is a dog behaving analogically when he chases his first skunk because he has habitually chased cats? Even more important, since the situation may represent a transition from simple association by contiguity to something called inference, is the dog who *refrains* from chasing his *second* skunk responding as if the second black-and-white animal is to the first, as one exceedingly unpleasant experience is to another? Or, is a man who forms the plural of *radio* by adding -*s* (*radios*) because most other nouns thus form their plurals, behaving, in essence, any more or any less analogically than the dog? What would one say of William James who associated *gas jet* and *moon* because of a common attribute, luminosity?

If examples like these are proper cases of analogy, are they essentially similar in principle to the figurative and literal analogy that the rhetorician finds at work in everyday discourse? Are they like analogy as it is understood by the scientist, the logician, the psychologist, and the linguist? In dealing with these questions, we hope to arrive at a re-definition of analogy, in part by reviewing the various uses of the term and in part by drawing on recent experimental investigations that seem to throw light on analogy as behavior. Then, with the new conception in mind, we shall suggest what implications it may hold for rhetoric.

§1

The logicians look at analogy in two ways. It may be regarded as a similarity or resemblance of relations, in which the resemblance lies in the qualities of two or more objects that are essentially dissimilar. The relationship, moreover, may be formulated as a proportion with four terms.[1] When, for example, one brings together such generically unlike objects as the tide and men's fortune, one has in mind a single identity of relationship that may be expressed conventionally by the statement "There is a tide in the affairs of men," or by the proportion, *ebb-and-flow of tide : ocean :: rise-and-fall of fortune : men's affairs.* The other way in which the logician sees analogy rests on the supposition that because two objects or events resemble each other in a number of points, they also resemble each other in some other point known of the first but not known of the second.[2] Event A, for instance, has attributes *1, 2, 3, 4,* and *5,* and event B, known to exhibit attributes *1, 2, 3,* and *5,* but not known to exhibit *4,* is nevertheless judged to possess the doubtful attribute also.

The natural scientist, represented by the biologist, uses analogy to denote a physiological or *functional* correspondence between things that are structurally unlike. Thus, the wing of a bird and the wing of a butterfly correspond only in that they serve the same function, flight. To the biologist, accordingly, analogy is opposed to homology, a term reserved to describe the *structural* correspondence between two or more parts.[3] The structural similarity, also, usually implies a genetic relationship. Hence it is that the arm of a man, the foreleg of a horse, and the wing of a bird are homologous, for they are not only structurally alike, but they have developed from corresponding embryonic parts.[4]

Although the biologist will not definitely associate structural similarity with analogical relationships, the chemist will admit structural similarity. He will apply analogy to a group of compounds whose atoms, though different as to substance, have the same power of attraction and thus combine in molecules in such a way as to give the molecules the same structure. "Isologues,"[5] for example, are one kind of analogous group, because although they differ in many properties they are alike in one respect, structure. But the chemist is not at utter variance with the biologist. His homologous series of compounds is thus named, first, because the members of the series reveal the same morphology, and second, because each member exists (or originates) apart from adjacent members in that it *differs* from them by the *same* "radical" or combining group.[6] The members of an homologous series, however, appear to be in one sense, analogous. Although the compounds as a group reveal similar chemical properties, each member has evident differentia; and although the physical properties of each member change with some uniformity as the series ascends, the uniformity is by no means constant, and accordingly, each member shows a significant difference. Seemingly, therefore, because here there is resemblance amidst significant difference, the chemist speaks of the members as being not only homologous, but analogous to one another.[7] Though unlike in some respects, they behave similarly in others. Indeed, it would seem that some unlikeness is essential to analogy, for wherever compounds show a correspondence that is all but complete they are termed "isomers" and "isotopes." In brief, then, both the natural and the physical scientist appear to associate analogy with similarity amidst dissimilarity. In doing so, they are like the logician who sees analogy as involving a correspondence among unlike objects and events.

Such views on analogy are not entirely acceptable to the psychologist and the linguist. Interested in the behavior of man and of language, they object because the logician-scientist's account implies that conscious discrimination is necessary to analogy. Actually, so they counter, analogy is another case of behavior, and since behavior is of a lower and a higher order—habitual or uncritical, and deliberate or discriminatory—analogy likewise may exhibit similar levels of behavior that can be accurately described in terms of stimulus-and-response patterns. The hen responds to the china eggs as if they were real eggs, and the dog responds to the skunk as if it were a cat; and in neither case, so far as we know, is the action discriminatory and analytical. Furthermore, the psychologist and the linguist take some exception to the scientist's conception of analogy because it puts too much emphasis on qualities and properties and not enough weight upon the essential relationship of every analogy—the *identity* of relationship between two unlike contexts. Accordingly, the psychologist seems to hold that *analogy is in essence an identity of response to two or more unlike stimulus-patterns.*[8]

The phrase "identity of response" is meant to point towards that behavior, consisting either of gross bodily adjustments or of speech symbols, whose stimulus is two unlike contexts. If one observes, say, first a seed and then an egg, he may throw the seed out of the window and fry the egg. The two unlike stimulus-patterns or contexts provoke different bodily responses. But if one perceives that the seed is to its parent and offspring in the plant world what the egg is to its parent and offspring in the animal world, then his intellectual response is the same to each situation. In other words, the seed has the same *identical relation* to the plant world as the egg has to animal life; the identity of relationship is thus the identical response in each case. Nevertheless, as significant as relations are to analogy, it is never relationship *as such* and alone that is perceived; always there must be concrete objects-, events-, or symbols-in-a-relation.[9]

The phrase "two unlike stimulus-patterns" is meant to indicate that the two contexts must be different. For example, if one says "moon" the word may be taken as referring to itself, i.e., the word *moon* is the word *moon.* Here the two contexts—the word *moon* on the one hand and the word *moon* on the other—show complete correspondence, and hence there is no analogy. If, however, one says "the moon is a gas jet," there are manifestly two unlike contexts that reveal but one common relationship: *gas jet : moon :: illumination of room : illumination of earth.* It appears, then, that strict identity in all respects, or sameness, is incompatible with analogy, even if it may be regarded as theoretically possible in the "real" world.

To define analogy as an identical response to two unlike stimulus-patterns seems to satisfy the purposes of the psychologist. Once he has brought analogy within his vocabulary, he points out, for the instruction of the rhetorician and the logician, wherein analogy differs from the symbol and from reasoning. In place of the usual definition of symbol as something that stands for something else, the psychologist describes it as that aspect of a behavior pattern which not only stands for the pattern but also upon re-occurence as stimulus calls up the pattern of which it was a part.[10] It is evident, accordingly, that analogy differs from the symbol in not being an invariable substitute for the contexts referred to. Rather, analogy *is* the identity of response between two unlike stimulus-patterns; it is not a substitute for that response.

Not only does the psychologist help in distinguishing symbolic activity from analogical behavior; he also throws some light on the relation of analogy to reasoning. As a result of a series of investigations, Maier concluded that "reasoning is primarily characterized by a new combination of old experiences which is adequate to meet a situation."[11] Whereas learning is acquired, habitual adaptation, reasoning involves a new integration whose stimulus is the problem-situation; and where the mechanism of learning is association by contiguity, the mechanism of reasoning is "spontaneous integration" or orientation. Although the precise character of such integration escapes them, the experimentalists seem to agree that the indispensable processes *prior* to integration are "equivalence reactions,"[12] or in our vocabulary, analogical behavior. The reaction is depicted thus:

stimulus-situation A B C D → response X
stimulus-situation E F B H → response X

It is this behavior that Maier has explored experimentally; he has interpreted his results thus:

If response X occurs we say the two situations are equivalent but they are not equal because the animal can differentiate the two situations and expresses this differentiation by showing much more hesitancy in the second than in the first situation. Problem solving of this sort is usually treated under the term transfer of training. Perception is the essential process in such transfer reactions. Only when B in the first situation is like B in the second situation can we expect the transfer to appear.[13]

The psychologists' work on analogy and related behavior, then, would appear to have made these contributions: (1) analogy starts from two or more unlike stimulus-patterns or contexts;

(2) it ends as a response that can be described as identity of relationship; (3) analogical behavior is not consciously discriminatory, except in moments of analysis; and (4) it should not be confused with reasoning *per se.*

As for the linguist's understanding of analogy, we need not delay long. Although the student of language makes no attempt at definition, his use of the term reveals his sympathy with the psychologist. By accepting analogy as an identity of response to two or more unlike stimulus-patterns, he can offer an adequate account of certain language behavior, especially where the apparent diversity of phenomena will yield striking relationships.[14] For instance, the order and form of sentence utterances he explains on grounds of analogy. The sentence, "I went home," is in the familiar form, *actor—action—goal of action;* so also is the statement "I drove downtown yesterday to buy a bushel of apples." Here, again, are the two unlike contexts whose identity lies in structure only. Similarly, the linguist accounts for the formation of new plurals by the addition of final *-s;* both in sound and in function, the new form, say *radios,* is like other plural forms. Analogy is seen also in the repetition and persistence of intonation patterns.

To look at analogy as an identity of response between two or more unlike stimulus-patterns may quite properly characterize the simple, low-order type of analogical behavior. But though the description will apply to all *analogy,* it is not sufficiently revealing for behavior that is more complex than the responses of hens and dogs, nor for the behavior of men who utter sounds analogically and unwittingly invent metaphors and similes and other charming figures. I refer to the analogy involved when one judges that the golden age of Rome was like the golden age of Greece, that life is a game of chess, that one drama follows the pattern of another; or the analogical process at work when a new chemical element is predicted because of the identity of pattern seen in the other members of a group or series, or when one discovers that the postulates of the solar system may apply also to the organization of the atom, or when the orator founds an argument on analogy. In all such cases one manifestly starts with two dissimilar contexts and ends with an identity of relationship between them. But instead of dealing with a single relationship as in the simple analogy, we are confronted with many relationships. Or more strictly, we perceive many identities of relationship in the two contexts. In the attempt to understand the nature of such analogies, the psychologist and the linguist are of little help. It is to the mathematical scientist one must turn.

Euclid defined analogy as a proportion.[15] A case in point is 2 : 4 :: 4 : 8; so is 3 : 5 :: 9 : 11. In the first proportion what is important is not the quantitative result indicated by the equation, but the literal fact that 2 stands in relation to 4 as 4 stands in relation to 8, for by virtue of the relationship manipulation becomes possible without destroying either the equation or the ratio. One can divide each side by 2 and still keep the identity of the ratio; one can multiply and divide each side by the same digit and preserve the ratio; one can change the order of the digits, either by the arrangement 4 : 8 :: 2 : 4, or by putting together the antecedents on one side and the consequents on the other. Or one can extend the series 8 : 16 :: 16 : 32 :: 32 : 64, and so on. In the second proportion, manipulation is still possible, although it cannot be carried on as extensively and as freely as in the equation. The first ratio differs from the second by a constant, 2. If one adds or subtracts any digit, the ratios still differ by the same constant; if one multiplies each member by the same digit, say by 3, the ratios, although they differ by a new constant, 6, still bear the same *relationship* to each other, for 9 obviously bears the same relation to 15, as 27 does to 33. Where division is possible, a similar change of constant occurs, but again an identity of relationship is the result.[16] Now if during all this manipulation, we should regard the digits as being purely formal symbols, then with each shift we would alter the *content* of the symbol. For when we say 2 : 4 :: 16 : 32, obviously the numerical symbols are different. Hence, it is evident that the *sensible content* has shifted with each manipulation while the relationship has remained identical.

This circumstance is so important to an understanding of the

higher order of analogy that it should probably be illustrated
further. Suppose that two chess players were to make a map or
diagram of the progress of their game, indicating the initial
positions of the men and recording every move. Then for each
position on the board and for each move in the game there is a
corresponding position and move on the map. If the king and
queen stand together in the back row on the board, they stand
in the same position on the map; if pawn No. 3 makes the opening move in the game, it moves likewise on the map; if in the
game the bishop moves according to one rule, the queen according to another, then on the map the two pieces behave
correspondingly. What is important to our purpose in this illustration is that the symbols on the map are not like the pieces
and moves of the game, and yet for each relationship on the map
there is an identical and corresponding relationship in the game.
Indeed, the relationships might not change significantly if the
game or its map became the charts of an individual's behavior
in society, of rival nations, of diplomats at play, or of the strategy
and tactics of an army. Here, though the domain or sensible
content of the contexts will change, there will still be a one-to-
one correspondence involving not merely a single identical relationship, but many.

When one context or pattern is conceived of as the map of
the other, it is significant that no matter how many similar relationships there may be, the corresponding points on the map
and its ground are different. If, for instance, the ground should
contain points R_1, R_2, R_3 . . . R_7, and the map should present
points r_1, r_2, r_3 . . . r_7, all the large $R's$ differ in content, and so
do all the small $r's$. Furthermore, the relationship between any
one pair of correspondences, say R_5 to r_5, is the same as for any
other pair of correspondences, say R_1 to r_1. Where two unlike
contexts "map on" each other and thus reveal one-to-one relationships, the mathematical scientist calls the relation *isomorphic*. And it is this relation of isomorphism that appears to be
the essence of analogy. Accordingly, we may perhaps conclude
that whereas the simpler cases of analogy may be described as
an identity of response (or of relationship) between two unlike

stimulus-patterns (or contexts), the complex analogy may be termed an isomorphic relationship between two unlike contexts.

If the complex analogy may be thus described, there appear to be at least two properties of the model-and-ground relationship that, although they may not be essential, are properties that accompany it necessarily. Of special concern to rhetoric, the first property is that of familiarity. The model or map is always more familiar than the ground or basis it illuminates, and thus aids in the ordering and communication of thought. In rhetoric this is seen readily in the fable, the parable, and the example.

The second property of the isomorphic relationship consists in the possibility of *extending* the map, once it is started, and thus bringing to light many unsuspected relationships. Once we perceive the analogy, $R_1 : r_1 :: R_2 : r_2$, then it is always possible to find other pairs of correspondences.

In pursuit of analogy, then, our conclusion, though perhaps not to be regarded as final, is this: In simple behavior situations analogy may be an identity of response to two unlike stimulus-patterns; in more complex situations where discrimination, analysis, and judgment appear, it is an isomorphic relationship between two unlike contexts in which the familiarity of the model or figure and the possibility of its extension are implicit.

§2

Such a description of analogy may have some interesting implications for the rhetorical theorist and the teacher. If the view is correct, it might lead to a different treatment of analogy by those who are concerned with argumentation and discussion. In the first place, the rhetorician might be led to discard the traditional division of analogy into two species, the figurative and the literal. In his *Elements of Rhetoric,* Bishop Whately adopts the view that analogy is "a resemblance of ratios" in which two things "stand in similar *relations* to some other things."[17] By so doing, he presents an accurate, though incomplete, discussion in which the unlikeness of the two contexts receives emphasis. Dissimilarities, the student learns, should prevent him from pushing the similarities too far and assuming

that there are identities where none exists. Differences, furthermore, test the alleged identities of relationship, and thereby reveal their propriety or impropriety. *Argumentation and Debate,*
by O'Neill, Laycock, and Scales, follows Whately part of the
way, but labels the Bishop's description as being limited to the
figurative analogy and then goes on to describe the literal analogy
as a "quite different" conception.[18] Most of the more recent books
on argumentation maintain the same distinction,[19] chiefly because of convenience and out of fear that figurative analogies
will not meet the requirements of proof.

Actually there would seem to be no good grounds for such a
distinction. If our earlier sketch of analogy be acceptable, the
"figurative" variety is a case where the two contexts are different
to the point of being outside their "normal" category, class, or
kind, and the "literal" variety is an instance where differences
between the two contexts are held to a more restricted area, the
traditional class. In the former, also, the identity of relationship
is usually single; in the latter, it is manifold. Put in this way, is
it not evident that in the figurative analogy the differences, no
matter how great, may yield a ratio that is just as sound or real
as any that obtain in the literal analogy? To say that *London* :
England :: *heart* : *body* may have the force of fact; whereas the
literal analogy with its many relationships may at best attain a
high degree of probability.[20] Is it not plain, moreover, that any
figurative analogy, though it may be first discovered as a single
relationship, is potentially many-sided? We can often extend it
and make its isomorph. Indeed, in the parable, the fable, and
the detailed example, we explicitly make the extension. In the
final analysis, it would seem that the rhetorician has dismissed
the figurative comparison brusquely and suspiciously because
he has found it hard to tell whether the resemblance is true or
false, whether the analogy is "sound" or "unsound."

It is in testing for the soundness of an analogy that our re-
definition may hold a second implication for the rhetorician.
Most of the usual rules for testing have doubtless been of practical aid to the student. He is counselled that "only *essential*
particulars have any weight," and that "an agreement or dif-

ference is *essential* when it is sufficiently important for the purpose at hand."[21] He is advised to select real similarities, and that these may be determined by "fundamental" differences.[22] He is told that "the points of likeness [should] outweigh the points of difference."[23] When such tests are illuminated by example, they become useful in guarding against error, though the student is perhaps not much wiser in knowing what is "important for the purpose at hand," and what essential similarities are.

On the other hand, if one were to emphasize the *ratio*-nal and proportional aspect of analogical relationships and the possibilities of extending the one-and-one correspondences in map-like fashion, the result might be some guiding questions that directly settle the matter of essence without abstruse discussion:

I. Where a single identity of relationship is under observation:
   A. Can the resemblance be expressed as a proportion? Where an explicit proportion cannot be set up, abandon the analogy. (This might at times be bad advice for the mature and experienced speaker and the poet!)
   B. Where one resemblance is established, can others be discovered? (Although extension of the map may give one greater confidence, it would not seem to enhance the accuracy of a single resemblance provided that it had been expressed as a clear proportion.)
II. Where more than one identity of relationship is at hand:
   A. Can *each* resemblance be turned into a proportion?
   B. Do not claim that because one context resembles another in some respects it must therefore resemble it in *all* respects. (In thus "generalizing," the difficulty lies not in the analogy itself, but in the hazards of the inference *from* analogy.)

Perhaps the attempt at re-definition suggests a re-evaluation of analogy in relation to the classical processes of deduction and induction. Although analogical behavior may not be the same as reasoning, as Maier's experimental work appears to demonstrate, certainly it is the ground of reasoning. The psychologists have testified to this point, as we have already seen; Schiller states a similar view for the logician:

Every argument, whether "inductive" or "deductive," is really analogical. In "induction" we argue from a number of "cases" to a "law" or rule. In "deduction" we . . . extend the rule's application to fresh cases. In both, therefore, several "cases" of a law are involved. But no two cases are ever absolutely "identical"; they are known to be only "similar," and their "identity" is always constituted by abstracting from their differences, which are judged to be irrelevant. Hence, every argument is from "case" to "case" according as the differences abstracted from turn out to be relevant or not.[24]

When the rhetorician is persuaded that analogy is the generator of reasoning and argument, he will at once give more attention to the case and the example. The example will be more widely recognized as a crucial point to both rhetorical theory and pedagogy. And as a result a fundamental question will always be posed: How does one know when an example is *typical* or *representative?* It is in determining the typical that the isomorphic attribute of analogy may prove useful. For there would appear to be no way of judging whether a case is representative except by comparing it with similar cases. This is seen at once to be a kind of measurement in which one situation is mapped on another, a second on the third, and so on; in other words, a number of one-to-one correspondences emerge in as many contexts as there are examples being examined. Such a procedure would give "character" to an example, in much the same way that an agent in drama attains ethos by being like his kind and by acting as other human beings act.[25] To the proper selection of examples, therefore, the principles of analogy may apply.

The processes of rhetorical proof, then, might be made more workable if the rhetorician were to treat analogy more exactly and at greater length, thus giving it the prominence it seems to deserve. The two properties of analogy, the familiarity of the model and the possibility of its extension, hold out much for rhetorical proof. Almost independent of grammatical and logical forms and symbols in which it is expressed, rhetorical proof may be in essence the revelation of identical relationships between two unlike contexts in such manner that one context is well within the experience of the hearer. Where the identity of relationship is single, there lie the metaphor and simile and many other tropes and figures; and where the identity is manifold, there lie the parable, the fable, and the example. Perhaps the greatest of these is the example, the *sine qua non* of deductive and inductive patterns.

NOTES

1. Cf. J. S. Mill, *System of Logic*, 2 vols. (London, 1851), II, 84-92; Sir William Hamilton, *Lectures on Metaphysics and Logic*, 2 vols. (Boston, 1860), II, 450-456; B. Bosanquet, *Logic*, 2 vols. (Oxford, 1888), II, 84; M. R. Cohen and E. Nagel, *An Introduction to Logic and Scientific Inquiry* (New York, 1934), pp. 222, 369; Aristotle, *Nicomachean Ethics*, V, 6, 7; Alexander Bain, *Logic, Deductive and Inductive* (New York, 1874), pp. 370-378; Scott Buchanan, *Poetry and Mathematics* (New York, 1929), p. 83.

2. Of the logicians mentioned above, perhaps Bain puts this relationship most concisely and accurately. *Op. cit.*, p. 373. Peculiarly, Hamilton suggests that from partial identity of the two objects, we infer complete or total similarity. *Op. cit.*, II, 454.

3. See Thomas Huxley's lecture on "The Lobster," *Discourses Biological and Geological* (New York, 1896), pp. 200-204.

4. It is interesting that "general homology" as one of the three species of homology is called "the relation of the organism, or any of its parts, to the general type or plan of such organisms or parts." *Century Dictionary and Cyclopedia*. That a logician should regard this relationship as analogical may be seen in Bosanquet's view that "analogy is essentially an argument about the significance of a type, or what in botany are called characters." *Op. cit.*, II, 84.

5. Isologues of water: H_2O, M_2O, M_2S, M_2Se, M_2Te, etc. M represents any metal.

6. A familiar homologous series is the alcohol group: CH_3OH, C_2H_5OH, C_3H_7OH, C_4H_9OH, etc. Each compound differs from its neighbors by a single constant, CH_2.

7. Like many technical experts the chemist occasionally employs his concepts without clear definition. He will insist that the members of an homologous series are analogous without quite knowing why. Perhaps the chemist's best attempts at definition are in *Hackh's Chemical Dictionary* (Philadelphia, 1937), and in A. F. Holleman, *A Text-Book of Organic Chemistry* (New York, 1930), pp. 37-39.

8. No psychological literature I have consulted flatly defines analogy in these words. Nor, for that matter, does any linguistic literature. I am partly indebted for this formulation to Mr. A. A. Hill, Professor of Philology and Linguistics at the University of Virginia. Among psychological sources, one study bears directly on analogy: M. L. Lemmon, "Psychological Consideration of Analogy," *American Journal of Psychology* LI (1938), 304-356. Sources bearing on processes closely related to analogy I have also found very useful: E. R. Guthrie, "Association and the Law of Effect," *Psychological Review* XLVII (1940), 127-148; N. R. F. Maier, "The Behavior Mechanisms Concerned with Problem Solving," *Psychological Review* XLVII (1940), 43-58; ———, "The Effect of Certain Aspects of a Problem Situation on the Reasoning Score of Rats," *Journal of Comparative Psychology* XXVI (1938), 527-544; ———, "A Further Analysis of Reasoning in Rats. II. The Integration of Four Separate Experiences in Problem Solving," *Comparative Psychology Monographs* XV (1938), 1-43; ———, "Reasoning in Rats and Human Beings," *Psychological Review* XLIV (1937), 365-378; G. H. S. Razran, "III. The Factors of Similarity, Proximity, and Continuity in Configurational Conditioning," *Journal of Experimental Psychology* XXIV (1939), 202-210; ———, "The Law of Effect or the Law of Qualitative Conditioning," *Psychological Review* XLVI (1939), 445-464; T. A. Ryan, "Mathematical Ob-

servations and Symbolizing," *American Journal of Psychology* LI (1938), 283-303; and K. L. Smoke, "Negative Instances in Concept Learning," *Journal of Experimental Psychology* XVI (1933), 583-588; ————, "An Objective Study of Concept Formation," *Psychological Monographs* XLII (1932), No. 4.

9. "Results . . . have given no indication that there is a psychological product which may be called *a relation*, apart from terms related. . . . Even when two analogical members of objects-in-a-relation were equated, it was never an abstracted relation which was identified; the relation was described as an apposition between general classes or orders which included the specific things named in the members." Lemmon, *op. cit.*, p. 349.

10. A symbol's context may be more important than its surrogate character, for since the context consists of symbol and the thing symbolized, the symbol itself is frequently, if not always, a part of the experience. As a part, of course, it is not entirely a substitute. Cf. W. S. Neff's notion of "symbolic reference," in his "Perceiving and Symbolizing: an Experimental Study," *American Journal of Psychology* XLIX (1937), 376-418, esp. p. 410. See also, Ryan, *op. cit.*, pp. 285-286.

11. "Reasoning in Rats and Human Beings," *op. cit.*, p. 368.

12. This is Maier's term. Krechevsky refers to the same reactions as "hypotheses"; Spence calls them "systematic response tendencies" consisting of trial-and-error. See Karl Duncker and I. Krechevsky, "On Solution-Achievement," *Psychological Review* XLVI (1939), 176-185; K. W. Spence, "Continuous versus Non-continuous Interpretations of Discrimination Learning," *Psychological Review* XLVII (1940), 271-288.

13. "The Behavior Mechanisms Concerned with Problem Solving," *Psychological Review* XLVII (1940), 47. Another view of the mechanism of analogy is Dewey's "comparison-contrast," a purely organic activity. See John Dewey, *Logic: The Theory of Inquiry* (New York, 1938), pp. 184, 186.

14. This judgment and the examples which follow are based principally upon Leonard Bloomfield's *Language* (New York, 1933), and L. H. Gray's *The Foundations of Language* (New York, 1938).

15. "Analogy, or proportion, is the similitude of ratios." *The Elements of Euclid*, ed. Robert Simson (Glasgow, 1781), p. 112. For the discussion that follows I am deeply indebted to the late Professor Carroll Mason Sparrow of the University of Virginia, particularly to his unpublished study, The Measurement of Measurement, in which measurement is regarded as analogical in character. As a consequence, even the most quantitative measurements of science and the symbols which express them are regarded as signs of analogical relationships. Cf. Dewey, *op. cit.*, pp. 202-214.

16. It should be observed that the proportion that is not an equation is the clearer illustration of analogy, for the equation complicates *qualitative* relationships with a *quantitative* product, whereas the non-quantitative proportion shows a single relation, i.e., *position*.

17. (Boston and Cambridge, 1855), p. 115.

18. (New York, 1915), p. 162.

19. E.g., A. C. Baird, *Public Discussion and Debate* (New York, 1928, 1937); H. L. Ewbank and J. Auer, *Discussion and Debate* (New York, 1941); W. T. Foster, *Argumentation and Debating* (New York, 1917, 1932); J. M. O'Neill and J. H. McBurney, *The Working Principles of Argument* (New York, 1932); and J. A. Winans and W. Utterback, *Argumentation* (New York, 1930).

20. Foster and the logicians seem to regard the literal analogy as deductive inference. "An argument from analogy is the inference that if two objects resemble one another in certain points, they also resemble one another in some other

point, known to belong to the one, but not known to belong to the other."
Argumentation (1932), p. 136. This is obviously the general premise of a hypothetical syllogism. The specific premise asserts that *these* two objects *do* reveal
a number of similar relationships. On this level Maier's equivalence mechanism
operates to yield the analogy, and the resemblances, having all the reality of
observation, are less open to doubt. But when it is finally drawn, the conclusion
of the syllogism, as is well known, derives its force from the proper conjunction of
the specific and general premises. Accordingly, since this conjunction has always
fostered error, we take the product as less trustworthy than observation. Cf.
Foster, who offers just the opposite evaluation: "An argument from analogy may
create an exceedingly high degree of probability, but it should not be regarded
as conclusive proof." *Ibid.*, p. 138.

21. Foster, *Argumentation* (1932), p. 138. In substance, so also Baird, *Public
Discussion* (1937), p. 166; O'Neill and McBurney, *op. cit.*, p. 133.

22. Ewbank and Auer, *op. cit.*, p. 165.

23. Foster, *Argumentation* (1932), p. 138. Winans and Utterback remark, however: "Two things that have more points of difference than similarity . . . may
still be essentially alike with regard to the point under discussion." *Argumentation*, pp. 133-134. O'Neill, Laycock, and Scales see the literal analogy as a
case of "generalization from a single instance." [*Argumentation* (1925), p. 166];
hence, their tests or "methods of attack" reflect those of the argument from
example.

24. F. C. S. Schiller, *Formal Logic* (London, 1912), p. 342.

25. Aristotle, *Poetics*, 1454^{a}16-25. It should be recalled that Aristotle thought
of the rhetorical example as analogical. *Rhetoric*, 1393^{a}30—1393^{b}4. Cf. *Prior Ana-
lytics*, 69^{a}13-19.

Contemporary Theories of Public Opinion

WILLIAM E. UTTERBACK

§1

THE problem of conceptualization has embarrassed the study of public opinion from its inception. Familiar as the air we breathe and nearly as amorphous, the phenomena of opinion baffle definition. How is the mind to lay hold of them? In what terms are they to be conceived? What, in short, *is* public opinion?

To this elementary question so many answers have been proposed that the body of contemporary writing on the subject presents a bewildering diversity of viewpoint and conception. Beneath current discussion at least twelve or fifteen basic theories may be distinguished. Interesting as examples of speculative ingenuity and important as sources of influence in the study of opinion, they invite a more careful examination than most of them have received.

The foundation of modern theory need not be sought in antiquity. Political observers from the earliest times have noted the influence of popular opinion on government; but while "the roots of the concept," as Palmer observes, "lie deep in the past," there was "no explicit formulation of it prior to the eighteenth century and no systematic treatment of it prior to the nineteenth."[1] For the early writers public opinion meant simply the weight of popular influence in government. Assuming that government involves two parties, the sovereign and the mass of subjects, they were interested in observing that the exercise of sovereign power is circumscribed by popular opinion. In so far as they conceptualized public opinion, most of them conceived it as will. Sovereign power having been traditionally regarded as an exercise of will, it may have been presumed that the sovereign's will could be limited only by the exercise of an opposing will, the will of the mass. Will is not readily susceptible of observation or analysis, and the early theorists made little attempt to describe or explain the processes through which the popular will is formed.

Before the rise of modern democracy there was, in truth, little in the political scene to direct attention to public opinion, and its serious study dates from the early nineteenth century. By then democracy had become a practical problem. It was already apparent that either the sovereign people is not always wise or its wisdom often miscarries. Preoccupation with democracy at work, eclipsing the theoretical speculation of the preceding century, generated a rapidly growing interest in the processes through which the popular will forms and expresses itself. Conditions were ripe for the study of opinion as a process of government.

The tendency to conceive public opinion as will persisted, though with diminishing force, throughout the new century. Taylor,[2] urging that opinion ought to rule in the United States; de Tocqueville,[3] insisting that in fact it does so; Austin,[4] denying that it is the sovereign power; Willoughby,[5] viewing it as an extra-legal force rather than a sovereign power; Ritchie,[6] calling it the political sovereign as distinguished from government, the legal sovereign—all explicitly or by implication conceived public opinion as the will of the people. So also did the much larger number of writers who with declamatory fervor exalted public opinion as the source of political wisdom or, like Bentham,[7] Jones,[8] and Godkin,[9] mingled a reasoned defense of democracy with objective description of the democratic process.

More characteristic, and increasingly so as the century advanced, was the conception of public opinion as opinion shared by a majority of the electorate. Such opinion, it was asserted, is, or should be, rational, and most writers sought the source of its rationality in the enlightening influence of leadership or of public discussion. Mackinnon,[10] Lewis,[11] and Maine[12] relied chiefly upon the influence of the leader; Lieber,[13] Stickney,[14] Giddings,[15] Bryce,[16] and Thompson,[17] upon the beneficent effect of public discussion. By the close of the century the new view prevailed: public opinion is opinion shared by a majority of the electorate.

The twentieth century opened a new chapter in the evolution of English and American theory of opinion. Already mounting rapidly, interest in the subject mushroomed in the most extraordinary volume of discussion, as sociologists and psychologists joined political scientists in the field. The conceptualization of opinion, recognized for the first time as basically important, began to receive adequate attention, and theories of public opinion appeared in great profusion and variety.

An explanation of this variety may be found in the intellectual climate of the time. The restless spirit of inquiry pervading the social sciences during the twentieth century has made each of them a storm center of conflicting currents of thought. In political science the philosophy of democratic individualism, still dominant in England and America, gives ground to the pluralistic and idealistic conceptions of the state. In sociology the most influential school, associated with the name of Tarde and popularized in America by Ross and his followers, discusses social life in terms of mental interaction between individuals. A rival school, regarding the social group as the significant unit, thinks in terms of interaction between groups rather than between individuals. In contrast with both, the bio-organismic conception regards the group as an organism possessing a continuous life, a unique personality, and in the opinion of some writers, a collective mind and will. In psychology, functionalism, influential at the turn of the century, is being eclipsed by behaviorism, purposivism, and various forms of dynamic psychology.

Such diversity of background and richness of conceptual material, brought to bear on the conceptualization of public opinion, should yield an interesting harvest. It has done so, the theories projected during the past forty years leaving few possibilities unexplored. A public opinion may be conceived as a phenomenon of human behavior or as an ideational entity capable of influencing behavior. Conceived as a form of behavior, it may be regarded as will, as opinion, or as action, and in any one of these views, as the behavior of a social group in process of making a collective decision, as the behavior of two or more conflicting subordinate groups within the larger group, or as the behavior of some aggregation of individuals within the larger group.[18] The variety of theories which it would be possible to frame is thus very great. Though no writer of this century has conceived public opinion as will, most of the other conceptions have been elaborated in some detail.

§2

Many contemporary conceptions of opinion bear little resemblance to those of the preceding century. Albert V. Dicey, in *Law and Public Opinion in England*,[19] blazed the first new trail, though not one destined to become a beaten path. More nearly than any other writer he regards a public opinion as an ideational entity capable in itself of influencing events. "There exists at any given time," he says, "a body of beliefs, convictions, sentiments, accepted principles, or firmly-rooted prejudices, which, taken together, make up the public opinion of a particular era, or what we may call the reigning or predominant current of opinion."[20] Displaying a certain logical unity and consistency, this ideational mass has often a common origin: "The opinion which affects the development of the law has, in modern England at least, often originated with some single thinker or school of thinkers."[21] Public opinion, in short, is the dominant social or political philosophy of the time.

In the legislative history of England during the nineteenth century, Dicey continues, three periods may be distinguished, each dominated by a public opinion peculiar to the period. From 1800 to 1830 the old Toryism induced an era of legislative quiescence. With the rise of Benthamism during the next four decades legislation was predominantly individualistic in tone, while under the influence of collectivism during the last third of the century, it became increasingly socialistic.

This attempt to establish a causal relationship between doctrine and law did not quite satisfy Dicey himself. Regarding the first period he remarks that Toryism was a sentiment of conservatism rather than a theory of legislation; the factor influencing legislation was a widely prevailing attitude, not a doctrine.

And the existence of collectivism during the third period, he confesses, is an inference rather than an observed fact: the inquirer can "prove the existence of collectivist ideas in the main only by showing the socialistic character or tendencies of certain parliamentary enactments."[22] For the second period only can he point to a definite body of doctrine as the source of legislation.

Dicey's difficulty illustrates the weakness in any theory conceiving public opinion as ideational entity: such an entity, if it exists, can neither be observed nor reliably inferred. Scientific explanation relates an event to known antecedent events. If the antecedent event is not an observable fact but must be inferred from other facts, the explanation is at best dubious. If it must be inferred from the very event to be explained, as in Dicey's third period, explanation fails completely. This difficulty of so conceiving public opinion as to make its phenomena accessible to observation was to embarrass most of Dicey's successors.

§3

The conception of public opinion as opinion, widely held in England and America, has taken many forms. Several writers, chief among them William McDougall, regard public opinion as opinion held by a group mind. In McDougall's view the nation-state is an organism. It "has a certain individuality, is a true whole which in great measure determines the nature and the modes of activity of the parts; it is an organic whole."[23] So much cannot be said of other social groups. The nation "alone is a self-contained and complete organism; other groups within it do but minister to the life of the whole. . . . Hence, the nation, as an object of sentiment, includes all smaller groups within it."[24]

Though organic in nature, the state is also a compact. As man develops from the primitive condition, the relation between individuals within a political society becomes more and more contractual. The modern nation-state, a product of this evolutionary process, is best described as a contractual organism. "This ideal of the contractual organism synthesizes the two great

doctrines or theories of society which have generally been regarded as irreconcilable alternatives: the doctrine of society as
an organism, and that of society as founded upon reason and
free will."[25]

To the nation-state we may ascribe a collective mind, though
consciousness is not one of its attributes. "We may fairly define
a mind as an organized system of mental or purposive forces;
and, in the sense so defined, every highly organized human society may be properly said to possess a collective mind."[26] "The
crucial point of difference between my own view of the group
mind and that of the German 'idealist' school . . . is that I re-
pudiate, provisionally at least, as an unverifiable hypothesis the
conception of a collective super-individual consciousness, somehow comprising the consciousness of the individuals composing
the group."[27]

The group mind deliberates, forms collective opinion, and
exercises a collective will. Public opinion is "a product not of
individual, but of collective, mental life."[28] It is

not a mere sum of individual opinions upon any particular question; it is rather the expression of that tone or attitude of mind
which prevails throughout the nation and owes its quality far more
to the influence of the dead than of the living, being the expression
of the moral sentiments that are firmly and traditionally established
in the mind of the people, and established more effectively and in
more refined forms in the minds of the leaders of public opinion
than in the average citizen.[29]

Only upon broad moral questions, however, does the group
mind form collective opinion: "The current use of the term,
in this country at least, does, I think, recognize that public
opinion properly applies only to the sphere of moral judgments
and can and should have no bearing upon the practical details
of legislation."[30]

An ingenious combination of diverse elements, McDougall's
theory stems from political idealism and bio-organismic sociology. The concept of the group mind, foreshadowed in Kant's
philosophy and formulated explicitly by Hegel and Treitschke,
reappears in the writings of the English idealist T. H. Green. It
is to Hegel and Green that McDougall is chiefly indebted. For

the conception of society as a contractual organism he goes to Fouillée, an exponent of the bio-organismic view of society.

The resulting theory has at least one virtue. Centering attention on collective behavior, it recognizes the significance of opinion as a group process. However important the individual's role in the formation of opinion, the object in view is the determination of collective action, and the decision reached is executed by the group's official representatives. This aspect of the process is often ignored by those who conceive opinion exclusively as the behavior of individuals or of conflicting interest groups within the nation.

Regarding the group as an organism and conceiving public opinion as opinion, McDougall is under the necessity of postulating a group mind as the only conceivable abode of public opinion. The necessity is unfortunate. Inaccessible to observation, the operation of such a mind, if one exists, must remain a mystery. And as in McDougall's theory, the conception leads almost inevitably to an unduly narrow definition of the area within which public opinion operates. A collective mind, viewed as the common denominator of the individual minds composing it and representing the traditional wisdom of the group, will operate, as McDougall insists, on broad moral questions only. It is hazardous to exclude from view so much of the total process of collective decision.

McDougall has had few followers, most English and American writers preferring to regard public opinion as opinion held by some aggregation of individuals within the social group. In spite of its popularity, the latter view presents serious difficulties. Individual opinion is unobservable, and its reflection in the press or in recorded votes is not always available or reliable. And the insularity of an individual's opinion is somewhat baffling. How is his opinion to be related to the collective action which it presumably influences? Among the many individualistic conceptions of public opinion as opinion we may trace a fumbling progress toward such precision of definition as will reveal how the weight of John Doe's opinion influences collective action.

Cooley began the quest with the conception of public opinion as the sum of all individual opinions on a controversial topic, whether in agreement or not, after discussion and reciprocal influence have resulted in a certain stability of view.[31]

The social ideas I have [he says] are closely connected with those that other people have, and act and react upon them to form a whole. This gives us public consciousness, or to use a more familiar term, public opinion, in the broad sense of a group state of mind which is more or less distinctly aware of itself. By this last phrase I mean such a mutual understanding of one another's points of view on the part of the individuals or groups concerned as naturally results from discussion.[32] . . . Public opinion is no mere aggregate of separate individual judgments, but an organization, a coöperative product of communication and reciprocal influence.[33] . . . It is not at all necessary that there should be agreement; the essential thing is a certain ripeness and stability of thought resulting from attention and discussion.[34]

Emphasizing the role of discussion and reciprocal influence in the formation of opinion, Cooley's view is congenial to sociologists of the "mental interaction" school. It is the view also of those interested in the measurement of opinion, and its influence is apparent in much of the work now appearing in *The Public Opinion Quarterly*. But while it recognizes the richness and complexity of the phenomena of opinion and affords an excellent basis for certain types of quantitative and descriptive work, the conception is too vague for a penetrating analysis.

Many writers, achieving somewhat greater precision of definition, regard public opinion as opinion shared by a majority of the individuals composing a social group. Three representative variations of the view, those of Ross, Lowell, and Young, illustrate the characteristic approaches respectively of the sociologist, the political scientist, and the social psychologist.

Ross[35] has much in common with Cooley. When alteration in the physical or social environment necessitates a change in the customary behavior of a group, vocal conflict may ensue. As discussion proceeds, the numerous private conflicts of opinion, becoming progressively fewer in number and more public in nature, coalesce in a majority opinion. The result, if discussion has run its full course, is a consensus integrating the originally conflicting views of those composing the majority. If the process is interrupted by the necessity of immediate collective action, premature decision in the form of a compromise must be accepted. In either case the majority opinion, since it determines collective action, is a public opinion. Essential to the formation of public opinion are freedom of communication and a common ground of belief among those participating in discussion.[36]

Members of the "mental interaction" school of sociology, both Cooley and Ross are interested primarily in discussion as the distinguishing feature of public opinion. Lowell,[37] writing in the tradition of the rationalistic philosophy of democratic individualism, is more interested in the mental processes, predominantly rational, by which the individual citizen forms his opinion on public questions. Unless an individual's belief is in part based on reasoning or has been adopted because in harmony with his *Weltanschauung,* Lowell says, it is not a true "opinion." When somewhat more than a mere majority share the same "opinion" on a public question and the minority is willing to see the majority prevail, we may speak of "public opinion." Absence of irreconcilable minority groups is thus a prerequisite of government by opinion. Mediating between the individual citizen with his opinions and the candidate with his desire for votes, the political party acts as a broker, its service consisting essentially in the formulation of alternatives, each representing a common denominator of opinion, on which the public can express a choice at the polls.

Lowell's conception of the political party as broker, grounded on realistic observation of political life, is a notable contribution to the theory of opinion. Of his theory as a whole less can be said. Like most views based on the philosophy of democratic individualism, it is highly rationalistic, the statement of an ideal rather than an interpretation of fact.[38]

Young, a social psychologist,[39] is interested in the individual personality as conditioned by, and reacting to, the social environment. Through a process of conditioning, the individual's inherited responses become integrated in complex behavior patterns. Not merely inert mechanisms, such patterns are often capable of operating "under their own steam." Under the impact of the social environment these "drives" form "attitudes," which largely determine the individual's behavior. An opinion is a "verbalized attitude"; shared by the majority, it is a public opinion. "The verbalized attitudes, beliefs, and convictions" which constitute public opinion "are essentially emotional," and "the amount of rational and scientific discussion in public opinion is small."[40] It is questionable whether Young's substitution of "verbalized attitude" for "opinion" makes the conception less subjective, and his view, based on Woodworth's dynamic psychology, differs little from that of Ross and Lowell except in regarding public opinion as non-rational.

Whether the views of Ross, Lowell, and Young represent an advance over that of Cooley it is difficult to say. Though the opinion of a majority, more tangible than the total mass of conflicting opinion on a topic, may seem more easily related to the collective action in which it issues, the advantage is less real than at first appears. Only occasionally is collective action determined by majority vote. The ballot is seldom employed under autocratic regimes, and even under democratic forms much governmental action, though undoubtedly influenced by opinion, is determined without recourse to popular vote.

The conception presents a more serious difficulty perhaps in holding out little promise of relating opinion to its ultimate determinants. Revealed most clearly in the organizational and promotional activities of interest groups, the determinants of opinion can hardly be discovered in the undifferentiated mass of anonymous individuals composing a majority. A more significant definition of the mass out of which the majority is formed might be helpful.

Seeking such a definition, some writers have regarded public opinion as opinion held by a majority of the "public," the nature of their theory depending upon their conception of the public.[41] The views of Wilson, Dewey, and Lasswell are especially worth noting.

For Wilson[42] the public is composed of those persons who

have the right to vote, and "public opinion is the content, in terms of the valuation and attitude, of the wills of those persons who compose the public."[43] The function of the concept is "ultimately to designate the area or body of opinion which will be given weight by any certain political organization. The political aspects of opinion arise logically, therefore, from the primary concept of the public."[44] Though useful in designating the theoretical source of political power in a democratic state, Wilson's conception throws no light on the genesis of opinion unless one makes the unwarranted assumption that the electorate has a common interest opposed to that of other elements of the population.

More promising is Dewey's view, based on a modified form of pluralism.[45] When a transaction between two persons or groups within the state entails consequences to other parties, the transaction is a public act and the outsiders affected are a public: "The public consists of all those who are affected by the indirect consequences of transactions to such an extent that it is deemed necessary to have those consequences systematically cared for."[46] Apparently Dewey does not mean that innumerable publics exist, each created by a particular transaction affected with a public interest. Rather the public acts characteristic of any period, having much in common, create a comparatively permanent public. This public, with the body of officials who safeguard its interest by regulating private transactions, constitutes the state. As modes of behavior change, especially modes of economic behavior, the incidence of public acts is likely also to change, and the new public thus created seeks to control government for the protection of its interest. By implication the author regards public opinion as opinion shared by a majority of the public at any given time.

As the first attempt to conceive public opinion as opinion and yet relate it to underlying group interest, Dewey's theory merits attention. It suffers perhaps from an unduly narrow definition of the type of interest generating opinion. The mischievous consequences of transactions affected with a public interest are but one of many factors prompting groups to organize for the control of government. More frequently than not the parties to the transaction themselves are conflicting interest groups, each seeking through public opinion to control government in its own interest, and their interest rather than that of the public created by them is the force molding opinion.

For Lasswell the public is composed of those participating in a political movement.[47] Political changes occur, he says, by unreflecting innovation, by private planning and adjustment, or by political movements, that is, by public opinion. When met by opposition generating conflict, the political movement includes four stages: unrest, symbolization and discussion, enactment, and a relatively permanent change in the political pattern. Associated with "that phase of a complex political movement which is characterized by debatable demands for action,"[48] public opinion is to be regarded as the prevailing opinion of the public, that is, of those participating in the movement.[49] More nearly than any other so far examined, Lasswell's conception affords a realistic approach to the study of the forces molding opinion, and it is unfortunate that the view has not been more fully developed.

No further attempt has been made to refine the conception of public opinion as opinion shared by an aggregation of individuals. All theories of this type encounter three primary difficulties: opinion itself is not accessible to direct observation; it is not easily related to the underlying forces which mold it; and except when the ballot is employed, it is not easily related to the collective action in which it eventuates.

§4

Deterred by the difficulties attending the conceptualization of public opinion as opinion, a growing number of writers have attempted to conceive it objectively. Here also a varied background of conceptual material has produced an interesting variety of theories. Viewed as overt behavior, opinion may be regarded as the activity of a group in process of determining collective action, as the activity of conflicting subordinate groups within the larger group, or as the activity of some aggregation of individuals within the larger group. All three paths have been explored.

Many sociologists, interested primarily in the patterns and processes of group life, find congenial the conception of public opinion as the activity of a group in process of making a collective decision. Regarding the group as a social unit adjusting itself to changes in the environment, they readily conceive opinion as one phase of the adjustive process. Carr, for example, believes that "public opinion from the point of view of the process involved may be defined as that type of coöperative interaction by which people in groups consciously readjust to change" when the established behavior patterns of the group do not afford a satisfactory adjustment.[50] Group adjustment conceived as a process, he concludes, must be our basic concept in the study of public opinion.[51]

Lundberg, feeling that the organismic conception of society has much to recommend it and that even the conception of the group mind may be salvaged, would restate the latter concept in terms of behavioristic psychology.[52] The concept is objectionable, he says, for the reason, and only for the reason, that the concept of the individual mind was objectionable. Both are sound if defined in terms of objective behavior.

It is "just as permissible," he continues,

to speak of public opinion as of individual opinion and as permissible to speak of the thinking, feeling, and acting of a group as it is to attribute these phenomena to individuals. In both cases, these words merely indicate a deliberative technique through which the unit referred to achieves a tentative adjustment.[53] . . . Public opinion is the tentative deliberative adjustment of a public to any situation. Any group which makes such an adjustment may be called a public with reference to the question on which it acts—actively or by acquiescence.[54]

In Lundberg's view a divided public opinion presents no difficulty. An individual opinion, as distinguished from a belief or conviction, contains an element of doubt. "If an opinion is the preponderance of positive reactions to a situation, the degree to which stimuli are present motivating the organism in another direction is essentially the question as to how unanimous an individual opinion is."[55] Eventually the individual must make up his mind; that is, he must make an adjustment; and the adjustment indicates his opinion, whether unanimous or not. A public opinion is one which "becomes the basis of the practical deliberative adjustment of the public,"[56] regardless of the degree of unanimity involved.

It is not clear that Lundberg's view adds anything to Carr's functional conception. Emerging from its disinfectant bath of behavioristic terminology, the group mind proves to be simply a social group making a collective adjustment. It may be doubted whether the behaviorist's satisfaction in using "group mind" and "public opinion" with a clear conscience is worth the trouble it costs. But the conception of public opinion as the process through which a group makes tentative adjustments is distinctly useful. Without postulating a group mind, it relates opinion organically to the total process of group government. Unfortunately it throws no light on the interest and pressure groups whose activities largely determine what collective adjustment is to be made. Bentley centers his attention upon the subordinate groups themselves.[57]

Political phenomena, he says, consist exclusively of the activities of conflicting groups within the nation. "The whole social life in all its phases can be stated in such groups of active men, indeed must be stated in that way if a useful analysis is to be had."[58] The group is to be conceived, however, "not as a physical mass cut off from other masses of men, but as a mass activity, which does not preclude the men who participate in it from participating likewise in many other group activities."[59] The opposition of such groups being an incident of social conflict, "we shall always find that the political interests and activities of any given group . . . are directed against other activities of men, who appear in other groups, political or other."[60] We may distinguish between the underlying interest group based upon a widespread aspiration or grievance and the smaller representative group which arises to arouse and lead it and to further its ends by promotional and pressure activities. Government is the phenomena of the "push and resistance between groups," and "the balance of the group pressures *is* the existing state of society."[61]

Public opinion, the promoting-talking-writing activity of groups in conflict, is better conceived as overt behavior than as opinion.

What a man states to himself as his argument or reasoning or thinking about a national issue is, from the more exact point of view, just the conflict of the crossed groups to which he belongs. To say that a man belongs to two groups of men which are clashing with each other; to say that he reflects two seemingly irreconcilable aspects of the social life; to say that he is reasoning on a question of public policy, these all are but to state the same fact in three forms.[62]

Occasionally exercising a directive influence, public discussion is more often a superficial phenomenon, reflecting rather than causing social conflict.

As the first attempt in English to conceive public opinion objectively, Bentley's theory possesses considerable interest. His sociological background is unusual in an American writer. Stepping quite aside from the main current of English and American sociological thought, he goes for a theoretical basis to those writers who discuss social phenomena in terms of interaction between groups rather than between individuals, his chief indebtedness being to Marx, Gumplowicz, and Simmell. Their conception, however, he greatly improves for his own use by defining the group as a mass of activity rather than as a fixed mass of individuals. Incidentally his view is based on a pluralistic conception of the state, though *The Process of Government* antedates those writings now described as pluralistic.

Bentley's theory deserves more attention than it has received from students of public opinion. His definition of opinion in terms of conflicting representative groups engaged in promotional and pressure activities strikes deeply into the realities of political life. More effectively than any other conception so far examined it relates the process of opinion to the underlying forces which control it. But it does so at the cost of ignoring almost entirely the significance of opinion as the process by which the national group modifies its collective behavior. Exposing the roots, it ignores the fruit of opinion.

Not all objective theories of opinion have been couched in terms of group process. Among individualistic conceptions that of Lippmann is most interesting,[63] and its examination may well conclude this review of representative theories.

Following McDougall's hormic psychology, Lippmann seeks an explanation of the individual's behavior in the instinct as modified by contact with the environment. An instinctive act has a threefold aspect, cognition, emotion, and response. While the emotional core of this complex remains relatively constant, through a process of conditioning both stimulus and response become greatly modified. "The whole structure of human culture is in one aspect an elaboration of the stimuli and responses of which the original emotional capacities remain a fairly fixed center."[64] Modification of the stimulus often involves substitution of a symbol, verbal or otherwise, for the situation originally prompting the instinctive act. Thus the individual accumulates a stock of symbols largely devoid of specific intellectual content but capable of arousing emotion and evoking response.

When through the manipulation of such symbols a political leader arouses and canalizes an emotion in an identical response at the ballot box, he has formed "a public opinion." A majority vote does not imply community of opinion among those composing the majority. Indeed the leader's technique consists primarily in securing the same vote from individuals holding diverse opinions on specific issues. Though Lippmann speaks of public "opinion," he apparently means merely the concerted act of a majority in casting an identical ballot at the polls.

In *Public Opinion* Lippmann means by a "majority" a majority of the electorate. But in *The Phantom Public* his "majority" is a majority of the "public." A controversy having arisen between two groups within the state, the public consists of those not parties to the dispute; it consists, that is, of bystanders, whose sole interest is in seeing the dispute settled according to some rule. "The public is not a fixed body of individuals. It is merely those persons who are interested in an affair and can affect it only by supporting or opposing the actors."[65] When such a controversy must be settled at the polls and a majority of those composing the public are induced by the influence of political leaders to cast an identical vote, a public opinion has been expressed.

Though suggestive, Lippmann's view encounters several difficulties. One it shares with all conceptions of opinion in terms of majority vote—it can relate the process of opinion and its product, collective action, only when action is determined at the polls. More often than not the pressure of opinion on government finds expression through other channels, and a definition in terms of majority vote, whether couched in objective or subjective terms, must unduly restrict the area within which opinion is represented as operating.

Even where the ballot is employed, Lippmann's theory can do little to relate opinion to the forces which control it. His account of the individual, drawn from McDougall's hormic psychology, does not explain why the individual's interest leads him to vote one way rather than another. Rather is it implied that his vote is determined solely by the political leader's manipulation of symbols. For the ultimate explanation of majority action one must therefore turn to the activity of the leader. But the leader is not regarded as representing an interest group. Apparently a *deus ex machina,* he operates from without upon an inert mass of voters for reasons known only to himself. This account misses entirely the significance of group interests as determinants of opinion.

Nor does Lippmann's use of the "public," based on a pluralistic view of the state, materially improve his account of the formation of opinion. The public, in his view, consists of those not parties to the controversy in question; its only interest is that of the spectator, who would see law and order preserved. Like Dewey's view of the public as those victimized by conflict, this conception is too vague to reveal the forces molding opinion, and we are still thrown back upon the inscrutable personal motives of the leader for an explanation of opinion.

§5

Viewed as a whole, contemporary theory of opinion exhibits extraordinary variety of conception with little internal coherence. No theorist has been noticeably influenced by his predecessors, and such paths of influence as may be traced lead directly to the adjacent fields of political science, sociology, and psychology. Split into conflicting schools, each field has made a wealth of conceptual material available to the student of opinion. In political science Lowell draws upon democratic individualism, McDougall upon idealism, Bentley, Lippmann, and Dewey upon pluralism. In sociology Ross and Cooley borrow from "mental interactionism," McDougall from bio-organicism, Bentley from the "group conflict" school, Carr from the functional sociology of group adjustment. In psychology McDougall's hormic psychology is utilized by Lippmann, Woodworth's dynamic psychology by Young, behaviorism by Lundberg. Built of materials quarried from sources so diverse, contemporary theories display little architectural similarity.

Three main types may, however, be distinguished. Owing little to contemporary thought in other fields, Dicey's conception of opinion as ideational entity stands alone, least popular of the three types. Most popular has been the view of public opinion as opinion. Among theories of this type, despite much diversity of conception, a certain continuity of direction is apparent in the succession of views projected. Setting on one side as *sui generis* McDougall's "group mind" conception, we may trace among views conceiving public opinion as the opinion of individuals a progressive refinement of the concept from Cooley's conception of the total mass of conflicting opinions, through the "majority opinion" views of Ross, Lowell, and Young, to the attempts of Wilson, Dewey, and Lasswell to think in terms of the majority opinion of a "public." Less popular but persisting throughout the period, the objective definition of opinion has produced three distinctive views, that of Bentley in terms of the activity of conflicting subordinate groups, of Lippmann in terms of the activity of individuals, and of Carr and

Lundberg in terms of the activity of the larger group adjusting its collective behavior to a changing environment.

No view has been generally accepted or is perhaps likely to be in its present form; all are open to objection on one ground or another. The conception of public opinion as ideational entity or as opinion, whether of a group mind or of individual minds, makes the phenomena to be examined unobservable. Conception in terms of individual behavior, objective or subjective, fails to disclose the ultimate determinants of opinion and, except where the ballot is employed, makes it difficult to relate the process of opinion to the collective action in which it issues. Conceived as the activity of conflicting subordinate groups, opinion cannot be related to the collective action of the inclusive group; conceived as the activity of the inclusive group, it cannot be related to that of the subordinate groups controlling it. If the objective conceptions of Carr (activity of the inclusive group) and Bentley (activity of conflicting subordinate groups) could be combined in a unified view, all requirements of a satisfactory theory would be met. Such a view is suggested in the following paragraphs.

According to the functional theory outlined by Carr, the nation takes collective action to adjust its behavior to changes in the environment. The utility of the conception depends very much on how "environment" is defined. Of slight value in the abstract, the concept has important implications when stated concretely. The environment to which national behavior must be adjusted consists, on the one hand, of the equilibrium, or balance of power, among the nation's own interest groups, and on the other, of the equilibrium among the various national powers of the world. The first may be called the internal, the second the external, environment.

The necessity of adjusting collective behavior to the internal environment arises from the group nature of political life. As Bentley insisted, the nation is a congeries of competing interest groups, each seeking to advance its interest by influencing governmental policy. "The push and resistance" between these groups is the essence of political life, and, in Bentley's words, "the balance of the group pressures *is* the existing state of society." To speak of the balance or equilibrium among the groups is not to say that they exert an equal pressure against each other but rather that they have achieved a *modus vivendi* based on their comparative strength. Much of custom and law is the socially sanctioned set of arrangements governing the relations between interest groups and reflecting the balance of power among them when the custom had its inception or the law was enacted. When custom and law reflect the existing equilibrium with reasonable accuracy, a political society is stable. But the equilibrium shifts constantly as various interest groups wax or wane in strength, and since custom and law change slowly, some maladjustment is a continuous feature of political life.

Political conflict arises chiefly from discrepancy between the existing equilibrium and the current customary and legal arrangement. In large part the function of government is to resolve the conflict by conforming behavior, individually and collectively, to the existing equilibrium. When organized labor has become strong enough to force a revision of the relationship between labor and capital, government registers the new balance of power and through a Wagner Act compels individuals and groups to adjust themselves to the changed situation. The shifting equilibrium among interest groups is thus a sort of internal environment to which the nation collectively must adjust its behavior.

Similarly a shifting equilibrium among national powers imposes upon government the necessity for a continuous revision of its foreign policy. When a sharp discrepancy develops between the existing balance of power among nations on the one hand and international law and treaty on the other, a conflict arises which, unless adjusted through diplomatic channels, leads to war. When Germany regained the status of a world power after her defeat in 1918, other powers were obliged to adjust national policy to the new equilibrium. The shifting balance of power among nations is thus also a part of the environment to which a nation must adjust its collective behavior.

National adjustment to a changing environment of internal

and external group pressures is accomplished by governmental action. But what action will be taken is determined ultimately by public opinion. The influence of economic and social conditions prompting political activity; the organizational, promotional, and pressure activities of interest groups; the discussion and propaganda accompanying such activity; the political party and electoral procedure; the response of government itself to these varied and conflicting influences—all are phases of the process determining collective action. For these activities "collective decision" is perhaps a better term than "public opinion." It designates the area of phenomena in question more accurately, indicates the nature of the process more clearly, and is free from the unfortunate subjective and individualistic implications of the more familiar term.

That collective decision in all of its phases as essentially a group process is nowhere more clearly revealed than in the political movement, which marks the evolution of an interest group. The indispensable condition of a political movement is the existence of what may be called an *interest area,* that is, a mass of individuals with a common grievance (or aspiration). The individuals may be unaware, or only dimly aware, that they share the grievance with others; it may never have occurred to them that political action might relieve their distress; the grievance may never have been the subject of public discussion. Such interest areas often exist for generations without leading to political action. But eventually, for reasons still little understood, a small compactly organized group arises to represent the interest area, and a political movement is under way. Organization of the representative group is often the achievement of a single leader with an idea, who gradually collects about him a few energetic men sharing his vision and ability as an organizer.

The first task of the representative group is to arouse the interest area: to make its members sharply aware of their grievance, to convince them that others share the grievance and that political action affords a remedy. Its second task is to formulate a program and to launch a campaign of propaganda for its promotion. Addressed at first to the interest area itself, propaganda is later directed to other groups, sometimes vaguely described as "the general public," which have enough in common with the interest area to be a potential source of support. The process at this point is often complicated by the fact that competing representative groups arise with rival programs of action, each attempting to organize the area behind its program.

Having organized the interest area and mobilized its political power in support of a program of action, the representative group begins to function as a pressure organization. It may either exert pressure at the polls by organizing as a political party and presenting its own platform and candidates, as the English labor movement has done, or by swinging its vote to the party most favorable to its program, as the Anti-Saloon League did; or through the lobby it may exert pressure on the government directly.

This brief sketch has indicated how the processes of collective decision and collective action in their entirety may be brought into a single unified picture and described in the same conceptual language, the dynamic and objective language of group activity. Taking its inspiration from Carr and Bentley and to a less extent from Lasswell, who first emphasized the importance of the political movement, it has sought to unite the most promising elements in contemporary theory.

NOTES

1. Paul A. Palmer, "The Concept of Public Opinion in Political Theory," *Essays in History and Political Theory in honor of C. H. McIlwain* (Cambridge, Mass., 1936), p. 231. Both Plato and Aristotle discussed the weight of popular influence in government, and occasional allusion to the subject can be found in writings of the classical Roman and medieval periods. Among later pre-nineteenth century writers who discussed public opinion, usually emphasizing its power, were Pascal, Voltaire, Hobbes, Locke, Hume, Rousseau, Necker, Wieland, Garve, and Fries.

2. John Taylor, *An Inquiry into the Principles of the Government of the United States* (Fredericksburg, 1814), p. 418.

3. Alexis de Tocqueville, *The Republic of the United States of America* (New York, 1856). The English translation first appeared in 1838.

4. John Austin, *Lectures on Jurisprudence* (London, 1861), Lecture V.

5. Westel W. Willoughby, *Examination of the Nature of the State* (New York, 1896), p. 294.

6. David G. Ritchie, "On the Conception of Sovereignty," *Annals of the American Academy of Political and Social Science* I (1890-1891), 401-402.

7. Jeremy Bentham, *Essay on Political Tactics* (1789); *Securities Against Mis-*

rule Adapted to a Mohammedan State (1822); *Constitutional Code* (1827).

8. Henry J. Jones, *The Rise and Growth of American Politics* (New York, 1898).

9. Edwin L. Godkin, *Unforeseen Tendencies of Democracy* (Boston, 1898).

10. William A. Mackinnon, *History of Civilization and Public Opinion* (London, 1846).

11. George C. Lewis, *An Essay on the Influence of Authority in Matters of Opinion* (London, 1849).

12. Sir Henry Maine, *Popular Government* (London, 1885).

13. Francis Lieber, *Manual of Political Ethics* (Philadelphia, 1838).

14. Albert Stickney, *Democratic Government* (New York, 1885).

15. Franklin H. Giddings, *The Principles of Sociology* (New York, 1896); *The Elements of Sociology* (New York, 1898).

16. James Bryce, *The American Commonwealth* (1888).

17. George C. Thompson, *Public Opinion and Lord Beaconsfield, 1875-1880* (London, 1886).

18. Cf. Robert C. Binkley's classification of conceptions of public opinion as naturalistic, introspective, and phenomenological in "The Concept of Public Opinion in the Social Sciences," *Social Forces VI* (March, 1928), 389-396.

19. London, 1905.

20. *Ibid.*, p. 19.

21. *Ibid.*, p. 21.

22. *Ibid.*, p. 68.

23. William McDougall, *The Group Mind* (Cambridge, England, 1920), p. 7.

24. *Ibid.*, p. 180.

25. *Ibid.*, p. 175.

26. *Ibid.*, p. 9.

27. *Ibid.*, p. 19.

28. *Ibid.*, p. 193.

29. *Ibid.*, p. 198.

30. *Ibid.*, p. 198. For a similar view of the nation-state as an organism possessing a group mind which is the abode of public opinions see F. J. C. Hearnshaw's *Democracy at the Crossways* (London, 1919), p. 318. Hearnshaw differs from McDougall in ascribing collective consciousness to the group mind.

31. Charles H. Cooley, *Social Organization* (New York, 1909).

32. *Ibid.*, p. 10.

33. *Ibid.*, p. 121.

34. *Ibid.*, p. 122. William Albig, in *Public Opinion* (New York, 1939), takes substantially the same view.

35. Edward A. Ross, *Social Psychology* (New York, 1908).

36. Many writers have gone farther than Ross in insisting that public opinion is the product of discussion, some requiring that the discussion be rational, others that it result in an integration, or "consensus," of individual opinions. See, for example, the following: Clyde L. King, "Public Opinion in Government," Introduction to Graves' *Readings in Public Opinion* (New York, 1928); Chester C. Maxey, *The Problem of Government* (New York, 1925), p. 353; E. B. Reuter and C. W. Hart, *Introduction to Sociology* (New York, 1933); Robert H. Gault, *Social Psychology* (New York, 1923), p. 176 ff; Emory S. Bogardus, *Fundamentals of Social Psychology* (New York, 1931).

37. A. Lawrence Lowell, *Public Opinion and Popular Government* (New York, 1913).

38. The rational nature of public opinion is similarly emphasized in Charles A. Ellwood's *The Psychology of Human Society* (New York, 1925) and in William Bauer's "Public Opinion," *Encyclopedia of the Social Sciences* (1934). In *Public*

Opinion in War and Peace (Cambridge, 1923) Lowell turns to functional psychology as a basis for his theory and takes a much less rationalistic view of public opinion.

39. Kimball Young, *Social Psychology* (New York, 1930).

40. *Ibid.*, p. 580.

41. A few writers, like Walter J. Shepard in "Public Opinion," *American Journal of Sociology* XV (1909-10), 32-60, define the public as those who share the same opinion on a topic. If public opinion is then defined as the opinion of a public, a meaningless circularity of thought results, depriving both concepts of any value. Morris Ginsberg in *The Psychology of Society* (London, 1921), pp. 137 ff., defines public in terms of community of opinion but avoids the circularity of thought by distinguishing between "public" and "the public." A "public" consists of those sharing the same opinion on a controversial question; "the public" includes all the minor publics interested in the question. A public opinion is that held by the numerically largest public.

42. Francis G. Wilson, "Concepts of Public Opinion," *The American Political Science Review* XXVII (June, 1933), 371-391.

43. *Ibid.*, p. 382.

44. *Ibid.*, p. 382. Henry W. Jones in *Safe and Unsafe Democracy* (New York, 1918) and James Bryce in *Modern Democracies* (New York, 1921), Ch. XV, also identify the public with the electorate. The view is common among political scientists.

45. John Dewey, *The Public and Its Problems* (New York, 1927).

46. *Ibid.*, p. 15.

47. Harold D. Lasswell, "The Measurement of Public Opinion," *The American Political Science Review* XXV (May, 1931), 311-326.

48. *Ibid.*, p. 313.

49. Robert E. Park and Ernest W. Burgess take a somewhat similar view in their *Introduction to the Science of Sociology* (London, 1921), defining the public as those who participate in the discussion of a controversial question.

50. Lowell J. Carr, "Public Opinion as a Dynamic Concept," *Sociology and Social Research* XIII (1928-29), 23.

51. Carroll D. Clark takes much the same view in "The Concept of the Public," *The Southwestern Social Science Quarterly* XIII (March, 1933), 311-321.

52. George A. Lundberg, "Public Opinion from a Behavioristic Viewpoint," *The American Journal of Sociology* XXXVI (1930), 387-405.

53. *Ibid.*, p. 396.

54. *Ibid.*, p. 401.

55. *Ibid.*, p. 397.

56. *Ibid.*, p. 399.

57. Arthur F. Bentley, *The Process of Government* (Chicago, 1908).

58. *Ibid.*, p. 204.

59. *Ibid.*, p. 211.

60. *Ibid.*, p. 222.

61. *Ibid.*, p. 258.

62. *Ibid.*, p. 204.

63. Walter Lippmann, *Public Opinion* (New York, 1922); *The Phantom Public* (New York, 1925). See also Floyd H. Allport, "Toward a Science of Public Opinion," *The Public Opinion Quarterly* I (January, 1937), 7, for a brief discussion of public opinion in terms of verbalized attitudes. Allport's general approach is behavioristic.

64. *Public Opinion*, p. 204.

65. *The Phantom Public*, p. 77.

The Forensic Mind

Richard Murphy

THROUGH the ages forensics has been revered as a means of deciding controversy and as a means of education. But in this century the methods of debate have been vigorously attacked. In the field of parliamentary government the revolt can be observed in the spread of administrative law and in the development of bureaus and boards which do not publicly debate and decide, but which investigate and administer. Frequently our lives are affected by specific measures, such as those fixing prices or rationing goods, which are not debated in Congress but are decreed and executed by agencies granted the power to act. "Already, in every democracy, important activities of regulation are outside the direct control of parliaments," says R. M. Mac-Iver. "If this process continues, parliaments and congresses may cease to be the main centers of national life."[1] In the field of education the vigor of the attack on forensics is seen in the development of *discussion* as an antidote for malpractices in *debate,* and in the suspicion directed toward debating in the schools. Instead of receiving gratitude for his efforts to teach students the traditional art of controversy, the teacher of debating now may have to spend a share of his time defending his subject.[2] He may be told by principal, colleague, or adult-educationalist that he is teaching habits of mind harmful to social welfare. In this dispute[3] forensics is at a disadvantage in having to defend herself; if successful she is denounced as artful and clever, and if she fails she fails in her own province.

Since the forensic method of handling conflict and of exposing information is built into the structure of many democratic institutions, re-evaluation of the habits of thinking associated with debate is demanded. We seek here a clarification of the forensic process in terms of modern thought. We look for answers to these questions: What have been the characteristic elements in forensic aims and methods? What virtues have been traditionally ascribed to the system? What has been the traditional explanation of malpractices in forensics? What is the nature of the modern attack upon forensics? To what extent do these attacks seem justified? What changes may be expected in the forensics of the future?

Traditionally forensics has been the art of attacking and defending a proposition for the purpose of reaching a wise decision. "The elements of forensic speaking," says Aristotle, "are accusation [and] defense."[4] The process occurs in "practical matters," where one "cannot be scientifically exact."[5] If the drawing of a proposition for attack and defense, and the taking of sides upon it can be avoided, it is best to do so, thinks Aristotle; it is better "to agree to arbitration rather than go to court." But it is better "that a difference shall be settled by discussion rather than by force."[6] The forensic method includes, of course, investigation of evidence, analysis, and whatever steps are necessary to promote a fruitful attack and defense. The processes occur most prominently in formal and parliamentary debate, and in procedures in the law courts; but forensics may be quite as evident in conversation, conference, or editorial—wherever men seek decision in disputed areas of thought. The decision reached may be that of judge, jury, popular vote, or it may be the conclusion one accepts after hearing the proposition exposed. This decision is not merely logical, according to Aristotle's interpretation, but is also psychological; the emotions are a part of the process. "The method of logic" will not suffice; "the most accurate scientific information"[7] will not move some persons. The psychological function of persuasion was applied to democratic government by Thomas Jefferson when he said it is necessary "to persuade men to do even what is for their own good."[8] Guiding attack and defense of propositions in a forensic system are rules of evidence, laws of thought, and procedures in presentation and refutation. In the main the forms of argumentation have become so standardized that any difficulties in procedure can be dispatched easily enough by referring to a textbook in classical rhetoric or logic, a manual of debating, or the rules of the union or of the court.

Traditionally the benefits of forensics were held to be obvious. That an accused person should be given a fair trial, that argument should replace physical combat, that evidence should be presented and weighed before action was taken, that honest conviction should be openly declared—these attitudes seemed to encourage rational behavior among men. Under protection of the commonplace of forensics, "both sides shall be heard," many problems were opened to discussion and deliberation which otherwise would have remained unquestioned. Even the church permitted the devil to present his case, provided, of course, that an advocate at least as strong, and preferably a little stronger, spoke in refutation. The local debating society frequently investigated useful problems, sometimes too audaciously, as the debating club in Ohio which was notified in 1827: "You are welcome to the use of the school-house to debate all proper questions, but such things as railroads are impossibilities, and are impious, and will not be allowed."[9] Because the very opening of questions to vigorous attack and defense was regarded as a virtue, any malpractices that developed in the process were tolerated.

In the older way of thinking, attacks on debate frequently were answered by explaining that abuses arose through violation of the rules. Jefferson recalled with revulsion "the morbid rage of debate"[10] he encountered in the Continental Congress, and instances in informal debate of disputants "getting warm, becoming rude, and shooting one another."[11] His recommendation, however, was not that forensics be discarded, but that it be refined through avoidance of petty dispute and through formalizing of parliamentary rules. In this way the ignorant might be exposed to evidence, and procedures might be fair. He counselled against arguing with people who "are determined as to the facts they will believe, and the opinions on which they will act." Argument with such people is futile; "Get by them . . . as you would by an angry bull."[12] Recognizing, however, that argument was essential in a democratic assembly, he drafted for the Senate a manual of rules, in which he asserted, "It is much more material that there should be a rule to go by, than what that rule is; that there may be a uniformity of proceeding in business not subject to the caprice of the Speaker or captiousness of the members."[13] Archbishop Whately cautioned against the "considerable dangers" in debating societies,[14] yet was a vigorous practitioner of forensics in both logic and rhetoric, even believing that a primary aim of logic is to investigate "the principles on which argumentation is conducted."[15] The obligation of a good man to know the rules and to work for their enforcement was emphasized by Aristotle: "It is the business of one who knows a thing, himself to avoid fallacies in the subjects which he knows and to be able to show up the man who makes them."[16] Granted knowledge of the subject under consideration and a sense of ethics, familiarity with the rules could direct forensics in the way of good practices, it was reasoned.

When Agamemnon had controversy with Achilles, he laid the blame on the goddess of discord and not on the methods of argument. Similarly the apologist for forensic method has been inclined to find the cause of much malpractice in the perversity of human nature. Matthew Prior, observing controversy in the early eighteenth century, commented that many difficulties spring from the "natural Frailties of our Minds." Deploring unreasoned partisanship, Prior noted: "We cannot see two People play but we take part with One, and wish the other should lose, this without any previous reason or consideration." The *party line* was found even in eighteenth century coffee houses by Prior, who saw there the "Party Man . . . an Animal that no Commentator upon Human Nature can sufficiently explain. . . . Without enquiring he Acts . . . implicitely according to the word of Command given out by the heads of his faction." But even for the "Party Man" Prior had sympathy, if contempt, for "such most of Us are, or must be."[17] In Prior's view, man, not the institution of forensics, was at fault.

The modern attack on methods forensic does not accept man's disinclination to follow the best rules or his mental and moral frailty as an explanation of his prejudices and contentiousness. Rather the attack is upon the method itself as an institution that guides man into error. Some objections, it is true, are not to the particular method of debate, but to any consideration of things controversial. Such a point of view shines through the sign in a fascist cafe, "Here politics is not discussed," and the slogan in a business office, "Nothing is gained by argument." The longing one hears to have the school inviolate, as "a haven of rest and a place where a child could go and learn something substantial and not always be attacking or arguing about something,"[18] may be a defense of the *status quo* or of authoritarianism. But substantial criticism of attack and defense as a method has been made by persons thoroughly eager to see problems exposed and solved. Alfred Korzybski, for example, whimsically remarks: "In the old days philosophers amused themselves with writing books on the art of controversy; it is equally amusing to study the reverse—the art of abolishing controversy."[19]

Much of the modern criticism of forensics has been directed at the device known as formal debate. "Why do people go to debates?" asked Henry Hazlitt after hearing Clarence Darrow and Gilbert Chesterton attack and defend religion. "Are they thirsty for knowledge or thirsty for blood?"[20] In a textbook widely used in adult education we read that "the debate should not be considered an adult method of education and should be completely discarded." The authors shift the burden of discovering any possible good in the process by declaring: "It should be left to those who can justify prize fights to explain the uses of the debate."[21] H. A. Overstreet is no less vehement when he says: "It is significant of the profound ignorance which prevails in schools and colleges . . . that debate, which is one of the most devastating forms of wish-thinking, is still highly respected."[22]

The danger in such sweeping denunciations is that they are too often directed at all forensics rather than at the extremes associated with formal debating. Overdeveloped in school tournaments and perverted by exhibitionists who use it as a vehicle for sophistical display, formal debate is losing its popularity and is being replaced by less formal patterns of forensic discussion. But so long as we have spokesmen and issues, we shall want to see men and beliefs come together. Some procedures for facilitating such public meetings must be provided. More profitable than excoriating debate as a duel, or eulogizing it as the method of Lincoln and Douglas, is analysis and evaluation of the criticisms that have been directed against forensic thinking and against the habits of mind displayed in the process.

What are the habits of mind that critics find objectionable in forensics? What is the "destructive spirit of debate"[23] that writers on conference find harmful? One criticism is that debaters are preoccupied with a temporary decision. This objection has emerged prominently in the philosophy of the discussionists (as distinguished from the followers of traditional argumentative method). Basic in the thinking of the discussionists has been the belief that *decision* in controversy is not sufficient, and that *solution* of the difficulty which gives rise to controversy should be the major aim. An example is prohibition, concerning which two mighty decisions, enactment and repeal, have been made, but with the basic problem of intemperance still remaining. "Decision should be regarded as only a temporary interruption of the quest for a common solution," writes Robert Leigh, reminding us that "a numerical preponderance of one set of ideas and prejudices over the other"[24] is in no sense a solution. A. D. Sheffield, pioneering in the field of discussion, thought that "any solution of a controversy which is really to prevail in a practical sense must get from the group something more than a majority assent."[25] More "co-operative thinking," less "spirit of belligerent advocacy" is recommended by a writer early in the debate-discussion exploration, who says that for "co-operative thinking, discussion far surpasses debate."[26] The attempt to reach solution rather than mere decision is, in a sense, a movement back to the practical aspects of forensics. Through the years the psychological functions, as Aristotle saw them, have to an extent become stereotyped and formalized into non-purposive logical patterns; debate at times has been a thing in itself, quite detached from the problem it originally sought to decide. But the movement is more than a return; it is an attempt to advance human relations by applying post-Aristotelian psychology and sociology, particularly in the effect institutions may have upon man's behavior.

Emphasis upon attempting to "*harmonize* the differing ideas advocated,"[27] is a great contribution of those who revolted against traditional methods in controversy. Whether as debaters looking no further than a victory, or as legislators thinking of making a law rather than of finding a solution, we have too often regarded decision as the end in dispute. The full implications of *search for solution* as opposed to *decision* are not always found in the discussion textbooks, however. John Dewey recognized one of the implications when he said, "One question is disposed of; another offers itself and thought is kept alive."[28] Even though we agree that our social aim should consist of "uncovering serious difficulties in their full depth and reach,"[29] we must realize that practical matters seldom give us the time or the evidence to search for a solution interminably. A man who has murdered his grandmother presents a case for decision; we may not be able at the moment to solve his problem or that of his kind. We have to decide what to do with him, and quickly. "There is nothing which a scientific mind would more regret than reaching a condition in which there were no more problems,"[30] says Dewey. Continuous problems and continuous search is a laboratory ideal, but in the humble affairs of practical concern we shall not be made unhappy by a scarcity of problems. When they do arise, we shall welcome quick and efficient dispatch. Life compels us to make decisions. If we delay too long, we lose the power to act.

A second charge brought against the forensic process is that thought and feeling are predetermined. H. S. Elliott regrets that in an argument "persons representing each side usually have their minds made up." In a true discussion, this author thinks, "folk come with open mind and with problems." But "if persons who have predetermined a question come . . . they come not to get light . . . but rather to put over their point of view on the group."[31] The habit of investigating a problem by first deciding what one shall think about it certainly need not be encouraged. We need not think backwards like Alice's Queen, who first inflicted punishment, then held trial, and finally waited for the crime to be committed. If "most of our so-called reasoning consists in finding arguments for going on believing as we already do,"[32] we must probe our methods stringently to exclude the processes of rationalization. The habit of fitting all evidence into a pattern proceeding from fixed generalizations has encouraged anticipating conclusion before all channels of investigation have been explored. This habit has been so much a part of forensics that some authors cite it as the distinguishing characteristic of debate.[33] Also tending to restrict investigation and to lead to a predetermined conclusion is the use of stock patterns of analysis, such as "disease and remedy," "theory and practice," "social, economic and political advantages." Modern thought has become increasingly suspicious of dialectic in which a person with a predetermined conviction justifies it by elaborate yet logical connections with fixed generalizations.

However much we favor open-minded investigation of evidence, we are compelled at times to work from axioms and beliefs, even if they are not more than the dogma of scientific method or the procedures which guarantee the validity of our process. Discussionists, eager for an open mind and the absence of any predetermined conclusion, often have taken too seriously Elliott's criticism of speakers who "come not only with their minds already made up, but also with their speeches prepared."[34] The result is that for years we have had to listen to speakers explore their minds in public while we wait for a statement determinate enough to be intelligible. Could we not learn by recalling Whately's distinction:

In the process of *Investigation* . . . by which we endeavour to discover Truth, it must of course be uncertain to him who is entering on that process, what the conclusion will be to which his researches will lead; but . . . in the process of *conveying truth* to others by reasoning . . . the conclusion or conclusions which are to be established must be present to the mind of him who is conducting the Argument.[35]

Willingness to declare one's belief, to present one's evidence as concisely as may be compatible with persuasion, and to change one's belief where investigation or argument may direct, have been characteristic elements in the forensic process. There seems to be no reason to discard them. Confusion has arisen because some participants in debate have been satisfied with incomplete or wishful investigation, and because auditors, hearing in any debate only a presentation of evidence, forget that the process of investigation has already been performed. If debate has devoted too much energy to the final stages of attack and defense, and too little to a fair investigation of the bases of conviction, the corrective is certainly not to avoid a determination of what one thinks or what one should do.

A third objection to forensics is that it puts a premium on "two-sidedness." "The naive assumption that all questions have two sides distorts debates at the outset,"[36] we read. The person who thinks bilaterally, in terms of affirmative and negative, rather than multilaterally, the accusation goes, not only fails to canvass the situation fully, but usually identifies himself with one of the two sides in a "two-valued orientation."[37] The fashion of choosing a position, or side, by chance or habit, and before one is aware of the basis of his choice, is a practice to be generally deplored. The Democrat who vilifies one of two candidates in the primary election, but in the general election unquestioningly supports him against any Republican, no matter how capable, is a good example of a bad confusion of loyalties; he puts party or side above intelligence and country. But in practical matters we are frequently faced with the choice of alternative actions. Our suspension of sides in the war, for example, by which we were not at peace and not at war, ended with our being very definitely at war. As we look for possible actions we quite naturally narrow our selection and finally adopt or reject a first or second choice. The error in method comes not in the narrowing, not in the desire to select the best possible candidate or course, but in starting with an incomplete choice. Some of the objection to "sidedness" in forensics comes from misunderstanding the use of propositions. In formal debate we "hear both sides," often with a view to a "yes" or "no" response. But "both sides" does not mean a literal "two" sides; often it means hearing unpopular, or minority sides. As evidence that the extremes of affirmative and negative do not necessarily restrict choice, we have only to look at practice. For decades in America propositions have been phrased in terms of laissez faire or government ownership; whereas decision (if not solution) habitually is in terms of regulation of public utilities. The practice to be worked for in the phrasing of resolutions for action is not to avoid propositions, but so to frame them that they provide for the best possible final choice. In parliamentary debate allowance for change in the statement to be voted upon is made through all the stages of consideration; a bill may be amended in almost any way to achieve the wisest wording. But finally, if one wishes to declare his opinion upon it, he must vote yes or no. The only way to avoid taking sides in such a case is to shun the problem. Since this course is disastrous, we can "suspend sides" only until all evidence is in, or until the time to act comes.

A fourth objection to forensics frequently raised is that it presents attitudes of conflict. Whereas Aristotle counselled against drawing a point of issue where avoidance was possible, he provided for a vigorous attack and defense if conciliation failed. The movement in modern discussion, however, has been toward the discovery of forms which might avoid actual clash of interests. It is true that one finds, in some authors, clear recognition of inevitable cleavage and suggestions for handling it. "The fact of disagreement should be recognized," we are advised; "when . . . an affirmative and negative appear . . . there is no wisdom in ignoring or glossing over the existing differences."[38] But a strong strain of pacifism ran through the conferences and discussions following the first World War. Conciliation and agreement, not argument and decision, were at the heart of the discussionist's creed. E. C. Lindeman, in 1926, agreed with H. A. Overstreet that a debater "represents 'militarism in the intellectual life' "; he thought "debates . . . follow rules but these are of no value to discussion," and maintained that "rules for discussion will . . . be compatible with the fundamental purpose of conference which is, *not to defeat any one,* but rather to arrive at a joint conclusion."[39] When, in recent decades, extreme holders of this doctrine met extremists of the militant school, we had the irony of one side deliberately seeking "clash," while the other as deliberately avoided coming to grips with an issue.

It is true that feelings often run high as issues are debated and decided. Attributing the conflict to the form used to settle it, however, is not a satisfying explanation; the very fact that a course of action is being settled brings out conflict. Certainly one's feelings are less tense as he ponders seven hypothetical possibilities than when he realizes the die is to be cast. If a union and the boss reach the stage of debate in their dispute, is it because the workers belonged to a debating society and the employer was a varsity debater in college, or is it because of a clash of basic drives, the one for a wage, the other for profits? Much as we may wish it were otherwise, observation leads us to agree with Havelock Ellis that "the great principles of conflict in life . . . are built into the structure of the world."[40] If in the discussion of human affairs we cannot change that structure, perhaps we can seek to avoid war and verbal battle, by working with a "vision of harmonious conflict . . . of opposite tendencies, each necessary to the other and supporting it, while compromise would merely mean weakness." If the rightists and leftists of politics cannot be conciliated or liquidated, perhaps they can, by refinements in method, become as the arch. "Here we see how in the conflict of two opposing forces each supports the other, and stability is insured. If the opposition ceased, the arch would collapse in ruin."[41] We must recognize and use conflict, not vainly seek to avoid it.

Objectors to forensic method vary in the degree to which they find obnoxious the elements of decision, predetermination, two-sided thinking, and conflict. They are agreed, however, on a method which should replace forensics. That is the "scientific," or "experimental," or "objective" method. A distinguished historian cites the aphorism, "Men begin the search for truth with fancy, after that they argue, and at length they try to find out."[42] He cautions against deciding human affairs on the basis of argumentation, and asks for scientific method. A noted contemporary educator tells teachers to "use primarily the methods of science rather than those of emotion, discussion, and persuasion."[43] The terminology, if not the method of objectivity, has been vigorously applied. The high school student in Kansas, who a generation ago might have been a member of a debating society, is now advised that "He will have the scientific attitude."[44] If one turns to the right books he can find full testimony to the value of objectivity, and even to its complete achievement. Louis Madelin found that in writing a history of the French Revolution he "approached this thorny subject without any preconceived views," felt he had "been just to everybody," and had "not found it difficult to observe . . . freedom of observation and appreciation." His formula, if others wished to follow him, was this: "to take his stand upon the wall of the threatened city and watch both besiegers and besieged."[45] Equally reassuring has been Pareto's declaration that through the writing of four large volumes he was able to maintain an attitude in which "we have no preconceptions, no *a priori* notions. We find certain facts before us."[46]

The attempt to substitute objective attitudes for forensic in matters of controversy has had its fortunate and unfortunate aspects. In so far as the "objectivists" have insisted upon fair and open-minded investigation, their methods need all the encouragement possible. Too often the forensic speaker or writer has taken proof as his first step, ignoring full investigation, and seeing only what he set out to see. The dream of applying the method of science to the practical affairs of life— a vision traditionally credited to Auguste Comte[47]—is a noble one. Its limitations and dangers, however, must be kept in mind. Attempting to maintain objectivity through all stages of controversy may result in deception. Trotsky, viewing Madelin's "stand upon the wall," saw it not only as impractical but as dishonest. "In a time of revolution," Trotsky observed, "standing on the wall involves great danger."[48] He feared Madelin's passive sightseeing on the barricade was as reconnoiterer for the reaction rather than as impartial observer. As more satisfactory than "treacherous impartiality," which presents for its verification good intentions for which only the spokesman can vouch, Trotsky recommended that the observer should reveal not only the positions in battle from which he worked, but also the extent to which his own interests were involved.

The advice was good, for the notion that objectivity can be attained is an illusion. It has long been recognized that an object or value may appear in one way to one person, but in another to another person. As William Blake explained, "I see Every thing I paint In This World, but Every body does not see alike." Blake's counsel in biblical vein that "As a man is, so he sees,"[49] has given way to the modern commonplace that we see the world not with our eyes but with our interests. Indeed, the notion that one's ideology may be revealed with the discovery of his economic interests has been prominent since Marx. If this is an extreme, so is its opposite, that one can look at an object not caring whether it be his or another's, nor what effect it may have upon his personal well-being. Declaration of objectivity does not guarantee its achievement. Charles Beard detected in Pareto's testimony the "assumption that no assumptions are made." Pareto's impersonal and detached "we," Beard discovered to be the "I" of "a man of great personal passions, convictions, dislikes and contempts, . . . a product of his time and his place, . . . not a timeless, placeless, universal 'I'." And that such a man "could reach the age of maturity required for the discussion of human affairs without arriving at any habitual assumptions must remain one of the seven wonders of the world."[50] A consistent trouble in applying the principle of objectivity to decision is that the method fails when we need it most. The closer to our interests a problem comes, the less objective can we be. An academic may look at a wage controversy in a mill and decide in some detachment what should be recommended. He is less objective, however, on the question of his own value on the payroll. In a relatively quiet world we may dream of labelling news reports as fact or propaganda. But what shall we do in war when we know every report is propaganda of a sort? Have we any safer process than a forensic method of putting evidence against evidence and weighing the result? Much yet needs to be done to understand why one line looks curved to one person and straight to another. But to hope that all can see the same thing from different positions involves either hypocrisy or illusion.

Yet another danger in the doctrine of objectivity is that it frequently leads to inaction. The attitude becomes a refuge, an excuse for not declaring oneself. There comes to mind Conrad's Heyst, a man who "in his fine detachment had lost the habit of asserting himself," and who regretted in the end that all his life he had been "a disarmed man." When one hears a scholar assert to a thousand people that he wishes "only to present," and that if his remarks might influence anyone present, he never again would make a public speech, one begins to fear detachment. Archibald MacLeish, alarmed at the slowness at which detached scholars showed concern with growing fascism, asked: "How could we sit back as spectators of a war against ourselves?"[51] The perils of deception, illusion and inaction, when one pretends to carry an objective attitude into areas of decision, have become increasingly dangerous. In an era of "rising above controversy," the words of an honest polemic are refreshing: "That we should care whether something is true or not true, chiefly, perhaps, is what makes us human beings."[52]

More attainable than objectivity is the basic forensic method of exposing all available evidence in terms of interests involved. Through the ages the debater has made his contribution to keeping the lanes of truth open by enforcing a doctrine of "both sides." We no longer think, however, that analyzing lines of argument in order to accept or reject them is a large enough goal. Aristotle insisted that we should know all lines of argument. His attitude, however, of surveying evidence with a view to successful persuasion and refutation,[53] is now regarded as too narrow. A statement by Karl Mannheim gives us a doctrine more in keeping with modern thought: "See reality with the eyes of acting human beings; . . . understand even . . . opponents in the light of their actual motives and their position."[54] In an attempt to get understanding we need not accept a program because its adherents claim objectivity, nor need we reject it because we detect partisanship. We cannot make patriotic organizations and chambers of commerce and labor unions objective, but we can learn to look upon their proposals as designed to meet their special interests. They, in turn, can learn to be more humble in asserting that their interests are necessarily those of total society. Given channels for detecting motive and evidence, we have a good start toward wise action.

The pattern of thought which gave rise to attacks on forensics was greatly changed with our entry into the war. The pre-war period marked a time of conciliation, of "problem-solving" that rarely did more than state the problem, and of discussion rather than decision. There was much talk of economic drives in behavior, but little coming to grips with the issues. It was a period in which people "sat around a table to talk things over." It was thought that if persons were not antagonized or thwarted they would behave reasonably. With war, an era in attitudes of conciliation came to an end. Dramatically we heard prominent "conciliators" denouncing Munich and appeasement. Suddenly they agreed with Lowell that "compromise makes a good umbrella but a poor roof."[55] Eschewers of conflict avowed they were not merely for victory but for total victory. "Objectivists" deserted their scientific attitude and boldly proclaimed their convictions. It was discovered that no technique of discussion had been devised which would make people with fundamentally different philosophies settle their strife unless fundamental adjustments were made in their lives. And it was reaffirmed that no improvement upon the convention that all people must abide by decisions fairly arrived at had yet appeared. The calamity of war was not needed to expose the extremes in the assault upon forensic thinking. It does, however, give occasion for revaluation. Should the shades of Aristotle and Whately appear, what "technique" can we reveal to them which improves upon the attack and defense of a proposition when it is necessary to accept, modify, or reject a proposal? The fact remains, above all the criticisms, that in matters of mutual concern we have to plan how we shall expose and test evidence in order to reach democratic decision. Such procedures are the essence of forensic thinking. A debate proposition is not quite a scientific hypothesis to be tested in the laboratory of public opinion, but it is the best attempt in that direction that has yet been discovered.

Above the criticisms of forensic method rise these traditional elements which today need to be re-affirmed:

1. The attempt to substitute even verbal battle for physical conflict.
2. Recognition of the conflicting drives among men, with the need for methods of attack and defense.
3. Recognition that man's judgments are both logical and emotional; decisions are determined in a process of persuasion.
4. Belief that democratic decisions are reached in the larger processes of debate, and not by mysticism (decisions arrived at by persons with positions in a holy of holies), nor by authoritarianism (decisions given by persons merely because they hold official positions).
5. Acknowledgment of the inescapable necessity of deciding upon propositions which will determine conduct in practical affairs.
6. Belief that, in fairness, clarity, and courage, the positions one works from had best be declared.
7. Belief that in asking for approval, the methods of proof should be indicated (as in the filing of the brief, the stating of the process the speaker uses to reach his conclusions, etc.).
8. Approval of granting tolerance to opposing views; one does not seek to silence but to answer.
9. The necessity of following some forensic procedures— even though they be perverted at times—as protection to minority positions.
10. The desirability of holding an active conviction based on

the best available evidence, with recognition that further investigation and debate may prove it false.

These basic elements in forensics, here separated from many incidental aspects, are traditional, but are not incapable of adjustment to evolving social thought. Although a hazardous task, it is interesting to speculate upon the directions in which forensic thinking of the future may move. One of the influences at work is multi-valued logic, a field the discussionists have drawn heavily upon in their criticisms of debate and in their positive suggestions. Argumentation has hewn close to the Aristotelian tradition, but the influence of the non-Aristotelians is already felt. It is not of concern, here, to judge whether the conflict between schools of logic is fundamental or not, or whether one system is superior to the other. The fact is that both systems are influencing forensic thought, the one largely through tradition, the other through reform. "The attacks upon the Aristotelian tradition come from several different sectors along the battle line, and have not come simultaneously,"[56] says O. L. Reiser in summarizing movements in experimental logic since Hegel. Our modern search has been for dynamic rather than static methods. The goal has been to guide an unfolding of the true significance of things and to avoid forcing understanding into conformity with set conclusions, patterns, and procedures. Especially under attack is the habitual following of precedent, on the assumption that any problem is necessarily a specific instance to be fitted under ancestral generalizations.

An example of reform is seen in "laws" which forensics in the past has leaned heavily upon; but which non-Aristotelian logic seeks to discard. One of these is the *Law of Identity*, with its applications in thought that "A word means what it means," and that "The meaning of a term must remain constant in any discourse."[57] Observing this "law," debaters have tried to define terms immutably and at the outset. In the preliminary analysis in debates, which includes definitions of the terms of the proposition, attempts are made to come to agreement on meaning before presenting issues. Although the debater finds frequently that he cannot set up definitions that his opponent will accept, or that he himself is willing to adhere to through any prolonged discussion, still he has accepted the "law" that meaning can be fixed once and for all. More flexible, and more real explanations emerge, however, if interpretations are maintained constantly, providing for accumulations of understanding as issues develop. The *Law of Identity* has been called upon frequently by those who insist that the Constitution means what it means, quite independent of the environment it may have at the moment of interpretation. A second "law" accepted in forensics but under attack by non-Aristotelians, is the *Law of Contradiction,* with its application "That a word does not mean what it does not mean." In the great debates on America's neutrality we applied this "law" vigorously, if unconsciously. "Neutrality" was construed in its literal sense of "refraining from taking part on either side." When a minority pointed out that such a "neutrality," in actual circumstances, meant giving aid to Franco at the expense of the Spanish Republic, and to Japan at the expense of China, the rejoinder was made, perhaps in less theoretical language: a term does not mean what it does not mean, and neutrality does not mean giving aid, but quite the opposite. A third "law" to which forensics has given allegiance but which is under question, is the *Law of Excluded Middle.* Frequently declared from the forensic platform are two applications of this principle, "A proposition is either true or false," and "Two contradictory propositions cannot both be true." The district attorney may declare the culprit to be "either guilty or innocent," but often he must suspect some of his subjects are a little guilty and a little innocent. Even in the midst of his appeal he must reflect that much depends upon the interests of the people who view the proposition. An example of a proposition that consistently receives a multi-valued response, and not an either-or one, is the statement that "high taxes are either good or bad." The answer depends upon who pays and who receives, for what purposes they are applied, and the attitudes held toward those purposes. Forensics has never been necessarily committed to these "laws."

Even in a formal debate, the most rigid pattern of forensic thinking, the negative has wide choice in its proposals, and the audience is frequently so "multi-lateral" in its thinking that it will have neither the affirmative nor negative position. But the "laws" have greatly influenced forensic thought, and less insistence upon them will make debate freer and more adaptable.

Whether we work as Aristotelians or as non-Aristotelians, our problem is to strengthen methodologies which encourage fair and thorough investigation, free hearings, and just, efficient decision or solution. Our idealism, however, will have to be tempered by the kind of world we find around us. Methods of thought useful in the laboratory or in a speculative consideration of the divisibility of matter, are not necessarily useful in practical concerns. The possibilities for improvement in the settlement of controversy are great. "Our logic in social and humane subjects" is archaic, says Dewey, adding: "For the most part the lesson of experimental inquiry has still to be learned in the things of chief concern."[58] Forensic procedures to come will surely have as elements, combinations of traditional virtues, constructive criticisms of the discussionists, and the practical fruits of experimental logic. Much of the academic exploration in controversy recently has been in terms of discussion *versus* debate. Viewed functionally and historically, however, they are parts of the same process, and there is no need to prolong a cleavage, nor to dissipate our energies in making sharp distinctions to demonstrate they are separate fields of effort. We shall move toward a common methodology in controversy as debate sheds some of its patness and belligerence, discussion its looseness and inaction. Who knows but that forensics of the future will:

1. Be less satisfied with *decision,* more concerned with *solution.*
2. Place less reliance upon precedent.
3. Prefer experimental evidence to the type of truism or generalization that Aristotle made the basis of the enthymeme.

4. Place less emphasis upon consistency as dictated by "laws of thought," and hence give less time to assailing opponents' fallacies or to insisting upon traditional logical patterns. Instead, search out a *whole* pattern of response to a *whole* situation.

5. Discard the traditional static definition of terms for ampler explanation and application of the proposal.

6. Abandon stock patterns of analysis such as *theory and practice, disease and remedy;* substitute fuller and closer description of the situation.

7. Search for areas of harmony more strenuously than for points of disagreement. Make greater use of devices, such as direct and cross examination, to explore evidence and belief, rather than as means of discrediting, humiliating, or confounding a witness.

8. Modify the practice of starting debate by stating a proposition; make greater use, particularly in parliamentary procedures and in forums, of discussion which precedes rather than follows statement of the proposition.

9. Place greater emphasis upon public consideration of the earlier stages of debate, such as exploring problems, and searching for evidence; feature less prominently the dramatic final stages of deciding issues. This would mean greater public participation in *shaping* and *directing* policy.

10. Rely less upon open debate of specific measures. Delegate more extensively the actual determination of solutions to boards and experts, who will use forensic procedure for arriving at their decisions. This would mean less public participation in *applying* policy.

Toward a day of relatively impartial investigation, co-operative conferees, and dynamic methods, we may be moving. For a "new attitude toward the constructive use of conflict"[59] rather than for any set of traditional rules, the practitioner in forensics must labor. He must avoid those methods which fan ignorance and prejudice into deep conviction. He should recognize that the essentials of forensics have persevered against misuse and criticism, and now must be protected from the attacks of those who do not understand them or are unwilling to face the actualities of conflict. His task is to maintain the courage, freedom, and honesty that have been achieved through parliamentary debate and forensic law, without seeking to perpetuate merely incidental forms. Of this we can be reasonably certain in the years to come: over conference-room, platform, and assembly where practical matters are determined, even though unlabelled and unsung, will continue to hover the forensic mind.

NOTES

1. R. M. MacIver, *Leviathan and the People* (University, Louisiana, 1939), p. 69.

2. See, for example, a defense of debating reprinted in the Kentucky Interscholastic League's *Bulletin* VII, No. 4 (September, 1928), 26-29.

3. For an example of debating turned on itself, see the author's article, "Debating, as Generally Conducted in American High Schools, is Educationally Harmful," *Scholastic* XVII, No. 4 (November 1, 1930), 16-17 ff.

4. *Rhetoric*, I, 3, 1358^b, trans. Lane Cooper (New York, 1932).

5. Aristotle, *Nicomachean Ethics*, II, 2, trans. J. E. C. Welldon (London, 1892).

6. *Rhetoric*, I, 13, 1374^b.

7. *Rhetoric*, I, 1, 1355^a.

8. Letter to the Rev. Charles Clay, *The Writings of Thomas Jefferson*, ed. A. E. Bergh, 20 vols. (Washington, 1907), VIII, 4.

9. Hervey Scott, *A Complete History of Fairfield County, Ohio* (Columbus, 1877), p. 298. (The railroad appeared in 1853.)

10. "Autobiography," Jefferson, *op. cit.*, I, 86.

11. Letter to T. J. Randolph, *ibid.*, XII, 199.

12. *Ibid.*, p. 200.

13. "Jefferson's Manual," *Senate Manual* (Washington, 1941), pp. 241-242.

14. Richard Whately, *Elements of Rhetoric*, 7th ed. rev. (London, 1846), p. 32.

15. Whately, *Elements of Logic*, 7th ed. rev. (London, 1840), p. 1.

16. *De Sophisticis Elenchis*, I, 165^a, trans. W. A. Pickard-Cambridge in *Works*, ed. W. D. Ross (Oxford, 1928), I.

17. "An Essay upon Opinion" [1719?], *Dialogues of the Dead and other Works in Prose and Verse*, ed. A. R. Waller (Cambridge, 1907), pp. 199, 201, 202.

18. The president of the San Francisco Board of Education, speaking on America's Town Meeting of the Air, March 4, 1940. Town Meeting *Bulletin* V, No. 21, p. 16.

19. Dated 1926 and quoted by Irving J. Lee, *Language Habits in Human Affairs* (New York, 1941), p. ii.

20. Henry Hazlitt, "Debate," *Nation* CXXXII (February 4, 1931), 130.

21. Dorothy Hewitt and Kirtley F. Mather, *Adult Education—a Dynamic for Democracy* (New York, 1937), pp. 161-162.

22. *About Ourselves* (New York, 1927), p. 74.

23. Frank Walser, *The Art of Conference* (New York, 1933), p. 22.

24. R. D. Leigh, *Group Leadership* (New York, 1936), p. 70.

25. A. D. Sheffield, *Joining In Public Discussion* (New York, 1922), pp. vii-viii.

26. W. E. Utterback, "The Group Discussion," in *A Course of Study in Speech Training and Public Speaking for Secondary Schools*, ed. A. M. Drummond (New York and London, 1925), p. 182.

27. Sheffield, *op. cit.*, p. ix.

28. *The Quest for Certainty* (New York, 1929), p. 228.

29. *Ibid.*, p. 251.

30. *Ibid.*, p. 101.

31. *The Process of Group Thinking* (New York, 1932), p. 18.

32. James Harvey Robinson, *The Mind in the Making* (New York, 1921), p. 41.

33. See W. E. Utterback's article, "The Appeal to Force in Public Discussion," *Quarterly Journal of Speech* XXVI (February, 1940), 1-6. The author says, for example: "Where debate is a subsumptive process based on logic, conference is a creative process based on procedure closely resembling that of scientific investigation."

34. Elliott, *op. cit.*, p. 19.

35. *Rhetoric*, p. 35.

36. E. C. Lindeman, *The Meaning of Adult Education* (New York, 1926), p. 190.

37. Lee, *op. cit.*, p. 104.

38. Leigh, *loc. cit.*

39. Lindeman, *op. cit.*, pp. 189-191. (Italics mine.)

40. *The Philosophy of Conflict* (Boston, 1919), p. 60.

41. Havelock Ellis, "Harmony in Conflict," *Nation* CXLVIII (April 22, 1939), 465-66.

42. Frederick J. Teggart, *The Processes of History* (New Haven, 1918), p. 162.

43. E. L. Thorndike, *The Teaching of Controversial Subjects* (Cambridge, Mass., 1937), p. 22.

44. From *The Kansas Program for the Improvement of Instruction. Bulletin,* Kansas State Department of Education (No. 6, April, 1939), p. 13.

45. *The French Revolution* (New York, 1916), pp. vii, viii.

46. Vilfredo Pareto, *The Mind and Society* [1923], ed. Arthur Livingston (New York, 1935), I, 75.

47. See, for example, McQuilkin De Grange's "The Method of Auguste Comte: Subordination of Imagination to Observation in the Social Sciences," *Methods in Social Science,* ed. S. A. Rice (Chicago, 1931), ch. 1.

48. Leon Trotsky, *The History of the Russian Revolution,* trans. Max Eastman (New York, 1937), preface, xxi.

49. Letter to Dr. Trusler, Aug. 23, 1799, *Poetry and Prose of William Blake,* ed. Geoffrey Keynes (Bloomsbury, 1927), p. 1039.

50. Charles A. Beard, *The Discussion of Human Affairs* (New York, 1936), pp. 34 ff.

51. *The Irresponsibles* (New York, 1940), p. 19.

52. Dorothy Thompson, *Let the Record Speak* (Boston, 1939), p. 285.

53. Note the attitude in the *Rhetoric* (I, 1, 1355^a): "We should be able to argue on either side of a question; not with a view to putting both sides into practice—we must not advocate evil—but in order that no aspect of the case may escape us, and that if our opponent makes unfair use of the arguments, we may be able in turn to refute them."

54. *Ideology and Utopia* (London, 1936), p. 146.

55. James Russell Lowell, "Democracy," *Democracy and Other Addresses* (Boston, 1895), p. 25.

56. *The Promise of Scientific Humanism* (New York, 1940), p. 59.

57. See Reiser (*op. cit.*, p. 60) for a table of interpretations of the "laws." The applications here given are taken from his chart.

58. *Op. cit.*, p. 251.

59. Walser, *op. cit.*, p. 3.